ADVENTISM IN AMERICA

A History

Edited by
Gary Land

WILLIAM B. EERDMANS PUBLISHING COMPANY
GRAND RAPIDS, MICHIGAN

Copyright © 1986 by Wm. B. Eerdmans Publishing Co.
255 Jefferson Ave. S.E., Grand Rapids, Mich. 49503
Printed in the United States of America

Library of Congress Cataloging-in-Publication Data:

Adventism in America.

  (Studies in Adventist history)
  Bibliography: p. 294
  Includes index.
  1. Adventists—United States—History. 2. Seventh-day
Adventists—United States—History. 3. United States—
Church history. I. Land, Gary, 1944-   . II. Series.
BX6153.2.A38 1986   286.7'73   86-29061

ISBN 0-8028-0237-0

Contents

Preface   vii

1   The Millerite Movement, 1830-1845   1
    by Everett N. Dick

2   Sectarianism and Organization, 1846-1864   36
    by Godfrey T. Anderson

3   Years of Expansion, 1865-1885   66
    by Emmett K. VandeVere

4   The Perils of Growth, 1886-1905   95
    by Richard W. Schwarz

5   Shaping the Modern Church, 1906-1930   139
    by Gary Land

6   The Church under Stress, 1931-1960   170
    by Keld J. Reynolds

7   Coping with Change, 1961-1980   208
    by Gary Land

Appendix 1   Seventh-day Adventist Statements of Belief   231

Appendix 2   Seventh-day Adventist Membership
   Statistics   251

Notes   254

Bibliographical Essay   294

Contributors   297

Index   299

Preface

Seventh-day Adventism emerged out of the social and religious turmoil of mid-nineteenth-century America, an era that also produced—directly or indirectly—the Latter-day Saints, Christian
Scientists, Jehovah's Witnesses, and Pentecostals. Like most of these
groups, Seventh-day Adventism had a charismatic figure, Ellen G.
White, who shaped its identity, and it has maintained its sectarian
character into the twentieth century. And, like all but Christian
Science, it carries on extensive mission efforts abroad.

In fact, despite what Sydney Ahlstrom calls its "made in
America" character,[1] the Seventh-day Adventist church has become
perhaps the most widespread Protestant denomination. From a sect
of about four thousand members when it organized in 1863, it had
grown to about 3.5 million by 1980. When it began, Seventh-day
Adventism was limited to the northeastern United States; by 1980,
Seventh-day Adventists lived in 190 countries nurtured by approximately thirty-two hundred missionaries.[2] As with most of its sectarian counterparts, the denomination's recent growth has occurred in
the emerging nations of the Third World rather than in its increasingly secular homeland.

Although a dynamic, if relatively small, entity on the religious
scene, Seventh-day Adventism has a history that is neither well
known nor well understood. This situation has come about largely
because, until recently, Seventh-day Adventists, who look to an imminent Second Coming of Christ, took little serious interest in their
own history. Over the years they have published a few general historical works, the most important being those written by J. N.
Loughborough, M. E. Olsen, and Arthur W. Spalding.[3] But these
books have been of limited use to the general reader and scholar,
for they have tended to be apologetic in nature and anecdotal in
form. Scholarly attention to the Adventist past was limited by the
fact that most of the denomination's historians taught in Adventist
colleges, which gave little time for research, and by the absence,
until 1973, of a central archive for the preservation and organization
of documents. Perhaps even more significant, the denomination's
successful effort to prevent the publication of Everett N. Dick's re-

vised dissertation on the Millerite movement discouraged nearly an entire generation of historians from studying Adventist history. The denominational leadership, it appeared, wanted to maintain ministerial control over the church's past. The publication in 1946 of Harold O. McCumber's dissertation on Adventism in California was a major exception to the general situation.[4]

Since scholarly Seventh-day Adventist attention to its own history has been slight, it is not surprising that those outside the church have given that history little attention. Two journalistic works, David Mitchell's *Seventh-day Adventists: Faith in Action* and Booton Herndon's *The Seventh Day*,[5] gave brief attention to Adventism's Millerite origins, as have several scholarly works treating mid-nineteenth-century society and religion. But for the denomination's development beyond the 1850s there are only scattered references in histories of American religion and brief sketches in reference works.

In the 1970s, however, Seventh-day Adventist historians began expressing a serious interest in their denomination's past. The reasons for this are complex: the denomination became more open to historical investigation, as when it published a considerably revised version of Richard W. Schwarz's dissertation on John Harvey Kellogg, a previously untouchable subject;[6] younger scholars, having come of age in the restless 1960s, felt a need to better establish and understand their denominational identity; theological ferment led to an investigation of earlier Adventist beliefs; and the growth of Seventh-day Adventist colleges brought about a growth in the number of professionally trained Seventh-day Adventist historians.

Out of this reawakened interest came *Studies in Adventist History*, a multivolume project conceived in the early 1970s. Recognizing the need for a comprehensive, nonapologetic history of the denomination, Ronald L. Numbers and Vern Carner, two historians then teaching at Loma Linda University, recruited a board of editors to direct the production of this work. Godfrey T. Anderson and William Frederick Norwood agreed to serve as senior editors on a panel that also included Everett Dick and Richard Schwarz. Anderson chaired the board, and Numbers acted as its executive secretary. Halfway through the project, Jonathan Butler and Gary Land, having accepted the responsibility of editing the projected two volumes, also joined the board.

This first volume is, I trust, the kind of history that the initiators of this project envisioned: accurate in scholarship, comprehensive in scope, and objective in tone. The paucity of previous scholarship and the still incomplete organization of the General Conference archives have, however, limited what the authors could accomplish. Consequently, the following history is based primarily on published sources and focuses on the institutional church in America. Little is yet known about the history of the Adventist people or the history of Adventist missions. Furthermore, this multi-author work makes no attempt to establish an overarching interpretation of the Adventist past.

This volume, therefore, cannot be regarded as a definitive history of Seventh-day Adventists. Rather, it synthesizes our present knowledge and lays a base for further investigation. If we have provided a book that is both interesting and authoritative and at the same time provocative of further inquiry, we will have achieved our purpose.

1 | The Millerite Movement 1830–1845

EVERETT N. DICK

Seventh-day Adventism developed out of a movement that seemed to end in ignominious failure. William Miller, during a widespread resurgence of interest in millenarianism, predicted that Christ would come in 1843 or 1844, and he gained a wide following in the northeastern United States. Although the announced event never took place, leaving the believers in bitter disappointment, the Millerite movement bequeathed a system of prophetic interpretation and biblical literalism that helped shape the character of the Adventism that arose from its ruins. In the Millerite movement of the 1830s and 1840s lie the roots of a Seventh-day Adventist Church that, though small by comparison with the mainline Protestant denominations, today circles the world.

As startling as Miller's prediction was, he worked within a time-honored Christian concern. Down through the centuries, the Second Coming of Christ in fulfillment of the prophecies had been the hope of Christendom. But the meaning of the Second Coming, and in particular the millennium—the thousand years when the expectant ones would dwell with Christ—had aroused considerable disagreement.

Although the early Christians expected the imminent bodily appearance of Christ, the post-Nicene Fathers interpreted the biblical prophecies allegorically. The most influential of these Fathers, Augustine, taught that the millennium was a long period in which the saints "reigned" with Christ through an inner spiritual triumph, the "Beast" was the community of unbelievers, and "God's image" was his simulation in those who did not live according to their professed beliefs. [1]

The allegorical approach to the prophecies dominated Christian thinking until the Reformation. The Protestants took the prophecies "literally," interpreting the 1,260 days of Revelation 12 as a period of 1,260 years that covered the whole history of the Christian church. Until the latter part of the seventeenth century, most Protestants took a premillennialist position, believing that Christ would come first and the millennium would follow. In the middle of the seventeenth century, however, another view emerged; it said that the millennium would occur before Christ's coming.

This view received its most influential expression at the beginning of the eighteenth century, when the Anglican clergyman Daniel Whitby in 1703 interpreted the prophecies to mean that the world was progressing toward the millennium. The Resurrection, he thought, meant the conversion of the world through a great surge of missionary activity that would result from the outpouring of the Holy Spirit. At the same time, pagan religions would be subdued, the Jews would be reestablished as a nation, and the papacy and the Turkish Empire would be overthrown. These events would usher in one thousand years of peace and happiness, which he called the "golden age" or the "good time coming"—the millennium. At the conclusion of this period Christ would return.

Partly because of reaction to the excesses of the Puritan Revolution, which had been premillennialist, this postmillennial theology soon dominated Christian thinking in both England and its American colonies, where Jonathan Edwards was its most significant exponent.[2] But the French Revolution, beginning in 1789, revived literal premillennialism by appearing to fulfill Daniel 7 and Revelation 13. Numerous voices arose in England advocating this line of interpretation. Among them were ministers such as Anglican George Stanley Faber and Scots Presbyterian William Cunningham, as well as laymen like James Hatley Frere and Lewis Way. Edward Irving became the most famous preacher of premillennialism; he translated the Chilean Jesuit Manuel Lacunza's *The Coming of Messiah in Glory and Majesty* in 1826 and played an important role that same year in the Albury Conference, which brought together many noted British millennarians. Irving, however, became an advocate of speaking in tongues, which broke out in his church in the early 1830s, and died in disgrace in 1834.

As a result of the annual Albury Conferences of 1826 through 1828, the prophetic interpreters came to substantial agreement on the fundamental doctrines of their eschatology. The six points, summarized by Henry Drummund, sponsor of the conferences, asserted the following: 1) the cataclysmic end to the age; 2) restoration of the Jews to Palestine during the time of the judgment; 3) the judgment would fall primarily on Christendom; 4) the millennium would occur after the judgment; 5) Christ would come before the millennium; and 6) the 1,260 years of Daniel 7 and Revelation 13 would be the period from Justinian to the French Revolution, the vials of wrath (Revelation 16) being poured out now, and the Second Advent would be imminent. Some participants predicted that Christ would come in 1843 or 1847, but all expected him to return within a few years. The major elements of this interpretation had taken form by 1830.[3]

Meanwhile, says Ernest Sandeen, America "was drunk on the millennium." Alexander Campbell, founder of the Disciples of Christ, speculated for several years on the prophecies, and Joseph Smith, prophet of the Latter-day Saints, taught a premillennial eschatology. In time, both of these men, however, were to lose their sense of the imminence of Christ's Second Coming. More extreme views appeared in two communal groups: the Shakers believed that Christ's return had occurred in the incarnation of God in Mother Ann Lee, and John Humphrey Noyes of the Oneida community taught that it had taken place in A.D. 70. But the most famous of all the American premillennialists was William Miller, a New York farmer.[4]

WILLIAM MILLER

Miller was born in Massachusetts in 1782 and was reared on the frontier at Low Hampton, New York, just south of Lake Champlain. His schooling consisted of the rudimentary education that the three-month wilderness schools afforded in the late eighteenth century. In spite of educational handicaps, Miller learned to read well. Fortunately, there were in the neighborhood several men of influence and some learning who took an interest in the lad and lent him books. He read these avidly, devouring ancient and modern European history, and thus became a well-read, self-educated man.

From his youth he had been taught by his godly mother to believe the Bible and to cherish the Christian faith; but when he married and went to live in Vermont, he was thrown among doubters. For the first time, he had access to a public library. There he met the community's better-educated men, who had accepted deistic teaching—which rejected Christ as the Savior of the world and allowed only that he was a good man. As a result of this association, Miller became a deist.

Miller served in the War of 1812, rising to the rank of captain. His faith in deism had begun to wane even before that time, however, and certain experiences during the war further weakened his deistic beliefs. When circumstances led him to compare the history of the children of Israel with that of the United States, he came to feel that God was watching over the army of the United States just as he had protected Israel from the armies of Canaan. A particular instance of this was the battle of Plattsburg, in which Miller fought. In this engagement fifteen hundred regulars and four thousand volunteers on the American side defeated fifteen thousand British troops. Before the battle, Miller and his comrades had felt that defeat was practically certain. The amazing outcome appeared to him as the workings of a power mightier than man.[5]

After his discharge from the army in 1815, Miller settled near Low Hampton on a farm close to the home where he was reared, and for a period he went through a tremendous spiritual and mental struggle. Of his experience he said: "The heavens were as brass over my head, and the earth as iron under my feet. *Eternity! —what was it? —and death —what was it?* The more I reasoned, the further I was from demonstration."[6]

Some months later, in 1816, he became reconciled to the Bible and to Christ as the Savior of men; he joined the Baptist church. A deist friend now taunted him about his faith in the Bible, asserting that it would not bear logical scrutiny. Convinced that the Bible must be consistent and harmonious if it is indeed the Word of God, Miller determined to harmonize all seeming contradictions in it, including the things his deist friends said were absurd, or else turn again to deism. So he began a reverent study of the Bible, comparing passage with passage, to make it explain itself.

Miller was familiar with Whitby's teaching of the temporal millennium, but his study of the Bible convinced him that post-millennialism was clearly contrary to the Book's plain teaching. Also, he was astonished to discover to his own satisfaction that the time of the Advent was revealed by the Bible prophecies. The Scripture passage that seemed to him to foretell the time of Christ's return was Daniel 8:14: "Unto two thousand and three hundred days; then shall the sanctuary be cleansed." Following the rules of interpretation used by standard commentators of the day, particularly the "day-year principle," and accepting the contemporary view that in the Christian Age the earth is the sanctuary, Miller understood the cleansing to be the purification of the earth by fire at Christ's Advent as it had been purified by water in the days of Noah. After diligent study he became convinced that the 2,300-day period began in 457 B.C. with the decree of Artaxerxes to rebuild Jerusalem. On that basis, simple arithmetic revealed that the prophetic period would end in 1843.[7]

Of Miller's biblical interpretation Whitney R. Cross says:

> His accumulating data pointed inescapably to a pre-instead of a post-millennial Advent. Aside from this change of emphasis, shared by several contemporaries, Miller achieved no startling novelty. His doctrine in every other respect virtually epitomized orthodoxy. His chronology merely elaborated and refined the kind of calculations his contemporaries had long been making but became more dramatic because it was more exact, and because the predicted event was more startling. On two points only was he dogmatically insistent: that Christ would come, and that he would come about 1843.[8]

Miller differed from his British counterparts primarily in his refusal to accept that the Jews would be restored to Palestine and his teaching that nonbelievers would not survive the Second Coming.[9]

Although Miller became convinced in 1818 of the time of the Advent, he continued to study until 1823 to be certain that he had tried every possible objection to his finding. Then he began talking cautiously with his friends and acquaintances. He was disappointed to find them uninterested in the Lord's return. Next he talked with some of his minister friends, hoping to find one enthusiastic enough to tell people about the glorious appearing of Christ and qualified to warn the world. Failing this attempt, he began to feel a personal responsibility to spread the warning message. But he excused himself on the ground that he was unqualified.

Finally, one Saturday morning the impression came to him more urgently than ever before: "Go and tell it to the world." The impression was so real that he promised God that he would tell the world if someone asked him to preach. Thinking there was no chance that such a thing would happen, he felt relieved of the anxiety. But within half an hour a boy rode up on horseback bringing an invitation for him to present his views on the prophecies to the Baptist congregation at Dresden, New York, the next day. At first he rebelled at the idea, but then he felt that it would be a sin to break his promise to God. After "struggling with God" in prayer, he "gained the victory" and accompanied the messenger.

Sitting in an armchair in the log house of his brother-in-law, Hiram S. Guilford, with the family Bible on his lap, Miller gave his first public lecture on the Advent on that second Sunday in August 1831. It was so enthusiastically received that the services were moved to the church. Miller stayed all week, and a spiritual revival took place. When he got home the following Monday, there was a letter on his desk from the Baptist minister at Poultney, Vermont, inviting him to preach in the church there. From that time on, Miller kept busy responding to invitations in the country churches of New York, New England, and Canada. Revivals followed, and before long he was unable to answer half the calls coming from Baptist, Methodist, and Congregational churches.[10] Thus was William Miller diverted from the plow to the pulpit in spite of himself.

Miller brought his message into a social atmosphere that was ready for new ideas. Beginning in the late 1790s, Americans were entering into a series of revivals in both the East and West that were collectively known as the Second Great Awakening. Dominated by an Arminian theology, this revivalism challenged the older ecclesiastical authorities in the direction of greater spiritual autonomy for the individual. Its most famous evangelist, Calvinist Charles Finney, learned from the Methodists and made popular a number of "new measures": the anxious seat, itinerancy, mixed praying, direct and colloquial preaching, sustained seasons of private and public prayer, and the protracted meeting. Although the revivals went through periods of growth and depression, influenced to some degree by economic factors and denominational schisms, the Second Great Awakening developed, according to Richard Carwardine, primarily out of a desire for and expectancy of revivals in the churches involved. The Methodists benefited most, but the proportion of Protestant church membership in general within the American population moved from 7 percent in 1800 to 15 percent in 1855.[11]

Prompted partly by the optimism of revival religion, but even more by the major changes taking place in American society after 1814, reform movements sprang up nearly everywhere. Territorial and population expansion, improvements in the standard of living, and the movement from a relatively elite to a relatively democratic politics were taking place so rapidly that many Americans felt that things were getting out of control. In response, they engaged in movements to bring about temperance, establish humane treatment of debtors and the insane, improve health, take education to the masses, and—most importantly—end slavery. A few declined to work within the existing system and sought instead to establish communal organizations, such as Robert Owen's New Harmony in Indiana, which would plant the seeds for a totally new society. All of these efforts, along with more negatively oriented ones such as anti-Masonry and nativism, were among the several means by which antebellum men and women, as Ronald G. Walters writes, "attempted to impose moral direction on social, cultural, and economic turmoil."[12]

Although reform pervaded the world in which Miller began to preach, he was not of the class of intellectuals seeking to make the world better by human effort. In fact, isolated as he was in the rustic environment of the Lake Champlain region, he was not in touch with those reformers whose background was urban. He had made a great discovery — that Christ was coming soon — and he felt a tremendous responsibility for warning people to get ready to meet the Lord.

PREACHING THE WORD

Miller's qualifications as a speaker came only from Bible study, sincerity, and the exercise of his talent; and he became a power in the pulpit. Ministers in the small towns in New York and Canada were happy to have him preach in their churches, because great revivals often followed. Few speakers have the power to hold an audience as Miller did: eager listeners hung on his words, spellbound for two hours at a time, and packed houses were the rule. The publication of his lectures and the reports of revivals that followed his preaching in the back country led to invitations to lecture on the New England coast.

In the spring of 1840, when Miller preached a series of sermons in Portsmouth, New Hampshire, David Millard reported in the *Christian Herald* that crowds flocked to hear him. And this was only the beginning. The meetings continued after he had left, and an intense feeling pervaded the congregation such as Millard had never before seen anywhere. The word spread from that congregation to the other churches in town, and the ringing of church bells for daily meetings gave the town the atmosphere of a continual Sabbath. The oldest inhabitant, said the writer, had never witnessed such a revival.[13]

A little later, Miller lectured in Portland, Maine, with the same happy community results. Lorenzo D. Fleming of the Christian Church reported that there had never been so much religious interest among the inhabitants of the city as at that time. At some of the meetings held after Miller left, as many as 250 believers "went forward." The prayer meetings of different denominations in every part of the city were held at almost every hour of the day. When he was in the business district on April 4, Fleming said, he found a prayer meeting of thirty or forty of the principal men of the town in a room over a bank at eleven o'clock in the morning! An almost total solemnity was felt throughout the city.[14] Thus there began among the various church faiths a revival movement that gained momentum until the maximum was reached at the time Miller expected Christ to return — 1843.

By the time Miller began preaching in the larger cities, he was fifty-eight years old and his health was only fair. His physical state, together with his plain dress, gave some the mistaken first impression that he was a mediocre preacher. Expecting a fashionably dressed evangelist, Timothy Cole was taken aback when he went to meet Miller at the train and found a plainly clothed old man shaking with the palsy. Cole was sorry he had invited such a person to preach in his church. At the first service, however, he found out how mistaken he was to judge by Miller's physical appearance.[15]

In spite of Miller's health problems, he was an untiring worker with an impelling drive to save the great multitudes who would be lost if they were not warned. Of this burden he wrote: "Those souls whom I have addressed in my six months tour are constantly before me, sleeping or waking. I can see them perishing by the thousands." In January 1844 he recounted: "I have preached about 4,500 lectures in about twelve years, to at least 500,000 people."[16]

Although it took time, Miller eventually gained a following among the clergy. The first outstanding cleric was Josiah Litch, a minister of the New England Methodist Episcopal conference who accepted Miller's message in 1838 and began to write about the Advent in his support. In his book *The Probability of the Second Coming of Christ About* A.D. *1843*, published in May 1838, Litch stated that, according to his interpretation of the prophecies, the Ottoman Empire "will end in A.D. 1840, some time in the month of August."[17] This interpretation and time prediction created wide interest in his prophecies and in Miller's date for the Advent; the public looked forward to seeing whether the prediction would come true. When the Turkish Empire, which was having a hard time keeping its independence, accepted the protection of the great European powers, Litch concluded that the Muslim nation had fallen. In his *Address to the Public and the Clergy* in 1841, Litch wrote: "I am now entirely satisfied that on the 11th of August, according to previous calculation . . . the Ottoman Supremacy departed; and on the 15th of August, the control of the empire was thrown into Christian hands."[18]

Charles Fitch, an orthodox Congregational minister and pastor of the Marlboro Chapel in Boston, also became convinced of the Advent message presented by Miller; but because of the determined opposition of his fellow clergymen, he stopped preaching it. After Litch visited him, Fitch again took up Miller's message. These two men then left their pastorates and gave full time to proclaiming the Advent.[19]

An even more outstanding leader was Joshua V. Himes, who invited Miller to give a series of lectures in his Christian Connection church in Boston after hearing him preach in the latter part of 1839. At the time Himes was a vivacious young man of barely thirty-five who, as a lieutenant of William Lloyd Garrison, was experienced in the dissemination of reform propaganda for abolitionism, temperance, nonresistance, and other reforms centered at the Chardon Street Chapel. Himes became convinced of the truth of Miller's message, and he told the latter to prepare for a campaign because, he said, doors would be opened in every important city in the nation. True enough: within four years Miller's name was a newsworthy one on the front pages of the nation's press.[20]

Because of his ability as a publicist, Himes furnished the major influence in the organization and propagation of the whole Advent movement of the 1840s. Although the leaders all looked on Miller as the head of the movement, it was Himes who provided the active field leadership. In February 1840, for example, Miller expressed the wish for a periodical publication in which to present his message. Himes went down the street to an abolitionist friend and arranged for such a paper, with the result that the *Signs of the Times* appeared as a semimonthly under the date of March 20, 1840. By the end of the year, it had a subscription list of fifteen hundred; and in 1842 the *Signs* became a weekly.[21] This and similar papers served as a bond to draw Miller's followers together.

A general conference similar to the Albury conferences in England and other reform conferences in America was called to meet in the Chardon Street Chapel on October 14, 1840. All who were looking for the imminent coming of Christ were invited. The leaders desired to study the whole subject of the Advent carefully and to determine how the last warning message might be carried speedily. In view of the past experience of reform organization, they feared grave differences might develop that could break the whole movement in pieces. Fortunately, this did not happen.

Henry Dana Ward, a Congregational minister and a born reformer who was editor of the *Anti-Masonic Review and Magazine* and active in the national anti-Masonic party, was the natural choice to be chairman of the conference. With a master's degree from Harvard, he was probably the best educated of the delegates. His keynote address traced the history of the Advent hope from the time of Christ and cited the statements of the church fathers and reformers to show their original faith in the personal Advent. Calling attention to the great reforms of the day, he declared that the conference had met to forward another reform of the times, the proclamation of the near return of Christ. A written address from Miller—who could not be present because of illness—was read, and reports were given of the rapid progress of the message in various places. Before they separated, the two hundred present, who were of many creeds and denominations, celebrated communion together. They allocated money to publish the proceedings of the conference and endorsed the establishment of the *Signs of the Times*. Now there was a greater degree of unity and indeed a vehicle to promote the Advent cause. [22]

A second general conference held at Lowell, Massachusetts, in June 1841 took on the look of a permanent standing committee, with subcommittees to raise money and carry on until another such meeting would be called. Recommendations for the conduct of Advent believers in promoting the message included personal consecration, conversing with others, forming Bible classes, and holding social meetings for prayer and exhortation. The conference further recommended that each church member question his pastor about the Advent and ask him to explain certain texts—until he was led to study the subject. Each Advent believer was to remain in his church, to practice liberality, but not to abandon his business. Finally, it was recommended that a set of books be printed, to be known as a Second Advent Library, which believers could buy and circulate among their friends. The believers were then exhorted to suffer scorn and reproach with meekness, gentleness, and patience. [23]

The publishing committee elected by this conference now assumed the authority of an executive committee, making essential decisions for propagating the Advent message. These general conferences occurred at decreasing intervals until the one held at Low Hampton, New York, in November 1841. Miller had been unable to come to the others, so this time the conference came to him. His presence gave impetus and solidarity to the work. Those present decided to hold more frequent conferences at different rallying points, where large numbers could come to catch the enthusiasm generated at such gatherings. The aim seemed to be to bring these assemblies to the more isolated places so as to permeate the back country and stimulate large attendance. Consequently, the word "general" was dropped from the title—except for the occasional important meetings—and conferences that were more local in character took place more and more frequently. These conferences became one of the most important promotional agencies of the movement. [24]

Perhaps the most significant general conference of all occurred in Melodian Hall at Boston in May 1842. Joseph Bates, formerly a sea captain, was chairman and Himes was secretary; Miller, Fitch, and Litch served as committee members. Although they drew the points of faith more sharply than they had before, the leaders did not arbitrarily demand acceptance of the year 1843 as the date of the Lord's coming. A number of outstanding men, including Ward, Henry Jones, and N. N. Whiting, declined to set a date at all. They tended to drop out of major leadership roles but nevertheless continued in cordial association. The conference did pass a resolution on the shortness of time:

> Resolved, that the time has fully come for those, who believe in the second advent of our Lord Jesus in 1843, to show their faith by their works. . . .
> Resolved, that we should keep it distinctly in mind, that we are this year to do our last praying and make our last efforts, and shed our last tears for a perishing world.[25]

As David Arthur states, "The time for discussion had ended, the time for unquestioning propagation had begun."[26]

REACHING A BROADER AUDIENCE

When he started preaching, Miller had no thought of founding a sect. He supposed that the churches would enthusiastically receive "the glorious doctrine" that was founded on Scripture and held forth the joyous hope of a soon-coming Savior. He was disappointed when "enemies" called the Advent leaders schismatics, covenant breakers, and disorganizers. Again and again the leaders denied any design to form a new church and, reflecting the antisectarianism of the time, rejoiced that the "blessed hope" had drawn together many from the various churches and had broken down sectarian walls.[27] But a dynamic built up that eventually led toward separation.

Until the beginning of 1844, the Millerite movement in the smaller towns was an interchurch movement. Some form of local organization was needed, however, and it was only one step from the prayer meetings recommended by the general conference of June 1841 to the Second Advent associations. Before the year 1843 had closed, these associations had appeared in almost every city of any size in the North. The constitutions that have been preserved indicate that the prerequisite for membership was belief in the imminent coming of the Savior and a desire to disseminate the knowledge of this event.

Each member was encouraged to give a sum monthly, "if the Lord will," to carry forward the objective of the association. The members of the association rented a meeting place wherever this was possible. They would continue to attend regular worship services in the churches where they held membership; but the urgency of hastening the news of the Advent's approach impelled them to meet between times at the lecture hall with their friends from other denominations. In some instances, when a minister accepted the Millerite teaching, he carried almost all his members with him, and his people were happy to support him on missions to carry the message to members of other faiths. In other cases, the conference to which the minister belonged asked him to withdraw and, bereft of church support, he was obliged to find his living from among those who believed in the Advent. Many laymen also felt impelled to travel and tell people of the Advent and the end of the world. Like Joseph Bates, some spent the savings of a lifetime to spread the message. Others lived off the country as they traveled, with believers caring for their needs and sending them on their way with the good news of Christ's coming soon.[28]

When he lectured at Chardon Street Chapel in Boston during the winter of 1839—40, Miller stayed at the home of Himes. Himes, who could not understand why the Advent doctrine was so little known, asked Miller why he had not been in other large cities. Miller replied that he had gone wherever he had been invited, but nobody had yet invited him to go into the cities. Himes asked, "Will you go with me where doors are opened?" Miller said he was willing to go anywhere and lecture to the extent of his ability. Said Himes: "I then told him he might prepare for the campaign; for doors should be opened in every city in the Union, and the warning should go to the ends of the earth! Here I began to 'help' Father Miller."[29] It was at this time that Himes arranged for the publication of the *Signs of the Times*.

Himes was as good as his word. Having worked tirelessly in the country and small cities for eight years, Miller was now introduced to the world by the indefatigable Himes, who became his mouthpiece—his amplifier. No longer could the simple farmer remain in obscurity. The searchlight of publicity was turned squarely upon him. Like magic, Himes opened the great cities to his captain, and within three years Miller's name and doctrine were on everyone's lips.

As early as 1840, the first work had already been done in New York City; but it was like trying to dig a well through solid rock. The lecturers had worked hard but with little result. Now, in May 1842, Himes determined to take the old master himself to the great metropolis to blast through the stony crust of indifference and prejudice so that his message, springing up like a fountain of living water, could revive the city. On their arrival, Himes and Miller found that the results of the previous visit had been so thoroughly obliterated that there was no one to invite them home for a night's lodging. They rented Apollo Hall at 410 Broadway at heavy expense and used an anteroom for lodging; they slept on the hard floor until they made friends who would bring cots. According to Litch, the impression had spread that the Advent people were monsters, and for several days women were frightened away from the meetings. Before the meetings closed, however, prejudice had given way, and the house was filled with attentive listeners—with the result that many of them became believers.[30]

PUBLICATIONS

The autumn of 1842 saw another, greater campaign in New York. Literature was needed for such an evangelistic drive, and the leaders determined to establish a daily paper in conjunction with it. They announced that this paper, to be called the *Midnight Cry*, would run for four weeks and be discontinued at the end of that time unless the people showed sufficient interest to support it permanently. Accordingly, ten thousand copies were published daily and given away or hawked by newsboys on the streets of the great city. The first number was dated November 17, 1842. The expenditures for two months exceeded the receipts by a thousand dollars; nevertheless, the courage of the promoters and the ease with which subscriptions were secured led to its continuation. At the completion of the first volume as a daily, a second volume appeared as a weekly. So wide was the distribution of the *Midnight Cry* at this time that it aroused great interest throughout the country, and thousands who had never heard a lecture accepted the Advent doctrine.[31]

After the success of this experience, the campaign made it a practice to start a paper and run it a few weeks at a given place in connection with a series of evangelistic meetings; they followed this more or less consistently. They selected vantage points for big campaigns, and they sent the paper into the surrounding country. Ordinarily the papers ceased publication after a short time; but in a few instances they were continued.

In the autumn of 1842, Litch started a crusade in Philadelphia, another strategic point. The message gained a precarious foothold there, but in the face of bitterest resistance.[32] Early in 1843, Litch started a penny paper called the *Trumpet of Alarm*. About fifty thousand copies were circulated during the life of its first volume. At certain places Himes supported more permanent papers—not because they paid their way but because they were located in advantageous places, and the spread of the message dictated the need. When Fitch started the *Second Advent of Christ* in Cleveland on little more than faith, Himes wrote encouragement to his fellow worker: "The paper which you have started is of the utmost importance to the cause, and must be sustained. . . . It can be made to speak trumpet tongues. I have sent you *one hundred dollars* to help sustain it; twenty-five of which was from a friend in Providence, R.I., the rest from the Lord's treasury, 14 Devonshire Street."[33]

The *Voice of Elijah*, published by R. Hutchinson at Montreal, was largely supported by Himes. Since transportation of papers between Canada and England was free, the Adventist leaders saw that every packet boat between Canada and England carried quantities of the *Voice of Elijah*. This paper, well supported by gifts from the believers in the United States, continued to spread the message until the autumn of 1844.

In Great Britain the Advent message as preached by Miller was initially disseminated entirely by printed matter. But at the first camp meeting held in the United States in 1842, a young Englishman named Robert Winter accepted Miller's message and returned to give it in England. At Bristol in 1844, he and an associate began to publish a weekly paper they called the *Second Advent Harbinger*. They also published copies of the *Midnight Cry* and many books on the Advent written by the movement's leaders in America. A number of camp meetings took place, and Winter declared in a letter to Litch that there was not a county in England where the literature had not been scattered. He wrote that great numbers of those who believed that the Lord was coming in 1843 were going from house to house exhorting sinners to prepare to meet God.[34]

The *Western Midnight Cry* was founded at Cincinnati and *Glad Tidings of the Kingdom to Come* at Rochester, New York. Both publications served their areas but did not have enough circulation to support them; however, the leaders felt that they were too strategically located to discontinue. And women were not left out: at Boston in 1844, Himes began the publication of the *Advent Message to the Daughters of Zion*, with Clarinda S. Minor as editor.[35]

A small hymnal entitled *Millennial Harp and Millennial Musings* appeared in 1842. Although some songs were new, the editors had selected mostly older pieces from Europe and America that contained sentiments on the Second Coming of Christ or on subjects related to it. As a rule, the tunes were plaintive, yet the sentiments were joyful. Lecturers with good voices made effective use of these songs to create an atmosphere for their subject. When Bates and his singing evangelist, H. S. Gurney, went into the South, Bates said the slaves who were allowed to attend the meetings would sing, "Gabriel goina blow! Gabriel goina blow!"[36]

Another kind of publishing that proved effective was the so-called 1843 prophetic chart. At the opening of the general conference at Boston in May 1842, Fitch and Apollos Hale presented the prophecies of Daniel and John through pictorial images they had painted on cloth. Portrayed were the great metallic image of Daniel 2, the numerous beasts of Daniel and of Revelation, and the beginnings and endings of various prophetic periods. The use of this chart device was thought to be in fulfillment of Habakkuk 2:2: "The Lord answered me: 'Write the vision; make it plain upon tables, so he may run who reads it.' " The conference gratefully received the chart and voted to have three hundred of them prepared — lithographed or printed on silk, cotton, or paper — to sell, from twenty-five cents to $2.50 each. The charts were nearly three feet wide and twice as long.

From that time on, a lecturer was considered incompletely equipped without the chart rolled up under his arm. Traveling on canal boat, river steamer, or coastal packet, the lecturer would hang the chart on a cabin wall and stand looking at the strange medley of beasts, figures, and diagrams. When a curious group had gathered around, he would launch into a full-blown lecture. Late in August 1844, for example, when Miller was on his tour into Ohio, about a hundred Advent supporters from Akron chartered a canal boat and went up to Cleveland to hear him preach. Miller and Himes accompanied them on their way back to Akron. The boat became a happy evangelistic vehicle, with singing, prayer, and a lecture by Miller enroute. But there was always the reminder that they had no time to be idle. The constant spur to energetic, zealous work was the exhortation that "time is short."[37]

A variation of the chart idea was the missionary writing tablet. On the top half of each sheet was a prophetic diagram; the bottom half was blank to give the writer space to explain the meaning of what was at the top. Believers used these tablets for corresponding with their friends: folded once, the sheet constituted an envelope. In the days before envelopes and stamps were used, the folded sheet was held together by a seal, or a "monitory wafer," similar to a Christmas or Easter seal and sold in sheets like stamps. Himes printed an Adventist version of monitory wafers, on each of which was an appropriate Scripture text or a warning to be ready for the Second Coming of Christ that was approaching.[38]

In addition, various writings of outstanding leaders were printed and bound together to form a volume (or volumes) known collectively as an "Advent Library." Depending on the number of volumes, these sold for between three and ten dollars and were meant to be taken home and lent to neighbors. The spoken word of the lecturers and the printed word thus went hand in hand: wherever a lecturer went, there was an immediate call for printed matter; and wherever the printed word was sent, there was a call for lectures.

To open the way for the lecturer, Himes would send out thousands of bundles of papers. Each postmaster and newspaper office in a state received a bundle containing instructions for the recipient to cut the bundle and distribute the papers to those who called for their mail or their paper. Workers placed bundles of papers on ships and requested the crews to drop them off at every port of call in the world. Thus papers went everywhere that English was read and reached all the known mission stations in this manner. The leaders felt that the gospel had reached the whole world and that the Great Commission was being fulfilled.[39]

Miller's people also used the public press. Himes would send religious printed matter to newspapers and invite them to reprint anything they wished. Newspapers often reported the sermons in detail when a big evangelistic effort, camp meeting, or conference convened. On occasion, an adherent would even buy advertising space to warn the world of its danger. Such an advertisement appeared in the *Philadelphia Public Ledger* in a prominent manner just before October 22, 1844: "Warning—I believe according to the Scriptures, that the Lord Jesus Christ, will be revealed in the clouds of Heaven, on the tenth day of the seventh month, which agrees with the 22nd inst. I therefore entreat all whom this may reach to prepare to meet their God. Clorinda S. Minor."[40]

CAMP MEETINGS

The general conference held in Boston in May 1842 discussed the holding of camp meetings. Many felt that the believers were too few in number and too poorly organized to try an undertaking as big as holding even one such meeting; but finally, after hesitation, the conference decided to hold three. Thereafter, the camp meeting concept spread like wildfire. At least 31 were held that year, 40 in 1843, and 54 in 1844—a total of at least 125 camp meetings in the three years they were held. The number of those attending varied, according to the reports, between four thousand and fifteen thousand. If one uses the smallest reported number—four thousand per camp meeting—as a basis for estimating the total, no fewer than half a million people attended Millerite camp meetings during the three years from 1842 to 1844.[41]

The camp meeting idea had originated on the frontier almost spontaneously during the Great Revival of 1800, when the pioneers, hungering for "spiritual food," assembled to hear the word of God and camped for several days to enjoy the "feast" of preaching and Christian fellowship. Those meetings were held in the forests under the boughs of the great trees. The Methodist Church, particularly, had continued the camp meeting as an institution; and it is quite evident that the Advent supporters took over the institution from them. The worshipers brought good-sized tents and pitched them in a circle perhaps twenty-five yards from the outer edge of the open-air meeting place. Known as the "circle of the tents," this area (something like the temple court) was considered sacred. The numerous tents were large enough to accommodate all the people from a given town or neighborhood. Three meetings—morning, afternoon, and evening—took place in the open-air auditorium. At other times "testimony" and prayer meetings were held in the community tents. If rain prevented the three general gatherings in the big outdoor arena, the people crowded into the living tents for these meetings. A "tentmaster" was in charge of each tent to hold morning worship and coordinate matters.

The first camp meeting—although it was not planned to be—convened at Hatley, Quebec, beginning on June 21, 1842, when Litch's visit to that area met with such a warm response that the people decided on the spur of the moment to hold a camp meeting. So great was the interest that another began a week later in the United States at East Kingston, New Hampshire.[42]

Disruption by irreligious people who came to cause trouble was often a problem at camp meetings, one the Methodists had wrestled with for years. Some states had passed laws forbidding the sale of liquor within a specified distance of the camp meeting. But in spite of these precautions, liquor was obtainable beyond the legal limits, and rowdies would come into camp to stir up trouble. Hiram Munger, who was a kind of perennial camp superintendent for the Advent believers, was equal to the offenders. On one occasion, anticipating a visit from the rowdies, Munger stationed some stout helpers in ambush at the entrance of the camp. The ruffians came into camp, tore down the tent of the worshiping black slaves, jumped into a rig, and galloped away in high glee. But Munger's men stopped the horses at the gate, seized the troublemakers, and tied them up. Then came a discussion about what should be done with them: they deserved to be turned over to the sheriff. The case thoroughly tested the nonresistance principles of the leaders; but finally they prayed with the rogues and let them go. [43]

Customarily a parting ceremony closing these great convocations included a song and farewell prayer. The senior minister would then lead, and all would follow in single file to form a great circle around the camp; then the column would break and double back so that everyone could shake hands with everyone else. The *Salem Gazette* editor, who witnessed "the parting" at a camp meeting in 1842, said that when brothers in Christ grasped the hands of other brothers, tears coursed down their cheeks and with choked voices they exhorted one another to be ready to meet at the next great camp meeting on the "sea of glass."[44] It is clear that the camp meetings, along with the publications and the conferences, contributed to a developing sense of community and identity, despite the leaders' desire to avoid forming a sect. [45]

The first United States camp meeting in New Hampshire voted to raise eight hundred dollars to buy a large tent to be used for lectures in the various towns. By this time, community opposition had risen to the point where it was difficult to rent a hall. But even if meeting places had been available, none was large enough to accommodate the huge crowds that gathered. Five hundred dollars was subscribed on the spot, and the "great tent," as it was called, was purchased immediately. Said to be the largest in America, the tent was 120 yards in circumference and had a center pole 55 feet high. Himes reported that it could seat four thousand people, and an additional two thousand could be crowded into the aisles (and presumably around the perimeter).[46]

The great tent was pitched eight times in 1842, and the advertising value alone was tremendously worthwhile. Because the size of the tent attracted even more interest than the camp meetings had, a combination tent meeting and camp meeting now developed. Pitched on a suitable spot near town, the great tent served both purposes. As was the custom of the Methodists, however, most of the camp meetings still used no large tent auditorium.

Big tent meetings, camp meetings, and city efforts were just part of the endeavor to warn the world. Overnight, doctors, school teachers, shoemakers, students, and housewives felt an irresistible urge to tell the people of their imminent danger. O. R. Fassett, who had a growing medical practice in western New York, and his wife accepted the Adventist doctrine, and he then tried his hand at holding a few meetings at a school house, never dreaming of leaving his practice. The people were so eager to listen, and he was so successful in telling them, that he never went back to his profession. Mrs. Fassett soon began to lecture as well, and together they preached and visited homes. Luther Boutelle, a shoemaker who had heard Miller lecture in a Congregational church, accepted the message and, filled with enthusiasm, abandoned his bench to give the "last warning." He started out on foot with "one penny and the promise of God," and went into the neighboring state. The man whose home he stayed at the first night was so impressed that he lent Boutelle a team and sleigh and even gave him money to pay for feed for the horses. The shoemaker-preacher was so well received that he continued on his lecture circuit. Schoolteacher Lucy Maria Hersey, a native of Worcester, Massachusetts, felt impelled to give the "call to repentance." She resigned her position to travel and preach with her father; and great revivals crowned her work.[47] The diversity of individuals preaching the Advent message, however, held dangers as well. As more people participated, it became more difficult to maintain the unity of belief and practice. But the expectation of the Lord's imminent return gave the movement its needed focus for the time being.[48]

With the dawning of 1843, Miller sent out a New Year's address to his followers that read, in part:

> This year, according to our faith, is the last year that Satan will reign in our earth; . . . let everyone of us try by persuasion, by the help and grace of God, to get one at least of our friends to come to Christ. . . . This year, a glorious year! . . . This year the long looked for year of years, the best, it is come. I shall hope to meet you all, through faith in God, and the blood of the Lamb. Until then, farewell.[49]

The year opened with perhaps the greatest campaign in the history of the Millerite movement—the "assault" on Philadelphia. Litch had started with a fair amount of success; but the result was that all of the churches had been closed to him. Now he secured the services of a committee of thirty men, each representing a different creed. With faith in the drawing ability of Miller (who preached nightly to overflow crowds), he rented the famous Chinese Museum, a mammoth hall said to hold fifteen thousand people. Even if one allows for great exaggeration, the museum was a large structure. The city was rocked from "core to circumference," said Litch. "Saints rejoiced, the wicked trembled, backsliders quaked, and the word of the Lord ran and was glorified. It is doubtful whether Mr. Miller gave a course of lectures with greater effect than at that time."[50]

THE DATE

William Miller never personally set a precise date for Christ's Second Coming. It appears that he felt it unreasonable to pinpoint a date when interpreting a time period that extended over hundreds and thousands of years. He said only that he expected the Lord to come "about the year 1843." Furthermore, he did not press this approximate date. The time simply emphasized the urgency of preparation of life to meet a holy God. His concern was to warn people to abandon their sins and get ready to meet Christ. "The hour of God's judgment is at hand—prepare to meet thy God," was his message.

Nevertheless, Miller's followers kept urging him to be more specific concerning an exact date. He had not studied Jewish chronology particularly, but he did know that the Jewish year began in the spring. Therefore, in response to questioning, Miller said that he thought the Lord would come in the Jewish year 1843, that is, sometime between March 21, 1843 and March 21, 1844.[51]

As the spring of 1843 opened up, there was marked acceleration in the tempo of the movement. The leaders resolved to open the West to the message, and they sent J. B. Cook by canal to Pittsburgh and from there down the Ohio River to Cincinnati. They planned, further, to reinforce Fitch at Cleveland and cover northern Ohio. A mission to Great Britain to be led by Himes was projected but never followed up on, perhaps because time was deemed too short and Himes was too busy in America. A collection was taken for work among blacks, and John W. Lewis, a black minister, was ready to give his full time to that. A marked accretion among ministers was also evident, including N. N. Whiting, a well-known Hebrew and Greek scholar, and Elon Galusha, president of the New York Baptist Association, both of whom actively propagated the message.[52]

Because the adherents in various places had no adequate meeting halls, the leaders in the early part of 1843 began to build tabernacles, dotting the East and all the sizable towns in Ohio with inexpensive, commodious halls, an activity that caused widespread comment in the papers.

The advertisements of the newspapers of the day indicate that the Advent message was common knowledge. One such advertisement under the caption "Astonishing News" pictured an angel flying "in the clouds of heaven" carrying a scroll on which appeared the words "The Time Has Come." The caption below the picture read: "When consumption may be classed with the curable diseases. Wistar's Balsam of Wild Cherry."[53] Another advertisement was even more to the point: printed in glaring, heavy type was THE WORLD DESTROYED; in smaller type beneath it appeared the explanation that a world of misery, distress, and disease had been destroyed during the past twelve months by the use of Dr. Halsted's Magnetic Remedies.[54]

The more scholarly religious world also took note of the Millerite teaching. An article entitled "End of the World" opened *Graham's Magazine* for March 1843. The speech of Dr. E. Nott before the National Institute at Washington, D.C., on April 4, 1844, addressed the "Origin, Duration, and End of the World."[55]

That spring also brought a flood of scoffing, abuse, and puns. The Millerites and their leader—"the end of the world man," "the great conflagrationist," "the world burner"—were the butt of many jokes. The *New York Sunday Mercury*, in mockery of "Parson Miller" and his chronology, proved that the world would end in 1843 by multiplying the wrinkles on the horns of a five-year-old ram by the twelve signs of the zodiac and that product by the number of seeds in a summer squash.[56] The Advent supporters saw such mockery as merely a fulfillment of the prophecies, for Peter had prophesied long ago that in the last days scoffers would arise.

One of the stories that was part of the poking fun of Millerites was that those looking for the Advent wore ascension robes, that they gathered in cemeteries robed in readiness to meet Christ and go home to heaven with him. The stories differed: some said the robes were made of white muslin, others that they were made of satin, and still others that they were made of drab mackintosh. In no place is there any record of Adventist teaching that any special garb should be worn. If there had been such instruction, Millerites certainly would not have denied it, for they stood firm for what they believed. But as early as 1842, critics were charging that the Millerites wore robes.

Francis D. Nichol, in his defense of the Millerite movement, *The Midnight Cry*, cites twenty-nine instances in which Adventist papers refuted the charge that Miller's followers wore ascension robes.[57] This tale was one of those stories that people love to repeat. There were many newspaper articles, but none was an eyewitness account. As a rule, such stories began with the words "it is said" or "it is reported." Then followed a story that in some locality, miles away from the place of publication, people were wearing robes. It is a historical fact that many people believed these stories; but church historians today generally agree with Himes, who, as one of his final acts, summed up the matter in his letter to the *Outlook* of October

1894 that "the ascension robe story is a tissue of falsehoods from beginning to end."[58]

FANATICISM

Akin to the ascension robe charges were the numerous reports of an upsurge of insanity among individuals attending Millerite meetings. Reports abounded that people lost their reason and killed themselves or their loved ones while in a religious frenzy. Some Millerites in their right minds were labeled insane by their neighbors. It is not strange that a man's neighbors, and especially his heirs apparent, might think him demented if he suddenly began to give away, right and left, what he had spent his whole life earning, toward the promotion of this new doctrine. It would also appear that opponents were all too happy to look for weak spots in the Millerite armor.

The superintendent of the Worcester Insane Asylum in Massachusetts, in his report of December 1, 1842, stated that some new views of religious truth had recently disturbed many persons and brought a number of patients under the institution's care.[59] The *American Journal of Insanity* in January 1845, upon recording and evaluating the reports of the various insane asylums for 1844, judged that Millerism was responsible for a substantial increase in religious insanity. In his defense of the Millerite movement, Nichol points out that methods of detecting the cause of insanity were in their infancy, and that in at least two asylums the official reasons recorded for a patient's derangement were the ones given by those who committed him. From the facts available one can presume that a rise in "insanity" supposedly caused by religious fervor accompanied all great religious awakenings. But the charges of wild excesses, suicides, homicides, and other disorders were actually exaggerations, gladly reported by those who wanted to scoff.[60]

As to whether fanaticism accompanied the preaching of the Advent message from 1831 to 1844, conflicting statements were made in all sincerity. The term is difficult to define: "fanaticism" means one thing to one person and something else to another person with a different background. The Methodists of that day, with a long line of frontier camp meeting experience, and the Christian Connection, to which Joseph Bates belonged, were informal in their worship. In the eyes of the Episcopal Church and other more formal groups, these informal churches were "extreme." Naturally, members of the informal groups brought their manner of worship into the Advent movement, which certainly was an interchurch movement in its beginnings. For example, the report of the Methodist (not Millerite) camp meeting at Plymouth, New Hampshire, stated that "the heavenly breezes were sweetly passing over us, and the grove, for a great distance around, echoed and reechoed with shouts of *Glory to God, Halleluja.*" In the same paper the report of the Glastonbury, Connecticut, camp meeting said: "We remember the rapturous songs of praise, and the deafening yet soul inspiring shoutings."[61]

The Methodists, from whose ranks most Millerites came, could hardly be expected to change their manner of worship overnight. An observer spoke of the confusion in the tents at the Salem Adventist camp meeting in 1842, stating that utter chaos reigned in the community living tents where the work for the unconverted took place. One man was shouting "Glory!" while another was praying; and when the dinner bell rang during a prayer, someone shouted, "Make a short prayer." Bates said of the same meeting that sometimes, hearing a "shout of victory" coming from one of the tents, the campers rushed to see who was converted. It was common also for a worshiper to swoon away—or "lose strength," as it was called. Bates said that at the 1842 camp meeting at Taunton, Massachusetts, when the invitation was given to come forward for prayer, "among the mourners were about thirty ministers who prostrated themselves, some of them on their faces, beseeching God for mercy, and a preparation to meet their coming Lord!" The report of the meeting at Palmer, Massachusetts, in May 1843 said that "God shook the whole encampment and many fell prostrate in front of the stand."[62] These things should be accepted for what they were: informal worship as practiced by certain churches.

The real problem, however, was that of fanaticism stemming from a deviation in the doctrine of perfection, or "entire sanctification." The idea was popular at this time at certain centers in the Congregational Church, especially at two college centers: Yale in New Haven, Connecticut, and Oberlin College in Ohio. The chief source of the problem in the Millerite context was John Starkweather, a graduate of Andover Theological Seminary, who had a reputation for "superior sanctity." Because Himes was occupied in general duties, he had installed Starkweather as assistant pastor of the Chardon Street Chapel. Starkweather soon demanded to be given joint control with Himes over the publishing business; when his demand was denied, he felt abused. By this time he was discovered to be teaching that, in addition to conversion, one needed a second work, "sanctification," usually manifested by the loss of physical strength. These bodily manifestations Starkweather called the "sealing power."

When Starkweather finally wore out his popularity, Himes was able to exclude him from headquarters but not from the movement—since there was no formal church organization. So Starkweather continued to work among the believers and took a leading part in some of the camp meetings despite the objections of Miller, Himes, and other leaders.[63] In the three 1843 autumn meetings in Connecticut, fanaticism appeared to be especially strong. While Starkweather preached, an individual who claimed to have a "discerning spirit" passed up and down the aisles with a green bough in his hand, waving it over his head and crying "hallelujah" and "glory" at the top of his voice. He began pointing toward certain ones, "sealing" them for eternal damnation. In order to be "sanctified," one had to discard all worldly items. People began to throw away brooches, safety chains, finger rings, and even a set of false teeth. Some women cut off their hair because they were persuaded that it was their "idol." Arriving at the camp, Litch declared from the lectern that these objectionable manifestations were "of the devil" and that the fanatics had to leave. Later, when he read the account in the *Philadelphia Public Ledger,* he wrote to Himes: "I find in the papers of this morning an account of the Second Advent camp meeting near Bridgeport, Ct. The picture is, to be sure, a dark one, but no more so than the truth will warrant." He continued that fanaticism was not peculiar to the present Advent movement; John Wesley had had to contend with it, and it had ruined the Advent cause under Edward Irving in England.[64]

Subsequent incidents at Philadelphia, in connection with the day of the Great Disappointment, were even more unfortunate, since they involved George Storrs, one of the more prominent leaders of the movement. A Dr. C. R. Gorgas, claiming to have the gift of prophecy, predicted that the Lord would come at three o'clock on the morning of October 22. Furthermore, he said, it was revealed to him that the righteous were to leave the cities before the day of destruction, just as Lot fled from Sodom. Storrs carried the three o'clock time message to the *Midnight Cry* editor, who, on the spur of the moment, published it under the title of "Midnight Cry Extra." Storrs later apologized and said he had erred in judgment because he had been mesmerized by the self-proclaimed prophet. In harmony with his message to withdraw from the cities, Gorgas led a group of about 150 people outside of Philadelphia, where they camped in tents to await the coming of Christ. The whole movement suffered a great deal of bad publicity from the acts of this little group, only a fraction of the estimated 6,000 believers in Philadelphia.[65]

Such incidents resulted from the diversity of participants and a lack of central control over the movement. As David Rowe writes,

> But considering the ease with which converts to the cause added their own ideas and notions to Adventist doctrine and the leaders' inability to know all that was going on under their auspices, such activities could have taken place without their knowledge. At any rate, if such stories were true for a small number of Millerites, they certainly were not for the vast majority, who were sober pious Christians.[66]

During the spring of 1843 the believers lifted up their heads in the expectation that their redemption was near. The *Signs* adopted a policy of receiving subscription money for three months only. Papers carried the information that a volume would be published "if time lasts that long." Camp meetings were announced for certain dates "if time continue" or "if time permit."[67]

SETTING THE DATE

Great revivals took place in the churches in many sections of the country. Between January and April 1843, the *Western Christian Advocate* of Cincinnati, a non-Millerite paper, devoted a large amount of space to reporting revival news from the West and Midwest. A correspondent of the *New York Herald* filed the story of the great revival in Dayton, Ohio, on January 12 under the title "New and Extraordinary Offensive and Defensive against the Devil." He explained that all the ministers of the various denominations met together once a week in league against the archenemy of mankind, planning to warn the world of Christ's coming. Occasionally, the congregations met together, and numbers were added to the churches daily. The Albany correspondent for the *New York Herald* said that the religious revival that began with the visit of the great tent in August 1842 still raged. Amusements of every kind had declined in popularity; nightly performances were given before empty seats at theaters and museums. Two or three members of the legislature had even been converted, he said.[68]

As the year 1843 progressed, pressure from opponents caused Miller's associates to reassess the exact beginning and close of the year 1843 as computed by the Jews. The Karaite Jews, reckoning the start of the year according to the letter of the Mosaic law, commenced the year with the new moon nearest barley harvest at Jerusalem. The Rabbinic Jews, who were scattered around the world and could not observe when barley is ripe at Jerusalem, started their year by astronomical computation. The Advent leaders' problem was to determine which was the logical biblical computation, and they decided that the Karaite method was the logical one. According to the Karaite ceremony, the Jewish year 1843 closed at sunset April 18, 1844; the Jewish year 1844 would begin at the same time. The Advent leaders thus set that time as the end of "the year 1843." This attempt to establish the precise bounds of 1843 was erroneously interpreted by a hostile press as setting a new date.[69]

The equinox passed, April 18 passed, and on May 2, Miller sent an address to the Advent supporters saying: "*I confess my error,* and acknowledge *my disappointment:* yet I still believe that the day of the Lord is near, even at the door." In the first week of May at the general conference at Boston he publicly apologized. He was disappointed, he said, but his faith in God was not shaken. Although the supposed time was past, God's time had not passed. He referred to Habakkuk 2:3: "If the vision tarry, wait for it." The Adventist papers talked courage. It was said that the time in which they found themselves was the "tarrying time" of the parable of the ten virgins (Matt. 25:5); the believer should have a supply of oil and should watch, keep his light trimmed, and burning, and be ready to go in to the marriage feast.[70]

In spite of rationalizations, however, there was the keenest disappointment. Gloom settled down on those who had so firmly expected to see Christ come at that time. Many left the Adventist ranks. But opponents, expecting that the whole movement would explode, were surprised to see the larger part of the group continue on with renewed courage and hope. To encourage the believers, leaders took the big tent out of storage at Cincinnati and started it on its way to the frontier West; they announced camp meetings; and lecturers gave the warning message that this was the "tarrying time," the closing scenes of earth's history. Miller made a western tour, visiting Rochester, Buffalo, Toronto, Akron, and Cincinnati; he intended to visit St. Louis, but floods and sickness in that area made it seem unwise to do so.[71]

In May 1843, Miller had pointed out that a number of observances of the Jews had taken place in the seventh month. He presented this information not as anything conclusive but as worthy of prayerful consideration; thus it was dropped. Writers in the papers had also called attention to the fact that in order to make the number 2,300 complete, it would take all of 457 and all of 1843. Therefore, if in reality the 2,300-day period began after the first of 457 B.C., it would end at just that point in 1844. This observation also passed without undue notice. All through the summer the adherents took the position that they were occupying the short period of time just before the coming of the Bridegroom. The waiting leaders were in an expectant attitude when a camp meeting convened at Exeter, New Hampshire, on August 12, 1844.

Joseph Bates said that he went to this meeting with the impression that he would "receive new light." On the third day he was invited to speak; but while he was speaking, a woman interrupted him to say there was someone on the grounds who had new light and should be given time to present it. Bates courteously yielded. Samuel S. Snow, the elder in question, then presented what has come to be known as the seventh-month message, or the "true midnight cry." Snow had published an article in February 1843 arguing that Christ would come in the fall of 1844 rather than in the spring. He was convinced that the Jewish Day of Atonement was a type of the Judgment Day: it would occur on the tenth day of the seventh month, or October 22, 1844. He presented the thought that the decree of Artaxerxes went forth sometime in the middle of the year, and if that was so, the 2,300-year period would end in the autumn. Furthermore, the parable of the ten virgins worked into this interpretation, because the virgins slept during the "tarrying time"; but at midnight, or roughly six months after the beginning of the year, the cry was made, "Behold, the bridegroom cometh; go ye out to meet him." Therefore, Snow argued, on the basis of the types and antitypes, the coming of Christ would occur on October 22, 1844. Bates said that the "true midnight cry" worked like leaven, and the people left the camp with the ringing cry: "Behold, the Bridegroom cometh! . . . Get ready! Get ready!"[72]

Snow published the *True Midnight Cry* at Haverhill, Massachusetts, on August 22, 1844. His February message, which had lain like a smoldering brand for six months, now ignited the tinder-dry territory of a waiting people, and it spread across the nation like a prairie fire. It met ready response from papers not under the direct control of Himes. The followers had moved ahead of the leaders. In his *Bible Examiner* editorial on September 24, Storrs said:

> I take up my pen with feelings such as I never before experienced. *Beyond a doubt,* in my mind, the tenth day of the seventh month will witness the revelation of our Lord Jesus Christ in the clouds of heaven. . . . I think the hour will be in the evening of the tenth day (of the seventh month). I incline to believe that those who watch for the day and hour will understand both, before they arrive.

Others elsewhere took up the idea. Said Isaac C. Wellcome: "The influence of this *time message* went forth like the released waters of a mighty river when the dam has given away." Miller and Himes, who were in the West and did not hear of the new interpretation until late, apparently were not inclined to accept it at first but were swept along with the tidal wave. Miller accepted it on October 6, and on the tenth the *Midnight Cry* yielded to the movement.[73]

Meanwhile, as opposition to Miller's message became more pronounced in the churches, Advent believers felt less at home there. The ministers who had espoused Millerism suffered especially by being expelled from their conferences and set adrift without a livelihood. Methodist ministers were particularly vulnerable because of their episcopal form of organization. L. F. Stockman of Portland, Maine, near death with consumption in 1843, was told that if he did not give up Millerism, he would be lost and conference funds reserved for families of deceased ministers would be withheld from his widow. He stood firm—and died leaving his family unprovided for.[74] As a result of instances similar to this and the antisectarian sentiments popular at the time, Adventists began to doubt the moral condition of churches that opposed them yet made no attack on slavery, liquor, or other evils of the day.

In Cleveland, Fitch published in the July 26 *Second Advent of Christ* the sermon "Come out of her my people," taking his title from Revelation 18, wherein a mighty angel cries, "Babylon is fallen," and a voice warns, "Come out of her, my people." Protestants had long taught that Babylon was the Catholic church. But Fitch, applying the title also to the Protestant churches that rejected the Advent message, advised those who were looking for Christ's return to leave their fellowship before the "glorious hope" was stifled within them. Thousands of members left the churches, either voluntarily or involuntarily. Miller deplored this course of action,[75] but it was the culmination of accelerating developments. David Arthur has written:

> Yet the Millerites were the initiaters, the aggressors. It was they who were propagating, indeed trying to force acceptance of, new views. They had expressed these vigorously in their churches and public meetings and had questioned ministers before congregations. They had established their own meetings, presses, associations, conferences, camp-meetings, despite assertions that they were not trying to disrupt or divide the churches or to establish a new one. Their spirit was sometimes ungenerous and censorious, causing the leaders to admonish their followers. While believing themselves to have laid aside sectarian views, they had in truth established their own.[76]

THE DAY

As the 22d of October approached, people prepared to leave the world bodily, just as someone going on a long trip gets his business affairs in order. Moreover, there was a sense of the utter lack of the value of possessions. Farmers refused to harvest their crops, merchants closed their stores, mechanics abandoned their shops, and laborers deserted their employers. People paid their debts, and those who had money left over freely shared it with fellow believers so that they too might settle up and owe no one anything. Large amounts of money were brought in, received, and disbursed without any accounting.[77]

At the last minute, some people gave quantities of money to help disseminate the warning; but it was too late, and these belated givers went away in despair because they had not given more generously before. Newspapers of the day record that banks, the United States Treasury, and other financial agencies received large amounts of money from those who had defrauded creditors. A reporter for the *Philadelphia Public Ledger* noticed the following in the window of I. T. Hough, the tailor, on Fifth Street: "This shop is closed in honor of the King of Kings, who will appear about the 22nd of October. Get ready, friends, to crown him Lord of all."[78] Methodists, Congregationalists, and Presbyterians, whose creeds do not require immersion, hastened to the water for that form of baptismal rite. The urgency of preparation is indicated by the following notice: "If any human being has a just pecuniary claim against me, he is requested to inform me instantly. N. Southard."[79]

The great tent was furled for the last time, never to be unrolled until "the heavens" were "rolled together as a scroll." With an enthusiasm akin to that of the Crusaders led by Peter the Hermit, the Adventists sacrificed their possessions, confessed their sins, and prepared for their journey to the Holy City, the New Jerusalem.

An eyewitness described the meeting of the believers at Rochester, New York, on October 22, the day of expectation. The day dawned bright and clear, and believers came to the meeting place early and continued to pray and testify of their faith. Speakers used such phrases as "last hours of time," "last moments of time," "we're living on the brink of eternity."[80] The day dragged on slowly—to noon, to sunset, to midnight. Finally, daybreak of October 23 came as on any other day, and the worshipers went home, worn out and bitterly disappointed. This day has come to be known among Adventists as the day of Great Disappointment.

Not only grief-stricken, the believers felt forsaken of friends.

Regarding the bitterness of that sorrow, even after years had passed, Hiram Edson of Port Gibson, New York, recalled: "Our fondest hopes and expectations were blasted, and such a spirit of weeping came over us as I never experienced before. It seemed that the loss of all earthly friends could have been no comparison. We wept till the day dawned."[81] James White said that when, "a few days after the passing of the time," Himes came to Portland, Maine, and told the group that they would have to prepare for another cold winter on this earth, "my feelings were almost uncontrollable. I left the place of meeting and wept like a child."[82]

Recalled Joseph Bates: "The effect of this disappointment can be realized only by those who experienced it." And again: "Hope sunk and courage died within them." At a time when one's faith in the Bible itself was tested and one needed friends, the neighbors and fellow townsmen loosed a flood of scoffing and mockery: "I thought you were going up yesterday" and similarly cruel gibes. The morning after the Great Disappointment, Bates went out to purchase some provisions for his family. Children followed, mocking him, and men pointed at him derisively. Of this humiliating experience he confided to a fellow Adventist minister some years later:

> You can have no idea of the feeling that seized me. I had been a respected citizen, and had with much confidence exhorted the people to be ready for the expected change. With these taunts thrown at me, if the earth could have opened and swallowed me up, it would have been sweetness compared to the distress I felt.[83]

William Miller wrote to Himes on November 18:

> Some are tauntingly inquiring, "have you not gone up?" Even little children in the streets are shouting continually to passers-by "Have you a ticket to go up?" The public prints, of the most fashionable and popular kind, in the great Sodoms of our country, are caricaturing in the most shameful manner the "white robes of the saints," Rev. 6:11, the "going up" and the great day of "burning." Even the pulpits are desecrated by the repetition of scandalous and false reports concerning the "ascension robes."[84]

A great flood of actual physical persecution burst forth on October 23. Mobs broke into meetings and dragged out the worshipers, meeting places were stoned, and it was reported that the tabernacles at Ithaca and Danville, New York, were destroyed.

Never did Himes show his generalship more favorably than in the hour of defeat. He rallied the broken forces and reorganized.

Within a week after October 22, he and his associates had recovered from their dazed condition and begun to publish the papers once more. As resourceful and efficient as ever, he immediately began to make provision for the needs of the destitute who faced the coming winter. He asked the believers in each city to aid their needy associates, and accordingly Philadelphia was districted. The leaders also urged the adherents to go to work and cease congregating to speculate on the time for the Advent.[85]

DIVERGENCE IN ADVENTISM

The ground of their specific day of expectation having been cut from under them, what were the believers to do? Although many left the Advent cause, others were simply perplexed and bewildered. Miller was as nonplused as were his followers. He wrote to Himes: "We have done our work in warning sinners, and in trying to awake a formal church. God in his providence, has shut the door; we can only stir one another up to be patient; and be diligent to make our calling and election sure."[86] This was merely a transitional thought in his hour of disappointment. He soon adjusted his thinking to the idea that he was mistaken again.

But others concluded that no mistake in the date had been made, and asserted that Christ actually had come in a spiritual way. Joseph Turner of Maine led a group in the belief that the Bridegroom had come, gone in to the wedding, and shut the door; thus there was no more probation for sinners. Turner traveled around promoting that idea. When Miller was urged to support this concept, he wrote Sylvester Bliss on February 12, 1845:

> But you ask why I do not show whether the probation for sinners is ended. I answer, it is a close point, and if handled at all, it ought to be done very wisely and with a great deal of humility. I would not grieve if possible to avoid it, one of Christ's little ones. There is much sensitiveness on this point among our good brethren; therefore I would much rather keep my views in my own breast, if I could and do right, than to run the risk of hurting the oil and the wine.[87]

For the next few years, however, some held what became known as the Shut-Door belief.

Others theorized that the world had entered the seventh millennium, the great sabbath, and that the "saved" should do no work. When some of these conscientious ones reproved the women who were getting the meals for not observing the great sabbath, the women quit cooking—a response that brought a sudden cessation to that teaching.[88] Some taught that they were living in the great jubilee in which the ground should rest and the poor should be supported without labor. Their advice was: "Sell what ye have, and give alms (to support these unfortunate ones)."[89] Still others acted on the principle that in the kingdom of God one must become like a little child. They would creep around in their houses, on the streets, across bridges, and even in church.[90] Others set new dates for the advent: April, July, and October 1845. These people Storrs called "Timeists."

Even certain of the lesser leaders in the movement were carried away with some of the vagaries of the times immediately after the Great Disappointment. Snow proclaimed himself to be "Elijah the prophet," "the Prophet like unto Moses," "the Messenger of the Covenant," "the poor wise man." O. J. D. Pickands, a minister of the Congregational church in Akron, had served a large body of Advent supporters in that city. He now went to Cleveland and started a paper entitled the *Voice of the Fourth Angel*, which taught that Christ was sitting on a white cloud (Rev. 14:16) and was to be prayed down. Enoch Jacobs, who was a power as editor of the *Western Midnight Cry*, became a Shaker.[91]

Among the variant ideas were two that had made their appearance before the Great Disappointment but now received more attention. First, Storrs, in six sermons as early as 1842, had urged the sleep of the dead in his paper, the *Bible Examiner*; and Fitch came out in favor of this teaching in 1844. As explained by its exponents, this doctrine asserted that the biblical term *soul* referred to the whole person. When one died, he returned to earth not to be awakened from his unconscious sleep until the Lord's return. Furthermore, because humans had no inherent immortality, the wicked would be annihilated rather than suffer eternal torment. Called the "life and death" view at the time, this complex of ideas eventually became known as "conditional immortality." Although opposed by Miller and several of his closest associates, it spread widely among the Adventists after 1844.[92] The second variant idea was the seventh-day Sabbath. A Seventh-day Baptist, Rachel Oakes Preston, had brought it forward and as early as the spring of 1844 influenced a group of Adventists at Washington, New Hampshire, to observe Saturday as their Sabbath. That same year, Thomas M. Preble accepted the seventh day as binding on Christianity and wrote an article favoring it in the *Hope of Israel* of February 28, 1845. Although Preble and J. B. Cook, another Millerite who taught the doctrine, soon dropped the practice, Hiram Edson and others continued as Sabbatarian Adventists.[93]

In the confusion that followed the Great Disappointment, everyone, it seemed, was going around trying to set everyone else straight. Miller said that in one week he had received seventeen different papers advocating various views, and all claimed to be Advent papers.[94] So great was the diversity of ideas that Miller, Himes, and some other longtime leaders felt that a general meeting should be called to harmonize differences and bring unity among the followers. Accordingly, the Mutual Conference of Adventists met in Albany, New York, on April 29, 1845. Unlike the "extremists" they condemned, this body admitted a mistake in the time but reaffirmed belief in the nearness of the Advent. Instead of forming a central ecclesiastical organization, they adopted a congregational form of church government. "We regard any congregation of believers . . . as a church of Christ."[95] This was the first studied attempt to form a new sect — the very thing Miller had tried to avoid during his entire ministry. The leaders had to proceed very gingerly in this matter. The cry "Fallen is Babylon. . . . Come out of her, my people" (Rev. 18:2, 4) was fresh in the minds of the rank and file, who considered the church a sinful, tyrannical organization. Many held that those who established a church organization would drink "of the wine of . . . impure passion" (Rev. 18:3).[96] The conference condemned what the majority felt were radical new theories, mentioning specifically the following:

> That we have no fellowship for Jewish fables and commandments of men, that turn from the truth, or for any of the distinctive characteristics of modern Judaism. And that the act of promiscuous feet washing and the salutation kiss, as practiced by some professing Adventists as religious ceremonies, sitting on the floor as an act of voluntary humility, shaving the head to humble one's self, and acting like children in understanding, are not only unscriptural, but subversive, if persevered in, of purity and morality.[97]

This conference, David Arthur says, had four principal results. First, it unified and strengthened the moderate Adventists. Second, it encouraged several who had been attracted to the new ideas and practices to drop them and return to what was regarded as the original Adventism. Third, it encouraged an elitist tendency, for generally those with the most education supported the moderates and rejected the extremists. And finally, it made more permanent the division among Adventists.[98]

* * *

Despite all the problems, Miller was not crushed by the Great Disappointment. In time, he took the position that the year of expectation was according to prophecy; but he suggested that there might
be an error in Bible chronology, which was of human origin, that
could throw the date off somewhat and account for the discrepancy.
He said: "Brethren, hold fast; let no man take your crown. I have
fixed my mind on another time, and here I mean to stand until God
gives me more light, and that is, *today*, *today*, and *today*, until he
comes."[99]

Years of traveling and preaching had sapped Miller's physical
strength. His trips grew shorter and less frequent. On December 20,
1849, with his fellow warrior, Joshua V. Himes, at his side, Miller
died. He had never given up "the blessed hope."

It is difficult to assess the impact of Miller's message on his
time. He himself estimated that about 200 ministers embraced his
views and that about 500 public lecturers were engaged in speaking.
He thought that a thousand congregations had been raised up, num-
bering about 15,000 believers. But Miller was a modest man, and
his estimate of numbers seems too low. A Millerite estimate of 1,500
to 2,000 public lecturers is more realistic.[100] At the time of Miller's
death, a news story in the *New York Tribune* stated that for a while
there were 30– 40,000 Millerites. A correspondent who spoke with
seeming authority corrected that item, saying that for a while there
had been 100,000 followers and that there were still 50,000 in
1849.[101]

Just as the total number of Millerites is elusive, so is their
social make-up. I have ascertained, however, that the affiliations of
174 lecturers (which can be considered a fair number as a basis for
estimating the membership of the movement as a whole) were as
follows: Methodist — 44 percent, Baptist — 27 percent, Congregational — 9 percent, Christian — 8 percent, Presbyterian — 7 percent.[102]

Furthermore, thousands of people, many influenced by Miller,
joined the various Protestant churches during this time.[103] Consequently, William Miller may justifiably be considered the greatest
evangelistic influence in the northeastern United States between
1840 and 1844. The fact that growth in the Methodist and Baptist
churches in that section of the country reached a peak the precise
year of Miller's "expectation" is scarcely a coincidence. On the other
hand, in the South, where Millerite lecturers were not welcome
because of their well-known antislavery views, there is no correlation
between the dates of Millerite expectation and the growth of these
two churches, which were most receptive to Adventism.[104] In his
recent study, Richard Carwardine concludes that the Great Awak-

ening, rather than ending in the mid-1830s, as many historians have believed, continued to develop during the next decade. "In strictly statistical terms," he states, "the peak of the Awakening came in this Adventist phase of 1843-4."[105]

But as meteoric as was Miller's rise to evangelistic power, the nature of his prophetic conclusions brought his brilliant career to an even more abrupt decline. The ultimate results were twofold. On the one hand, the failure of his prophetic interpretation created great prejudice against any kind of millenarian thinking, particularly of a historicist nature.[106] On the other hand, the movement spawned several Adventist sects, of which Seventh-day Adventism would become the largest and most widespread.

2 | Sectarianism and Organization 1846–1864

GODFREY T. ANDERSON

The call to "come out of Babylon" that was initiated in 1843 led not only to Millerite separatism but contributed also to opposition against setting up any kind of organized church. Organization was associated with sectarianism, sectarianism with creeds, and creeds with unbiblical man-made beliefs. Wanting to restore pure biblical Christianity, many Adventists fought against any attempt to formalize and systematize either beliefs or association. As a result, progress toward the formation of Adventist denominations was slow and, even when organization was accepted, the choice of a name that did not seem sectarian aroused intense discussion. Although the Sabbatarian Adventists followed their own separate path, their experience took much the same pattern as did the other Adventist churches.

Despite efforts at Albany and subsequent conferences to hold the Adventists together, the profusion of ideas and conflict of personalities following the first Great Disappointment led to the division of what David Arthur calls moderate Adventism into three major groups. These interests emerged not only around particular doctrines but also in particular geographical areas where individual papers held sway.

In the Boston–New York area, where Joshua V. Himes published the *Advent Herald*, a group was formed that regarded itself as adhering to the "Original Advent Faith." Involving such prominent Adventist preachers as Himes, I. C. Wellcome, Josiah Litch, and Sylvester Bliss, these people rejected the creation of new doctrines, particularly conditional immortality, and time setting. Beginning with the organization of sectional conferences in 1853, they moved toward formal church organization, an objective achieved in 1858, when at Worcester, Massachusetts, the annual conference adopted a constitution for an American Evangelical Advent Conference. Known as the Evangelical Adventists, this group asserted the literal premillennial Advent of Christ, the purification of this world by fire, and the personal reign of Christ with the saved on this new earth.

A second group appeared in the Hartford – New York territory and at first coalesced around the *Second Advent Watchman*, edited by Joseph Turner and W. S. Campbell. These individuals advocated conditional immortality, the ultimate annihilation of the wicked, the millennium past, and the sonship of Christ—and disagreed on the issue of church organization. The *Watchman's* opposition to a movement predicting Christ's return in 1854 led to the latter's publication of a rival paper, *World's Crisis*. Shortly thereafter, the *Watchman* folded; in time, *World's Crisis* became the chief publication for these Adventists. In 1858, discussions concerning church organization began. With the *Crisis* leading the way, conferences took place that culminated in 1860 with the formation of the Advent Christian Association. That same year, Joshua V. Himes, increasingly independent of the Evangelical Adventists, started publishing *Voice of the Prophets* and pursued missionary work in the Old Northwest. In 1864 Himes began another paper, *Voice of the West and Second Advent Pioneer*, and he led in forming the Western Christian Publishing Association. The *World's Crisis* favorably observed these developments and called for a joint meeting, which took place in 1865. The delegates at that time organized the American Advent Mission Society, which included the annual delegates, officers, and ministers of both the eastern and western associations. Such cooperation continued until the two groups combined in the 1880s.

The third group, known as the Age to Come Adventists, congregated originally around Rochester, New York, and supported Joseph Marsh's *Advent Harbinger and Bible Advocate*. The Age to Come idea, which Marsh first published in 1849, asserted that "the end" referred to the termination of the millennium rather than the Second Coming and argued that some of those who had not accepted Christ would escape destruction at his Advent and be gathered in during "the age to come." These believers, who also came to accept the return of the Jews to Israel, held a conference in 1853 at Rochester, where they formed an Evangelical Society. But opposition to organization was too strong, and the Evangelical Society—along with George Storr's provisionary committee—were abandoned a year later. Discussion concerning church order continued in the *Prophetic Expositor and Bible Advocate*, the successor to the *Harbinger and Advocate*, and in 1855 another conference was held in Indiana and organized the North Western Christian Conference of the Church of God. Conferences in other states were established, but no national organization developed until 1888, when the Church of God of the Abrahamic Faith took form in Oregon, Illinois.

These three divisions arose out of those Adventists who had met at Albany in 1845 and had condemned what they considered to be extremist positions, including the doctrine of the cleansing of the heavenly sanctuary, the seventh-day Sabbath, and the manifestation of the spirit of prophecy in the person of Ellen G. White. These three beliefs, developing in different places, gradually coalesced and, along with other doctrines, became the basis of the Sabbatarian Adventist movement, the only permanent group to arise out of the so-called extremists.

THE SABBATARIAN ADVENTISTS

The Sabbatarian Adventists felt alienated to a great degree from both society at large and their fellow Adventists. Their attitudes toward society were an inheritance of the Millerite movement's description of the Protestant churches as fallen Babylon and a general pessimism regarding the improvement of society. Their attitude toward their fellow Adventists stemmed from the rejection of Sabbatarianism. Not invited to the Albany conference of 1845, the Sabbatarians from that time on referred to the other groups as "nominal Adventists," a term reflecting their belief that the latter had rejected God's truth. As a result of these attitudes, the Sabbatarians moved toward establishing not only distinctive doctrines but also a set of social institutions that would enable them to maintain a degree of separation from the world. Progress along all lines, however, was slow and difficult.[1]

Soon after the 1844 Disappointment, Joseph Bates—upon reading Thomas M. Preble's article on the seventh-day Sabbath—concluded that keeping the seventh day was necessary to salvation. In May 1845, he personally contacted the Washington, New Hampshire, Sabbatarian Adventists at the home of Frederick Wheeler, their pastor, and confirmed his conviction. The next year he published a tract on the subject and influenced James and Ellen White, who were to become central figures in Seventh-day Adventism, to accept the belief late in 1846.[2]

Another strand in the tapestry of beliefs that would become Seventh-day Adventism was the recognition of "spiritual gifts" in the church. In Portland, Maine, Ellen Gould Harmon, a conscientious and deeply contemplative young woman of seventeen years with a Methodist background, experienced a "vision" in December 1844. Describing this experience, she wrote, "The Holy Ghost fell upon me, and I seemed to be rising higher and higher, far above the dark world." She saw the Advent believers moving toward the heavenly city, some falling off the path through weariness and discouragement. But when circumstances seemed darkest, "a small black cloud appeared . . . which we all knew was the sign of the Son of Man." The graves were opened, the dead arose, and all entered the cloud and ascended to heaven with Jesus. After experiencing the delights of paradise, Ellen was told, " 'You must go back to earth again, and relate to others what I have revealed to you.' Then an angel bore me gently down to this dark world."[3] In effect, the vision assured the Advent believers of eventual triumph despite the immediate despair into which they had plunged.

Other visions followed, and Ellen Harmon began traveling among small groups of Adventists giving assurances and guidance. On these travels she met James White, formerly a school teacher and itinerant Millerite preacher, who accepted her visions as coming from the Lord and began to accompany her. In the summer of 1846 they married and continued their efforts, though not without opposition, gradually binding together a following. Together with Joseph Bates, they stood out as the staunch triumvirate whose faith, foresight, and influence would become a major force in the formative years of the Sabbatarian Adventists.

Concurrent with the acceptance of the Sabbath doctrine and the recognition of spiritual gifts in the person of Ellen White came the development of another basic belief in western New York. This doctrine addressed the problem of the "Disappointment" by restudying the Millerite interpretation of Daniel 8 ("then shall the Sanctuary be cleansed") as referring to the earth. Hiram Edson of Port Gibson, New York, after a bitter reaction to the Great Disappointment, diligently studied the prophecies and with O. R. L. Crozier set forth the view that the sanctuary spoken of in Daniel was neither the earth nor the churches but, as indicated in Revelation 11:19, was located in heaven. The cleansing of that sanctuary, they argued, symbolized Christ's activity in blotting out sins — in contrast to his earlier forgiving of them — that would precede his Second Advent to the earth. This concept, another version of the spiritualizing interpretation of the 1844 experience, gave new cause for hope.[4]

Edson invited Bates to a conference at Port Gibson late in 1845, at which Bates became particularly interested in the relationship between the sanctuary and Sabbath doctrines. The Whites and

Bates spent most of 1845 – 48 traveling, proclaiming their new-found beliefs and nurturing the scattered groups of believers. In 1848 they called a series of Bible conferences, and those attending carefully studied the Sabbath, the sanctuary, and other doctrines. Fifty persons attended the first conference, which took place in April at the home of Albert Belden in Rocky Hill, Connecticut. At this meeting Bates presented studies on the law of God and on the Sabbath, and James White explored the meaning of the "third angel's message" of Revelation 14.

At the second of the 1848 conferences — held in August in David Arnold's barn, in Volney, New York — James and Ellen White met Edson for the first time. For a while, discord prevailed among those attending regarding the sanctuary doctrine, but when Ellen received a vision affirming its truth, the matter was settled. As James wrote later, "Here the work of uniting . . . on the great truths . . . commenced."[5] Several additional conferences followed. Throughout this time, however, the few Sabbatarian Adventists had difficulty getting a hearing for their views. Matters were further complicated for a time by the group's adherence to the Shut-Door idea. This doctrine, first proposed by Joseph Turner as a way of addressing the problem of 1844, had spread quite widely among the Adventists. In brief, Turner had asserted that salvation was open now only to those who had accepted the Advent message before October 22, 1844. Joseph Bates, Hiram Edson, and James and Ellen White held this doctrine until about 1852, by which time they realized that many outside Adventism desired to know God's will. Meanwhile, these "Seventh-day Door-shutters" were held in derision by the moderate Adventist groups; and in the pages of their publications all sides engaged in frequent and often acrimonious debates.[6]

Things began to change at mid-century. By 1851, James White could write: "Now the door is open almost everywhere to present the truth, and many are prepared to read the publications who have formerly had no interest to investigate."[7] White had begun to publish the *Present Truth* in 1849; the following May he added the *Advent Review,* and in November 1850 he replaced these periodicals with the *Second Advent Review and Sabbath Herald,* which upon the organization of the church became the official Seventh-day Adventist journal.

Also by 1850, the basic doctrines of Seventh-day Adventism had taken shape. Although there were differences of interpretation among the Sabbatarian Adventists on a number of points, the leaders of what was to become the Seventh-day Adventist Church had by this time accepted the Bible — and the Bible only — as their rule of faith and duty; the law of God as immutable (including the binding obligation to observe the seventh-day Sabbath); the imminent personal Advent of Christ; the conditional immortality of the soul; and the ministry of Christ in the heavenly sanctuary after 1844 in the blotting out of sins. Furthermore, they gained impetus to spread these beliefs by reading the message of the third angel of Revelation 14 as descriptive of the work of Sabbatarian Adventists to reestablish the Sabbath and prepare a remnant ready for Christ's Second Coming. In addition to these basic beliefs, by mid-century—a dozen years before the formal organizing of the believers as a separate church body—this small group was agreed on such practices as baptism by immersion, the ordinance of footwashing, and the Lord's Supper. By mid-1852, the editor of the *Review and Herald* could write; "We are a united, happy people. . . . We are united, and have a harmonious system of truth to present."[8]

CRYSTALLIZING BELIEFS

Some adherents of Adventism, however, continued to set new dates for Christ's return. One of the first such dates after the Disappointment was the fall of 1845, and James White for a time subscribed to this prediction.[9] The next date advocated by some was 1846, and then 1849. J. C. Bywater (not a Sabbatarian) proclaimed 1850 as the fateful year and developed a chart showing a line of reasoning on which he based his belief. In a study on the sanctuary published in 1850, Joseph Bates held that the Lord would appear in the autumn of 1851, a conclusion he based on the priest's sprinkling of the blood on the altar seven times in the typical cleansing service. These seven symbolic acts he interpreted as seven years: the addition of seven to 1844 led to the year 1851. Other dates suggested by individual Adventists included 1854, 1858, 1866, and 1877. In 1850, however, Ellen White discouraged the Sabbatarian Adventists from further date-setting, saying that "time had not been a test since 1844, and that time will never again be a test."[10] Following her lead, the Sabbatarian Adventist leaders eschewed the setting of another definite time for Christ to reappear, although they emphasized consistently the imminence of his return.

One detail of doctrine that remained to be worked out was the time period of the weekly Sabbath observance. Bates had drawn from his knowledge of Scripture and astronomy and his experience as a maritime navigator to set forth the view in 1851 that 6:00 p.m. was the biblical hour to begin and end the Sabbath.[11] Other leaders agreed with his position at that time. Six weeks after the Bates article appeared in the *Review and Herald,* John Nevins Andrews, a studious young minister, wrote that "the fixed point from which to reckon day and night is at six."[12]

But the question continued to come up. Some cited the practice of Seventh-day Baptists, which called for sundown as the proper and biblical time to mark the limits of the Sabbath. So James White asked Andrews to explore the question thoroughly, and the conclusions resulting from his research appeared in the December 1855 *Review and Herald.* Now Andrews unequivocally supported sundown as the proper time to begin and end the Sabbath.[13] After some hesitation by Bates and Ellen White, this time pattern became the accepted practice of Sabbath observance, and the matter was no longer an issue with Sabbath-keeping Adventists. In reply to a critical letter, James White commented on this change of position.

> We have reason for humble gratitude that the clear light
> has come out on this subject. Those who have walked accord-
> ing to their best light, are worthy of praise rather than censure;
> and those who have been unsettled, but have patiently waited
> till the subject is made so clear that all can move on in union,
> have acted an admirable part.[14]

Healthful living also gained increasing attention. Although alcoholic beverages were apparently little used among the Sabbatarian Adventists, strong sentiment against tobacco did not firm up until late in the 1850s. Ellen White wrote in 1848 about the harmful effects of not only tobacco but tea and coffee as well. Five years later, the *Review and Herald* began carrying articles (some excerpted from other periodicals of the day) discouraging the use of tobacco.[15] "I have seen in vision," wrote Ellen White, "that tobacco is a filthy weed, and that it must be laid aside or given up."[16] In 1855 the Sabbatarian Adventist believers in Vermont went on record to make the use of tobacco a test of church fellowship.[17]

Although the Vermonters modified this strong position the next year, the conviction developed that the human body is the temple of the Holy Spirit, and therefore tobacco, tea and coffee, and unhealthful dress came increasingly under question.[18] Andrews wrote on the importance of denying oneself the "inexcusable worldly lust" developed by becoming habituated to tobacco, thus defiling the "temple of God," the human body.[19] Leaders such as J. H. Waggoner, M. E. Cornell, and R. F. Cottrell published articles that were unequivocally against the use of tobacco.[20] The Minnesota believers voted: "That this conference do urge upon the members of the different churches the necessity of abstaining from the use of tobacco, tea, coffee, and [wearing of] hoops."[21] The growing feeling was reflected by Joseph Clarke of Portage, Ohio, in a piece published in the *Review and Herald* in 1857.

> Greet ye one another with a *holy* kiss. Here comes two Brn. [brethren] perhaps, one a chewer, and the other a smoker of tobacco, both otherwise fair, it may be. They keep the Sabbath, but alas, the greeting. *Ugh!* I ask, can such comply with Paul's exhortation? What have we come to! an age of tobacco! tobacco! TOBACCO! in the mouth, in the nose, on the beard, its taint in the breath, and the blood, in the air, borne on the winds; the store, the shop, the kitchen, the parlor, rendolent *[sic]* with its fumes, and to cap the climax, the breath of the saints.[22]

These Adventist attitudes toward healthful living were similar to — and often drawn from — the popular health reformers of the day, including L. B. Coles and Sylvester Graham. But for the Sabbatarian Adventists, healthful living took on special significance in light of the expected Second Coming. As one scholar writes, "They were convinced that the event of the Second Coming demanded a thorough preparation for perfecting the physical as well as moral powers of man so that they would receive the seal of the living God."[23]

Another major area of belief remaining to be settled at this stage of development was the Trinity. Although there were differences in details on the understanding and acceptance of the Trinity, in general most of the leaders at this period, and for some time afterward, were anti-Trinitarians. They identified the doctrine of the Trinity with other "errors" that Protestants brought away from the Roman Catholic Church — errors such as the counterfeit Sabbath, baptism by sprinkling, and immortality of the soul.[24] J. H. Waggoner, early evangelist and author, wrote the following on the Atonement:

> The great mistake of Trinitarians, in arguing this subject, seems to be this: They make no distinction between a denial of a trinity and a denial of the divinity of Christ. They see only the two extremes, between which the truth lies; and take every expression referring to the pre-existence of Christ as evidence of a trinity. The Scriptures abundantly teach the pre-existence of Christ and his divinity; but they are entirely silent in regard to a trinity.[25]

The background of some of these leaders in the Christian Connection at an earlier period probably explains, to some extent, their anti-Trinitarianism. The term "Christian Connection" was applied to a group whose members, for the most part, were originally from a humble level of society on the New England frontier. The movement, founded by Vermonters Abner Jones and Elias Smith, advocated a return to the "primitive gospel." This persuasion fused several schismatic groups who were strongly anti-Calvinist, revivalistic, and anti-Trinitarian.

A fourth area of concern was Ellen White's visions, which gained increasing acceptance during the 1850s. Accounts of her visions did not appear in the *Review* between 1851 and 1855, although during this time the journal published five articles by her that contained no references to visions. James White, who was then editor, explained in a special edition of the *Review* that he was not publishing the visions because many held prejudice against them. In the future, he said, the visions would be related in extra editions published for the benefit of those who accepted Ellen White's prophetic role.[26] However, only one "extra" appeared.

Because of his cautious approach to this matter, James White received criticism from some writers of letters to the *Review*; they felt that he had a lesser estimate of the visions than did the Advent believers in general. In reply, White reaffirmed his belief that the source of the visions was divine; but he made it clear that the Bible, and the Bible only, was the test of faith and practice.[27] "The Word should ever stand forth in front, as the rule of faith and duty."[28]

Increasingly, leaders of the developing body of believers emphasized that acceptance of the prophetic counsel as a "gift of the church" was important so that all in the fellowship of the Sabbatarian Adventist group would be in unity. By the time the church was ready to be officially organized in the early 1860s, J. N. Loughborough, D. T. Bourdeau, Uriah Smith, and other leading figures were suggesting that acceptance of the visions was essential to identify fully with the group.[29] As Smith put it: "It is a fact that those who reject the gifts do not have true union with the body. From the very nature of the case they cannot have it."[30]

However, confessions appearing later in the *Review* indicate that such early leaders as Andrews, Wheeler, and Samuel W. Rhodes did not support the visions consistently at the outset.[31] It appears that the lay members may have been ahead of the ministerial leaders in acceptance of the prophetic gift. Merritt Cornell reported after a tour of central New York, for example, that "more than three-fourths of all I saw on this tour heartily acknowledge the gifts."[32]

Late in 1855 (the year that the *Review and Herald* was moved from Rochester to Battle Creek, Michigan) a conference was held in Battle Creek to consider ways of fostering progress. Ellen White had a vision at the close of this meeting, and the Battle Creek church voted to request its publication. In addition, this November conference voted to request that Bates, Waggoner, and Cornell be appointed, on behalf of the conference, "to address the saints . . . on the gifts of the church." The statement prepared by these men and reported in the *Review* indicated that it was not enough to regard the visions as from God and in harmony with the Word, but that "we must acknowledge ourselves under obligation to abide by their teachings, and be corrected by their admonitions."[33]

The publication of this statement, Everett Dick writes, was "the first official pronouncement through the *Review* regarding the manifestation of the gift of prophecy in the remnant church. It marks the beginning of a public recognition of the special gift bestowed on the church through revelations to Mrs. White and of frequent allusions to her work."[34] The Battle Creek conference in late 1855 thus may be regarded "as marking the close of the critical, formative period in the work of the Sabbathkeeping Adventists, and as a turning point in their history."[35]

The political controversy over slavery also influenced developing Adventist ideas. Although the *Review and Herald* gave infrequent consideration to political issues, it was clear that the sympathies of the Advent believers were with the North in the debate over slavery. To a large extent, the views the believers held, as with those of the Millerites before, were similar to abolitionism in general. When the matters of slavery or the government's handling of related problems appeared at all, the *Review* referred to the nation as the "two-horned beast" (Rev. 13) and held out little hope for finding a man-made solution, especially since the church leaders believed that prophecy indicated otherwise. Jonathan Butler calls the Sabbatarian Adventists of this period "political apocalyptics"; for, although completely pessimistic about political actions changing the national situation, they did criticize the nation on the basis of an assumed political platform.[36]

Three articles on "the two-horned beast" in the *Review and Herald* of March 1857 reviewed "that monster of human iniquity," the Fugitive Slave law, "the abrogation of the Missouri Compromise in 1854," "flames, rapine, robbery, desolation and death on the plains of Kansas," and "the Dred Scott case." The author then raised these questions:

> In view of the facts thus far noticed, what may we not look for in the future? Can any one candidly consider these things, and tell us what atrocities, however dragonic and devilish, we have not reason to expect from the precedents already given us? Who may tell us that the voice of a dragon is not frequently heard issuing from the halls of Congress?[37]

One regular *Review* correspondent in Ohio, Joseph Clarke, listed his reasons for not meddling in political affairs, among them that the United States government legalized Sabbath-breaking (with its mail contracts), sanctioned slavery, and degraded and deceived the Indians.[38] A year earlier R. F. Cottrell had expressed the prophetic determinism that characterized Adventist views:

> Our government is just upon the eve of a political contest [the presidential election of 1856] which will finally result in the formation of the image [to the beast] for the next thing in the prophecy is the image completed and issuing its decrees of death and starvation against all who will not bow down to its authority, and receive the mark of the first beast, or take a share in the great number of his name.[39]

Such language indicates that Sabbatarian Adventists were already developing an apocalyptic outlook that saw Sunday observance, the image of the beast, about to be legally enforced nationwide. Political chaos, in their view, would lead the national government to take strong action to maintain unity. In doing so, it would trample into the dust civil and religious liberty, the two horns of the lamblike beast of Revelation 13, which had characterized American origins. Abolitionist views thus combined with Sabbatarianism to produce a unique apocalyptic.

CHURCH ORGANIZATION

The social alienation reflected in these views of the state also expressed itself in opposition to denominational organization, a characteristic of other Adventist groups as well. One of the "nominal" Adventists wrote in alarm: "I discover that the 'organization' fever is fairly up again. Brethren, beware! Would to God that the huge monster had gasped and expired in death at its birth. My prayer is, Lord cripple the monster. Amen."[40] Most of the opposers took seriously the counsel of George Storrs, who wrote in the *Midnight Cry* in early 1844: "Take care that you do not seek to manufacture another church. No church can be organized by man's invention but what it becomes Babylon the moment it is organized."[41]

This antipathy to organization, stemming in part from the Millerite experience, resulted in a lengthy struggle to structure a new denomination that did not culminate until 1863. Bringing order to the chaos of the scattered believers, examining and agreeing on the beliefs they would hold in common, and selecting a name was a long ordeal that severely tried the faith and patience of all concerned. Some who had strong feelings against this trend chose to separate from the group rather than support the move to form an organization.

Those who were in the middle of the struggle, including such intrepid leaders as James White, received much criticism for their stand, even though Ellen White wrote many of her messages in support of organization. Later James said that he had expected the believers to examine the need for organization with Christian candor; but "in this we were disappointed," he recalled. "Some of our best men opposed, and stirred up that element of insubordination and lawless independence which has ever followed us as a people, and not a few distinguished themselves in heaping their anathemas upon us for suggesting such a thing as organization." He revealed the depth of his agony over this question in these words: "We feel at least four years older than two years since, and sometimes fear that we never can fully recover from the effects of those heart-rending discouragements which so nearly drove us from the brethren, and from that cause which was dearer to us than life."[42]

The Whites believed that organization was needed for a number of reasons, which included support of the ministry and evangelism, the holding of church property, protecting the church from unworthy members and preachers, and the stabilizing and legalizing of the publishing activity.[43] The arguments in favor of formalizing an organization that would provide outlines of belief and practice and would protect business and legal interests are reasonable and convincing from the vantage point of more than a century later. But only a few with vision and foresight accepted these views at the time.

The chief argument against the proposed structure rested on the concept held by some Sabbatarian Advent believers that any move in this direction would automatically transform the body of believers into a "Babylon"—a world-conforming apostate body. Their feelings are understandable in view of the fact that many of them had been dropped from various other churches at the time they had accepted Miller's teachings; after 1844 they found themselves un-churched. Their belief that the popular churches were "harlots" (and simply daughters of the mother harlot, Rome) in the symbolic biblical sense gave them pause when it was suggested that they organize themselves as a church body and take on a denominational character. They had no desire to become the youngest daughter of such a questionable family.

No doubt the overriding conviction that Christ's Advent was imminent led many believers to question the need for anything as permanent as organizational plans seemed to call for. Also, there were those who feared that organization would lead to settling down and devoting time to matters that were not as urgent as the actual disseminating of the Advent message far and near. As a result, opposition was deep and persistent. Only great persevering effort accomplished each step in the organizing process.

James White recognized these varied reasons for opposition to his organizational plans and, his patience growing thin, satirized them in Bunyanesque terms:

> We are aware that these suggestions, will not meet the minds of all. Bro. Over-cautious will be frightened, and will be ready to warn his brethren to be careful and not venture out too far; while Bro. Confusion will cry out, "O, this looks just like Babylon! Following the fallen church!" Bro. Do-little will say, "The cause is the Lord's, and we had better leave it in his hands, he will take care of it." "Amen," says Love-this-world, Slothful, Selfish, and Stingy, "if God calls men to preach, let them go out and preach, he will take care of them, and those who believe their message."[44]

As early as 1851, steps had been taken toward a rudimentary form of organization for individual congregations. That year, in one instance, a member was set apart by the "laying on of hands" to designate him as qualified to administer the ordinances of the Lord's house. Also, that same year, James White began speaking publicly on church order, and disciplinary actions were being taken against erring members. In the next few years a number of churches chose deacons. Progress along these lines was such that Cottrell would write in 1856: "Order in the Church of God has been vindicated by different writers in the *Review*, and has been established to a considerable extent by the ordination of officers in the churches."[45] Nevertheless, the Whites believed that more needed to be accomplished.

In the fall of 1853, when dissension and controversy were taking place among the small groups meeting as churches in New York and New England, Ellen White wrote a "Testimony" (the term given to her messages of guidance for both individuals and the church) on "church order." She pointed out that now as never before there was need for order among the believers. "The church must flee to God's Word and become established upon gospel order, which has been overlooked and neglected."[46]

On the basis of Ellen's testimony, James, while still editor of the *Review and Herald*, wrote four articles on the subject of "gospel order," which appeared in successive issues of the *Review* in December 1853. These were general in nature but directed attention to the subject and provoked thought and discussion.

> We go for order and strict discipline in the church of Christ. And while we reject all human creeds, or platforms, which have failed to effect the order set forth in the gospel, we take the Bible, the perfect rule of faith and practice, given by inspiration of God. This shall be our platform on which to stand, our creed and discipline.[47]

The following spring, James White returned once more to the subject of "gospel order" in a lengthy editorial. He defined gospel order, or church order, as "that order in church association and discipline taught by the gospel of Jesus Christ by the writings of the New Testament." He mentioned two extremes on the question: resorting to human creeds, on the one hand, or acting independently of the views of the leaders, on the other. "Our Advent brethren, in coming out of the churches, in breaking away from human organizations and creeds, did well; but their sad mistake has been in not being subject to the order of church association and discipline delivered to the church by inspiration of God." White felt that now many hearts were beginning to beat in unison.[48]

Developments in specific lines of interest by the Sabbatarian Adventists during the 1850s added to the mounting evidence that progress depended on having an organizational entity by which to plan and finance whatever projects were undertaken. The publishing activity was experiencing a healthy and steady growth. The conference held in 1852 at Ballston, New York, gave the leaders authority and support to purchase a power printing press. That same year a paper for young people, the *Youth's Instructor*, was established, and it was soon experiencing a steady growth in subscriptions and popularity among the believers. After an early irregular schedule, the *Review and Herald* had begun appearing on a weekly basis, and before long, over two thousand of each issue were going out. Some readers were now saying that they prized the *Review* next to the Bible as the dearest possession that nurtured their spiritual lives. Tracts, pamphlets, and, in time, books were being published. The tracts dealt with such subjects as the sanctuary, the twenty-three hundred days, the seven churches, the open or shut door, and the messages of the angels of Revelation 14. The publication of Ellen White's pamphlet "Experiences and Views" was announced in the *Review* late in 1851. Four years later, Andrews published his *History of the Sabbath*. As time went on, other studies appeared in various languages, including German, Norwegian, and French.

A forward step took place in 1855, when the publishing plant was moved from Rochester to Battle Creek. Henry Lyon (Mrs. M. E. Cornell's father) played a key role in having the printing equipment moved to the new location. Lyon, with help from Cyrenius Smith, J. P. Kellogg, and Dan R. Palmer, provided the funds to ensure the move. At Battle Creek the publishing program was established on a firm basis, and it would continue there for half a century. Thus, legally incorporating a publishing association became one of the important matters to be faced without delay. James White repeatedly brought the urgency of this need to the attention of others. In 1855, when White asked to be relieved of some of the many burdens he was carrying, Uriah Smith, at twenty-three years of age, received the appointment as resident editor of the *Review and Herald*.

A second area was public evangelism. In 1854 the Sabbatarian Adventists began to follow a practice already employed by other Adventist bodies, the use of large tents for evangelistic purposes during the summer months. Loughborough and Cornell held the first tent meetings in Battle Creek for the general public early that summer; and from that time on the practice became a regular feature of Sabbatarian Adventist evangelistic methodology. Before long, five large tents (the one in Iowa was fifty by eighty feet) were in use in many states during the summer. This kind of undertaking required not only financial support but advance planning to make the maximum use of the investment during the limited season that a tent could be used. For the summer of 1855, Loughborough reported his expenses to "operate" a tent at about $270, including the cost of a horse and wagon for transporting it.[49] Some kind of general support and planning was necessary.

Although not organized as a church, the Sabbatarian Adventists were developing many churchly functions, some of which needed more formal oversight. An immediate problem was the credentialing of ministers, because unauthorized preachers were going around to the churches, often with bizarre interpretations of Scripture. Some of the early Sabbatarian Adventist leaders had previously been ordained in other churches. In 1853, Loughborough received a ministerial card signed by James White and Joseph Bates, and cards signed by "leading ministers" were issued subsequently to others. This haphazard arrangement met the need to a degree until a more orderly system of ordaining and credentialing ministers would come into being.

Local churches were also adding Sabbath schools to the preaching service. Beginning in 1852, the leaders began laying plans for such schools. James White took the lead in preparing the first Bible lessons, and the Advent believers in Rochester and Buck's

Ridge, New York, organized the first schools in 1853 and 1854. After the *Review and Herald* moved to Battle Creek, Merrit G. Kellogg organized a Sabbath school there.[50]

As local groups formed to worship together, the need for meeting houses arose. Originally, when the "traveling preachers" came around, the believers had met in schoolhouses, private homes, churches of various denominations, and outside when weather permitted. As opposition developed, however, the churches were often no longer available. Beginning at Battle Creek in 1855 and extending to various places where Adventist Sabbath-keepers were congregated, the believers constructed small, simple meeting houses. Some opposed such an expenditure on the principle that the limited funds should be used for more urgent "soul-winning" purposes. Nevertheless, the building of meeting houses went on for the rest of the decade. Disagreement continued as plans to build a larger meeting house in Battle Creek drew strong criticism, even though the building, which was to be only twenty-eight by forty-four feet and to cost under five hundred dollars, was badly needed for conferences and a growing membership.[51]

The question of the ownership or title to these meeting houses became an issue as well. Sometimes individuals made available their property as building sites; but in several such instances, either through the death or the apostasy of a person, embarrassment came to the group of believers. For example, the loss of a meeting house because a title was not held by the church occurred in Cincinnati. Some Adventists built a tabernacle on a believer's lot there and then "Satan tempted this brother, he yielded, got possession of the key, locked out the congregation, and the place built and consecrated for the worship of God was turned into a vinegar establishment."[52] In time, the need for an overall organization that could hold title to the property of such meeting houses became obvious.

Worship services also required hymnbooks. James White, who enjoyed singing and who sensed the importance of hymns for worship and for teaching the principles of the word of God, showed an early interest in developing hymnbooks for the Advent Sabbath-keepers. In 1849 he compiled a hymnal called *Hymns for God's Peculiar People*; and three years later he published another book, entitled *Hymns for Second Advent Believers Who Observe the Sabbath of the Lord*, a volume containing 139 hymns; a supplement gave 38 more. Other hymnals followed a little later. White and other leaders at the time recognized that the hymns in general use by the established churches contained many views that to their minds were out of harmony with the teachings of the Word of God. They wished to stress the ideas they believed. Speaking of the next collection to be produced, White explained the reason for putting out hymnals: "As most Hymns sustain some one or more of the popular 'fables' of the times, it will be seen that our task of selection is difficult."[53]

REGULATING BENEVOLENCE

The "ministering brethren" who led out in these varied activities required support. During the first part of the decade those who preached received freewill offerings from the people to whom they ministered. The amounts varied from almost nothing to barely enough to live on. Some who preached had to drop out certain times of the year to earn their living in order to get enough ahead to go out and preach again. Waggoner published a note in the *Review* calling for the payment of pledges that had been made to assist him so that he could go out and preach again: "If it would be more convenient to pay in clothing or provisions it would be equally acceptable, as it would enable me to leave soon for important fields of labor. Can I be relieved, or must I work out these pledges with my hands?"[54]

The Panic of 1857 adversely affected the believers' giving. After an early show of liberality, gifts for the support of those ministering fell off noticeably about that time. White and others persistently called for some systematic manner of supporting those who had been called to preach. White himself was becoming weary of writing appeals for funds in the *Review*. "The real friends of the cause," he wrote, "will respond a hearty amen, and look about for a better way, while the careless and stingy will say amen, and do nothing. Well, what shall be done? . . . Something must be done more definite and effectual."[55]

The need for a "definite and effectual" plan culminated in the appointment of J. N. Andrews in 1858 to lead a study group in thoroughly examining the whole matter of economic support. This group concluded that the biblical method for the support of the ministry required regular and proportional giving by the believers. The Andrews study group proposals, as modified by the conference session at Battle Creek in the early summer of 1859, suggested a scaled plan of donations that became known as "systematic benevolence." Men between the ages of eighteen and sixty were to lay aside, on the first day of the week, between two and twenty-five cents; and women of the corresponding ages were to lay aside between one and ten cents. In addition, another small amount suggested was based on the value of the holdings of the individual member. It was recognized that a few—the widows, the infirm, and the aged—might not be able to participate in the plan.[56]

A short-lived paper called the *Good Samaritan*, which was designed to promote systematic benevolence, touched on the principle of the tithe late in the 1860s when it said: "We propose that the friends give a tithe, or tenth, of their income, estimating the income at ten per cent on what they possess."[57] The fact that 10 percent was the rate for interest on savings at that time gave an added reason for proposing this as an equitable basis for contributing to the support of the emerging church system. Not until two decades later, however, did the Seventh-day Adventist Church officially adopt the tithing system.

The adoption of systematic benevolence was an extremely significant development in the successful operation of the church in the next few years. James White consistently praised the manner in which the system operated. Gone were the days when Loughborough (and others like him) would labor in the interest of the Sabbatarian Adventists for four months in the summer and receive board and traveling expenses and twenty dollars in cash. Gone were the times when he would labor from January to April in northern Illinois and receive, besides his board, a buffalo skin, a ten-dollar overcoat, and ten dollars in cash—after which he would have to walk a distance of twenty-six miles carrying his heavy satchel on his back so that he might have a little money when he arrived at his destination.[58]

Another step taken to implement the plan of systematic benevolence was to have each church appoint someone to collect the funds. The *Review* office prepared special "blank books of ruled foolscap" for each individual to keep account of his gifts (the date and the amount); and each "first day," a designated peson went around to collect the monies from those participating in the plan. One by one the churches adopted systematic benevolence, and soon the practice became firmly established. The home church retained a certain amount of the funds for its needs, and other amounts went to support such general projects as the tent fund and the book fund. The modern-day apportioning of contributions between the needs of the home church and those of the conference organization has its roots in these early practices.

In addition to these more specifically religious activities, the Sabbatarian Adventists in 1853 began some feeble and short-lived attempts at operating church schools. The first of these schools opened at Buck's Bridge, New York, with the support of five families. The next year Ellen White touched on the importance of keeping one's children separate from "the world" and the "company of wicked children."[59]

Other abortive attempts in the decade were made to open church schools at Battle Creek and elsewhere. One attempt at Battle Creek experienced a stormy three-month period and failed. But the school idea received support from James and Ellen White. The former spoke out against the "immorality" of the common schools and held that "our children may be separated from the poisonous influence of both school and street associations by home-schools emphasizing the Christian virtues."[60]

In spite of this kind of counsel, the establishing of schools on a firm basis by the various churches proved to be an idea whose time was not to come until 1872, when Goodloe H. Bell opened the first official Seventh-day Adventist church school with "twelve scholars" on June 3 in Battle Creek.[61] It appears that a church organization was necessary before church schools could become a success.

Meanwhile, the geographical concentration of the church was changing. What was to become the westward course of Sabbatarian Adventism was signaled first by the move of the publishing activities from Rochester, New York, to Battle Creek in 1855, apparently because the Whites regarded the West as more fertile territory for their message. Soon after this, James White began urging believers and workers in New England to move west. With the same effort, he said, twenty converts could be won in the West to one in the Northeast. "No consideration whatever, excepting a sense of positive duty, could induce us at present to labor in the gospel-hardened shores of New England, while so much can be done in the wide West."[62] Some friction arose when Adventist workers in the East objected to their subordination to those in the West, but it seems not to have developed into a serious issue.[63]

In what seems to be a reversal of views several years later, White appealed for support of the church work in New England, in late 1863, and this appeal was endorsed by the major leaders at Battle Creek. White went so far now as to express a willingness to go to New England personally for a year or more if necessary. He also recommended Loughborough, Cornell, or Moses Hull as highly qualified for this assignment.[64] When sent there, Loughborough and Hull reported smaller congregations than in the West; "sectarian bigots," they indicated, were not easily converted in the East.[65] In any case, repeated warnings appeared in the *Review* against settling in centers of believers, whether Battle Creek or elsewhere: "This is not the time to huddle together for the sake of the society of believing friends."[66]

SPIRITUAL DECLINE

Evidence for the geographical shift of Sabbatarian Adventism appears in reports printed in the *Review*. An Adventist believer in the Dakota Country wrote the *Review* a letter in 1855, and in the same year a California believer, who had heard White preach while he still lived in the East, also wrote to the *Review*. Roswell F. Cottrell reported that he had preached the "third angel's message" to the Seneca Indians, and that a small company of Sabbath-keepers could be found at Kickapoo Center, Bad Axe County, Wisconsin, as a result.

The trend of changes in regional totals of *Review* subscriptions in this period also indicates greater interest in the movement west. In 1858, New England had a net increase of 1 subscriber, New York State a decrease of 9, Ohio and Michigan an increase of 125, and further west an increase of 120.[67]

But serious defections were also taking place in the West, principally in Wisconsin and Iowa. About thirty believers had moved to Waukon, Iowa (in the northeast corner of the state), some of them—including Andrews, Loughborough, and Butler—in poor health and a discouraged state of spirituality. In the dead of the winter of 1856–57, James and Ellen White made a memorable and dangerous journey through snow and rain, precariously crossing the Mississippi River on water-covered ice, to Waukon to hold revival meetings there. White reported later that "these meetings were the most powerful we had witnessed for years, and in many respects the most wonderful."[68] Loughborough at once, and Andrews and Butler later, were influenced by these meetings to return as workers in the Sabbatarian Adventist cause. "Altogether, this meeting at Waukon was one of the decisive points in the development of the work in the Middle West."[69]

Despite all the apparent progress, however, the leaders saw the 1850s as a period of spiritual decline. At a conference in Battle Creek in November 1855, a feeling existed that the earlier ardor had been lost. "Strong desires were expressed, and fervent prayers were offered to Heaven, for the return of the Spirit of consecration, sacrifice and holiness once enjoyed by the remnant."[70]

By 1856, the Sabbath-keeping Adventists agreed that God would judge first the righteous dead before taking up the cases of the living. This concept tended to lull believers' consciences and to give them a sense of complacency; and hence a decline in spiritual zeal set in.[71] Precisely at this time Ellen White saw in a vision that the church was not the biblical "Philadelphia" (brotherly love), as they

had believed, but "Laodicea"—lukewarm, self-satisfied, and great
in need. Until this time the Sabbatarian Adventists had thought that
the "nominal" Adventists constituted Laodicea. The emphasis now
placed on their own Laodicean condition created a deep and widespread reaction. In the period between November 1856 and December 1857, the *Review* contained 348 references to the Laodicean
message.[72]

Recognition that the Laodicean message was applicable to
themselves raised the tone of spirituality among the Sabbath-keeping
believers. But it also had some adverse results. Looking back on this
experience, James White wrote:

> Some, when this subject [the Laodicean message] was dwelt
> much upon a few years since, seized upon it to give force to
> their fanatical ideas of selling and disposing of property. Others
> used it to enforce their extreme notions in regard to plainness
> of dress, while some others, who were perpetually dwelling
> upon others' faults, instead of searching for their own, took
> fresh courage in their blind work. These deceived persons ex-
> erted a sad influence on the conscientious, and the church
> generally where their influence reached.[73]

With all their interest in spiritual reformation, however, the early
leaders stood aloof from the Great Revival of 1858, which was surg-
ing across much of the nation, though at the outset it was essentially
an urban movement. The *Review* reported a result of fifty thousand
conversions a week.[74] Bates complained that the revivals were affecting the attendance at his meetings in the Worchester-Clinton-
Lancaster area of Massachusetts: "They seem to be so much absorbed in the work of revivals now all over the land, that they have
no time to heed the claims of God's holy law, or even to hear about
the second coming of Christ."[75]

An unusual interpretation of the Great Revival of 1858 was
offered by another contributor to the *Review*:

> A feeling of melancholy and gloom steals over me, as I think
> that a revival of the religion of this nation, is only deepening
> the death-wail of humanity, and enabling demons to feed on
> the virtue, life-hope, and blood, of the crushed millions that
> slavery plunges in the dark starless night of oppression, and
> binds unrelenting chains.[76]

Cottrell offered another interpretation:

> The great Deceiver has a definite object in this movement.
> That object I believe, is to increase the *political strength* of the
> nominal church, and thus prepare the way for the last perse-
> cution against the people of God. He wants more stringent
> laws to enforce the observance of his favorite institution.[77]

Their prophetic interpretation and their distinction from the larger society brought about by their emphasis on the Sabbath, which sometimes took them into conflict with Sunday laws, led the Sabbatarian Adventists to expect nothing good from their nation. This feeling of distinctiveness perhaps added another psychological push in the direction of organization. Although such organization was in itself something of a compromise with the world, it appeared to several of the leaders that only through organization could the movement maintain the cohesion to fulfill its God-given task.

SELECTING A NAME

Persevering on their course toward achieving an orderly church system, Sabbatarian Adventists held a series of general conferences at Battle Creek in November 1857. In addition to examining "gifts of the church," they took up such matters as the book fund, tent evangelism, needs of the publishing activities, support of the ministry, and other "wants of the cause." Further, the conference

> Resolved, that a Committee of Revision be appointed, through whose hands all matter designed for publication in book form shall pass, and under whose sanction it shall be issued; by which means an individual responsibility in the publication of books will be avoided, and confidence be placed in whatever shall be thus published, as the voice of the body.[78]

This movement toward greater centralization also appeared in the summer of 1859, when James White proposed that state yearly meetings be held as a sort of "half-way house" toward full organization, thus anticipating the local conference sessions of a later date.

Virtually every step taken in the direction of an official church organization met opposition from the believers. Cottrell was one vigorous and effective opponent. In answer to James White's call in the *Review* for suggestions of ways of meeting the need for organization, Cottrell wrote:

> I think it would be wrong to "make us a name," since that lies at the foundation of Babylon. I do not think that God would approve of it. The work in which we are engaged is the Lord's and he needs not the aid of insurance companies to take care of his property. I think it is for us to take the best care of the property we can and then trust it with the Lord. We want no name with the twohorned beast; and it would close my mouth in regard to the spiritual fornication of Babylon with the kings of the earth, should it be retorted: "*You* look to the civil arm for aid and protection"—I should be mute.[79]

And the issue that seemed to generate the most controversy — perhaps symbolizing the larger question of a church organization — was the selection of a name for the church. The debate had its roots deep within not only the Sabbath-keeping Adventists but throughout all the so-called nominal Adventists as well.

A writer in the *Advent Harbinger and Bible Advocate*, for example, had commented on this question from the standpoint of non-Sabbatarian Adventists, arguing in favor of the name "Christian" rather than Adventist or any other sectarian name. He objected to the name "Adventist," he said, because it was unscriptural, "because of its tendency to raise and perpetuate a party in the body of Christ," and finally because if the name belonged to anyone, it belonged to Himes and his associates rather than those who had split off from that group. "If you must use the name Adventists," he wrote, "use an adjective to distinguish you from those already in use of the name. The group might be called the 'Second Second Advent Church' or the 'New York Adventists' or the 'Hartford Adventists' or something of that nature to distinguish them."[80]

Actually, the Sabbath-keeping Adventists had been referred to by many titles since their first identification as a separate group. They were designated as "Seventh-day People," "Sabbathkeeping Advent Believers," "Seventh-day Believers," "Sabbath-keeping Adventists," "Advent Sabbathkeepers," "Seventhday Door Shutters," "Seventh-day Brethren," "Shut Door Seventh Day Sabbath and Annihilationists," "Sabbath-keeping Remnant of Adventists," and even as "The Church of God." The latter was a name that White and a number of others favored up to the time of the 1860 conference.

One historian of the Seventh-day Adventist Church has commented that the name "Seventh-day Adventist" "indeed had already been applied to them as much as any other."[81] As early as 1853 the term "Seventh-day Advent People" had appeared when a representative of the Seventh-day Baptist group wrote to James White for information about the Adventist Sabbatarians. The letter stated: "At the sitting of the Seventh-day Baptist Central Association in Scott last month, it was 'resolved that we instruct our Corresponding Secretary to correspond with the Seventh-day Advent people, and learn their faith.' "[82]

Loughborough reported another instance of the use of this term. He heartily endorsed the choice of the name "Seventh-day Adventist" after its adoption, for he felt that it was "the most natural and appropriate name we could take." Then he added that four years earlier, in 1856, he had come across a handbill at Hillsdale, Michigan, where the believers were going to have a conference, which

read: "There will be a conference of the *Seventh-day Advent people*
held in Waldron's hall." He continued: "This name I suppose was
used in the handbill because everybody would know at once who
it meant."[83] A further indication of the natural fitness of the name
emerged in a letter a Vermont woman wrote to the *Review* about
fourteen months before the name was officially adopted: "I found
no difficulty in deciding in favor of the Seventh-day Adventists."[84]

Individual churches had already begun to choose names for
themselves, irrespective of the overall body, a state of affairs that
could have led to some confusion. In Parkville, Michigan, believers
took legal steps in May 1860 toward organizing a religious society
that might hold property in a lawful manner. The signed articles of
association stated: "We, the undersigned, hereby associate ourselves
together as a church with the name of Parkville Church of Christ's
Second Advent: taking the Bible as the rule of our faith and discipline."[85] And late that summer a church in Fairfield, Iowa, organized "by subscribing to 'the Bible as the only rule of faith and
practice,' and surnaming themselves 'The church of the living
God.' "[86]

The time for decision had come. White called for a general
conference to convene in Battle Creek. In issuing this call, he sensed
strongly the significance of the conference, its paramount importance to the organization of the church: to settle the question of the
legal holding of church and publishing house properties and to
choose a name.

The conference assembled on Saturday evening, September
29, 1860, to organize for the transaction of business. Joseph Bates
was appointed chairman, and Uriah Smith secretary. The discussion
of a name began that night and continued throughout Sunday and
Monday morning. On Monday afternoon, October 1, at the fifth
business meeting, Bates posed the question: "Shall we adopt some
name?" Some of those who had opposed the whole idea now signified a change of position and were ready to move ahead. One
delegate suggested that going without a name would be like publishing books without titles or sending out a paper without a heading.
White indicated that earlier he had veered away from the selection
of a name, at a time when the believers were few in number. "But
now large bodies of intelligent brethren are being raised up, and
without some regulation of this kind all will be thrown into
confusion."

White then reviewed the opposition they had encountered —
first against publishing a paper, then against issuing pamphlets, against
having a set office, against the sale of publications, against church

order, and against the purchase of a power press. But all these things, he said, had been essential to the prospering of the Adventist cause. And now, he felt, the believers were confronting a similar matter at this meeting. The motion to adopt a name passed, although several declined to vote.

The discussion turned to the question of what the name should be. Some had suggested and zealously advocated the name "Church of God," a name to which James White and others at the publishing office were partial. Others objected that this name was already used by some denominations and that it would present to the world an appearance of presumption. Finally, the name "Seventh-day Adventist" was proposed as one that would be descriptive of the basic tenets of faith of the body of believers. After some additional remarks, David Hewitt, Bates's first Battle Creek convert, offered the resolution: "*Resolved,* That we call ourselves Seventh-day Adventists." After lengthy discussion, the conference adopted the revised resolution. T. J. Butler of Ohio dissented from this vote (and later withdrew from the body), and four abstained, including J. N. Andrews (though after hearing further explanation, he signified his assent to the action). The conference then voted to recommend this name to the churches generally, and to publish the proceedings of the meeting in the *Review.* [87]

There followed a period of discussion in the various churches, but soon the name was widely accepted. Subsequently, it received the endorsement of Ellen White, who credited God's leadership in the choice. "No name which we can take will be appropriate but that which accords with our profession and expresses our faith and marks us a peculiar people. The name Seventh-day Adventism is a standing rebuke to the Protestant world."[88]

In the months that followed its adoption, the name Seventh-day Adventist began appearing regularly in announcements and notices in the *Review and Herald.* Individual churches officially adopted the name, usually by unanimous vote. However, a few—even among the leaders—felt so keenly against organizing and choosing a name that they withdrew from the group. The deep convictions of some of those who were opposed appeared in a letter Waterman Phelps of Wisconsin wrote to the editor of the *Review.*

> Advent people are very dear to me. I have felt that their trials have been my trials, and their prosperity has been my prosperity. But I have not that unison of feeling at present. I feel that the union is broken, for I do not sympathize with the body of Adventists in relation to organizing under the name, Seventh-day Adventists, and enrolling names under that head. As

I feel, I never could consent to have my name enrolled on any class-book, or church-book, under any sectarian name. [89]

ORGANIZATION ACHIEVED

The choice of a name soon led to further organizational steps. The following May, the publishing activity was organized and incorporated as the "Seventh-day Adventist Publishing Association," a stock company under the then existing Michigan law. This was the first legal institution of the Seventh-day Adventist Church. [90] That same month, James White set forth some of the advantages to be gained by further organization. These included giving endorsement to qualified ministers, protecting the believers from "conceited, self-called messengers of the third angel's message," and keeping proper records of the members. "It should be definitely known at all times who are and who are not considered members, and then the welfare of all may be looked after and the erring may be reclaimed by timely action, or the unworthy withdrawn from in a manner to save the cause from reproach."[91]

But opposition continued. After a tour of New York State, White returned home "stung with the thought that the balance of influence is either against, or silent upon, the subject of organization." He resolved to "never consent to risk another eastern tour" until there was a change in sentiment. Then he concluded: "We shall be greatly disappointed if the number of Sabbath-keepers does not decrease for the next twelve months."[92] Waggoner also reported resistance to organization in Iowa. [93] Others who had seen the need for organization from the outset were running out of patience with those who continued in opposition. Joseph Clarke of Ohio, an early supporter of organization, who wrote often and forcefully on a variety of timely topics, expressed himself with feeling late in 1862:

> Is it possible, we exclaimed, as we read the article on Organization in No. 18, by Bro. White, that anti-organizationists still are hesitating? Why don't you come up, to a man, in this business? When I think, after all that has been said and done on this matter, how Bro. White is tantalized, how the testimony is trampled on, how the church is trammeled, how the good Spirit is slighted, oh, it is provoking, it is sickening, it is discouraging, it is positively flat, nauseous as the lukewarm water from the stagnant pool. [94]

The 1861 Battle Creek conference took on action binding the members together in a covenant: "We, the undersigned, hereby associate ourselves together, as a church, taking the name, Seventh-day Adventists, covenanting to keep the commandments of God, and the faith of Jesus Christ." Because the vote on this resolution was incomplete, White requested further discussion and suggested that all participate in the vote, including the women who were present. He called for a unanimous action on this resolution, for, he said, "We pledge ourselves only to do one thing, to keep the commandments of God and the faith of Jesus. There can be nothing more in Christianity. We pledge ourselves to help each other along the Christian journey, no one can call this a creed or articles of faith."[95]

This same 1861 assembly recommended that the churches in the state of Michigan unite as a conference. The conference was to be composed of ministers and delegates from the churches; the officers were to be a chairman, a clerk, and a standing committee of three. The first chairman was Bates, who presided at the Battle Creek conference then in session. In a sense, this veteran reformer and preacher of the Advent cause became the first local conference president in the young denomination. Finally, the conference voted that "our ministers' papers consist of a certificate of ordination, also credentials to be signed by the Chairman and Clerk of the Conference, which credentials shall be renewed annually." Further, the delegates outlined procedures for organizing a single local church, with officers' duties described in some detail.[96]

An editorial entitled "The Cause," appearing in the *Review* in the spring of 1862, reflected a brighter picture than James White had presented the previous year:

> Prosperity attends the cause generally. There never was a time when our people were so ready to sustain it with their means as now. The subject of organization has finally triumphed, and the real friends of the cause feel relieved of a great burden on this subject, and now see good fruits. Systematic benevolence is a perfect thing. It has been a hard struggle to bring these about, but now we have the joy of seeing the good results. We as a people had gone as far as we could go without them. Without them, the future was hopeless. . . . But the day is gained, and victory is again on the side of truth.[97]

The first meeting of the Michigan Conference held at Monterey in October 1862 received 17 organized churches. It decided that henceforth ministers were to receive a fixed sum for their services; in turn, they were to report their activities and expenses to the conference.[98] Other states followed suit, and by the time of the National Conference in 1863, there were six local conferences operating, thirty-five hundred members, twenty-two ordained ministers, eight licensed ministers, and 125 churches.[99] There may have been more ministers than indicated here, for D. T. Taylor's comprehensive study of all Adventist ministers, Sabbatarian and non-Sabbatarian, reported that fifty-seven of those responding indicated that they observed the seventh-day Sabbath.[100]

The capstone to the organizational structure of the Seventh-day Adventist Church came with the General Conference that convened in Battle Creek, May 20– 23, 1863. Twenty credentialed delegates attended from New York, Ohio, Michigan, Wisconsin, Iowa, and Minnesota. Of the state conferences then in existence, only Vermont lacked representation. The brief constitution adopted for the overall church entity consisted of nine articles stipulating the following: sessions were to be annual; the officers were to be a president, a secretary, and a treasurer; all were to be elected for one-year terms; an executive committee of three was to be chosen. The duties of the committee and of the treasurer were spelled out in some detail. Amendments were provided for, with a two-thirds vote of delegates present needed to change the organic law of the body. A constitution of eight articles was adopted and recommended as a model for consideration by the state conference, and the churches were to obtain all ministerial help from the local conference organization. Amendments to a state constitution could be made by two-thirds of the members present, "provided such amendment shall not conflict with the constitution of the General Conference."[101]

The first list of officers suggested by the committee on nominations included James White as president, Uriah Smith as secretary, and E. S. Walker as treasurer. Because he had been active in promoting organization, White declined to serve; the delegates then invited John Byington of New York to be the first president. He served for two terms, until 1865.

The spirit of this general meeting in 1863 was excellent from the outset; the greatest hurdles had already been passed. Writing about this meeting, Smith said: "Think of everything good that has been written of every previous meeting, and apply it to this. All this would be true, and more than this. Perhaps no previous meeting that we have ever enjoyed, was characterized by such unity of feeling and harmony of sentiment."[102]

The culmination of the long and trying struggle to organize the overall Seventh-day Adventist Church had special significance for James and Ellen White. In an editorial soon after the 1863 conference closed, James White wrote: "Organization has saved the cause. Secession among us is dead."[103] Whereas in certain areas churches that had persistently opposed organization were now languishing, he thought, churches that had supported the official establishing of a national organization were prospering. The Battle Creek church was a case in point. With its ninety-seven members, two elders, and two deacons, it was "in a healthy condition, united and prosperous."[104]

The tenor of correspondence published in the *Review* after the May 1863 conference favored the organizational steps taken and very likely reflected the feelings of the believers generally. One typical correspondent referred to the progress made this way: "My heart responds a hearty amen to it, for it does seem to me the Lord is setting his seal of approbation, by giving among his people a spirit of union."[105]

The feelings that had run deep in the ranks of Adventist Sabbath-keepers on the question of choosing a name and organizing a church entity, however, continued to an extent after 1863. Those whose consciences sincerely would not permit them to go along with the organizational developments "walked no more" with their brethren. Those who had serious questions chose to abide by the counsel of articulate, persuasive leaders and accept the moves in good grace. Answering the critics of James White—particularly with reference to his sharpness in dealing with Cottrell's earlier opposition to organization—Cornell wrote in the *Review:*

> Bro. White had occasion to use sharpness. The cause he loved, and for which he had suffered so much, had been wounded in the house of its friends. A spirit of rebellion had been kindled up against one of the most important steps ever taken in this great work. Bro. W. saw at once that such articles would do great damage, and therefore made decided efforts to counteract their influence.[106]

Reminiscing on the struggles over organization, Waggoner, a participant in the conflict, wrote twenty years after the 1863 conference:

> Brother and Sister White were far in advance of the body of Seventh-day Adventists in regard to the nature and magnitude of our work, and the necessity of a perfect organization to carry the message to the world. I heard him introduce the idea of an organization at least five years before he could induce his brethren to take any steps in that direction. Almost all Adventists of all classes were opposed to organization.[107]

Waggoner correctly saw the essential elements in the movement toward organization: it was James White, with the support of Ellen's testimonies and in conjunction with other leading ministers who had provided the moving force in both the development of doctrinal unity and church organization. The latter had come about only after a long struggle against deeply held convictions that were formed during the Millerite period. In part because organization had thus developed from the top down, so to speak, Seventh-day Adventists chose a system more episcopal than congregational, one operated largely by ministers rather than laypeople.

By organizing in 1863, Seventh-day Adventists, many of whom were confused regarding combat service in the Union army, were able to speak as a body to the government and take advantage of the noncombat provisions then in force. J. N. Andrews, empowered by the General Conference executive committee in August 1864 and armed with recommendations from the governor and the military agent of Michigan, presented the official request in Washington. In response, the U.S. Provost Marshal, on September 1, 1864, determined that Seventh-day Adventists could serve as noncombatants, thereby establishing a precedent for the young church. [108]

But these Adventists had more on their minds than the Civil War. Believing that they were called to the task of preaching God's "present truth," they were beginning to talk about mission work in Ireland, Europe, and Russia. [109] The debate over organization seems to have contributed to an enlarged vision of a world work. But just as it had taken time to move from talk about organization to its implementation, it would take time before the dream of overseas mission activity became a reality. A basis for permanence had been established by 1865, and it now remained to determine in just what direction the new denomination would move.

3 | Years of Expansion 1865–1885

EMMETT K. VANDEVERE

The struggles of the 1850s and early 1860s had brought general agreement on doctrine and organization of the Seventh-day Adventist denomination. But the young church was small, about four thousand members, and geographically limited primarily to the Northeast and the "Old Northwest." From the 1860s to the 1880s this situation would change. Following largely the patterns of western settlement into the Great Plains, California, and the Northwest, Seventh-day Adventism expanded geographically by appealing to people uprooted from home, family, and church. At the same time, European immigrants who had learned Adventism in America took the message back to the old country and soon pulled the denomination into overseas mission activity. Though still small in number, Seventh-day Adventists by the mid-1880s were gaining a world-encompassing vision that they would pass on to later generations of believers.

As their concept of mission enlarged, Seventh-day Aventists also began developing ideas, techniques, and institutions to carry out what they regarded as their God-given task. The social alienation that had characterized them before church organization in 1863 had expressed itself primarily in negative denunciations of the social order; now their approach began to take on more positive dimensions. Regarding themselves as reformers, these Adventists adopted dietary, dress, and medical reforms and founded a periodical and an institution to both propagate and put into practice a new manner of living. Development of schools not only allowed them to remain separate from the world but offered the opportunity to establish educational reforms that to them more fully reflected God's will. By the mid-1880s, Seventh-day Adventists were both creating a considerably isolated subculture and attempting to penetrate the larger society through evangelism. P. Gerard Damsteegt has described the process by which Seventh-day Adventists came to understand the function of these varied activities:

> At first the mission of restoration was seen as a mission to restore certain spiritual principles. Later the restoration aspect began to be interpreted in the context of man's spiritual and physical restoration as necessary preparation for the kingdom. Finally it led to the realization that their mission was to proclaim a message of the complete restoration of "the principles that are the foundation of the kingdom of God" with the ultimate goal of restoring in man the image of God.[1]

THE LEADERSHIP

But in the beginning the resources for fulfilling such an expanding purpose seemed meager. One essential human resource of the church was its leadership. A score of its foremost ministers (at that time called "missionaries" or "traveling brethren") were aggressive men with fire in their bones, among them James White, Joseph Bates, John N. Andrews, John N. Loughborough, Stephen N. Haskell, George I. Butler, and others.[2] Of these White (1865–67, 1869–71, 1874–80), Andrews (1867–69), and Butler (1871–74, 1880–88) served terms as General Conference president.

James and Ellen White were an invaluable team.[3] Ellen shared with James her wisdom based on her revelations; he acted vigorously to implement what she advised and what to him seemed common sense. She was certain that the strength of the church lay in its families, and she endeavored to "perfect" them in every respect, particularly in healthful living. In financial matters she strove for economy and generosity. Ellen White herself was an effective evangelist, so her statements to the ministers were poignant. She pled for deep, genuine piety. And by 1885 this messenger was emphasizing and reemphasizing the world mission of the young church, the vastness of the task, and the need for hundreds of youthful church workers.[4]

To help fill the need, an optimistic delegate at the 1881 General Conference session introduced a resolution "that females possessing the necessary qualifications to fill that position, may with perfect propriety, be set aside by ordination to the work of the Christian ministry." The proposal was referred for further study to the General Conference executive committee, however; and in failing to "report it out," the committee gave the idea its most effective possible burial.[5]

Before severe illness struck in 1865, James White was *the* general—in the tent and on the field. One contemporary described him this way: "He was a man of a remarkable mind. In some respects I never saw his equal. . . . As an organizer, and in laying the foundation of an enterprise, his mind was far-reaching, and he could see the bearing and connection of things with surprising clearness."[6]

At the level just below the major leaders was an increasing number of persons who were assignable as administrators and usually served in the local conferences. Their offices might be their homes. Some of them wisely endeavored to absorb the ideas and customs of the different parts of the country; they included people like R. F. Andrews in Illinois, John Byington in Michigan, Robert M. Kilgore in Texas, John H. Morrison in Iowa, Elbert B. Lane, his wife Ellen,[7] and his brother Sands in Indiana, James M. Rees in Indiana, and Isaac D. Van Horn in Oregon.

Gradually, as the conferences grew, next came apprentice ministers or "licentiates," some of whom began their careers as caretakers of the evangelistic tents. Many of these young men were listed in the conference directories only briefly, but others stayed by and rose in the ranks: Arthur G. Daniells, Roscoe C. Porter, Wolcott H. Littlejohn, Irwin H. Evans, Henry P. Holser.

Another rank, composed of colporteur evangelists (canvassers) who worked closely with the tract and missionary societies, sold gospel literature door-to-door. This literature came from Seventh-day Adventist presses. The principal physical printing resource of the church all along had been the Seventh-day Adventist publishing plant located south of McCamley Park in Battle Creek. Considering this press to be a "mission," church members worked in it both diligently and sacrificially. By 1885 the plant employed 115, was valued at $150,000, and topped $61,000 in annual sales.[8] It was becoming the largest printing establishment in Michigan. In fact, as more church members moved to Battle Creek, many to work in the press, its managers sought to make the enterprise more commercial. Naturally, other Adventist publishing houses located elsewhere—five by 1885—drew inspiration and some sustenance from this central "printing office."

Church members felt the weekly impact of the *Advent Review and Sabbath Herald* and the *Youth's Instructor,* and of *Good Health* each month. Under Stephen A. Haskell's leadership and drive, they joined various organizations, such as the General Tract and Missionary Society (forerunner of Adventist book centers), with headquarters at South Lancaster, Massachusetts, helping distribute periodicals, tracts, and pamphlets. In 1875 they reported giving over eight thousand Bible studies with these materials. Adventists were elevating evangelism of the print medium to a high level.[9]

THE HEALTH EMPHASIS

Another evangelistic institution arose out of the Adventist interest in healthful living. Born in the midst of a world of reform, Adventism was influenced by the ideas of such health reformers as Sylvester Graham, L. B. Coles, and James Caleb Jackson. Although Joseph Bates was the first prominent Adventist to adopt dietary reform — including vegetarianism and abstinence from alcohol, tea, and coffee — other Adventists were picking up bits and pieces of reform ideas in the 1850s. By the early 1860s, Adventist publications discouraged the use of tobacco, tea, and coffee, and several church members were practicing vegetarianism.

In addition to concern with diet, Adventists also took a disparaging view of contemporary medical practices, particularly the extensive use of drugs. Early in her career, Ellen White, relying on prayer, had brought about some miracles of healing, and in 1848 she advised Adventists not to go to regular physicians. By 1860, however, she was suggesting that the services of human physicians might be necessary in certain cases. Whatever the changes in Ellen White's attitudes, some Adventists were by that time experimenting with drugless remedies, including hot baths and cold packs, which offered an alternative to orthodox medicine.

These scattered ideas and practices developed into a system when, on June 6, 1863, Ellen White, shortly after the organization of the General Conference, experienced a vision at Otsego, Michigan, regarding healthful living. The vision impressed on her that physical and mental health were intimately related and therefore the maintenance of one's body was a sacred duty. Fifteen months later, she published an essay on health that, among other things, condemned meat eating and the drug-oriented medical profession, advocating instead a simple diet and drugless hydropathy.

In 1864 the Whites went to Dansville, New York, to observe the practices of James Caleb Jackson at his health retreat, "Our Home"; they returned when James White suffered a stroke in 1865. After a lengthy stay, Ellen White, disapproving of such amusements as the dancing and card playing that took place at the institution and believing that her husband needed exercise instead of complete bed rest, took James back to Battle Creek. Impressed by her Dansville experience and drawing from another vision that she received in December 1865, Ellen White called on the General Conference in

1866 not only to instruct the people more vigorously in healthful living but to establish a health institution of its own.

Responding positively to the call, the General Conference created a paper, *The Health Reformer* (later *Good Health*), edited by Dr. H. S. Lay, who had recently come from Dansville, and called for funds to establish the Western Health Reform Institute at Battle Creek. Opened in September 1866, the institute expanded too rapidly and came close to bankruptcy two years later; but by the early 1870s its situation appeared promising. Needing trained personnel, James White sent his sons, Edson and Willie, and Merritt and John Harvey Kellogg to R. T. Trall's Hygieo-Therapeutic College in New Jersey in 1872 to obtain a quick "medical" education. John Harvey Kellogg then went on to study orthodox medicine for two years at the University of Michigan and the Bellevue Hospital Medical School in New York. He returned to Battle Creek wishing to turn the water cure into a scientifically respected medical institution. Successfully obtaining Ellen White's support for such an establishment, he had a medical and surgical sanitarium erected on the grounds of the old institute.

When it opened its doors in 1878, the sanitarium on Washington Street had about two acres of floor space. Combining hydropathy with more orthodox medicine, a corps of physicians and allied health workers under Kellogg's supervision offered "unrivaled" treatments and care. Together, the water cure and the large sanitarium attracted more than ten thousand patients between 1867 and 1885, thereby presenting Adventism to many who otherwise would never have heard of it.[10]

CHRISTIAN EDUCATION

The impulse to reform and the belief that they needed to remain separate from the world also led Adventists to establish their first private educational institutions. In 1868, Goodloe H. Bell, who had been converted during a stay at the Health Reform Institute, began a private "select school" in Battle Creek. After the denomination took over the school in 1872, Ellen White called for a Christian education for practical life. To fulfill this purpose, she said, a correct school should offer its students agriculture and other trades as well as the normal school curriculum. Seeking to create a college to fulfill these objectives, denominational leaders, after considerable discussion, obtained land, began construction of a building, and secured Sidney Brownsberger, a graduate of the University of Michigan, to head the new institution. But despite Ellen White's counsel,

Battle Creek College, which opened in 1874, taught a curriculum little different from that of other educational institutions. This was largely because Brownsberger, according to his own testimony, knew nothing about operating a program that included industries and farming.

Although Battle Creek College did not institute the reform ideas that had prompted its planning, it was a considerable success and—though it was closed in 1882–83 because of personnel problems—became for a few years the largest church-related school in Michigan. About half of its college-level students prepared to teach in public schools, yet the institution propelled scores of "graduates" into branches of church work. Its faculty saw themselves, from within the church, as evangelists seeking to influence the entire body. [11]

One product of the college, Drury W. Reavis, looking back, saw Preparatory Principal Bell as

> a severe disciplinarian, a far too stern one in their [the students'] judgment; but in view of the fact that he had a conglomerate student body, the great majority of whom were full-grown men and women from socially neglected places, who had acquired a loose decorum, even severe discipline was necessary if reforms were to be achieved, for some were so calloused in their ways that a mere hint or suggestion was not sufficient to work any change in them. In fact, the whole spirit of the entire denomination at that time was reformatory in every detail of life. [12]

"Christian education," as sketched by Ellen White, was ideally reformatory, practical, and thoroughly religious: mind, heart, and hands were to be used to the glory of God. The results of education at Battle Creek College, though in some respects not the ideal, so attracted Seventh-day Adventists that they soon founded other institutions, including Healdsburg College in California and South Lancaster Academy in Massachusetts, both in 1882. [13]

Battle Creek was also home to the largest Seventh-day Adventist church building. The "tabernacle," which was erected west of McCamley Park in 1879 and had a capacity of thirty-two hundred, accented the skyline with its steeple and clock. Commonly called the "Dime Tabernacle," because a "march" of dimes helped finance it, this edifice served its congregation and the large convocations of the new denomination and of the city.

Thus by the mid-1880s the leaders in Battle Creek, with the support of members of the church, had designed and cut a "Battle Creek pattern." They believed their "plan" heaven-sent: evangelism, composed of preaching, teaching, healing, and publishing, should predominate wherever the church expanded. But these things required funds. Church giving in the 1860s and 1870s was less than sufficient, having evolved from gratuities and pledged sums to amounts proportional to one's tangible properties. The inequities and inadequacy of these "plans," however, were so clear that the leaders searched the Bible for a scriptural system. [14]

Tithing was the ancient rule, and careful scrutiny, particularly of 1 Corinthians 9:14, convinced the Adventists of these latter decades of the nineteenth century that the tithing system was applicable to their era too. In 1876, therefore, the General Conference session voted "that we believe it to be the duty of all our brethren and sisters, whether connected with churches or living alone, under ordinary circumstances, to devote one-tenth of all their income from whatever source, to the cause of God."[15] In 1881 the donations of members was $74,185; by 1885 the amount had reached $112,641, with the Michigan, California, Iowa, Minnesota, Kansas, Wisconsin, and Ohio conferences supplying the largest sums. [16] The tithing system tapped the financial resources of the Adventist people and assured a slender income to the conference.

MISSIONS

While they were systematizing their ideas and developing new institutions, Seventh-day Adventists were also expanding their vision of the task to which they believed God had called them. The fact that Christ had not yet come continually forced Adventists to reevaluate their understanding of their mission. As a result, they moved gradually from the "Shut Door" theology of the 1840s to a recognition that they had been called to evangelize.

At first it was the apocalyptic impulse—the belief that people had to be warned that the judgment hour was at hand—that propelled them into evangelistic activity. But by the mid-1870s, a nonapocalyptic emphasis on Christlikeness began receiving increasing attention, as Ellen White, particularly, called on Adventists to be selfless and sacrificial in working for the salvation of others.

As their theological motive for mission changed, they also enlarged the geographical scope of their work. Whereas in the 1850s Seventh-day Adventists believed that they were fulfilling God's command to teach all nations by preaching only in North America, a land of immigrants, by the 1860s they were realizing that this was not enough. Prompted partly by the success that Protestant missions were having abroad, but even more by the contacts converted immigrants in America had with their families in their home countries, Seventh-day Adventists recognized that they had a worldwide task. Damsteegt has written: "The basic structure of the theology of mission only slowly emerged to a view of a world-wide outreach. Thus it was not until the 1870s, when the theology of mission had sufficiently matured, that the increasing interest in the SDA message on other continents led to the sending of missionaries to areas outside of North America."[17]

At first the strategy of church expansion adopted by the Seventh-day Adventists called for a general holding pattern in the eastern states and aggressive campaigning beyond the Allegheny Mountains. They chose to do this because the people in the older East generally wanted to hear nothing more of an imminent Advent of Christ, whereas those in the newer West, torn from their traditional relationships, wanted to attend all meetings possible—of whatever sort. So the westward movement in the nation was joined, in accordance with Ellen White's alert that "tenfold more has been accomplished [by 1857] in the West than in the East with the same effort, and . . . the way is opening for still greater success . . . in Wisconsin . . . in Illinois . . . in Minnesota and Iowa."[18]

The figures for growth supported her view. In 1867 the New England Conference, plus those of New York and Pennsylvania, reported 1,936 members; in 1885 only 2,774. The cradle area of Adventism had not even increased its numbers by 50 percent in twenty years.[19] By contrast, when the Adventist leaders fastened on Battle Creek as the headquarters for their expanding organization, they found an inviting situation. The general exodus of "pure" Yankees from New England and New York to raw Michigan had been just right: the lower third of the state became the most "New England" of all the newer states and territories. But apparently these settlers were more adventuresome than those who stayed in the East, and they were reasonably susceptible to religious impulses.[20]

For twenty years the operating funds of the Michigan Conference were about half those of the General Conference, but its membership total leaped forward: 1,308 in 1867; 2,226 in 1875; 3,809 in 1885. This state was unquestionably a great reservoir for the development of Adventism, and its ministers and finances were continually drawn on to nourish other conferences, missions, and institutions. When the General Conference asked A. O. Burrill to leave Michigan to assist in Vermont in 1880, the Michigan delegates finally protested the "bleeding" of their conference. Thereupon the call was rescinded in deference to "the propriety of claims for help from a State [Michigan] which has furnished so many men for important fields and posts of labor."[21]

Wisconsin, Ohio, Indiana, and Illinois fell behind the pace set by Michigan. Settlers in these states were not as receptive as were the "Yankees" between the lakes. In 1885, Wisconsin had 1,525 members, Ohio 944, Indiana 920, and Illinois 729. Nevertheless, this "Old Northwest" fortified the new faith.

On the heels of "conquests" north of the Ohio, the Adventists next tackled the states of the trans-Mississippi region that lay northward. Two preachers, Washington Morse and William B. Hill, left memoirs that reveal much about Adventist life in the West of that era. Migrants from states stretching from Maine to Michigan, plus immigrants from Germany and Scandinavia, were the early settlers on the flatlands of southern Minnesota, in the Minnesota River Valley, and in arcs curving out from St. Paul and Minneapolis. Topographically, the area was much like what New England and northern Europe would have been without their granite teeth.

The Washington Morse family of Vermont migrated to Deerfield in Steele County, Minnesota, in 1856, where Morse was postmaster, farmer, and preacher. During the Indian War of 1862, Morse's place sheltered "scores" of refugees whose names and home localities he jotted down. "Some became so interested [in our faith] that we made appointments to come and hold meetings in their houses, and in the coming winter we walked long distances to fill such appointments with marked success. Thus it was that even through the great trouble with the savages the seeds of present truth were sown."[22]

In July 1863, in a state meeting at Deerfield, the churches in Minnesota organized a conference of about 150 members under Morse's presidency (1863 – 65). James and Ellen White attended the first two conference camp meetings, staged at Eagle Lake in 1869 and 1870, to encourage and advise. In one season (1873), Dudley M. Canright and Charles Lee helped increase state membership by a third, and there was considerable optimism.

HARDSHIPS OF GROWTH

The progress of growth would not be easy, however, as William B. Hill's detailed autobiography reveals.[23] A farmhand and logrunner who at age twenty-two followed his family from Michigan to Minnesota in 1865, Hill found Sabbath-keeping neighbors who handed him literature depicting "present truth," and he converted to Seventh-day Adventism. After periods of farm work and school teaching, he accepted an invitation to become a licentiate minister in 1873.

That decision led to a life of almost constant travel as he preached Adventism in Minnesota and the Dakotas. Typical of the physical struggle he endured was a trip of two hundred miles that he took to the southwestern corner of Minnesota in the spring of 1877. The country was raw, wet, and cold. When he forded the swollen Big Cottonwood River, the opposite bank was so steep that his valise full of clothes and books fell back into the water. Both man and baggage were thoroughly soaked by the mishap. Two weeks of meetings at Luverne, however, won eighteen adherents to the Adventist faith. The return trip was wetter still. Sloughs and streams overflowed, and roads stretched like ribbons of mud; baggage had to be carried by hand across streams. The horse became so worn she would lie down when she entered a slough, and there was nothing Hill could do but unhitch her and pull the buggy by hand. As the minister was to recall later, "In weariness and painfulness, was the cause built up in those days."

The expansion of the church in Iowa matched that of Minnesota. Actually, the membership there increased faster at the outset, but then slackened. Nonetheless, the Iowa Conference, fully organized in 1863, was a continuous reinforcement source in the movement west. Two prominent developments in Iowa after 1865 were the fall of B. F. Snook and William H. Brinkerhoff and the rise of George I. Butler. Snook was the first president of the conference, and Brinkerhoff was secretary-treasurer. Craving money and unrestrained power, these men rebelled against the General Conference, attacking the believers at Battle Creek as slack and worldly and decrying Ellen White's visions. James White and Loughborough hoped to quell the uprising, but they withdrew from the state exhausted. So it fell to Butler to meet the crisis.[24]

Scion of an able Vermont family, Butler migrated to Waukon, Iowa, and rose rapidly in the church after his conversion from skepticism.[25] In about a year's time he was farmer, deacon, elder, ordained minister, president of the Iowa Conference, and healer of defection. Late in 1865, Butler began to counteract the hurtful effects of Snook and Brinkerhoff, who took nearly one-third of the members and churches of the Iowa Conference with them when they left the Adventist faith. Butler later recalled: "I drove my span of colts through the wintry cold from church to church, instructing . . . [until] no other conference in the denomination was more thoroughly instructed or more perfectly and harmoniously united in *all* the precious truths of the message." As a result, excellent growth was ensured in Iowa thereafter, and it was usual to admit from four to six churches to the conference each year. The total number of members soon ranked second or third to that of Michigan.

The memory of Adventist fervor in Iowa remained vivid in Butler's mind: "I can never forget the joyous reunions which took place [at the camp meetings], as hundreds, alighting from the incoming trains met one another. . . . It used to affect me to tears to see them embrace one another . . . after a year's separation; I have failed to see such a degree of affection in most of our camp-meetings since."[26]

Geographically adjoining Iowa, the states of Kansas, Nebraska, and Missouri had winters that were somewhat less paralyzing and settlers who were reputed to be more Bible-minded. Consequently, in twenty years the upper trans-Mississippi West grew remarkably in Adventist numbers. State memberships looked like this in 1885: Minnesota — 1,488; Iowa — 1,460; Kansas — 1,313; Missouri — 563; Nebraska — 500; Dakota — 488; Colorado Mission — 195.

Soon the former Confederacy, including the Border States, received evangelistic attention. More than any other but Michigan, the Indiana Conference supplied ministerial personnel to enter the adjacent South. Hence one finds Jacob Hare, Squire Osborn, Elbert B. Lane and his wife Ellen, Sands H. Lane, and James M. Rees among the early "missionaries" venturing south and east of the Ohio. But it was Robert M. Kilgore of Ohio, a Civil War veteran, who led the advance into Texas. Several times his life was threatened, but he had lived dangerously in war and was fearless in fighting the "battles of the Lord." By remaining in Texas until 1885, Kilgore demonstrated that Yankee "carpetbaggers" who wished to evangelize in the South had to settle in the region as "Southerners." In northern Texas the Adventists established themselves in the vicinity of Cleburne.[27]

The "infiltration" of the South usually occurred picket post by picket post. Statistics in 1885 showed Texas with 300 members, Tennessee with 119, Kentucky with 113, Virginia Mission with 105, and the General Southern Mission with 201.

PROSELYTIZING THE WEST COAST

Although the Canadian northland was likewise difficult territory (there were only 127 members of the Adventist faith in Canada during these same two decades), the far West seemed to offer greater possibilities for growth. California had burst on the United States scene in 1848. Spanish-speaking people who had searched for gold in other parts of America had not at first suspected that there were rich deposits in California. But after the "strike" on the American Fork, the nation's frontier leaped the eastern mountains. And when California was admitted to the Union in 1850, it was a state more richly born than any other. Thousands of feverish men tore into the diggings, even though there was some question about whether the Pacific Coast could become linked to the East. The empire-building thing to do was to connect the West Coast to the nation's heartland by means of transportation. This came with the completion of the Union and Central Pacific railroads to California in 1869.

As for the young Adventist church, who would have the drive to put it over the Rocky Mountains? One member of John Preston Kellogg's family had helped establish the church headquarters at Battle Creek. In 1859, another Kellogg son, cabinetmaker Merritt G. Kellogg, and his wife trekked overland to San Francisco, arriving there with their feet in Indian moccasins and their purse empty except for a dollar.[28]

By 1864, Kellogg was lay leader of a dozen or more Sabbath-keepers. One spokesman for the group, B. G. St. John, declared: "This is really a good missionary field for a man filled with the spirit and love of God, of strong faith, and mighty in the Scriptures."[29] The ever-restless Kellogg appeared before the General Conference at Battle Creek in the spring of 1868 as a doctor (having taken the abbreviated "medical course" at Florence Heights, New Jersey) and as a petitioner in boots, begging for "missionaries" for the distant West. By July of that year, a tent and two ministers, John N. Lough-borough and Daniel T. Bourdeau, had arrived in San Francisco by way of the Isthmian route, and the Seventh-day Adventist "rush" for converts on the Pacific Coast had begun. Loughborough, the leader of the two, was a wiry man who was calm in the face of opposition; he was to be the primary builder of the church in the Golden State during the ensuing ten years.

News that tent evangelists had shipped for California raced ahead of the two men, prompting two "independent" religionists to invite them to begin tent meetings in the Petaluma area. One of these dreamed he saw two men successively starting five radiant "gospel fires" north of the Bay: he interpreted this dream to mean that the independents were to help these incoming ministers. Another of this independent group located the newcomers in San Francisco within thirty minutes of their arrival. The next day at Petaluma, the dreamer recognized the two men of his "vision," and at once he and his friends aided them by locating a site and raising a tent for the meetings.

An action-packed year later, a series of lectures had raised up churches in Petaluma, Windsor, Piner, Santa Rosa, and Healdsburg. Such successes argued for a temporary organization in the state to unify the churches and to plan for further expansion. In April 1872, this "synod" met at Santa Rosa in the first church edifice and expressed gratitude to the General Conference for having invested $1,755 in the Pacific mission. It concluded that Californians themselves could discharge the responsibility thereafter. There was $500 in the treasury.

This same organizational session resolved to endeavor to establish a health institution, undertake a publishing enterprise, and create a $10,000 book fund. A total goal of $1,500 in pledges was soon overshot by $425. California, it seemed, saw no reason not to have all that Michigan had: press, sanitarium, college! Then, as a climax to the meeting, the delegates voted to invite James and Ellen White to spend the winter of 1872–73 among them. Their entreaty, reinforced by $300 and pledges, impressed the General Conference.[30]

Hoping to shed their cares for a while, and naturally interested in California's plans, the Whites agreed to go to the West. On the Kansas pairies en route west they saw cattle being taken on the Long Drive, as well as herds of buffalo and the carcasses of those shot for their hides. They spent a number of weeks touring cool Colorado. One morning they awoke to find that their horses and lone cow were no longer nearby. Armed with revolvers and bowie knife, two of the guides forthwith pursued a band of two hundred Indians who had passed by the day before. Several hours later, the guides returned with the "strayed" animals.[31]

The Boulder Pass route led the party into Boulder Park, where the mighty heights and the beauty of the tapestried valley floors in the Rockies fascinated them.[32] On one occasion Mrs. White's pony, frightened by a loosened pack, pitched his rider head first to the ground; but her bones were unbroken, and progress resumed a short time later. After that, Ellen rode in the baggage wagon through hazardous places.[33] Arriving in California in September 1872, the Whites happily feasted their eyes on the beautiful flowers and their palates on an array of fruits. They thought that the California settlers were both healthy and buoyant.[34]

Another statewide church meeting of Adventists convened in February 1873. The annual tithe stood at $2,151. Now the delegates courageously declared conference status, elected Loughborough president, and asked for membership in the General Conference. Their request was granted. Later in 1873, the delegates again took up the discussion of plans for a health institute and a publishing plant. They sent a communication asking the General Conference to relinquish the Whites, who were once more recuperating in Colorado, to come to the West Coast for service during the coming winter.

When it became evident that the Whites were determined to do their utmost for the Adventists on the Pacific Coast, the General Conference dipped into its scanty manpower reservoir and sent California the following persons for varying terms of service: George I. Butler, Dudley M. Canright, John O. Corliss, Merritt E. Cornell, Lucinda Hall,[35] Stephen N. Haskell, Charles H. Jones (permanently), Joseph H. Waggoner, J. Edson White, and William C. White. As membership increased, the more experienced evangelists combed the churches for local persons who could be trained on the job. And they did well, nurturing such people as A. W. Bartlett, William N. Healey, a Minnesota convert of W. B. Hill, Mendel C. Israel, and Merritt G. Kellogg (as a medical lecturer).

Naturally, the villages and towns south and north of the San Francisco Bay were the recipients of church endeavor. Thus towns such as St. Helena, Oakland, San Jose, and Sacramento entered the list of Adventist place names. Eventually, California south of Tehachapi Pass received attention too, with churches springing up in Los Angeles, San Bernardino, and elsewhere. A church group was even established in Reno, Nevada.

The city preaching series most strategic to the Seventh-day Adventist Church expansion, however, were those successively conducted in 1873 and 1874 in Oakland by Loughborough, Cornell, and Canright. Might this city accommodate the often-discussed office of publication? The Whites believed it could. James White acted quickly: he rented a small second-floor printing office in Oakland and founded the *Signs of the Times* (beginning on June 4, 1874), a religious paper that was much like the *Review and Herald* in format but was slanted toward western Seventh-day Adventists and priced at two dollars a year. A month later, he bought out the printer's space and typesetting equipment, though for a while the presswork was done several blocks away.

During the summer of 1874, James and Ellen White hastened eastward to attend the August General Conference gathering at Battle Creek. If the Easterners would raise $6,000 to help establish a publishing house, they reported, the Westerners would overmatch it with $10,000; so an agreement was reached. At the Yountville, California, camp meeting, gold and pledges reached $19,414; by the due date of January 1876, $20,000 was in hand.

The Whites returned in February 1875 from Battle Creek, accompanied by an editor, Joseph H. Waggoner. They secured a lot on Castro Street in Oakland and soon constructed a brick building (in the shape of a Greek cross) to house the Pacific Seventh-day Adventist Publishing Association, which had been organized on April 1, 1875.

Now James White sped to New York for presses and equipment. To raise more money, he sold his home in Battle Creek and withdrew his funds from the *Review* establishment, thereby almost paralyzing it.[36] Five young people trained in Battle Creek accepted western positions. As their train left the depot in Michigan, scores of comrades at the *Review* hung out of the windows so both groups could wave handkerchiefs in godspeed.[37]

Initiative at the new Pacific Press successively passed from James White to his son, Will White, to editor Waggoner, and to manager Charles H. Jones. But too often they had to cope with financial adjustments, friction among workers, an inadequate work force, and the problems occasioned by non – Seventh-day Adventist employees who used tobacco.[38] At times Waggoner was still at his desk at two or three o'clock in the morning. By the end of 1879 he feared bankruptcy. But by July 1885, Jones gave a satisfactory business report.[39] To balance budgets, however, the press had to handle many jobs unrelated to church concerns. Nevertheless, Oakland served for many years as the western headquarters for a rapidly increasing Adventist church constituency.

The establishment of the Pacific Press was the last of James White's major contributions to the cause he so passionately loved. He had not been himself since a stroke had felled him in 1865. As Waggoner pointed out, "They who knew him only since that time cannot realize with what strength and energy he labored in the cause previous to that time."[40] But the intense James had become increasingly obdurate in dealing with associates who disagreed with him, probably a result of his earlier stroke. Butler wrote him: "Nothing would be more pleasing to me than to see you [us] in perfect union if I knew how to. But I am sure I do not." Waggoner wrote: "If we cannot work without personalities and hard feelings I am resolved to stand clear in the matter." And Haskell explained: "He said in substance I had run things long enough and now he was going to run them and me [too]."[41]

Unfortunately, James White finally became so obtuse that, despite Ellen's efforts to soften him, he persisted in wanting to maneuver himself and Canright into the posts held by President Butler and Committeeman Haskell, and he wrote that his wife had been "ruined" (perhaps he meant that she had been unduly influenced) by those two men.[42]

When malaria suddenly ended his life at the age of sixty at Battle Creek on August 6, 1881, those who recognized the real dimensions of James White in his prime, and at his best, deeply mourned his loss. A telegram reached Haskell in Washington, New Hampshire. As he remembered: "Wife and I had gone to bed. I dressed myself and went out in to the room where the folks were and we sit *[sic]* in comparative silence . . . nearly an hour. We seemed spellbound. . . . All the unpleasantness of [the] past especially that which . . . related to him [seemed] instantly obliterated from my mind."[43]

Washington Morse in Minnesota reacted similarly: "When the news broke upon my ears that he [White] was dead I drop[p]ed my tools aw[e] stricken. And sat down bathed in tears. I did not know how much I loved him until he was gone."[44] Said President Butler in summation: "Now his reputation is secure."[45]

Some people supposed that the Seventh-day Adventist Church would disintegrate now that this man of rare capability and strength of will was gone. But as the Battle Creek *Daily Journal* observed in 1885: "He was a man of great ability, and of sterling integrity. After his death many looked for a reaction in Adventist ranks. But he had built so well this did not occur."[46]

* * *

Meanwhile, the health institute so much a passion of the Californians became a reality in June 1877, when the Rural Health Retreat (now the St. Helena Hospital and Health Center) opened near Crystal Springs on the Pratt ranch, a few miles from St. Helena. Merritt Kellogg was among its initial planners, and Ellet J. Waggoner, son of Joseph, was on its medical staff until he joined his father in editorial work at Oakland in 1884. The institute staff persuaded the Pacific Press in 1885 to begin issuing the *Pacific Health Journal*.

By 1881, the Westerners were also moving ahead with their educational aims. They would open a school that featured a combined study-work program and emphasized the common branches: classics, Bible study, and the manual arts (such as printing, carpentry, domestic arts, and the making of tents, brooms, and shoes). A committee purchased cheaply an adequate structure of a defunct institute in Healdsburg at a good price. Will White then hurried to Cheboygan, Michigan, where Sidney Brownsberger, who had left Battle Creek College, was teaching high school. White persuaded Brownsberger to leave teaching amid the northern snows and to come and be the head of Healdsburg College, which opened on April 11, 1882.[47]

The college founders were so concerned for the preeminence of Bible instruction that they established a vigorous religion department headed by Ellet Waggoner, who divided his time between college teaching and editing at the Pacific Press.[48] The founders were also very much interested in conditions for the students while they were on campus. Accordingly, in 1883 they made provisions for a students' home and boarding hall. Nevertheless, the future of this educational institution did not look favorable, because of the increasing settlement of too many insufficiently committed Adventist families in the school area at Healdsburg.

THE PACIFIC NORTHWEST

Even before the burgeoning of California, prairie schooner migrants from the eastern states had begun to settle Oregon. Walla Walla, in the shadows of the Blue Mountains of Washington Territory, became a prospectors' capital for the "inland empire." And beyond the Cascades, a Douglas fir paradise attracted land claimers and loggers. Yet the Pacific Northwest eventually came partially into the California orbit. Thus captains guided their vessels northward from San Francisco to Portland, and drovers herded stock northward into the Palouse country. Seventh-day Adventists naturally accommodated themselves to these patterns.

A spin-off from California evangelism was the presence of a few Adventist adherents in the Walla Walla Valley by 1871, some of whom had come by wagon from California. When tithes and pleas for a minister from "the church in Milton" reached the leaders in California, they took notice. In turn, the California Conference repeatedly asked the General Conference to send a missionary to the Pacific Northwest; they, in turn, agreed to supply a tent and the necessary funds.

Isaac Doren Van Horn and his wife, Adelia, who had lived as a "daughter" in the White home, were chosen. Late in March 1874, a ship brought the Van Horns and the tent from San Francisco to Portland; they reached Walla Walla in April. The town of twelve hundred was still the largest in Washington Territory, with new Fort Walla Walla nearby.

Van Horn, a handsome and affable man, began tent meetings in Walla Walla and generated confidence immediately. Of him, Franklin Wood, one of Van Horn's fellow believers, wrote: "Brother Van Horn is a worker. We are not at all ashamed of him as a representative of our ministers. [Wood had met other Adventist ministers in California.] He has preached every night, and twice every

Sabbath and Sunday, since the tent was pitched, and yet he holds out all right."[49] In May 1875 the first baptism was conducted and the first church organized.

The Van Horns were impressed with Sergeant Alonzo T. Jones, a young soldier from the garrison of eastern Ohio parentage who had enlisted in the United States army seeking excitement. Van Horn left an armful of Adventist books for Jones to feast on; but Jones did more than feast—he digested. His memory seemed remarkably retentive. Adelia Van Horn wrote: "For weeks he has been earnestly seeking the Lord, and a few days since received bright evidence of sins forgiven. After being buried in Christ he arose exclaiming with upraised hands, 'Dead to the world, and alive to thee, O my God!' "[50] On his discharge from the army he married Frances Patten, Mrs. Van Horn's sister, and began to preach in Washington and Oregon, with fruitful results for the church.[51]

By 1877, Jones was elected the first president of the North Pacific Conference, though he was not ordained to the ministry until a month later. Haskell heard him speak on the Walla Walla campground and rhapsodized: "Bro. Jones is a splendid man. Think he will make a stir worth something. Give him a country and he will cut his own fodder."[52] As matters worked out, however, Jones reported for editorial duties at the Pacific Press in the summer of 1884.

Other companies and churches—a dozen or more—developed around Walla Walla and Milton in the ensuing ten years. And evangelists succeeded in an equal number of places in the Willamette Valley also, such as Oregon City, Portland, and Salem (the last being the largest city in the Northwest at the time with a population of six thousand). The North Pacific Conference organized at Walla Walla in October 1877. Three years later, however, the constituent churches wished to divide because they were separated by the Cascade Mountains. Van Horn favored the idea, and in May 1880 the Upper Columbia Conference (eastern Oregon and eastern Washington) was detached.[53]

Three times—in 1878, 1880, and 1884—Ellen White defied the rigors of travel and came to encourage these Adventist believers.[54] Recalling her visit of 1878, Mrs. Van Horn wrote: "Sister White was so ambitious when here, when contemplating work that was to be done, that it really seemed that she forgot her years. Her visit to Oregon was of the most valuable benefit to the work of Present Truth here."[55]

The Van Horns's letters to the Whites about financial matters in the Northwest provide an amazing picture of financial "prestidigitation" involving the General Conference, the printing offices, book sales, and mission expenses. At any rate, in late 1876, Van Horn confided to Will White: "We are here among strangers without any friends in the truth who can be relied upon for support, and our means running low, having only about $50. on hand. . . . Had it not been for the books . . . sold here, over $100.00 worth, we should be in want now." When the North Pacific Conference organized, it paid the Van Horn's mission expenses and their wages so that they could clear debts all around and have $400 in wages, with $200 in books left over. What they actually received for their pioneering was almost $15 per month. Thus the North Pacific Conference paid its own birth costs.[56]

At the outset, the missionaries suspected that Westerners were being de-Christianized by frontier hardships. "The people of this coast," lamented Van Horn, "have the smallest conscience of any I have met with anywhere. Full half of the people are convinced of the truth, but still they go right along in the old track, and do not attend meetings, so we can get hold of them."[57] But two years later he was in a happier frame of mind. "It has taken considerable time and labor to accomplish what has been gained," he told the Whites. "But we expect to see the work progress faster in the time to come than it has in the past."[58]

SURMOUNTING LANGUAGE DIFFICULTIES

Expansion to the west coast had accelerated; membership accessions had flourished. The tally in 1885 showed California with 1,587 members (second to Michigan); North Pacific — 237; Upper Columbia — 180. At the same time, the Seventh-day Adventist Church was beginning to learn that it was more difficult to surmount language barriers than mountains. Language problems were acute in areas to the north, east, and west of St. Louis, Missouri. In Illinois, Minnesota, Iowa, the Dakotas, Nebraska, and Kansas, particularly, immigrant settlers — about six million of them — were attacking the woods or the prairie sod. These sturdy folks had severed ties with the "old countries." As one Swede remembered: "Mother went with us as far as to the churchyard, so that she could say that she had followed us to the grave [as we left our ancestral home]."[59] After that the hold of the old state churches on them was less strong. Yet the Adventists got into the scramble for immigrant converts only because they were nudged into it.[60]

Principally, at first, it was a young Danish woodchopper, John Gottlieb Matteson, who pushed the young church on. His parents had started a farm near Manitowoc, Wisconsin, where he helped clear the land. "It was a beautiful sight," he recalled, "to see ten or twelve large piles burning . . . fine maple logs. [Because] cities and saw mills were . . . [too] far distant. So we worked hard to destroy . . . the hard work made me more sober."[61]

So serious was Matteson that he turned to God while reading his Bible alone in the woods. He then conducted schoolhouse meetings and stirred his neighborhood with many conversions. To further his preparation, he studied in a Baptist school in Chicago, and there he was ordained to preach. In the spring of 1863, Matteson met a Seventh-day Adventist neighbor of the Poy Sippi church, P. H. Cady, who spent the Sabbath with him studying Scripture. Six months later, all the families except one in Matteson's congregation became Seventh-day Adventists—and the membership had doubled.

Matteson's labors thus far had been in English, but now he proceeded to preach and "publish" a handwritten church paper in Danish. Two Sabbath-keeping Norwegian families, the Olsens and the Johnsons, strongly encouraged him, especially during four hard years when the Seventh-day Adventist organization paid him a total of only twenty dollars. In the meantime, his wife, Anna, supported the family. The conferences at this time were cool toward "foreigners." For example, President Butler confided: "They [the French-speaking ministers] are so peculiar. . . . I tell you, the French in this country will not amount to much, they are the poorest show of any of our foreign population. They have not got the stamina in some way." And later: "I am getting suspicious of foreigners, I confess."[62]

Despite such attitudes, Matteson formed a Danish Seventh-day Adventist church in 1868 near Albert Lea, Minnesota; and in 1871 a Norwegian church was formed under his ministry in Chicago. His preaching in Iowa resulted in the organizing of three churches. Congregations in Kansas, Wisconsin, and Missouri also regarded Matteson as their establisher. Matteson's successes led the administrators to scrutinize every foreign-speaking church member to discover persons with potential for church work. The Olsen, Johnson, and Serns families in Oakland, Wisconsin, responded with eight, Ole Andres Olsen being among them. Soon most conference rosters contained foreign-language ministers. Butler clearly saw, however, that "there are more Germans among us [in the United States] than any other nationality and many of them can be reached."[63] But where could German-speaking proselytizers be drawn from? From the woods too? From among the pastors tucked away in the conferences?

In 1878 a German woodchopper of twenty-two named Louis Richard Conradi, who was clearing land near Afton, Iowa, secured board and attic sleeping quarters with an Adventist family. His own home was in Karlsruhe, Germany; so this humble cabin with its religious atmosphere, including the children's prayers for him, impressed him. Uriah Smith's *Thoughts on Daniel and the Revelation* turned him to Bible study at two o'clock one morning; and his attendance at a camp meeting led to baptism. Counselors persuaded him to enroll in Battle Creek College, where he finished the four-year literary course in about a year's time and graduated in 1880.

By late summer 1881, Conradi was experienced enough with meetings to begin publicly to plant Adventist ideas among the Russian-German Mennonites of Brotherfield and Childstown near Parker, South Dakota. At nearby Milltown he helped heal a factious German company of religionists so effectively that the first German Seventh-day Adventist congregation was formed there. In September the Brotherfield congregation followed. The young licentiate collected a company of believers also at Immanuel Creek,[64] whereupon the Dakota Conference ordained this dynamic evangelist.

Because Germans of Mennonite-Russian background were open to Seventh-day Adventism, which was comfortably compatible with Mennonite beliefs in many ways, the leaders decided to team ministers of that background with Conradi. So they plucked Henry Schultz from the presidency of the Nebraska Conference to join Conradi in 1883 in the first tent lecture series among Germans at Sutton, Nebraska. Between 1883 and 1885 the leaders linked a longtime church worker, Joseph S. Schrock of Indiana, who was of Swiss ancestry, with Conradi; and the two shuttled between Pennsylvania and Kansas. The evangelistic series in western Kansas was especially fruitful. Understandably, Conradi felt that he was now prepared to enter Germany itself; and this the General Conference asked him to do late in 1885.

To help in proselytizing among the immigrants, the Seventh-day Adventist Church began to issue foreign-language periodicals: the Danish-Norwegian *Advent Tidende* (1872); the Swedish *Svensk Advent Harold* (1874); the French *Signes des Temps* (1876) in Europe; and the German *Stimme der Warheit* (1879), later changed to *Zeichen der Zeit.*

The General Conference delegates became so enthusiastic about immigrant accessions that they resolved that all Scandinavian ministers should serve among the Scandinavian settlements.[65] One estimate placed Scandinavian converts at eight hundred in 1877, and German converts at about seven hundred.[66] Proportionately, perhaps about a tenth of the Adventist church of that time was composed of foreign-language members. Butler noted these developments when he described a church rally in the Minnesota Conference: "Had a mixed meeting here last Sabbath. Lee, Swede; Olson, Norwegian; Rosie, German [;] Downer and Butler, Yankee. All in a pile."[67] The overall church was thus diversified, enriched, and cross-fertilized by these people. Each nationality contributed its characteristics — qualities needed in a movement searching for people, money, and measures.[68] In addition, the connections these immigrants maintained with their homelands called the Seventh-day Adventist Church into mission work beyond North America.

MISSIONS ABROAD

Actually, the return to the "old countries" began sooner than most of the church anticipated: the denomination was drawn there, unintentionally, ahead of time. The one responsible for this inadvertence was Michael Belina Czechowski, a Polish Catholic priest converted to Protestantism and then to Seventh-day Adventism in 1857. His career — in Europe, America, and back in Europe again — reads like fiction, with its swift, exciting, and unexpected decisions, movements, and escapes. Unfortunately, neither Czechowski nor the official Adventist church understood each other's financial "system," with the result that when he returned to Europe in 1864 it was as a representative of the Advent Christian group.[69]

Czechowski's mental image of Protestant Waldenses attracted him to Torre Pellice in Piedmont, northern Italy, where he preached biblical faith according to the Seventh-day Adventist understanding. Few Waldenses accepted his beliefs; but they evidently gave him leads — in Switzerland, and perhaps elsewhere — to people who had retained some Anabaptist traditions. Thus, before he left Switzerland to proselytize in Rumania (and later to die in Austria), Czechowski had formed a "Seventh-day Adventist church" at Tramelan in Neuchatel and had established a printshop in Basel.[70]

Before long the Tramelan church, learning of the existence of a Sabbath-keeping church based in Battle Creek, sent petitioners to the General Conference. As if in a dream, the leaders in Michigan were confronted by "Macedonians" — James H. Erzberger in 1869 and Ademar Vuilleumier in 1870 and 1872 — who entreated them to come over to Switzerland and instruct that church with the complete Adventist message.

Because Americans gave deference to European learning, the Adventists selected their most scholarly minister and writer to rep-

resent the church in the Central European mission: John Nevins
Andrews, the author of *The History of the Sabbath and the First
Day of the Week*. Widower Andrews, along with his son Charles,
his daughter Mary, and their friend Ademar Vuilleumier, left for
Europe on September 15, 1874. In the ten years thereafter, though
it was deprived of the skills and efficiency of Andrews after his death
in 1882, the mission prospered moderately well in strategic Switzerland—at Tramelan, Basel, and elsewhere. Companies and churches
of adherents in Germany, France, Italy, and Rumania also appeared.

By 1885, many of Europe's inhabitants could read the Adventist message in their own language periodicals issued by the church
from the Imprimerie Polyglotte at Basel. By this time, the converts
to Adventism were also given a sense of unity when a Continental
"council" was fashioned. An early action of that council was to ask
Conradi to come from America to superintend in Germany and
eastern Europe. The Americans stoutly hoped they could rely on
such frontier methods as holding tent meetings and sending "gospel"
colporteurs door-to-door like Yankee peddlers. But Continental conservatism and neighborhood cohesiveness were not receptive to these
American modes. The means that proved most acceptable in Europe
proved to be advertisements placed in broadly circulated newspapers.[71] Haskell in 1882 and President Butler in 1884 came among
them as inspirers and strategists representing the General Conference
headquarters. These men, however, could not completely satisfy
those Old World believers, who wished to see, hear, and "savor"
Ellen White for themselves—and they plainly said so.

The next attempt at foreign missions by the young church was
on the Scandinavian peninsula, the chief apostle being Matteson.
By 1877, this versatile man shipped for Denmark, responding to
pleas generated by reading matter sent from the United States to the
folks "back home."[72] Matteson's preaching and church organizing
among three Scandinavian nations succeeded rather well. Adventist
evangelists in America tended to shy away from the state capitals;
but Matteson, early in his work in Scandinavia, organized churches
in Copenhagen, Christiana (Oslo), and Stockholm. Two brothers,
Andrew and Knud Brorsen, helped Matteson nurture interests in
Denmark; John P. Jasperson and John P. Rosqvist supported him in
Norway and Sweden. Christiana was chosen as the site for a press,
and the Christiana Publishing House, under the management of
A. B. Oyen, was born in a building remodeled to serve as hall and
printing office. A hand press gave way to a cylinder press, and shortly
thereafter, three different Scandinavian periodicals began publication there—and thousands of tracts as well. As 1885 ended, a new

building for the combined mission hall and printshop was under construction in Christiana. If ever an apostle returned to his own to be well received by them, it was John G. Matteson. Said an observing friend: "He was . . . a real father to his people."[73]

Because the British Isles presented no language barrier, American Adventists anticipated expansion there with pleasure and high expectations. Had not the inhabitants heard the Advent message around 1844? However, though the leaders in 1878 directed William Ings, an English-born, American-reared Adventist, to evangelize in England, and in the years thereafter reinforced him with seven more church workers, accessions to a handful of churches or companies — such as Southampton and Grimsby — were scanty. Perhaps the most expansive achievement of these evangelists was the publishing of *Present Truth* after 1884, and the gratuitous dispatch of printed materials on ships bound all over the world. Generally, however, the British were cool toward Seventh-day Adventism, viewing it as upstart Americanism, too representative of Revolutionary War rebels, too challenging of Anglican state-church complacency.

When General Conference statisticians looked at Europe in 1885, they counted members in Denmark at 160; Sweden — 160; Central Europe — 224; and England — about 100. Europeans were evidently not entirely open toward people whom they viewed as "men with the bark on." In contrast, perhaps far to the west, across the Pacific, the frontier lands of Australia and New Zealand might be more open. Adventist leaders had a strong hunch that this might be true, for in a vision in 1874, Ellen White had "seen a large work" in Australia.[74]

With this in mind, the General Conference in November 1884 asked that Haskell "as soon as possible go to Australia to superintend the establishing of a mission there," and that "J. O. Corliss and other laborers who may be selected go at the same time to labor in the mission." They selected William Arnold, Mendel C. Israel, and Henry Scott, and the group left San Francisco in May 1885. By the end of that year, these ministers, colporteurs, and a printer had tested the temper of Australia sufficiently to convince them that Seventh-day Adventism ought to become solidly and broadly based there.[75]

* * *

This activity, both in North America and abroad, had increased the church from about 4,000 members in 1865 to 20,092 twenty years later; the average net gain had been close to 800 believers annually. The pattern of expansion had been one of considerable growth in

newly settled sections of North America, whereas the eastern United
States and Europe, where people had not been as uprooted from
their traditions, were more resistant to the "third angel's message."
Up to this point, Seventh-day Adventists had tended to go to countries that either spoke English or had sent large numbers of new
immigrants to settle the American West. Nations whose immigrants
had moved to the American cities did not much attract the attention
of the rural-oriented Adventists; nor did the non-European peoples
of the world. A full understanding of what world mission meant
would take time.

QUASI PAPALISM REJECTED

Despite the apparent growth of the denomination, however, not all
was well with Seventh-day Adventism in its homeland. General
Conference delegates were quick to notice that adherents, preferring
to isolate themselves into the Adventist subculture, tended to settle
around ("colonize") three main centers: South Lancaster (Massachusetts), Battle Creek (Michigan), and Oakland (California). Realizing this, the leaders passed resolutions discouraging such localism,
instead counseling church members to live in areas where they could
evangelize.[76] On the other hand, this colonization was helping
church unity, a direction that was further encouraged by a move
toward bolder common beliefs, the study of Ellen White's "Testimonies," the transfer of ministers among the state conferences, and
the effectiveness of the "traveling brethren." Partly because the denomination was becoming more close-knit than formerly, a squall
arose over a tract entitled "Leadership" that President Butler prepared
in 1873. Seeking to exonerate the ailing James White for taking
prerogatives that were not really his, Butler reasoned: "There never
was any movement in this world without a leader; and in the nature
of things there cannot be. . . . Efficiency is the result of wise leadership." Butler defended White by citing biblical precedent through
the examples of Moses, Joshua, Gideon, and David, and by recognizing White's earlier successful record.[77]

   Had the "Leadership" ideas prevailed, White (and perhaps his
successors) would have become responsible for nearly all denominational behavior. James White sidestepped the issue; and Ellen
counseled modification of Butler's ideas, so that the voice of the
General Conference, collectively through its executive committee,
would be the official (or authoritative) one — but not so authoritative
as to override individual conscience. Finally, General Conference
administrators agreed with Mrs. White. Butler burned all the tracts

he could buy back, and he hoped that the affair had helped clarify church polity.[78] In effect, the denomination had looked at quasi papalism—and backed away from it. Wolcott Littlejohn, the blind preacher who thought he had "sighted" in Butler's tract a potential inclination toward "kingly power," thereupon returned to the ministerial fold.[79]

Although Butler had been thinking primarily of the institutional affairs of the church in writing "Leadership," the most important role of the leadership was in guiding its religious development. The spiritual tone of the church members derived in a large measure from meetings, *many meetings*: evangelistic lecture series, Sabbath school, Sabbath worship service, midweek prayer service, the quarterly sacramental service, and General Conference sessions. Undoubtedly the most important meeting of all, however, was the areawide or statewide camp meeting, the first of which was held in thirteen tents pitched in 1867 at Johnstown Center, seven miles south of Milton, Wisconsin. That year it was called a "State Convocation."[80]

CAMP MEETINGS

Administrators planned their camp meeting seasons as generals would plan military campaigns. Every time Butler attended a state encampment, he assumed that the people sorely needed a revival, one that would renew and intensify their conversion experiences. When Canright tried a format that differed slightly from the usual, Butler was skeptical of its genuineness. At the Michigan camp Canright arranged for assisting ministers to go among the people to "urge them forward." But then a too unemotional minister called the responsive ones to the speaker's stand to speak "one by one in regular rotation." Declared Butler: "I was sad. . . . I suppose this is Canright's way à la Moody. I shall never learn these new-fangled ways: I am doomed to be an old fogy."[81]

Butler's description of the sort of "melting meeting" he was looking for reflects the Iowa camp meeting of 1885:

> I think I never felt freer in my life. A good many were in tears quite a portion of the time. When we came to call them forward for prayers, about one hundred and fifty came forward without much urging, and seemed ready to speak, and many good testimonies were given. Indeed, we really had a blessed season. . . . Some who had been long out of the truth broke all down and wept freely. All felt that it was a very profitable day.[82]

The meetings that counted most to secure new members, of course, were the lecture series in new areas. Tents, schoolhouses, halls, houses, churches, served to "tabernacle" the lectures. Tents seemed the most novel and schoolhouses the most community-centered. Ellen White advised the speakers not to pound the pulpit nor contort the body in these meetings; hence "contortional religion," once common on the frontier, was absent.[83] Although these activities played an important role in attracting new members and developing church unity, they had some negative side effects.

WRITING THEOLOGY

Because the members were involved in a constant round of meetings, and because the denomination was undergoing constant change and expansion, nearly all ministers and leaders of this period were people of action, not much given to contemplation, research, and writing. Only editors such as Uriah Smith and Joseph Waggoner were paid to write. As a result, there was little significant theological development during the two decades after church organization.

What little theology Adventists did write, however, followed the same assumptions and mind-set that had characterized Adventism from its beginning. The rationalist interpretation of the prophecies presented by William Miller received further development in the hands of Uriah Smith, editor of the *Review and Herald.* Following such historicist assumptions as the year-day principle, Smith put forth *Thoughts on Daniel and the Revelation* (combined into book form in 1881)—after exhausting many lamps full of midnight oil. This was a verse-by-verse study of these two prophetic books of Scripture, with emphasis on the all-engrossing struggle between Christ and Satan; on the Second Advent of Christ; and on the earth made new after the millennium. Almost overnight, Smith's book became a "best seller" with the church colporteurs. The volume's popularity tended to retard further elucidation of the prophetic topics that intrigued Seventh-day Adventists.[84]

The rationalism assumed in the interpretation of prophecy also led to debates over seemingly minor matters, such as whether the particles of the body would be resurrected from the dusty sleep of death or whether God would speak a new body into existence.[85] A more significant result of this approach to religious problems was the support that it gave to Adventist tendencies toward legalism. Joseph Harvey Waggoner, using the proof-text approach common to Seventh-day Adventists and other conservative Christians, strongly argued that Christians must keep all ten of the Commandments in order to be saved. Both law and gospel were necessary, he stated, for the former pointed out sin while the latter provided the remedy. And "the Son saves only those who return to the allegiance to the Father." Furthermore, where people keep the law they receive the gifts of the spirit, including the spirit of prophecy as manifested in Ellen G. White. Drawing his argument to a close, he asserted, "The Seventh-day Adventists have from the beginning maintained these two unpopular ideas, of keeping *all* the commandments of God and *all* the faith of Jesus, not rejecting the 'Spirit of Prophecy.' "[86]

A few years later, Waggoner worked out more fully the implications of this view of Christology. The denial of the Trinity implied in his earlier work appeared clear now. *"The Son is not the Father,"* Waggoner declared, "but rather the divine and preexistent Son sent to do the work and will of the Father." This viewpoint in turn led to a view of the atonement that supported Waggoner's argument for the necessity of law. According to him, Christ's death on the cross, by fulfilling God's requirement that blood must be shed for the remission of sins, opened the way for man's reconciliation. However, "if we are not reconciled to God; if we do not so accept the offering of Christ as to appropriate it as our own, and to cease our violations of the divine law, that offering avails nothing for us." Atonement occurs only after this reconciliation, in fact only at the time of judgment preceding the Second Coming. As Waggoner put it, "If we are justified or reconciled, and so *continue to the end,* we may hope that our sins will be blotted out when the times of refreshing shall come from the presence of the Lord."[87]

Waggoner's legalistic, rather than Christ-centered, approach may have encouraged a general spiritual coolness that seems to have crept imperceptibly over leading Adventists. But it was also true that overwork among them was a habit. As far back as 1873, Butler had decried the necessity of it: "I find that a constant round of meetings (we generally held thirty or more every week) has a strong tendency to bring the mind into a dull state, where the freshness and life of religion gives place to a spirit of mechanically plodding wearily through a round of duties."[88]

Right along, Ellen White warned her coreligionists against "Laodiceanism" and "discussions" or debates. Under such influences, too many of the sermons had become cut and dried.[89] Hoping to sweeten the people, she began to open before them the matchless person of Jesus, teaching them righteousness by faith. In 1883 she told the General Conference session that some, although repenting and believing their sins were forgiven, were not claiming the promises of God. "They do not see that Jesus is an ever-present Saviour;

and they are not ready to commit the keeping of their souls to Him, relying upon Him to perfect the work of grace begun in their hearts," she said. "While they think they are committing themselves to God, there is a great deal of self-dependence."[90] But her hearers, it seems, were too busy running the organizational "machine" to grasp the deep-down goodness of God. Although perceptive church folks often sensed an approaching crisis, they did not know how to prepare for it.[91] Too many Seventh-day Adventists were indeed spiritually luke-warm. Geographical and institutional expansion had become the essence of Adventism. The time was coming when, encouraged by Ellen White, Seventh-day Adventists would reexamine the state of their church.

4 | The Perils of Growth 1886–1905

RICHARD W. SCHWARZ

The trends that had become apparent in the two decades following denominational organization gained momentum as the nineteenth century waned. Development of health and educational institutions and expansion of mission activities absorbed increasing amounts of Seventh-day Adventist energies and finances. It was clear by the 1890s that the organizational structure was inadequate for the growing church.

Just as the institutional structure was experiencing growing pains, so was Seventh-day Adventist theology. As a Christian sect, the Adventists had tended to emphasize their distinctive beliefs, which, shaped by a theological rationalism, resulted in an increasingly legalistic religion. Rumblings of a theological earthquake were heard in the early 1880s, and before the decade ended, Seventh-day Adventists were trying to absorb the doctrine of "righteousness by faith" and understand what it meant for their theological identity.

The Adventist emphasis on health was also creating particular problems: John Harvey Kellogg, director of the Battle Creek Sanitarium and the denomination's leading expert on medicine, was increasingly unwilling to follow ministerial direction. Personality conflicts, theological aberrations, and disagreements over the role of the medical work led to increasing tensions between Kellogg and the General Conference officials.

As the denomination sought to gain control over these myriad problems, Ellen G. White gave counsel and direction. With her husband gone, Mrs. White now emerged as the central influence on Seventh-day Adventism. Although she held no office and was abroad for part of the time, her "Testimonies" on personal, theological, and organizational matters deeply impressed the church leaders, particularly A. G. Daniells, who had become close to her while both were working in Australia. As a result, when Seventh-day Adventists reorganized their denominational structure and addressed theological and personnel dissensions, they did so under Ellen White's guidance. By providing what was regarded as divinely inspired counsel, she gave the leadership an authoritative basis on which they could act to meet the mounting crises.

SUNDAY LAWS

One of the crises that they faced, Sunday legislation, confirmed their apocalyptic stance and pushed Seventh-day Adventists into limited political activity. Events during the 1880s stimulated their belief that they were "about entering upon the times we have long been expecting."[1] Study of Bible prophecies, especially Revelation 13, convinced Adventists that, just before the Advent, "dignitaries of Church and state will unite to bribe, persuade, or compel all classes to honor the Sunday [and] . . . legislators will yield to the popular demand for a law enforcing Sunday observance."[2] Activity in widely scattered parts of the United States indicated to Adventist leaders that they were on the verge of such a long-anticipated crisis, "the magnitude . . . [of which could] scarcely be appreciated."[3]

Ever since its formation in 1863, the National Reform Association (NRA), an interdenominational organization, had been attempting unsuccessfully to secure an amendment to the U.S. Constitution that would specifically designate the United States as a "Christian nation." Disturbed by the increasing secularization of society and by the lax attitudes of recent immigrants toward Sunday, the NRA began to push for stricter Sunday-law enforcement in about 1879. This movement received increased support in 1887, when the Women's Christian Temperance Union (WCTU) added a Sabbath observance department, and the Reverend William Crafts organized the American Sabbath Union party. The following year the Prohibition party added its voice to those calling for strict enforcement of Sunday as a "civil regulation."[4]

Although Adventists were not the specific object of Sunday legislation, they were victims of its enforcement. Five Adventists were arrested in Arkansas in the autumn of 1885 and were convicted of the crime of working on Sunday. The presiding judge in one case informed the defendant that no one had the legal right to follow his views when they conflicted with the laws of the state.[5] The next year, similar cases developed in Tennessee. From 1885 to 1896, "over one hundred Seventh-day Adventists in the United States and about thirty in foreign countries were prosecuted for quiet work performed on the first day of the week, resulting in fines and costs amounting to $2,269.69, and imprisonments totaling 1,438 days, and 455 days served in chain gangs."[6]

In general, Adventists convicted of Sunday violations followed the advice of church leaders by refusing to pay the fines levied, believing that "to suffer imprisonment" would have a good moral effect, call attention to the injustice suffered, and focus public attention on the claims of the seventh-day Sabbath.[7] Meanwhile, the General Conference of Seventh-day Adventists began an engergetic lobbying and publicity campaign that included the launching of a monthly journal dedicated to combat religious persecution and the formation of the general and state press committees to rally newspaper support for the Adventist concept of maintaining the separation of church and state.[8]

Continued agitation by Sunday-law advocates resulted in the introduction of the "Blair Sunday-Rest Bill" in Congress in 1888 and again in 1889. To meet such challenges more effectively, Adventists organized the National Religious Liberty (NRLA) in July 1889 in Battle Creek, Michigan. After helping defeat the Blair Bill, this association joined the successful opposition to the Breckenridge Bill, which in 1890 proposed to ban Sunday labor in the District of Columbia.[9] Toward the end of the century, the association's vigorous efforts helped to detach the temperance groups from the ranks of Sunday-enforcers. The wave of arrests for Sunday work also virtually disappeared.[10]

Commenting on this move by Seventh-day Adventists toward limited political activity, Jonathan Butler writes:

> Encouraging Adventists toward the ballot box, petitions, temperance rallies and, on occasion, public office, Mrs. White typified the *political prophetic* that brought Seventh-day Adventism within the borders of the political process. The Adventists, as a prophetic people, were to use their voice to sustain the Republic as long as possible. The irony of their position, of course, involved them in a particular vocational hazard. They wished to delay the end in order to preach that the end was soon.[11]

INTERNAL CONTROVERSY

Just when "persecution" and threat of persecution were causing Seventh-day Adventists to draw more closely together, theological differences resulted in hard feelings that delayed a vigorous evangelical thrust. The differences involved two areas in which Adventists were particularly sensitive: the interpretation of prophecy and the perpetuity of the moral law.[12]

In California, two young men in their early thirties, Ellet J. Waggoner and Alonzo T. Jones, became convinced that the law Galatians 3 referred to was not the ceremonial law of types and ordinances abolished by the Cross, as Adventists generally held, but rather the moral law that was to last forever. It was the purpose of this law to demonstrate man's utter helplessness and thus draw him to Christ for salvation, they believed. An enthusiastic student of history, Jones also challenged the traditional Adventist list of the ten successor kingdoms to the Roman Empire, described prophetically in Daniel 2 and 7. He believed the Huns had been wrongly included in place of the Alemanni.[13]

If Waggoner and Jones had simply kept their views to themselves, there would have been no controversy. Instead, they used their positions as coeditors of Adventism's West Coast weekly, the *Signs of the Times*, to promote the new ideas. They also taught these ideas at Healdsburg College, where they were part-time Bible lecturers. These activities stirred the ire of both George I. Butler, president of the General Conference, and Uriah Smith, editor of the *Advent Review and Sabbath Herald*. As elder statesmen, they feared that the public introduction of divergent views would prove embarrassing and upsetting to many Adventists. Butler fired off a letter to Ellen G. White, then on a mission to Europe, in an attempt to find out whether she had any divine enlightenment on Galatians 3.[14]

When no immediate word was forthcoming from Mrs. White, Butler aired his concerns before the 1886 annual meeting of the General Conference delegates. As a result, that body established a nine-member committee (which included both Butler and Waggoner) to investigate the matter. After hours of debate, the committee was divided five to four in support of the traditional Adventist views. Waggoner was the only member of the committee who thought that it had been wise to publish the variant view of Galatians 3 in the *Signs of the Times* before church consensus on the change had been reached. And even he declined to back Jones's vigorous promotion of the Alemanni to replace the Huns. Since their vote was so close, the committee decided not to publicize their disagreement before the entire conference. Subsequently, the delegates voted that any doctrinal discussions that might cause dissension should not be introduced in the schools or journals of the church.[15]

Several months later, Ellen White reproached all the major participants in this debate: she reproached Waggoner and Jones for their overconfidence and lack of caution in publicly agitating matters of secondary importance; she admonished Butler and Smith to remember that they were not infallible and advised them not to take an overly sharp attitude toward younger men.[16] An open and frank discussion of the entire matter, Ellen stated, was now imperative; but she did not take a position on either of the points at issue.[17]

Perhaps because of Mrs. White's suggestion for an open discussion, both Waggoner and Jones were invited to make special presentations at the 1888 General Conference meeting in Minneapolis. Jones presented his research on Daniel 7 at the Bible institute that preceded the main sessions; Waggoner gave a series of devotional studies throughout the conference period proper. Ill from overwork, malaria, and "nervous exhaustion," Butler was forced to remain in Battle Creek. His views were ably championed, however, by Uriah Smith and J. H. Morrison, president of the Iowa Conference.[18]

Many delegates had arrived in Minneapolis prepared to see the young preachers from the West put in their place. Hostile feelings toward them were not relieved by a letter Butler had received from California shortly before the conference, implying that Waggoner, Jones, and William C. White (Ellen's son) were conspiring to make a major move at the meeting.[19] The rather disparaging way in which Alonzo Jones, on one occasion during the institute, referred to Uriah Smith, probably then Adventism's leading authority on the prophetic books of the Bible, further alienated some delegates. It made them more receptive to a Butler telegram urging them to "stand by the old landmarks."[20]

However, to the surprise of many, Waggoner's presentations greatly differed from what they had expected. Refusing to be drawn into debate, he focused on man's inability to save himself and on Christ's willingness to clothe the repentant sinner with his own righteousness. This was not simply a cleansing from past sin, he declared, but a providing of power for victory over sin to whoever cultivated sufficient faith. Many delegates were captivated by Waggoner's reasoned biblical presentation.[21] Even his opponents were stymied by Ellen White's strong words of approval and by her indication that Waggoner's presentation was what she had been trying to get across for over forty years. When a delegate moved to discontinue the discussion of "righteousness by faith" until Butler could be present, Mrs. White promptly squelched the idea.[22]

The traditionalists secured time for J. H. Morrison to present their views on the law in Galatians. Seeking to deal with the interest Waggoner had aroused, Morrison, first asserting that Adventists had always believed in righteousness by faith, proceeded to place heavy

emphasis on man's duty to keep the moral law. Other Butler supporters sought to discredit the position of Waggoner and Jones through
private ridicule and jest.[23] The young Westerners' unusual reply to
Morrison—which consisted solely of their alternating reading of
sixteen Bible passages—added to the impact of Waggoner's earlier
sermons.[24]

The conference did not take a formal vote on the theological
issues in question. One may infer the deep division among the delegates, however, from their selection of officers for the subsequent
year. Butler had announced that he could not continue in the presidency because of his health. Probably on the theory that the best
way to heal the threatening division was to select a president who
had not been clearly identified with either faction, the delegates
named Ole Andres Olsen to lead the church for the next year.[25]
Formerly president of the Minnesota Conference, Olsen at this time
was helping to introduce Adventism into Scandinavia. But tradi-
tionalist strength showed itself in the election of Uriah Smith as
General Conference vice president and of another Butler supporter,
Dan T. Jones, as secretary. By a vote of forty to thirty-nine, Butler
was retained on the General Conference executive committee. However, he turned down this assignment and retired to Florida to nurse
his sick wife. William C. White was subsequently asked to serve as
acting president until Olsen's return to the United States.[26]

The opposition expressed toward Waggoner and Jones during
the session caused Ellen White deep distress. She believed that the
Waggoner-Jones presentations were just what Seventh-day Adventists
needed, and she determined to use her considerable influence to get
this new emphasis on righteousness by faith before the members.[27]
Her initial visit to Battle Creek, a Butler stronghold, was disappoint-
ing; but subsequent meetings in Massachusetts, Washington, D.C.,
and Chicago were more successful.[28] The next summer she was on
the camp meeting circuit, frequently accompanied by Waggoner or
Jones. Their reception in some states, such as Iowa, was cool; but
in others, genuine spiritual revival followed the righteousness-by-
faith presentations.[29] In addition to her counsel to denominational
leaders and her public speeches, Ellen White published several
works emphasizing the revived doctrine. Particularly important were
Steps to Christ (1892) and The Desire of Ages (1898), which by their
very existence ensured that righteousness by faith would continue
to interest Adventists.

The discussion in Minneapolis, coupled with a perennial concern over the lack of theological preparation among Adventist ministers, led the 1888 General Conference delegates to call for yearly

Bible institutes in each state as well as a national institute conducted under the sponsorship of the General Conference. Three nationwide institutes were held during 1889–91, the last running for nearly four months. In all three, either Jones or Waggoner served as one of the instructors, as did Smith. The Westerners also took part in many of the state institutes, and they were frequent speakers at subsequent General Conference sessions down through 1901.[30]

As late as 1895, one observer reported that there were still "quite a number of men in Battle Creek" who saw no light in the views emphasized at Minneapolis.[31] Gradually, however, resistance to placing major emphasis on righteousness by faith disappeared from the Adventist ministry, although pockets of resistance continued until early in the twentieth century in Texas and parts of the Plains States and the West Coast.[32]

For many, accepting the fact that the new emphasis did not necessarily negate the importance of obedience to the Ten Commandments, including the seventh-day Sabbath, seemed easier than forgetting the feelings of rancor toward the men who had introduced the emphasis. For example, as late as April 1893, Butler was writing that he still could not believe that God had led Waggoner to "deluge the denomination" with the Galatians preachment at Minneapolis. Yet, a few lines further on, he could agree that "great good" had come from the new light on justification by faith in Christ's righteousness.[33] Two months later he publicly admitted that, though he thought he believed in these newly emphasized concepts before 1888, now he was well satisfied that "additional light of great importance has been shining upon these subjects, and [he] fully believe[d] that God has greatly blessed it to the good of those who have accepted it."[34] The following year he joined Alonzo Jones in presenting the major discourses at the Florida camp meeting.[35]

Others in the conservative camp had preceded Butler in admitting a wrong attitude toward their preacher associates in 1888. During the 1891 Bible institute, after much personal persuasion by Ellen White, Uriah Smith made private and public confessions of a change of view.[36] And in 1895, Smith gracefully relinquished his longtime role as editor-in-chief of the *Review and Herald* to Alonzo T. Jones; he continued to serve harmoniously as the latter's associate editor for four years.[37] Morrison made "the most thorough confession" of a number of delegates who at the 1893 General Conference session sought to repair the damage done at Minneapolis.[38] Dan Jones later went so far as to admit that his wrong attitude toward Jones and Waggoner had even extended in some part to William

White and had nearly led him to discard his faith in Ellen White's prophetic calling.[39]

THE STATE OF THE CLERGY

It may well be that part of Butler's opposition to any change in Adventist teachings can be traced to his concern over the state of the Adventist clergy. He had had to deal with cases of the unethical—if not immoral—conduct of several prominent Adventist preachers.[40] At the same time, he feared that all too many of the younger ministers were satisfied with a policy of "drift."[41] Could such persons really handle changes in theological emphasis? he wondered. Butler's concern was shared by his successor. Olsen found Adventist preachers as a whole "exceedingly weak" and, in many areas, behind lay members.[42] He almost feared placing young ministers with older, more experienced men, because the latter were "so defective" that it was hardly safe to allow them to guide the younger.[43]

Nor did the situation seem to improve during the next decade. When Arthur G. Daniells returned to America after years of service in New Zealand and Australia, he found it "a perfect astonishment . . . to see how the leadership in this country has degenerated. No one by language could have conveyed the situation to my mind."[44] Several years later he expressed the belief that the young Adventist ministers of the previous decade had been, at best, "a third rate lot."[45] As General Conference president, Daniells concluded that nothing was "demanded more urgently today in our denomination than the improvement of our ministry."[46]

If the opinions of these three General Conference presidents were correct, it should not be surprising that a wide variety of aberrant theological views surfaced during the two last decades of the nineteenth century. Seventh-day Adventists might be especially prone to such a tendency, since, in the words of another General Conference president, "we as a people are so likely to go to extremes on, well, almost everything."[47] Stephen N. Haskell, veteran Adventist leader and roving troubleshooter, commented that he had never "seen such a time as now, when there seems to be a special burden on the minds of so many of the people to get something 'new.' "[48] Haskell believed that the new ideas led to fanaticism and perverted the righteousness-by-faith ideas that had come to the forefront in 1888.[49] Daniells saw things in much the same way and interpreted them as being the "work of the devil" seeking to make the 1888 theological message "of none effect by swinging many of our ministers away from the fundamental truths for this time." "It certainly is not necessary," he continued, "to abandon the prophecies, and drop the distinctive features of the message in order to lead people to receive the righteousness of Christ."[50]

Since fanaticism had plagued the church in its formative years, Adventist leaders were continually apprehensive about its recurrence. A genuine spiritual revival seemed to turn easily to the promotion of extreme positions and to the criticism of church leaders. This had happened in the autumn of 1885, when a group in the large Healdsburg Adventist church professed to have attained an exclusive experience, verging on sanctification, as the result of their repentance and confessions. They subsequently became critical of taking offerings on the Sabbath day, and hence critical of local conference leaders.[51]

Among the theological aberrations that troubled Adventism in the 1890s was a flirtation with faith healing. This was especially troublesome because it involved Jones and Waggoner, central figures in the 1888 controversy, and William W. Prescott, a leading Adventist educator.[52] A number of ministers became fascinated with George Fifield's teaching that probation for sinners would not terminate just before the outpouring of the seven plagues described in Revelation 16, as Adventists generally believed, but would extend up through the first six plagues.[53] The somewhat similar views that arose in western New York were carried even further: their proponents held that all sinners, including Satan, would eventually be saved.[54]

At the other extreme, some Adventist ministers began to preach that just before the Second Coming, the seal of God could not be placed "on any person of grey hairs, or any deformed person, for in the closing work, we would reach a state of perfection both physically and spiritually where we would be healed from all physical deformity, and then could not die."[55] Strangely enough, Waggoner came close to this teaching when he professed to believe that the sanctuary was a type of the human body, and the sanctuary's cleansing (Dan. 8:14) related to the development of health teachings among Seventh-day Adventists. Another Adventist preacher, Albion F. Ballenger, also developed divergent views on the distinctively Adventist doctrine of the heavenly sanctuary.[56]

The turn of the century, particularly, seemed to be a time for some of the wildest ideas to rear their heads. One Battle Creek member professed to have discovered that the angels and the Holy Spirit were one and the same. Wolcott H. Littlejohn, former president of the Adventist Battle Creek College, was captivated by the idea that the International Date Line should pass through the Garden of Eden, which he located in present-day Armenia.[57] One of the most bizarre theories was promoted by some of the staff of Battle Creek College: since all life was sacred, they held, it was wrong to kill any living thing, even insects, snakes, or rodents. They wanted to trap the college rats and release them outside the city limits![58] Never at a loss for new ideas, Waggoner suggested at the 1899 General Conference session that all who kept God's commandments should also have the spirit of prophecy.[59] Most of these variant views failed to attract large followings; they were irritants rather than dangers.

In 1900, however, the entire state conference of Indiana seemed about to be taken over by a type of perfectionism known as the "holy flesh" or "cleansing message." Haskell called it the "greatest mixture of fanaticism in the truth" that he had ever seen. The conference president and nearly all his ministers promoted the idea that there were two kinds of sons of God: the "adopted" sons must die because they lacked "translating flesh"; the "born" sons were without sin and thus possessed "holy flesh." These would not die but would go up "to heaven on the underground railroad." Through a highly emotional use of music at the state camp meeting, ministers encouraged the believers to be sure that they were "born" sons of God.[60] Prompt disciplinary action by the General Conference leaders and counsel from Ellen White calmed the situation, and within a year's time almost no evidence of that incipient movement remained.[61]

In the end, few of those who promoted their pet theological ideas separated from the main body of Adventists. Albion Ballenger was one who did. Although he attracted some followers, he did not organize them into a separate church.[62] By far the most damaging deserter of Adventism in the late nineteenth century, however, was Dudley M. Canright, evangelist, author, and debater. In 1887, after more than twenty years as an Adventist minister, Canright decided that he could no longer accept Adventist doctrines on the Sabbath, the imminence of the Second Advent, the heavenly sanctuary, soul sleep, and much of Adventist prophetic interpretation. He became particularly bitter toward Ellen White, whom he characterized as a "religious enthusiast and a fanatic" whose visions were simply "the result of nervous disease, a complication of hysteria, catalepsy, and ecstasy."[63]

This was not Canright's first apostasy from Adventism. On four or five earlier occasions he had likewise expressed doubt; but after discussions with Adventist leaders, he had seemed to regain his faith and had taken up the ministry once more. These frequent turnabouts, however, had caused Adventist leaders to doubt his reliability; and despite Butler's support, he was not reelected as a member of the General Conference executive committee in 1886.[64] Although professing a desire "to go in peace with no unpleasantness," Canright was soon severely attacking Adventists. His book *Seventh-day Adventism Renounced* became the chief weapon used by Evangelicals against Seventh-day Adventists; and Canright himself, afterward a Baptist minister, was frequently called upon to speak in an area where Adventists were beginning to make progress.[65] Canright's attitude of superiority toward Adventist ministers and his inability to resolve his differences were obvious to those who knew him. Both his published matter and his private letters show his antagonism toward James and Ellen White.[66]

CONTROVERSY AND ELLEN WHITE

With Ellen White playing an increasingly prominent role in the church, the question of whether or not she was divinely led in a supernatural way became a "sticking point" with other Adventist ministers, abroad as well as in the United States. A major defection occurred in Australia in 1897, and another in 1902 in both the United Kingdom and the Netherlands. In each case, Mrs. White's role in the church came under attack. The chief Australian dissidents, McCullagh and Hawkins, advanced a series of wild charges against Ellen White (who was then ministering in Australia) that ranged from flagrant dishonesty to enriching herself at Adventists' expense. Her teachings on healthful living, which ran counter to their own inclinations, particularly upset these men.[67]

Mrs. White's prominent role and influence also led some church members with special causes to seek her support. Many times they misused her published statements to further their own interests and ends. The case of A. W. Stanton, a Montana layman, is one example. Convinced that the Adventist church in the early 1890s had become "Babylon" and was rejected by God, Stanton circulated a call for the faithful to "come out" of Adventism, at the same time dispatching a "disciple" to Australia to secure Mrs. White's cooperation. But she had already sent a letter to Stanton reproving him for his teachings, and subsequently she denounced them in articles in the *Review and Herald*.[68]

Still other Adventists aspired to share Ellen White's prophetic role. As early as 1884, Anna Garmire of Petoskey, Michigan, claimed visions that she said revealed, among other things, that the earth's probation would close in October 1884. Mrs. White rejected Anna's "inspiration," suggesting that it came principally from her father; but the Garmires persisted. Although they did not succeed in convincing many Adventists, their influence smoldered until as late as 1900, when it had a brief flare-up in Arkansas.[69]

More troublesome was the case of Anna Phillips Rice, a young religious worker in Ogden, Utah, who began having "visions" in 1891, shortly after Mrs. White left America to be in Australia for nearly a decade. Rice appeared to be an earnest Christian, and soon her "visions" and "testimonies" were accepted by such leading Adventists as Jones and Prescott. Even the old hand Haskell was inclined to think that God was giving Anna personal guidance, although he doubted that she was receiving advice intended for others.[70] Eventually, word from Ellen White convinced these leaders that Anna was sincere and well-meaning, but mistaken. The influence of Jones and Prescott was temporarily lessened by this experience. Rice accepted Mrs. White's guidance and remained a dedicated Adventist church worker.[71]

Around the end of the century, Fannie [Frances E.] Bolton, a former literary assistant of Ellen White's, began to claim divine revelations. So did several other Adventists of a more emotional and dramatic inclination. One, a man named Parmer, claimed to be Elijah and to have a commission to follow Haskell around and give him "special light." A Swedish-American named Nelson had to be arrested when he was found to be carrying a dagger and engaging in wild talk about the need to "thrust people through" who did not accept his views.[72] None of these persons made more than a fleeting impression, since at this point Adventists were already preoccupied with new ideas on the nature of the Godhead as it was being espoused by some of their most influential leaders, a controversy in which Ellen White played a prominent role.

KELLOGG AND PANTHEISM

Most Adventist laymen were probably unaware of the fact that many of their prominent ministers had long held unorthodox Arian or semi-Arian views of the Godhead. During the 1890s, these ministers began to shift toward the orthodox Trinitarian position, particularly after the appearance in 1898 of Ellen White's *The Desire of Ages*.[73] In this work White expressly emphasized the equality and coeternity of Jesus with God the Father.[74] At about the same time a pantheistic or semipantheistic current of thought began to be expressed, most notably at the 1897 General Conference session. The leading exponents of these new views were Prescott, Waggoner, and foremost

John Harvey Kellogg, physician-superintendent of the mammoth Adventist Battle Creek Sanitarium.[75]

Kellogg seems to have held pantheistic views for nearly two decades; but on the advice of Ellen White he had refrained from pushing them.[76] Just why these ideas surfaced at this time is not clear, nor can it be ascertained which of the three men influenced the others, or if each began expressing these ideas on his own initiative. Some years later, Daniells blamed Waggoner as "really the leader in this teaching." Waggoner, Daniells said, "has done more than any other living man to give these ideas a permanent root in this denomination. Dr. Kellogg is not the aggressor in this. He has picked up his ideas, or at any rate has picked up his courage in promulgating them, from Dr. Waggoner's aggressive attitude."[77]

Whoever was the promoter of the idea that God was in all men and all objects in nature, it was Kellogg who soon became most clearly identified with this teaching. Many ministers became concerned, for, as one wrote, "with the swing that Dr. Kellogg has among so many of our young people, it seems to me that there is a wonderful danger in the teaching that he is promulgating."[78] In what appears to have been a delicate attempt to counter Kellogg's teaching, Mrs. White sent a special communication to the 1899 General Conference session pointing out that, though God is the author of nature, nature provides only an imperfect view of the Creator. Few of those attending seem to have connected this statement with the new pantheistic ideas in circulation. Prescott may have, because soon he dropped this line of thinking and became critical of it.[79] Shortly after Daniells became General Conference president in 1901, he heard Kellogg expound his philosophy of God before a number of Adventist teachers. Daniells didn't "like the flavor" of these ideas; but he held his peace, since he was anxious to have accord with Kellogg—something his predecessor had found nearly impossible to do.[80]

The pantheism issue came to a head in 1902, when Kellogg injected his ideas into his book *The Living Temple*. The state of affairs became crucial when the author proposed mobilizing the entire body of Adventists to sell half a million copies of the book, with all profits going toward financing the rebuilding of the Battle Creek Sanitarium, recently destroyed by fire. The General Conference executive committee agreed to the proposal provided that none of Kellogg's particular ideas of God should intrude into the work, but that the book should deal strictly with physiology and hygiene.[81] When galley proofs of *The Living Temple* were ready, they were submitted to several prominent Adventist theologians, including

Prescott and Jones, for criticism. Largely on the basis of Prescott's adverse comment, the General Conference executive committee decided in the fall of 1902 to call off the project. Furious, Kellogg ordered five thousand copies printed immediately. The destruction of the *Review and Herald* printing plant by fire prevented this from taking place, but the work continued to circulate in galley proof form.[82]

Within the next few months, Adventist leaders split into two camps on the matter of the teachings of *The Living Temple*. Joining Prescott and Daniells in opposition were such old-time leaders as Haskell, Butler, and, most important, Ellen White. They were backed by most of the Adventist clergy, especially those who were leaders in the local and union conferences.[83] On the other side, Kellogg's position was supported by Waggoner and Jones (the "heroes of 1888"); by leading Adventist educators Edward A. Sutherland and Percy T. Magan; and by most Adventist physicians, who were marshaled by David Paulson.[84]

The pro-Kellogg forces came to an important council of Adventist leaders held in the fall of 1903 in Washington, D.C., determined to get their views accepted. They were making considerable headway when letters arrived from Ellen White, then in California, that pointedly denounced the ideas in *The Living Temple* and called them a "snare" prepared by the enemy. After these documents were read before the assembled church dignitaries, a pronounced shift took place. Paulson, a leader of the Kellogg forces, "was profoundly impressed." Not looking for such a turn of events, he seemed to be "thoroughly stunned with the force of the statements."[85] Jones, Waggoner, and Paulson all indicated acceptance of Ellen White's words as counsel from God that must be adopted, and Kellogg agreed not to put *The Living Temple* on the market.[86]

Kellogg had always declared that his teachings were not pantheistic. Now he took the position that he believed just what Ellen White, Jones, and Waggoner had taught for years, but that his problem had been in correctly understanding the Trinity. It must be "God the Holy Ghost, and not God the Father, that filled all space, and every living thing."[87] For a time he attempted to revise the theological portions of *The Living Temple* in order to make the book acceptable to Adventist leaders, but he was unsuccessful, primarily because he had not changed his basic ideas.[88] Kellogg fought a rearguard action, later bringing the book out in revised form as *The Miracle of Life*. Acceptance of his semipantheistic views by the main body of Adventists, however, was no longer a real danger. And Waggoner, though he appears to have continued to hold similar views, had personal marital problems that largely destroyed his influence among Adventists. Jones, who was soon to be openly opposed to Adventist leaders, dropped discussion of the nature of the Deity and focused on other points of difference.[89]

The crises of these years of theological turmoil resulted in moving Seventh-day Adventists closer to traditional Christianity. The rejection of pantheism, the move away from Arianism, and the growing emphasis on righteousness by faith brought about a theology that focused more on Christ than on the Decalogue. Ironically, in light of Evangelical criticism claiming that Seventh-day Adventists have made Ellen White an extrabiblical authority, it was she who played a key role in resolving these issues. Through her writing, speaking, and personal counsel, she nudged the denominational leaders toward Christ-centered religion. Without Ellen White's authoritative voice, the outcome may have been very different. These theological controversies, though weakening the thrust of the church, failed to stop Adventist efforts to promulgate their beliefs and essential "message." Continuing to expand their concept of mission, Seventh-day Adventists broadened their evangelistic activities both in North America and abroad.

URBAN EVANGELISM

During their early years, Adventists had made their "most significant progress . . . among the country people" of rural and small-town America.[90] In 1874, however, Ellen White had called attention to the fact that Adventist beliefs had to be expounded in the cities as well. In response, two Adventist evangelists, Merritt E. Cornell and Canright, successfully conducted tent meetings in Oakland, California. From that time on, Adventist attention gradually turned to the large cities of America.[91] Throughout the next few years church leaders established evangelistic missions in a number of major cities, and by 1888 twenty-two such centers were in operation. The original Adventist city mission was not directed toward welfare work for the underprivileged but was concerned with attracting interested persons from all walks of society to Adventist beliefs. The normal plan was to establish a mature couple in a respectable residential area and gradually add to this "home base" others especially interested in working in city evangelism. Door-to-door selling, loaning, or giving away of Adventist books and pamphlets provided an introduction. As these canvassers found interested persons, they made appointments for Bible instruction. At meetings held in the homes of prospective church members, the Adventist mission worker directed systematic study of some religious topic through the consideration of numerous Bible texts. In this way Adventist churches were established in many major cities where there had been none before.[92]

In 1884 the General Conference established a mission training school in Chicago to improve the preparation of workers for urban areas. During the next few years this school gave in-service training to over one hundred people, who then scattered throughout eighteen states and six foreign countries. Meanwhile, these students had converted over one hundred people to Adventism in Chicago. By 1888, Eugene W. Farnsworth, a coordinator of city mission work, reported that during the previous nine months city mission workers had held "12,037 Bible Readings with 16,339 persons" and had "sold, loaned and given away 1,560,111 pages of books and tracts." Selected members were also being taught to give simple home treatments to persons they discovered to be ill and in need of help.[93] The Chicago training school continued until the mid-1890s, and it enrolled as many as fifty students at one time.[94]

In some city missions, special efforts were made to reach the various ethnic groups clustered there. Language schools were opened to attract Chinese and Japanese youth in particular. Adventists were eager to convert people of these nationalities so that they might be sent to initiate work in their own homelands.[95] Not all city missions were successful. Much depended both on the caliber of the directors and on their perseverance. Ellen White believed that much effectiveness was lost because workers would "loose up the work too soon and go to a new field."[96]

During the 1890s, Adventist city missions underwent a dramatic change in emphasis. This began in 1893, when Kellogg acquired the Chicago Mission Training School and transformed it into a branch of the Battle Creek Sanitarium. At the same time, he organized a welfare-type mission at the south end of the Chicago Loop. This "medical mission" included a free dispensary, a laundry, an area for baths, and visiting nurse services for the poor and unemployed in the area. Begun later were a penny lunch counter, free kindergarten for working mothers, and an educational program designed for mothers struggling with the problems of child rearing.[97]

Kellogg was able to expand his operations after 1895, for in that year he launched the American Medical Missionary College. The last two years of study were conducted in Chicago, with the mission enterprises serving as a laboratory for the medical students. As a result, Kellogg also established the Workingmen's Home, a cheap but sanitary rooming house. A portion of the building was used to provide temporary employment at carpet weaving and broom making for those seeking permanent jobs. Another building on Chicago's South Side was purchased to serve as a combined dormitory for the medical students and a settlement house where a day nursery, free laundry, health school for area residents, and other social services were provided. Special work was inaugurated for alcoholics, juvenile delinquents, and prostitutes.[98]

A skillful promoter, Kellogg had convinced the General Conference in 1893 to organize the Medical Missionary and Benevolent Association to coordinate and direct all Adventist health facilities and such other social service organizations as church-sponsored orphanages and old people's homes.[99] With Kellogg as its president, this association began to encourage the development of welfare-oriented missions in a large number of cities across the United States. Kellogg had hoped to finance these social service activities from the profits of Adventist health institutions, but these profits proved woefully insufficient. Forced to turn to the public for contributions, he began to emphasize the nonsectarian orientation of the missions. This emphasis, along with his appeals to the none-too-prosperous Adventist members for funds, brought him into conflict with church leaders and drew severe disapproval from Ellen White. As the financial burdens grew, and as controversial theological and organizational stances brought Kellogg into increased contention with Adventist leaders during the early years of the twentieth century, his ability to promote these varied mission activities sputtered.[100]

Although Mrs. White had always supported work for the poor, sick, and unfortunate, she was concerned because the mission activities that Kellogg was promoting placed a disproportionate emphasis on this line of endeavor. She recognized that many other Christian and non-Christian groups would carry on welfare programs. But these groups were not interested in promoting the Adventist doctrine of an imminent return of Jesus and the need to prepare people who loved him well enough to keep all his commandments, including the seventh-day Sabbath. Thus she called for a return to the original evangelistic kind of city mission.[101]

One result of the crucial 1901 General Conference session was the decision to make a major attempt to recapture the evangelistic city mission momentum lost by the diversion of the 1890s. Pioneer evangelist and organizer Stephen Haskell, who originated the individual Bible study method, and his wife were invited to develop a "demonstration" program in the city of New York. Haskell was convinced that it was possible to adapt some of the activities of the 1890s to support an evangelistic thrust. He favored establishing small sanitariums, vegetarian restaurants, and cooking schools as additional ways of attracting the interest of persons through the avenue of Adventist health teachings.[102]

The Haskells and a number of helpers, principally young women, initially had success using the old door-to-door method of distributing religious literature and soliciting prospects to take Bible studies. Through one such success they were able to rent a large hall in mid-Manhattan, where two young ministerial assistants held a public evangelistic campaign. Six months after starting the program, Haskell secured the services of a female physician, Dr. Carolyn Geisel of the Battle Creek Sanitarium, to give health lectures and run a cooking school. Opportunities also developed for special work among blacks, Jews, and Germans in Brooklyn.[103] One outgrowth of this mission endeavor was the birth of a new periodical, the *Bible Training School*. When Mrs. Haskell began receiving numerous requests for copies of the Bible "readings" she had prepared, the Haskells decided to combine a number of these with other things (Bible quizzes, brief articles on biblical questions, and tips on healthful living and home nursing) and to print them in a monthly journal. Later the *Bible Training School*, which sold by the thousands on city streets, proved to be an additional way of getting the Adventist message to the attention of the general public.[104]

Not everything went smoothly for the Haskells. They discovered that the ugly demon of race prejudice kept many from attending their services once large numbers of blacks began to attend. They regretfully turned to separate meetings for whites and blacks, a move that drew criticism that would hamper their work.[105] Even more damaging was a disagreement over methods of evangelism that persisted between Haskell and Elmer E. Franke, another evangelist who had worked in the New York area for several years. Franke, who was a gifted public speaker, favored extensive and sensational advertising to attract a crowd; but Haskell thought Franke's methods attracted people to himself as much as — or more than — to the message he preached.[106]

When Franke opened a large evangelistic crusade in Carnegie Hall, a few blocks from the site of the Haskell group's meeting, the mission workers found much of their audience "stolen away." Haskell decided to shift operations to Brooklyn; but now Franke became more open in his criticism of the Haskells, publicly threatening to "run them out of New York City."[107] By the end of 1903, Haskell had had enough. At seventy years of age, he no longer felt able to carry on strenuous work, especially in the face of fierce and running criticism. The Haskells withdrew, first to Nashville and later to California, where they continued to conduct training schools in methods of personal evangelism.[108] A few months afterward, Franke's continued un-Christian conduct resulted in the General Conference's withdrawal of his ministerial credentials and his separation from the Adventist faith.[109]

Even before Haskell left New York, Daniells recognized that, with the exception of the Washington, D.C., area, the General Conference had not done much to promote Adventism in the large cities.[110] Ellen White was sad because of the neglect, and she wrote: "The favorable time for our message to be carried to the cities has passed by, and this work has not been done. I feel a heavy burden that we shall redeem the time."[111] She continued to promote activities in the large cities for the remainder of her life.[112] But another need for missionary endeavor lay heavily on Mrs. White's heart during the 1890s: the black population of the American South.

MISSION TO SOUTHERN BLACKS

Seventh-day Adventists had been slow to take their message to the southern states. The formal organization of the Adventist Church just at the outbreak of the Civil War, and their small numbers and resources, prevented them, in spite of the abolitionist background of many of their members, from joining the educational and evangelical movement sponsored in the South by the major Protestant bodies in the postwar period.[113] Only a scattered handful of Adventist believers, mostly recruited by laymen who had moved to the South, appeared in the former slave states during the 1870s and 1880s. In Missouri and Texas several of these Adventists attempted to conduct primary schools for the freedmen, but these schools did not last long.[114]

Early in 1891, Mrs. White began to publish appeals for Adventists to increase their efforts in the South. She even went so far as to say that "sin rests upon us as a church because we have not made greater effort for the salvation of souls among the colored people."[115] For several years her words had little effect. Then in 1893, Edson White, Ellen's second (the eldest surviving) son, had a deep spiritual awakening: he determined to leave private business in Chicago and, along with his wife, engage in self-supporting educational and evangelistic work for blacks in the deep South. The Whites recruited old friends, Will O. Palmer and his wife, to join them in this work.[116]

Edson White was blessed with an innovative mind. He conceived and prepared a *Gospel Primer* that could be used for teaching illiterates to read and at the same time for presenting Bible messages in simple form. Its widespread sale provided funds White needed to finance his next project, a river steamer to be used as a base of operations along the lower Mississippi River and its tributaries. By mid-1894 this boat, christened the *Morning Star*, was ready to leave Kalamazoo, Michigan. Accompanied by several helpers, the Whites and the Palmers took off on their great adventure.[117] Initially, there was a certain amount of uneasiness about this operation at church headquarters. But after White and Palmer agreed to accept supervision by the General Conference executive committee and from H. S. Shaw, its supervisor of work among southern blacks, the mission proceeded with the church's official blessing.[118]

The *Morning Star* company chose Vicksburg, Mississippi, as its first bridgehead in the black belt. After receiving a cordial welcome in the black community, they soon launched a night school for old and young alike. More than fifty students attended on the first evening, and soon the number passed one hundred; they then opened a second school several miles outside the city.[119] Although particular Adventist doctrines were not promoted in these schools, several students soon discovered the beliefs of their teachers, and before long a number joined the Adventist group in forming a church. For a time it met aboard the *Morning Star*; later they rented a hall; and finally, after many difficulties, they built a small chapel.[120]

From Vicksburg, White's group decided to expand into the rich cotton lands of the Yazoo River Delta. The *Morning Star* chugged upriver to Yazoo City, where they repeated the Vicksburg experience. Here, however, opposition from the white planters was more intense. After several threats of lynching, the white members of the group found it expedient to withdraw and entrust their educational and evangelistic endeavors to black converts.[121]

In 1898, Edson White and his associates organized the Southern Missionary Society to coordinate and help finance their growing ministry for Mississippi blacks. Finances had always been a problem. Only White and Palmer drew salaries from the General Conference; others had to be supported from sales of the *Gospel Primer* and similar books written and printed by White. An Iowa Adventist, C. W. Smouse, manufacturer of a variety of notions, became an earnest supporter of White's riverboat project and dedicated the profits from his creations to "the Southern Work." At Kellogg's suggestion, White also began to issue a small paper, the *Gospel Herald*, which publicized his work and brought donations of money and used clothing for distribution to needy blacks.[122] Through the *Review and Herald*, Ellen White made a public appeal for financial aid for her son's work. In response, Adventist churches across the land donated over eleven thousand dollars from Sabbath school of-ferings to this cause. But the money failed to arrive! Because of a change in General Conference officers and a complicated mix-up in bookkeeping, the money was given to other church projects.[123] Later the fund was partially made up, but meanwhile the riverboat work had to be curtailed.

While White and his helpers continued in Mississippi, other Adventist projects were also being launched throughout the South. Undoubtedly the most important one was launched by the 1895 General Conference decision to start an industrial training school for blacks, which was patterned somewhat after Booker T. Wash-ington's Tuskegee Institute. Late that year it secured a run-down plantation near Huntsville, Alabama.[124] Funds for this school were hard to come by, but Adventist leaders were determined to get it going. Even the General Conference president, Ole A. Olsen, spent a few days in his blue overalls helping plaster the buildings. George A. Irwin (who was then directing Adventist church work throughout the South, but would soon succeed Olsen) acted as tender, "mixing mortar and carrying it up stairs."[125]

Within a year, the Oakwood Industrial School, the institution established on the Huntsville property, had twenty-three boarding and fifteen day students attending evening classes. The days were spent in practical work: agriculture, masonry, and carpentry for the boys; cooking, sewing, laundering, and gardening for the girls. The students did most of the construction of the new buildings that gradually appeared. Schoolwork was carried on at the elementary level because of the poor preparation of those who came. In its second year of operation, Oakwood's student population rose to fifty; and it fluctuated between fifty and a hundred for the next decade.[126]

The students trained at Huntsville, both the black and the white Vicksburg associates of Edson White, and recruits sent by Kellogg's Medical Missionary and Benevolent Association—all fanned out across the South initiating projects in dozens of different com-munities. After the 1901 General Conference, White moved his river steamboat and the Southern Missionary Society to Nashville. From there he directed an expanding church work for blacks. When the supervision was turned over to the newly created General Con-ference Negro Department in 1909, the society was sponsoring fifty-five primary schools in ten southern states, in which over eighteen hundred pupils were enrolled. Medical facilities for blacks were be-gun in Nashville and Atlanta, and the number of black Adventists in the South had increased from around fifty to over nine hundred. When White retired to Michigan in 1905, he was succeeded, as president of the society, by George I. Butler, who had come out of retirement in 1902 to head the Adventist church work in the South. [127]

From the start of their operations in the South, Adventists had been troubled about the problem of whether or not to integrate their churches and meetings. Determined not to recognize any color line, leaders who were trained in the North soon found that when they invited "the colored people to share freely and equally with the Whites, then the result [was] that the White population [stayed] away."[128] In some places like Knoxville, Tennessee, it was possible for whites and blacks to meet together and "get along nicely." In Atlanta, however, there was a "tussle" over "the color question."[129] Although in the early days it was possible, at least in the upper South, to hold camp meetings that included both racial groups, the leaders came to the pragmatic conclusion after several years of frustration that the best course was to have separate congregations. White people should work for whites; and blacks should work for blacks, but under white supervision. Ellen White reluctantly agreed. [130]

THE OVERSEAS MISSION

Although the decades 1885—1905 proved to be ones in which Seventh-day Adventists in the United States modified their methods to increase the emphasis on urban centers and among southern blacks, it was overseas that the greatest challenges appeared and the greatest advances were made. Adventists had been slow to accept the idea of disseminating their message in *all* the world. By the mid-1880s their mission efforts were limited: Europe, Australia, and New Zealand, and in 1887, South Africa and British Guiana. At the same time, half a world away, Abram La Rue, a sixty-five-year-old Adventist layman with a "burden" for China, arrived in Hong Kong in 1888 to work among the seamen in the crown colony. Here he supported himself by selling Adventist books and importing dried fruits. Although he had been turned down by the General Conference foreign mission board, before his death in 1903 he had succeeded in interesting some Chinese in Adventism and had arranged to have the first Adventist tracts printed in Mandarin.[131]

Another Adventist layman, Theodore Anthony, a Greek cobbler who had been born in Turkey and immigrated to the United States, sold his business for two hundred dollars and in 1889 returned to Constantinople. Here he opened a shop, and in it he also held seventh-day Sabbath services. Soon he converted Zadour G. Baharian, who became an active propagandist for Adventism throughout Turkey until his imprisonment by Muslim authorities.[132]

In 1894, Adventists opened their first mission station among "pagans" when Cecil Rhodes's South African Company granted them twelve thousand acres in Matabeleland. This transaction caused much misgiving and a certain amount of opposition back in Battle Creek. Perturbed about the Adventist position on church-state relationships, Alonzo T. Jones and others feared the consequences of accepting government favors.[133]

The 1890s also saw the opening of Adventist church operations in such diverse places as Argentina, Jamaica, Finland, India, Japan, Iceland, and Egypt. It used an imaginative way to begin the Japanese bridgehead: William C. Grainger, former president of Healdsburg College in California, took a young Japanese student convert with him and opened an English language school in Tokyo. A chance acquaintance of one of their converts with a visiting Korean led to the latter's conversion to Adventism. The Korean convert had brought together a group of more than seventy Sabbath-keepers before the first American Adventist arrived in Korea in 1904.[134]

How does one explain the sudden foreign mission activity of Seventh-day Adventists in the late 1880s and 1890s? It may, of course, be viewed as part of the general American evangelical mission thrust of those years.[135] Yet it was undoubtedly more than that, since Adventists were not exactly in the mainstream of American Protestantism. Much of the sudden interest may be connected with the increasing exposure of Adventist leaders to the world outside America. Butler, the first General Conference president to leave the country while in office, visited Europe in 1884. Ellen White, Adventism's preeminent leader, was influential in her work in Europe from 1885 to 1887 and in Australia and New Zealand from 1891 to 1900. Olsen was working in Scandinavia when he was asked to head the General Conference in 1888. George A. Irwin visited Australia during his General Conference presidency (1897– 1901). Arthur G. Daniells, Irwin's successor, visited South Africa and Europe on his way home to America after spending fourteen years in Australia and New Zealand.

Haskell visited Europe in 1882 and several times thereafter, he pioneered the Adventist church work in Australia and later spent several more years there, and he served in South Africa during the 1890s. Along with a young secretary, Percy T. Magan, he made a world-circling tour in 1889– 90 to survey the prospects for Adventist missions. Magan's graphic accounts of their journeys were published in the church's *Youth Instructor*.[136]

Adventists themselves saw their sudden overseas expansion as part of God's prophetic plan, depicted vividly by the "loud cry" of the angel of Revelation 18.[137] Certain it was that Adventists were sending more church workers overseas. The increasing tempo of sending church workers overseas is shown in the mid-1890s: 62 went overseas in 1893, 65 in 1894, and 140 in 1895.[138] At the same time that the General Conference foreign mission board was dispatching salaried church workers overseas, it was encouraging farmers and skilled workers to immigrate to such areas as Australia and West Africa to establish themselves as self-supporting witnesses.[139]

In 1890, with the help of funds raised by Adventist Sabbath schools, the foreign mission board built a 120-ton schooner to use in evangelizing the islands of the Pacific. Christened *Pitcairn* to celebrate the acceptance of Adventism by all the residents of that tiny island in 1886, the ship was used for a decade to carry missionaries throughout the South Pacific until better steamship connections became available.[140]

From their earliest beginnings Adventists had experienced success in arousing interest by selling and distributing printed matter in all parts of the United States. They found this method equally effective among literate populations overseas. Camp meetings were held too, not simply to encourage the members and reinforce new believers but to draw the curious and expose them to Adventist teachings.[141] Once an interest developed in an area, however, a new problem arose. Should the missionary be kept there to strengthen and confirm the new converts, or was it his duty to move on immediately to warn the millions yet to be reached?[142]

One possible answer involved attempting to train local Adventists to fill responsible positions in all kinds of church endeavor. This practice would be acceptable also to nationals, because frequently they looked on Americans as "sharp" or "pushy." Both Irwin and Daniells believed that Adventism failed to sustain its early successes in Scandinavia because too much dependence on America and Americans had been practiced there.[143] By the turn of the century, Adventist world leaders had accepted the view that in the long run it was better to concentrate immediate efforts on places like Australia and Great Britain, so that these more prosperous areas could help provide funds and personnel for "weaker areas." They also believed it important to keep major positions at the General Conference level filled by people who had served overseas and thus knew from broad experience the heavy needs outside North America.[144]

Adventists soon discovered that methods used to build up the church must necessarily vary so as to be intimately connected with the culture and progress level of the people. A strong program of preaching and publishing worked well in literate areas; in nonliterate areas, however, it seemed necessary to establish schools and educate the nations in Western ways first. Aging pioneer Haskell found the very thought of such a "detour" frightening; it would take "a millennium" to evangelize these fields in this way, he opined.[145]

FINANCIAL PRESSURES

Perhaps the most persistent and troubling problem connected with the rapid expansion was how to finance it satisfactorily. This problem proved particularly vexing to Adventist leaders during the 1890s, when the United States staggered under one of the most severe financial depressions in its history.[146] However, at least one leader, George A. Irwin, soon to be at the helm of the Adventist church, saw these financial straits as a blessing in disguise. He wrote that the financial shortages would teach Adventists "to husband our resources and bring our expenses within [or] below our income; and it may be the means of teaching some, that even to work with their hands is not dishonorable. I have thought for some time, that some of our laborers were getting rather high toned."[147]

Too much money had proved to be a curse in at least one far-off segment of the Adventist organization — South Africa. Here the Wessels family, the earliest of Advent believers in the Cape Colony, had contributed $125,000 (from the sale of their farm for diamond mining) to start church enterprises in their homeland. The handful of Adventists, only around two hundred in 1895, got ambitious ideas about establishing a college, a publishing house, an orphanage, and a sanitarium to equal those developed at the Adventist headquarters in Battle Creek. Even so, they could not use all the money given them: $50,000 was kept in South African banks at a time when Adventists in other parts of the world were in desperate need of funds. But the South Africans' prosperity did not last; by 1900 their money was largely gone, and most of their overbuilt institutions were heavily mortgaged.[148]

The depression of the 1890s called attention to the dangers of another long-standing financial practice of the church. For years Adventists had been encouraged to loan money, interest free or at nominal rates, to the General Conference or to one of the Adventist publishing houses or sanitariums. This had seemed to be a practical and cheap way to get needed cash. However, when the Wessels family suddenly asked for repayment of $73,000 they had loaned the General Conference Association, it proved to be extremely difficult to repay it. By the beginning of the twentieth century, the total of loans ran into several hundred thousand dollars—all of which was subject to the same recall as was that of the Wessels.[149] What the church really needed to do was to increase its income from gifts.

During the 1870s, Adventist leaders had become convinced that God's answer to church financial problems was the tithing system instituted in the Bible. Thus they began to teach tithing as a moral duty incumbent on each Christian. Although this practice did make for a steadier church income, constant encouragement of the people to pay an "honest" tithe was necessary.[150] The amount of tithe paid varied greatly, both within a state and between states. In 1884, for instance, the amount of tithe paid per capita in Battle Creek was about double that paid throughout the state as a whole. In turn, Michigan Adventists paid about one-third more tithe per person than did adherents in neighboring Indiana. Thus Michigan had a surplus of nearly $5,000 over what was needed to pay its ministers, whereas Indiana barely scraped by. However, there was no "machinery" or agreed-on interconference policy for transferring surplus tithe funds from one local conference to another.[151]

To meet special financial needs, such as the building of a school or a sanitarium, Adventists depended largely on appeals made through their periodicals or at camp meetings or other large gatherings. Individuals would respond with gifts, and delegates at a conference might vote to give a certain amount of surplus tithe or Sabbath school offerings toward a specific project. During this period, local conferences controlled all the tithes and Sabbath school offerings collected in their territory, except for a tithe of their tithe, which they passed on to the General Conference to use in paying its employees.[152]

As Adventist mission work expanded, it became necessary to devise regular offerings to support it. At least from the beginning of the period 1885–1905, a special offering for missions was taken at Christmas. Beginning in 1887, the "First-day Offering" was also instituted. Every Seventh-day Adventist family that was "really true to the cause" was encouraged "to systematically lay by something every first day morning, for the advancement of our foreign work." The Christmas offering, which amounted to only about $20,000 in 1885, had increased to nearly $40,000 by 1893. That same year, the first-day offering amounted to $17,510; by 1897, however, first-day offerings were declining. Some felt this slackening was due to increased calls for funds to support the welfare-type missions that Kellogg and his associates were sponsoring in major American cities.[153]

Beginning in 1885, the Sabbath schools in Oregon and Washington decided to give all their regular offerings for mission work. Other conferences were slow to follow, although most did begin to set aside a portion of their weekly collections for this purpose. Still, by 1902 slightly less than 60 percent of the Sabbath school money went to support mission enterprises, the rest being retained for local expenses.[154] Toward the end of the century the General Conference foreign mission board began a campaign to get all Adventists to contribute ten cents a week for foreign missions; sometime later a special mission offering was scheduled to be collected in all churches in mid-July.

A total of $200,000 per year was now required to support the foreign mission program, and by November of each year General Conference officials were hard pressed to meet overseas payrolls. William A. Spicer, General Conference secretary at the time, drew only enough of his own salary during these months to meet his bare expenses; many other headquarters officials did likewise. Some missionaries took time to sell Adventist books in an effort to help meet their expenses, and because of these heroic efforts no missionaries were returned to America. But Adventist leaders considered the raising of finances to sustain the expanding work to be one of the most distressing matters facing them.[155]

The desperate financial picture led a former General Conference president to advance the idea of selling Adventists on the plan of setting aside a second tithe for missionary purposes. Daniells believed that the solution lay in simply getting all Adventists to pay an "honest" tithe in the first place. He noted that British Adventists generally had smaller incomes than did Americans; yet if American Adventists would pay a tithe equal to that of the average Briton, there would be some $220,000 extra available per year. Studies indicated, Daniells pointed out, that an honest tithe from North American Adventists would bring in an additional $450,000 annually—more than enough to finance mission needs satisfactorily.[156]

The General Conference tried various expedients in an effort to solve the church's financial needs. The Review and Herald Publishing Association found that its large plant was not kept busy doing the printing work of the church alone; so the publishers turned to an increasing amount of commercial work. Part of the profits from such work were then loaned to mission fields and Adventist institutions in need.[157] Haskell suggested encouraging missionaries to make direct appeals to their home churches and conferences. This could increase interest and the feeling of personal responsibility. The Haskells tested this idea on their return from Australia in 1899 and reported that many of the employees at the Battle Creek Sanitarium cashed in their meal tickets and went without food in order to have money to send to Australia.

Although Daniells certainly favored church expansion "down under," he was wary about the kind of program Haskell suggested, since it would lead, he feared, to a competition between overseas areas to see which could best reach the hearts and purses of American Adventists.[158] A program somewhat akin to Haskell's was suggested by Prescott in 1896: he called for letting state conferences choose a needy foreign field and send out and support one or more of their own workers in this area. This plan was actually tried to some extent and with limited success after 1900.[159]

As part of an effort to economize to meet overseas needs, Irwin, on the advice of Ellen White in 1899, promoted a pay cut of approximately 25 percent for church employees. Irwin proposed taking an even larger cut himself but was persuaded that to do so might bring undue pressures and hardship on others to do likewise. After the cut, the average Adventist minister was paid fifteen dollars weekly; office employees drew considerably less. This move seemed generally well accepted, particularly by Adventist laymen, many of whom pledged to increase their own giving as they saw their leaders sacrifice.[160] During these years, Spicer—and probably a number of other ministers—wore cheap suits (twelve to fourteen dollars) during the week in order to save his "preaching" frock coat for many years of service. In spite of a heavy traveling schedule, Daniells usually chose to ride train coach rather than Pullman in order to save the church's money.[161]

Late in 1899, a financial panic in Scandinavia (after years of rather poor judgment by the managers of the Adventist publishing plant in Christiana, Norway) placed a special strain on general church finances there. Creditors suddenly demanded nearly $70,000 on obligations, many in the form of notes the publishing house had cosigned. Some Adventist leaders favored declaring bankruptcy and forcing the creditors to take whatever could be realized from a sale of assets. But Ole Olsen, then in Norway, was horrified at the proposal; he was sure such a solution would forever stain the name of Seventh-day Adventists throughout Scandinavia. Finally, after great effort, he worked out a plan to pay off the entire amount over a three-year period.[162]

Even before the Christiana debacle, the Adventist General Conference was in a very precarious financial position. Irwin H. Evans, president of the legal organization that held Adventist properties, told Ellen White in 1898 that the General Conference was $366,000 in debt. When Daniells became General Conference pres-

ident three years later, he found that the organization was between
$16,000 and $20,000 behind in paying its personnel. At the same
time, the Australian branch of the church was about $150,000 in
debt. It is small wonder that Daniells, feeling he could not tolerate
this state of affairs, said, "We must bring our General Conference
expenses within our income."[163] Having decided to set his face "like
a flint against the creation of further debts," Daniells carried the
General Conference executive committee along with him. A "no-
debt" policy was inaugurated to prohibit the borrowing of money to
establish or expand church educational, medical, or publishing institutions. Although this policy brought him under attack from Kellogg and his associates, Daniells refused to capitulate.[164]

In an effort to help relieve some of the church's financial
overload, Ellen White advanced a promising idea late in 1899. She
proposed to donate all royalties from her new book, *Christ's Object
Lessons*, if the Adventist publishing houses would work out a plan
to print it cheaply and, if church members would sell it widely, all
profits would go to reduce the indebtedness of Adventist schools and
colleges. Through an energetic promotional campaign, the church
sold several hundred thousand copies of the book; in three years'
time about $263,000 of a combined school debt of $350,000 was
paid off.[165] Daniells was so pleased with this accomplishment that
he proposed a similar campaign for Waggoner's book *The Everlasting
Covenant* as a means of wiping out the General Conference debt.
This would also serve a second purpose: it would bring a clear ex-
position of the righteousness-by-faith teaching before the people.
Unfortunately, nothing came of this proposal.[166] Haskell used a
modest version of this plan when he published a special issue of his
Bible Training School and dedicated the proceeds of its sale to sending a missionary couple back to India when the Adventist foreign
mission board found itself unable to do so.[167]

INSTITUTIONAL PROBLEMS

Much of the financial pressure felt by Adventist leaders in the 1890s
and early 1900s was caused by the rapid development of church
educational, medical, and publishing institutions during these years.
Increasingly, the denomination embodied its message in institutions,
for past experience had shown that they were effective means of
evangelism. But in addition to the ever-present problems of finance,
church administrators had the never-ending task of finding institutional managerial and operational personnel with the right qualities
for their positions.

There was also a constant struggle to keep Adventist schools sufficiently different from their secular counterparts to justify their existence. From the beginning, Adventist educational philosophy had dictated schools that would be both practical and theoretical; yet few educators seemed to know how to operate such schools. Furthermore, for people who justified their existence and teaching by heavy reliance on Scripture, the Adventists would expect their educational system to be noted for outstanding instruction in the Bible. Yet Daniells wrote in 1902: "I am deeply impressed that the greatest need of our educational institutions in America, and everywhere else, is better Bible teaching."[168]

A different set of problems developed with the publishing houses. The original *Review and Herald* plant in Battle Creek, which by this time had grown to be the largest printing business of its kind in Michigan, was of particular concern.[169] Problems seem to have increased in direct proportion to the increase in size. Managers became overly concerned with profits, skilled workers with wages; both seemed to have lost much of the evangelical fervor that had dictated the establishment of an Adventist publishing house to begin with. According to the estimate of an observer not of the Adventist faith, by 1899 only 40 percent of the printing done at the *Review and Herald* was of religious material, 20 percent was of sanitarium materials, and 40 percent was of strictly secular matters.[170] Attempts to improve the situation seemed to get nowhere. In 1901 the new manager admitted that the business was "quite largely with the outside advertising commercial work." Commenting on this, Daniells expressed displeasure over the fact that the *Review* had "their solicitors in Chicago and other places driving like Jehu to secure commerce."[171]

Medical institutions brought a special kind of headache: masses of technical details that the clergymen's background had not prepared them to understand. This view was pointedly—and repeatedly—expressed by Kellogg, who had become a virtual "czar" over Adventist sanitariums and was determined not to take direction from clerical leaders. "Self respecting medical men are willing to work on an equal footing with preachers even though they may be of inferior education and ability," he said, "but it is not human nature that they could be willing to be slaves to such men while doing their own professional work."[172] It is not surprising, then, that Daniells should remember these years as a time when there was "more or less conflict between the General Conference President and the head of the medical work. No matter who was president there was conflict."[173]

Toward the end of his term, General Conference president

Olsen probably expressed the feelings of many of his associates when he wrote: "It is utterly impossible to give proper care and attention, and to follow and successfully develop so many different enterprises."[174] Others were thinking the same thing. Thus church leaders were soon wrestling with the problems of organizational restructuring, of simplifying and shortening decision making, and ultimately, as developments indicated, with the problems of relocating the headquarters. Questions of organization and administration seemed to surface at almost every General Conference gathering. To some extent at least, these questions resulted from repeated recommendations by Ellen White that church leaders grant more responsibility to subordinates and encourage their initiative, in order to develop a larger number of experienced persons able to advise and assist on difficult matters.[175]

ADMINISTRATIVE RESTRUCTURING

Expansion had increased the complexity of Adventist enterprises and had overloaded the president. So the 1887 General Conference delegates attempted to lighten the president's load by creating the post of corresponding secretary to help him with his paperwork. Three additional secretaries were provided to supervise specific activities: education, foreign missions, and home missions.[176] The first two of these posts continued through 1896, but the last was phased out in 1889.

In 1888 the newly elected General Conference executive committee decided that it would be profitable to subdivide the United States and Canada into four large districts and make one member of the committee responsible for supervising and coordinating activities in each district. On Olsen's recommendation, the last annual gathering of the General Conference in 1889 (thereafter to be biennial sessions) formally approved the districting plan but set the number at six rather than four, as follows: East, South, Central, Northwest, Southwest, and Pacific Coast states.[177] The make-up of the districts appears to have taken into consideration both the geographic factors and the size of the Adventist constituency.

Shortly after this plan was adopted, the General Conference executive committee instructed each member selected to "superintend" a district to attend all the annual conferences in his district, plan for competent instruction for the ministerial institutes and camp meetings in his district, advise the leaders of local conferences and Adventist organizations in his district, and take special care to encourage weak portions of his territory. Each superintendent was to

keep the General Conference executive committee informed of matters that needed their special attention.[178]

At the 1893 General Conference assembly, Olsen spoke of the
opinion in some circles that the complexity of Adventist organization
was hampering the work, and he suggested the disbanding of some
of the separate entities: the American Health and Temperance Association (established in 1879); the Foreign Mission Board (1889);
the International Sabbath School Association (1878); the International Tract and Misssionary Society (1874); the National Religious
Liberty Association (1889); the Seventh-day Adventist Educational
Society (1873), the legal body responsible for Battle Creek College;
the Seventh-day Adventist Publishing Association (1861), the entity
managing the *Review and Herald* plant; and the General Conference
Association (1887), the legal corporation to hold church institutional
properties. Doubting his own executive abilities, Olsen had been
frustrated for some time by the complicated overall organization. He
felt particularly lacking in background for dealing with all the concerns of a "business character," which were becoming more and
more numerous.[179] As it turned out, the 1893 gathering did not
dispense with any of the separate organizations; instead, it added
another, the Seventh-day Adventist Medical Missionary and Benevolent Association. Established to coordinate and direct Adventist
health and welfare activities, this new organization did absorb the
American Health and Temperance Association.

But more came of a second Olsen proposal: formalizing the
district division as a grouping of several local conferences into one
unit to be "intermediate between the General Conference and the
state conferences." These new district conferences would coordinate
the work of the various Adventist associations within the region, hold
title to Adventist property in the region, hold biennial sessions during
alternate years with the General Conference biennial sessions, and
name delegates to attend the latter. Provision was made for two
overseas districts, one composed of Australia and New Zealand, the
other of Europe.[180]

The American district conferences failed to develop into genuine administrative units; instead, they devoted most of their time
and effort to theological and evangelical instruction. But overseas
it was a different matter. This was particularly true in Australasia,
where Daniells and William C. White, with a strong executive committee, developed an effective organization that included subject
departments devoted to publishing, education, medical, and religious liberty interests.[181]

As Olsen's presidential term at the General Conference progressed (1888–97), he came to lean more and more for advice on two businessmen who had become prominent in the financial operation of the church, Archibald R. Henry and Harmon Lindsay. Although these men were able and shrewd financiers, they gave the impression of feeling superior to Adventist ministers and tended toward sharpness in dealing with them. Many of their actions drew severe criticism from Ellen White, and this helped to convince both Olsen and others that a new president not connected with Henry and Lindsay and their policies had to be elected.[182]

The 1897 General Conference delegates attempted in several ways to follow Ellen White's recommendation to divide responsibility among top leaders. During the tenure of Olsen and his predecessors, the General Conference president had also been president of the Foreign Mission Board, the General Conference Association, the International Tract Society, and the SDA Publishing Association. But when George A. Irwin (the superintendent of the southern district) was elected General Conference president in 1897, other officials were elected for these added positions that the president had previously held. In addition, three administrative subdivisions of the overall church were established according to geographic areas: the United States and Canada, Europe, and Australasia. Furthermore, the General Conference executive committee was increased from nine to thirteen members, and the headquarters of the Foreign Mission Board was moved from Battle Creek to the Atlantic seaboard. Other actions favored the organization of new union conferences in Europe and the United States on the Australian model and the choosing of businessmen to direct the business interests of the church.[183]

On the surface, these changes seemed to be significant. But events proved that the hopes of 1897 would go unfulfilled. Irwin was no more successful than was Olsen in organizing the districts into genuinely autonomous administrative subdivisions. The Foreign Mission Board's removal added confusion rather than strength; and administratively, the church was worse off rather than better off. "The facts are, that no one can ever know the sad condition that things are in here on this side," wrote the president of the General Conference Association. "Even we, who pretend to be in the light, cannot agree on many things among ourselves, letting alone those who are disaffecting and sowing discord. What we need at the present time is unity in our midst. There is a prevailing feeling that every man should do as he pleases."[184]

Although conscious that the hopes of 1897 had not been realized, the delegates attending the 1899 General Conference gathering were not yet ready for a major overhaul of the machinery. They *were* ready, however, to point out mistakes in the existing structure. Complaining of mismanagement of funds intended for mission fields, Prescott suggested that the church's administrative structure was interfering with the Lord's work by coming between God and his people. This criticism led Alonzo T. Jones to quote a letter from Ellen White indicating that for several years she had not considered the General Conference in session to be "the voice of God." Referring to prominent leaders by name, Jones called on them to repent of their actions and attitudes. This triggered a season of prayer and elicited statements by Irwin and others asking their associates' forgiveness for wrong attitudes.[185]

At a later session, Waggoner blamed organizational problems on the failure of Adventists to give more than lip service to the doctrine of righteousness by faith. The organization men had tried to devise a suitable structure in their own strength, Waggoner believed, whereas any kind of organization would operate well if the Spirit of God had been allowed to work in each one. Agreeing, Prescott, who had been closely associated with Waggoner in England since 1897, went on to criticize the overcentralization of the church, which he believed had resulted in virtual ecclesiastical despotism.[186]

THE GENERAL CONFERENCE ASSEMBLY OF 1901

During the next biennium a number of Adventist leaders became convinced that the organizational structure and administration of the church had to be the major issue for the 1901 General Conference assembly to consider. They were also convinced that Ellen White had to attend, for her repeated calls for reorganization might have more impact if she were to be there in person. They knew that preliminary plans had to be made carefully. As Daniells expressed it, "It will be a great calamity to have this conference go through as the last one did."[187] The day before the 1901 meetings began, Mrs. White, who had recently returned from Australia, addressed a large group of Adventist leaders representing nearly every line of church endeavor. She sounded a call for an "entirely changed" management — "newly organized." Leadership had to be broadened and entrusted to a committee "not composed of half a dozen men, but of representatives from all lines of our work, from our publishing houses, from our educational institutions, and from our sanitariums."[188]

A further appeal by Ellen White at the opening session was followed by Daniell's motion for the formation of a large committee representative of "organizations and institutions, and fields in all parts of the world" to prepare "the business to bring before the delegates."[189] After a week of study, this large committee recommended placing the leadership of the General Conference not in the hands of a single president but in an enlarged General Conference executive committee of twenty-five members, specifically to include six chosen by the Medical Missionary and Benevolent Association. This obvious effort to placate Kellogg and silence the opposition he posed by making him a part of the team drew criticism from some who saw it as favoritism to one branch of Adventist endeavor. But the plan was speedily adopted when Ellen White supported it.[190]

In other important actions, the convened delegates voted to discontinue the separate associations — with the exception of the Medical Missionary and Benevolent Association — and to form constituent state and national conferences into union conferences and three union missions. Church educational institutions were to be subject to the union conferences in which they were located. The enlarged General Conference executive committee was to have charge of all mission work, including that of a medical nature.[191] Almost as a postscript to the session, again on the initiative of Mrs. White, the delegates voted to move the church's first institution of higher learning, Battle Creek College, to a rural location. A storm of protest developed among local Adventists, as Olsen had predicted it would when relocation had been suggested five years earlier. But Edward A. Sutherland and Percy T. Magan (president and dean of the college respectively), who had wanted to make such a move for some time, quickly took steps to put this action into effect. Within a few months (mid-July 1901) the institution was reestablished as Emmanuel Missionary College near Berrien Springs in southwest Michigan.[192]

DANIELLS VERSUS KELLOGG

Probably as important as the administrative changes voted on in 1901 was the selection of the man who bore chief responsibility for implementing them. In deference to the strong views of Jones and Prescott, the 1901 delegates did not select a president; but when the General Conference executive committee organized itself for operation, they named Arthur G. Daniells chairman. At this time, even Kellogg believed that Daniells was "certainly the man for the place."[193] At the age of forty-one, Daniells was in his prime. He was a natural administrator, "a clear and independent thinker," who "when he believed that a certain course was right . . . upheld that course with his whole heart."[194] A practical man, Daniells soon recognized the need for the General Conference to have a titular head when dealing with business firms, and he began signing himself as president on official papers. His action was ratified, in effect, two years later, when the 1903 General Conference delegates formally voted to reactivate the office of president. Although Prescott by this time was reconciled to such a development, Jones, Waggoner, and others objected vigorously.[195]

During his early months at the helm, Daniells worked at a tremendous pace: twelve major meetings and ten thousand miles of travel during the summer of 1901. After nine months of such hectic activity, he seemed ready to step down as chairman of the executive committee at the end of a year. Shortly thereafter, however, the honeymoon with John Harvey Kellogg was over. In the fall of 1902, when the doctor's supporters in the executive committee attempted to substitute Alonzo T. Jones for Daniells as chairman, the latter rallied his supporters and weathered the challenge. Convinced that he was fighting to save Adventism from forces that would destroy it, Daniells was determined not to surrender. Kellogg's attempts to unseat Daniells at the 1903 general convocation failed completely.[196]

Over Kellogg's vigorous objections, Daniells and his associates got the 1903 delegates to pass a resolution declaring that all Adventist institutions should be owned directly by the church members — through a state conference, a union conference, or the General Conference.[197] Daniells also succeeded in getting the General Conference constitution amended to provide for the formal departmentalizing of the various lines of Adventist endeavor. But it took two more years of struggle with Kellogg before a medical division that would be subordinate to the General Conference executive committee was formed to take the place of the Medical Missionary and Benevolent Association.[198]

The wide support Daniells received from Adventist leaders was undoubtedly due in part to his ideas on the management of local affairs, particularly those in areas far from headquarters. To the president of the Adventist conference in Cape Colony, South Africa, he wrote in 1901: "All we can do in this country is to make suggestions for consideration and study. When you come to deal with the situation face to face, you must use our suggestions just as far as they prove to be wise."[199] Although a firm supporter of union conferences, Daniells was less successful than he had hoped to be in getting them operating at the desired efficiency. In 1905 he still regarded "the strengthening of our union conferences in North America" as one of the most important challenges facing the worldwide church.[200]

THE MOVE TO WASHINGTON

The 1901 General Conference delegates had voted to move Battle Creek College. Now the 1903 delegates decided to relocate the General Conference office headquarters and the *Review and Herald* publishing plant. For over a decade Ellen White had been critical of the growing concentration of Adventists in Battle Creek; she had long opposed any expansion of church institutions there. Other leaders were concerned over the gossip and criticism that seemed to envelop the church headquarters. "If an angel from Heaven should appear in the streets of this place," wrote Hetty Haskell, "I fear he should not escape evil remarks."[201] After the 1901 conference, when an invitation was extended to Charles H. Jones, long-time manager of the Adventist Pacific Press in Oakland, to assume a like position with the *Review and Herald*, Jones refused. "He writes," reported Daniells, "as though Battle Creek were about to be given over to the enemy, and as though the *Review and Herald* would probably be burned up soon for its great sins. . . . And he closes his terrible description of our situation with statements to the effect that Sister White confirms all this, and warns him not to come near."[202]

Fire did come to Battle Creek. On the night of February 18, 1902, the main sanitarium buildings burned; and ten months later, on December 30, it was the *Review and Herald* publishing plant that went up in flames. These two events caused Adventist leaders to pay special attention to the things Ellen White had been saying. Thus, at the 1903 General Conference session, when she renewed her plea for dispersal, the delegates voted to shift both the church headquarters and the publishing plant to a site somewhere in the eastern United States. Such a move would make it easier to keep in touch with the rapidly growing foreign mission endeavors of the church.[203]

Less than two months after the 1903 general meeting ended, a search committee was out examining possible sites, centering their attention on the New York City vicinity. They hoped to find suburban property on a main railroad. At first they were favorably impressed by Elizabeth, New Jersey; later, interest shifted to an estate about sixty miles up the Hudson River, near the village of Fishkill. Receiving word from Ellen White not to overlook the advantages of Washington, D.C., Daniells and another committee member went there to scout out the possibilities. After four days they concluded that the little village of Takoma Park (astride the boundary separating Maryland and the District of Columbia) had just what they needed: it was on the main Baltimore and Ohio Railroad line and also had street-railway service to downtown Washington. Land was available at a reasonable price, and they found the village officials cordial.[204]

Moving quickly, church leaders purchased fifty acres of land in Takoma Park. Then they hurried back to Battle Creek, packed two railroad cars with office equipment and files, and by mid-August 1903 they were operating out of temporary headquarters at 222 North Capital Avenue in downtown Washington. By fall they had decided to use the fifty-acre site in Takoma Park for a sanitarium and a college, and to purchase two more acres just inside the District of Columbia for the General Conference office building and the *Review and Herald* plant.

Most Adventist leaders were enthusiastic about the move and immediately set out to raise funds to construct the needed buildings.[205] Most—but not all. The Seventh-day Adventist Publishing Association had been founded as a stock company, and now a group of disgruntled stockholders led by Archibald Henry threatened to seek an injunction that would block the moving of the printing plant. It proved necessary for church leaders first to organize a new corporation in the District of Columbia and secure for it a majority of the stock in the old organization; then, at considerable expense, they bought out the obstreperous stockholders. Of all the skilled plant employees, only an apprentice typesetter agreed to move with the managers to Takoma Park. At first it was necessry to hire printers who were not Adventists to produce the one monthly and three weekly journals that continued publication without interruption. Slowly a production staff was built, and an increasing stream of religious materials rolled off the presses. From the start, church leaders determined that the new *Review and Herald* publishing plant would solicit no secular business.[206]

After fifteen months of frenzied effort and at considerable more cost than expected, Adventist leaders were able to open Washington Training College with fifty students and a faculty of seven on November 30, 1904.[207]

Kellogg's growing feud with Daniells and associates added to the difficulty of establishing a medical facility on the new property. The Battle Creek "rumor mill" circulated reports that a sanitarium could never succeed at the Takoma Park site, because the site adjoined the town sewage farm and was full of malaria, and because Dr. George A. Hare, who had been persuaded to develop the new institution, was a "crank." Therefore, construction did not begin until 1906. Meanwhile, on Iowa (now Logan) Circle in downtown Washington, the church rented an old mansion (formerly occupied by General Ulysses S. Grant) early in 1905 and began sanitarium treatments there. Early talks with the families of several important senators, including William B. Allison of Iowa and John C. Spooner of Wisconsin, convinced church leaders that an Adventist medical institution in the nation's capital would bring great opportunities for "witnessing in high places."[208]

The move to Washington placed tremendous strain on the three major church officials involved in administering the affairs of the church from its new headquarters: President Daniells, Vice President Prescott (also editor of the *Review*), and Secretary Spicer. Despite working fourteen to eighteen hours daily to keep the ecclesiastical machinery running, these men also launched a lecture series to acquaint the public with Adventist beliefs during their first two winters in Washington. A fair attendance, and good coverage by the capital press, convinced them that the effort was worthwhile.[209] In early spring 1905, Prescott was deeply involved in an effort to block a proposal by leading Washington clergymen to introduce a course of religious instruction in capital schools. This proposal, which failed to gain the approval of the Washington school board, appeared to Adventist leaders as an advance move toward a church and state union that they so much feared would soon result in religious "persecution."[210]

THE KELLOGG PROBLEM

It was not "Caesar," however, who was causing the Adventists the most difficulty during these early years of the twentieth century. Rather, it was one who had long been a chief ornament of Adventism, probably its most widely known adherent, the major proponent of Adventist health teachings — John Harvey Kellogg, M.D. A number of matters on which Kellogg differed with the Adventist mainstream have already been recounted: the nature of welfare versus evangelistic city missions, the financing of church enterprises, and the control and direction of Adventist church medical interests.[211] As early as 1886, President George Butler (1871–74, 1880–88) had expressed concern about the state of Kellogg's religious experience and the failure, under Kellogg's administration, to maintain strict observance of the seventh-day Sabbath at the Battle Creek Sanitarium. Butler was also irritated when, over his objections, Kellogg pushed a resolution through the 1886 General Conference session advising the executive committee to train and send out men to promote health reform principles among Seventh-day Adventists. To Butler this was evidence that Kellogg was getting unbalanced and was determined to push his views of healthful living above all else.[212]

At about this same time, Kellogg had a sharp disagreement with veteran Stephen Haskell, whom the doctor suspected of spiriting away both a prized stenographer and two of his medical associates.[213]

During the years of Olsen's presidency there was a minimum of friction between Kellogg and the General Conference. This was due in part to Olsen's frank admission that Adventist clergymen had not practiced and promoted health principles as much as they should have. This failure was a perpetual grievance of Kellogg's. Olsen attempted to work closely with Kellogg and helped to get him speaking appointments at major Adventist camp meetings, and the doctor proved to be an energetic health "evangelist."

Illness during 1891–92 seems to have led Kellogg to increase his dependence on God. As he shared the strength that came to him from this deepened spiritual experience, the prejudices of many Adventists were dispelled.[214] By 1895, however, though still firmly committed to the promotion of health principles, Olsen found that there were matters connected with the Battle Creek Sanitarium "which perplex me exceedingly." In subsequent months he became more and more disturbed over the increasing size and "worldliness" of the sanitarium.[215] Anyone who made a criticism of the sanitarium touched a sensitive nerve in Kellogg; he had given himself unstintingly to build it to its position of eminence, and he was determined to manage it as he alone saw fit.[216]

Within a year after taking the top position in Adventism, George Irwin was echoing George Butler. The health interest was getting out of proportion to the rest of Adventist endeavors, Irwin felt, and in the end this was bound to hurt the entire church cause. Sensing the intensified strain in the matter of the church versus Kellogg and his associates, Ellen White appealed to Irwin to unify the diverging groups—something that he professed a desire to do but found impossible to do because "the Doctor will not permit it."[217]

Shortly before the 1899 General Conference convened, Irwin was encouraged by an interview with Kellogg during which the doctor admitted that "unconsciously to himself" he might have sown seeds of doubt among his medical and nursing students as to the importance of basic Adventist doctrines. Irwin believed that they had established a basis for better cooperation. Yet within six weeks, Kellogg was in a "dreadful state of mind," threatening to resign all his connections with Adventist institutions and organization. Although he was persuaded to abandon these plans and appeared to enjoy a renewed spiritual experience during the 1899 gathering, Kellogg was becoming more and more disturbed about communications he had been receiving from Mrs. White.[218]

Ellen White had always been frank to point out what she considered Kellogg's shortcomings to him. But she had also strongly supported his endeavors since he was a youth. Now, during the last years of the century, she became even more frank in suggesting to Kellogg that he was overly ambitious; was selfish and misguided in his efforts; was neglectful of basic Adventist doctrines; and was critical and unwilling to accept the recommendations of others. Kellogg tended to blame Irwin for poisoning Mrs. White's mind against him.[219]

At first, hesitating to attack Ellen personally, Kellogg blamed others for feeding her false information, and he accused William, her son, of "tampering" with her letters to him. At one meeting with General Conference leaders, Kellogg reportedly said that "whenever anything came from Australia, the brethren would take it, and say that 'NOW THE LORD HAS SPOKEN' (that is, speaking of it in a contemptuous way, raising his voice above the natural pitch), 'when' he 'said it was nothing under the heavens but Will White.' " Kellogg seemed convinced that Ellen White had been made his enemy and that she was determined to "drive him to the wall." He resolved to fight with all the strength that he had.[220]

During 1900, Haskell spent a good share of the year in Battle Creek. He had long since made up his difficulties with Kellogg. Now he was disturbed over the doctor's attitude toward Ellen White. Haskell believed that she alone could convince the doctor that she was not his enemy. Others shared this view, and there was wide rejoicing when Kellogg accompanied Daniells to California for a visit with her shortly after Mrs. White returned from Australia.[221] Harmony seemed to be restored, especially after Ellen accepted Kellogg's invitation to stay at his home while attending the 1901 General Conference gathering. As noted above, special efforts were made at the 1901 session to see that Kellogg was included in the top echelon of Adventist administration. Daniells, who succeeded Irwin, even repressed his aversion to a separate organization to promote Adventist medical interests and agreed to specific representation from this organization on the General Conference executive committee. For a time it seemed that harmony had been achieved. According to Daniells, Kellogg "says that he had had a glorious time wherever he has gone since the Conference, and that there is a splendid spirit manifested everywhere."[222]

But this happy state came to an abrupt end in the summer of 1902 when Daniells refused to modify his no-debt policy to allow English Adventists to borrow money to establish a sanitarium. Later he was to remember that, as Kellogg tried to talk him out of this stand, the doctor simultaneously fed him doubts concerning the reliability of Ellen White's inspiration and the admonition she gave as coming from God. "You do not know," Daniells later wrote, "how nearly I was brought to ruin by the cunning insinuations of doubt that man sowed in my mind." It was not against Ellen White alone that Kellogg attempted to "poison" Daniells's mind, but against "nearly every minister in our ranks." The doctor tried the same tactics on Prescott and Spicer, Daniells reported, and "nearly succeeded" with them all.[223]

The controversy over publication of *The Living Temple* followed hard on the heels of the no-debt disagreement. But it was on the issue of Mrs. White's role as a leader who was divinely inspired that Daniells determined to take an uncompromising stand. Just before the 1903 General Conference assembled, Daniells became convinced that God had particularly commissioned him to defend Ellen White and her "gift" and lead all Adventists to accept and appreciate it. He saw his reelection as General Conference president in 1903 as confirmation of this commission.[224] Although the breach between Daniells and Kellogg seemed to have healed in the spring of 1903, by the start of 1904 it was reopened—to remain so until Daniells's death in 1935. Central to the disagreement was Daniells's position that "the only way we could possibly look for peace and concert of action is to do exactly what the Lord has pointed out in these Testimonies [Ellen White's letters]."[225] Rather than do that, Kellogg set himself on a deliberate course among Seventh-day Adventists, both at home and abroad, to undermine confidence in Ellen White and her writings—or so Daniells believed.[226]

There were certainly many other actions by Kellogg that Daniells and his associates disapproved of. They disliked hearing him "cover the General Conference Committee with smut and mud" in the presence of young people who were "innocent as babes of the grave situation we are in." Kellogg had a knack for biting criticism; and when he went on hour after hour, his opponents' patience was tried. By 1905, Adventist officials were convinced that it was "useless for us to meet him any more." From then on, all dealings were carried out through legal counsel.[227]

Since at least the last days of the Olsen administration, Adventist ministers had feared that Kellogg's overemphasis on medical and philanthropic programs was diverting Adventists from the particular message they believed God intended for them to give the world. They believed Kellogg was luring too many talented Adventist youth into becoming doctors and nurses by promising them everything from financial independence to freedom from "persecution" in the "last days." This made it practically impossible to recruit capable ministerial students or salespeople for Adventist publications.[228] If Kellogg had urged Adventist medical personnel to make the religious doctrines and theology of Adventism prominent, church leaders would not have been worried. They believed, however, that he did just the opposite, teaching his students "to keep the doctrinal features in the background." When Kellogg sought to reestablish a Battle Creek College two years after the original had moved to Berrien Springs, church leaders were highly suspicious of his motives and accused him of seeking to corrupt Adventist youth.[229]

Daniells also believed that Kellogg was subtly continuing to sow discord and heresy in Adventist ranks through the pages of the *Medical Missionary* magazine, which he controlled and which he was actively promoting in 1905. Haskell was quoted as saying that the *Medical Missionary* was the "most subtle, deceptive and dangerous publication ever put out by this denomination."[230] Daniells thought that Kellogg demonstrated vindictiveness when he threatened to start a rival sanitarium in Washington just when the General Conference officers were attempting to establish a medical institution there.[231]

One of the things that worried the Daniells group the most was what they regarded as Kellogg's efforts to get "absolute power" over all Adventist medical interests by close ties to the Medical Missionary and Benevolent Association, which he controlled absolutely. This, they held, caused "confusion and strife and in the end [would] bring about separation."[232] Thus it was with relief that they learned in 1904 that Kellogg was ready to disband the MMBA. But this relief turned to consternation shortly thereafter, when they learned that Kellogg and his compliant associates had transferred all MMBA assets to corporations the doctor firmly controlled, such as the Battle Creek Sanitarium. He passed over to the General Conference some eighty thousand dollars in liabilities, many in the form of notes given to Adventists who had loaned funds to the MMBA. Kellogg saw nothing amiss in these actions. "You have killed the baby," he told Daniells, "and you must pay the funeral expenses."[233]

Particularly disturbing to Adventist leaders was the role Alonzo T. Jones played in consenting to Kellogg's actions in the dissolution of the MMBA, for at this time Jones was the nominal head of the association. Propelled by motives that would become clear only in later years, Jones had completely cast his lot with Kellogg. Daniells could not understand this. "I had such great confidence in his keen perception, and his deep reasoning," he wrote, "I felt sure that if the facts could be but stated to him, he would size them up, and take his stand like a strong giant for the right. It took me many months to awaken to the fact that he was either a very partial man . . . or that he was completely blinded by some influence that was brought to bear upon him."[234] It hurt Daniells to find both Waggoner and Jones, the "heroes" of 1888, in opposition to him.

The local Adventist congregation in Battle Creek did not get around to expelling John Harvey Kellogg from church membership until 1907. By the end of 1905, however, any hope for a lasting reconciliation between the doctor and the church leaders was virtually gone. The Kellogg controversy had proved acrimonious and costly; for years Adventist leaders were diverted from major progress in evangelistic endeavors. Virtually no growth in Adventist membership in the United States took place during the first half-dozen years of the twentieth century.[235]

* * *

As the Kellogg controversy came to an end, it appeared that the Seventh-day Adventist Church was about to enter an easier time. The two decades between 1885 and 1905, although they had seen dramatic denominational expansion abroad, had also been fraught with theological controversy, financial difficulties, and personal rivalries. During the process of the resolution of these problems, Ellen White played an increasingly important role in denominational affairs. In receiving her criticism and advice, the leadership found her outspoken support necessary in order to gain passage of their proposals. As Ellen White was thus drawn into the denominational controversies over reorganization and John Harvey Kellogg, she became an issue herself. Although a measure of order was brought to a chaotic situation when the church embarked on major reorganization, the issue of the "spirit of prophecy" lay simmering.

5 | Shaping the Modern Church 1906–1930

GARY LAND

The leaders of the Seventh-day Adventist Church faced an immense task after the General Conference sessions of 1901 and 1903. The delegates had voted for reorganization. Now this reorganization had to be implemented. Furthermore, implementation had to take place in the face of increasing dissent that led to serious questioning of Ellen G. White's authority in the affairs of the church. It was clear that both structural and theological progress would be difficult.

DANIELLS AND WORLD MISSION

One man dominated the church from 1901 to 1922. Arthur G. Daniells, the General Conference president who led the church through the organizational and theological changes of that period, had greater influence on the Seventh-day Adventist Church than had any other president, according to one student.[1] An Iowan born in 1858, Daniells had left the United States for New Zealand in 1886 as the first Adventist missionary to that country; he served in the New Zealand and Australian area for fourteen years, ten of them in administrative positions. This experience had considerable effect on Daniells and, through him, on the development of the church. The administrative experience he gained in Australia included the presidency of the Australian Union Conference (later called the Australasian Division), the first union conference to be established by Seventh-day Adventists.[2] His organizational ideas, which seem to have stemmed from those developed by Asa T. Robinson in Africa, influenced the adoption of the union conference plan at the General Conference of 1901[3] and the choosing of Daniells as the chairman of the General Conference executive committee that same year.

It was also in Australia that Daniells was closely associated with Ellen White, whom he had previously served as a secretary, and with her son William C. White.[4] This relationship contributed to his emergence as a General Conference leader in 1901 and affected his position in the later dispute over the inspiration and authority of Ellen White's writings. Daniells and his associates— particularly William White and William A. Spicer—differed from most previous leaders of the General Conference primarily in that they had had significant foreign mission experience. Daniells took the position of General Conference executive committee chairman, he said, "to get things in order here so as to benefit the weak fields. That is my hope. I can do more for Australia from here than from there."[5] This interest in foreign missions was one of crucial importance to the Adventist church in the twentieth century, for under Daniells the church shifted from its nineteenth-century emphasis on North America to its twentieth-century worldwide emphasis on the basis of Christ's gospel commission to go into all the world.

The increase of foreign mission emphasis had its roots in two major aspects of church thought, both of which had existed for some time but now gained greater significance. First, Seventh-day Adventists, as they had from their beginnings, regarded themselves as uniquely "chosen," as having a special purpose to fulfill. Explaining why Seventh-day Adventists existed as a separate church, Francis M. Wilcox, editor of the *Review and Herald* (1911–44), set forth the idea that the church was "to act the part of heaven's messengers to the people of this generation, proclaiming the special truths now due the world."[6] Other articles spoke of Adventists as "the church,"[7] one that had "been entrusted [with] great light."[8] In a world gone astray, another *Review* editor argued,

> it is time for us to make known and make prominent God's purpose and plan. With one great religious denomination, which numbers its adherents at over two hundred million, denying the Word of God to its members, and with the leaven of the infidelity of Higher Criticism eating like a cancer at the vitals of the other denominations, we cannot be too earnest or too industrious in proclaiming to the world God's last message of warning and of mercy.[9]

This writer also touched on the second major theme of the Adventist mission idea: that the church was called to a worldwide proclamation of the gospel, an idea that had emerged in the 1860s and 1870s and was now echoed many times in Adventist publications. Calling for more funds in 1905, Spicer said that "the truth will march on, and will annex still more territory. This message is going to the world."[10] Ellen White spoke of the third angel's message as a "worldwide message."[11] According to a 1913 writer in the *Review*, "In our missionary endeavors we have the world as our field, and the hasty but effective preaching of the gospel to all people in it as soon as conditions and earnest labor can make it possible."[12] Although Seventh-day Adventists may not have spent much time developing a systematic theology of mission, they did not question that they had the specific purpose to finish "the gospel message in this generation."[13]

The worldwide mission idea and Daniells's organizational ideas were separate yet connected influences, and together they shaped the church during the first third of the twentieth century. That they were linked is illustrated by Daniells's forceful advocacy of the mission idea, both in preaching and in organizational leadership. That they were separate is indicated both by the earlier history of the mission idea in Adventism and its continuation when Spicer took over as president after Daniells stepped down from office in 1922. The reorganization inaugurated in 1901 and carried out under Daniells's leadership provided the vehicle that made the missionary vision effective and permanent.

DEPARTMENTS AND MINISTRIES

The move of the General Conference office headquarters from Battle Creek to Washington, D.C., in 1905 attracted much attention. In contrast, the structuring of General Conference departments, which proved to be equally important, developed in a relatively quiet way. As Daniells said in his address to the General Conference delegates in 1901, "The growth and extension of our cause demonstrates more clearly each year the value of thorough organization."[14] By that year, seven departments had been developed: Sabbath School, Publishing, Medical, Education, Religious Liberty, Young People's, and Foreign Missions.[15]

The creation of departments in the General Conference unquestionably enhanced "the efficiency of the management of the work."[16] But this advance likewise expressed the growing missionary concern of the church as a whole and of Daniells personally. Although much of the reason for bringing the medical work into the sphere of General Conference governance arose out of the experience of the church leaders with John Harvey Kellogg, emphasis on the missionary purpose of the medical work held a significant place in the discussion and final resolutions at the General Conference session of 1909. As Daniells said, those working in the medical setting were to be treated as those in the gospel ministry, a concept embodied in the name of the department—Medical Missionary Council—and the decision that the medical department would receive the same financial support and care as other branches of the General Conference. The departmental objective, the organizing resolution stated, was to advance the medical missionary interests of the church in all the world by developing a comprehensive policy and cooperating with and advising union and local conference departments.[17]

Two other departments organized during this period also illustrate the renewed missionary impulse of the Adventist church. America's large immigrant population, then relatively unreached by the Adventist message, presented a challenge to the "home" missionary efforts. Therefore, at the 1905 General Conference meeting, the North American Foreign Department was created to supervise work among the German and Scandinavian groups first, with other groups to be added as needed. The choice of these groups seems to have come about because of their concentration in the Midwest, where Adventist church members were also concentrated, and because some evangelism had already taken place among them. The church gave little attention to the southern and eastern seaboard of the United States.[18] In a related effort, the 1909 General Conference council, after being urged by Ellen White, voted to establish three foreign language schools. As a result, a Danish-Norwegian seminary was begun at Hutchinson, Minnesota, a German seminary at Clinton, Missouri, and a Swedish seminary at Broadview, Illinois.[19]

The Adventist young people were another unreached group, a fact that Milton E. Kern, a teacher at Union College, became aware of when he made a survey of his area and found that most of them were not in church schools. After Kern told Daniells of his findings during a casual dining room conversation, the General Conference president began to push for a youths' department.[20] In 1907 the General Conference council held in Gland, Switzerland, responded by recommending that such a department be established. A few months later, a convention in Mount Vernon, Ohio, voted "unanimously" to organize the "Seventh-day Adventist Young People's Society of Missionary Volunteers."[21] One of those attending, L. Flora Plummer, later recalled: "As we caught a view of the accumulative power and self-propagating force of our army of youth, organized and trained for service, it seemed that we had suddenly come into possession of a gigantic dynamo of energy and spiritual power, with which to finish the work of the Lord in this generation."[22]

The creation of these departments reflected concerns that had long been in the church. However, when the committee on plans at the 1909 General Conference session introduced a resolution to establish a North American Negro department,[23] the church ventured into rather new and controversial territory. Although some work had been done among blacks,[24] by 1909 there were probably not more than a thousand black Seventh-day Adventists. Furthermore, the high racial tensions in the South, after the failure of the Populists at the end of the nineteenth century, made work among southern blacks especially difficult.[25]

The lack of progress among the blacks prompted concern for a Negro department, a concept that received impetus when Ellen White, speaking at the 1909 General Conference meeting, called for greater efforts in the South. After her appeal, the resolution to establish a Negro department was enacted and favorably received, with one delegate describing the southern blacks as a "great mission field at our very doors." Several persons, pointing to the tense racial situation in the South, where lynchings and Jim Crow laws were on the increase, argued that such a department would "loosen our hands." Some of the blacks raised questions about the representation of their race in the department, and James K. Humphrey, a black minister from New York, called attention to the needs of both northern and southern Negroes. Page Shepard, a white delegate, raised the only objection to the idea of such a department when he said that Europeans had given the gospel to the world, and Ethiopia had not rejected them for being white. But these objections were overcome by the recognition that the establishment of a Negro department would forward the mission work of the church. The resolution — a "mission resolution," in the words of delegate Louis A. Hansen — passed "unanimously."[26]

The question of representation that the blacks had raised, however, remained a problem. The General Conference session of 1913 specified that two members of the advisory committee of the Negro department be Negroes.[27] Later, in 1926, it was decided that Negro departments of the Southern conferences include three Negroes each.[28] But these actions were not satisfactory, and a call for Negro conferences began to develop. Humphrey, who emerged as a major leader in this movement, became so dissatisfied with the role of Negroes by 1929 that he led his Harlem congregation out of the Seventh-day Adventist Church.[29] By that time, however, the racial question had shifted from mission emphasis to internal political relationships.

The establishment of two further departments in the next few years expressed strong missionary interests. The Home Missionary

Department was organized in 1913 in recognition of the need to promote local church missionary work in addition to public evangelism.[30] This step was taken in a relatively uncontroversial climate. Establishing a ministerial association, however, raised the question of authority within the Seventh-day Adventist Church and took until 1922 to accomplish.

As with his predecessors, Daniells for some time had recognized the need to improve the quality of the ministry. Since most Adventist ministers had little or no education of college level, they tended to emphasize particular "Adventist" doctrines to the neglect of basic Christian truths. In 1905, Daniells had announced that improvement of the ministry had to be a major goal of the church.[31] The General Conference took the first steps in this direction in 1910 and 1914, when its executive committee voted to begin holding periodic regional institutes[32] for ministers and when the Education Department introduced a ministerial reading course designed to help ministers "in the field."[33]

When a General Conference ministerial department was proposed in 1918, a number of questions as to its scope and authority were raised. For example, the delegates did not want the department to have executive power over ministers. Despite Daniells's urging that the action be passed, the delegates voted to send the recommendation back to the General Conference for further study.[34] Voting four years later on a more sharply defined proposal, the General Conference delegates established the Ministerial Commission, assigning it duties in three areas: to collect facts on the ministers and their problems, to serve as a medium of exchange for ideas and methods, and to encourage youths to prepare for the ministry.[35] The 1922 autumn council of the General Conference appointed Daniells (then no longer General Conference president) to be secretary of the commission and a year later changed the name to Ministerial Association.[36]

This action in 1922 brought to a close, for the time being, General Conference efforts to carry out the 1903 recommendation to establish departments that would advise and give direction to the various lines of church activities. Under Daniells's presidency, the General Conference thus largely completed its modern departmental structure.

DIVISION CONFERENCES

Of equal significance to the structuring of departments was the creation of division conferences. This process began in 1913. Although not envisioned by the 1901 reorganization proponents, the division conferences were a natural outgrowth of the development of the system of local conferences (usually individual states) and union conferences (groupings of states), for they gathered under one umbrella the unions within large geographical areas. After the division conference plan had first been suggested by Seventh-day Adventist leaders in Europe in 1912, the General Conference, at its autumn council of 1912 and at a special meeting in January 1913, considered the idea. The first proposal was to organize only a European division conference. But soon some of the North American leaders expressed the judgment that it was a propitious time to organize a North American division as well.[37]

When the request for a European division conference first came before the General Conference delegates at the May 22, 1913 meeting, Daniells, who had earlier opposed the idea, argued strongly in favor of it. He stated that the European Adventist leaders saw the "need of some kind of binding, uniting, authoritative organization" that would "enable the brethren from all those states and kingdoms to aid one another in meeting crises and in carrying forward the work committed to them." As an example of a situation calling for such an organization, he cited the heavy mortgage carried by the Christiana, Norway, publishing house and the help voluntarily given by Adventist leaders in Germany. Somewhat defensively, Daniells argued also that the creation of divisions was not really different from the creation of union conferences and that it would in no way lessen the authority of the General Conference.[38]

In response, the delegates expressed the opinion that more bureaucracy might be necessary and that the development of divisions, in effect, might diffuse the usefulness of the central authority of the General Conference. Daniells had already answered the latter objection; in reply to the former, he said that the growth of the church in Europe justified creating new positions. Roscoe C. Porter summed up the attitude of most delegates by saying, "I believe it will facilitate the hastening on of our work in the European Division." The proposal passed that afternoon.[39]

During discussion of a European division, some of the delegates raised the question of a North American division. Both Daniells and Spicer replied that such an organization was unnecessary because the General Conference headquarters was located in the United States.[40] Nevertheless, four days after voting to authorize the European Division, the union conference presidents in the United States and Canada petitioned for organization of a North American division. William T. Knox, General Conference treasurer, agreed with them, arguing that to establish this division would perfect the worldwide organization and enable the General Conference to give more time and funds to the mission fields. Although the president and vice president had opposed the idea, the motion to establish the North American Division passed.[41] After the division was organized, with Irwin H. Evans as president, Daniells announced his support of the new organization and its officers.[42]

Five years later, however, the General Conference administration, influenced by the disrupting effects of World War I, recommended discontinuing division *conferences* but not divisional organization. Integrating the divisions into the General Conference, the delegates voted to elect General Conference vice presidents, subtreasurers, and assistant departmental secretaries for each division, all of whom would be members of the General Conference committee.[43] Richard Schwarz comments that the church leaders wanted to preserve worldwide unity of the church and avoid the possibility of a split that would produce a European or an African Seventh-day Adventist Church. They were also afraid that an independent division might no longer feel responsible for supporting Adventism financially in any other section of the world. The new plan would curb any possible move toward independence by keeping the selection of the leadership of all the various divisions in the hands of the entire General Conference. Under this new arrangement, the General Conference session voted to accept the Asiatic and South American divisions that had been organized during the five-year interim.[44]

During the 1922 General Conference session, the Inter-American Division was organized,[45] and a new constitution and bylaws for the General Conference were adopted incorporating the new divisional structure.[46] The growing mission work was further reflected throughout the remainder of the decade as the African, China, and Far Eastern Divisions were established.[47] The coordinated worldwide church that Daniells had envisioned thirty years earlier was now a reality as far as formal organization was concerned. These organizational changes were made for the stated purpose of advancing and increasing the efficiency of the church.[48] The United States, of course, continued to be the center of Seventh-day Adventist efforts; until the 1920s it had the largest membership and always contributed the most money. Church growth occurred in all areas of the United States (see Fig. 1)—for the most part slowly. One chronological exception was the 1914—19 period, when membership increased by twenty-seven thousand—which was more than twice the growth for any other four-year period. This startling increase resulted primarily from an evangelistic exploitation of World War I, an event Adventists confidently described as a prelude to Armageddon.

Geographically, the largest growth took place in the West, California in particular, where membership nearly doubled between 1914 and 1929. Membership between 1903 and 1929 grew most slowly in the South and the Northwest, increasing slightly over a thousand members during each four-year period, except for 1914– 19. The Midwest continued to hold the largest portion of the membership, but clearly it was not growing at the same rate as were the Northeast and Southwest. The relocation of General Conference headquarters to Washington, D.C., probably influenced the growth of the church in the Northeast. The membership increase in California resulted, at least in part, because the state itself was growing rapidly and, as had happened before, uprooted people were more willing to change their religion. Furthermore, publishing activities, hospitals, and a college had been established in California during this period. Meanwhile, membership in Canada grew very slowly.

The increase in the number of church employees in each geographical area appears to have been directly related to the increase in church membership, although in areas of good church growth the number of employees increased at a slightly faster rate. This relationship indicates that the church administrators followed a policy of assigning personnel where church growth seemed most likely to take place.

The membership figures for divisions outside North America (see Fig. 2) indicate clearly that church leaders were sustaining the missionary emphasis. Most important, by 1926 church membership outside North America had exceeded that of the homeland. In actual figures, Europe — except for the years of World War I — was adding the most members to the church roster; but the non-Christian continents of Asia and Africa, as well as Catholic Latin America, showed the most rapid rate of growth in the 1920s. As in North America, leaders of divisions everywhere sent personnel to the areas most likely to produce converts.

Included were both missionaries sent out from North America and workers native to a given area. Yet steady growth in all areas of the world indicates that the church leaders were systematically attempting to make the worldwide missionary vision of the church a reality. With but one exception, increase in the number of missionaries sent from the United States continued throughout the period 1905– 30:

FIGURE 1
Growth in SDA Church Membership and Workforce:
United States and Canada

	NORTHEAST	SOUTH	CENTRAL	NORTHWEST	SOUTHWEST	CANADA
MEMBERS						
1903	8,116	2,541	34,271[1]	9,761[2]	3,047	1,103
1909	11,351[3]	3,196[4]	27,174	7,440[5]	4,353	1,669
1914	13,405	5,514	26,528	8,676[6]	15,019[7]	2,873[8]
1919	20,255	9,211	34,289	11,533	19,137	4,998
1926	21,961	10,305	36,756	13,262	24,612	5,330
1929	23,182	11,655	38,478	14,126	29,791	5,937
WORKFORCE						
1903	132	52	734	231	109	22
1909	316	232	670	189	128	74
1914	374	214	678	228	445	117
1919	631	295	912	273	668	162
1926	440	296	961	278	686	124
1929	486	345	708	331	830	125

[1]Lake, North, and Central Union Conferences.
[2]The entire Pacific Union Conference.
[3]The Atlantic and Columbia Union Conferences included from here on.
[4]The Southern and Southeastern Union Conferences included from here on.
[5]Some territory seems to have been removed at this point.
[6]California no longer included from here on.
[7]New Pacific Union Conference included.
[8]Western Canadian and Canadian Union Conferences included from here on.

Statistics compiled from *SDA Yearbook* issues for 1906, 1910, 1920-21, 1926, and 1931.

FIGURE 2
Growth in SDA Church Membership and Workforce: *Worldwide*

	NORTH AMERICA	EUROPE	AUSTRAL- ASIA	ASIA	LATIN AMERICA	AFRICA	MISC
MEMBERS							
1903	57,839						18,715
1909	60,807	17,362		601			10,184
1914	72,015	35,146		2,689			18,683
1919	99,623	35,245		7,657[1]	8,657[2]	2,200	5,650
1926	112,255	80,000	9,813	17,648	24,501	6,185	175
1929	123,169[3]	100,822	11,490	29,180[4]	33,586	15,160	
WORKFORCE							
1903	1,280						543
1909	1,770	403		136			461
1914	2,364	743		141			641
1919	2,741	502[5]		751	265	154	474
1926	2,585	922	387	1,194	491	367	
1929	2,761	1,370	463	1,830	671	761	

[1]Far Eastern and Southern Asia Divisions included from here on.
[2]South America, Central America, and Mexico included from here on.
[3]Central, Northern, and Southern European and Soviet Divisions included.
[4]China Division included.
[5]A figure of 800 would probably be closer to fact. Several union conferences did not make reports, probably because of World War I.

All membership figures would be increased if members in "companies" not organized as churches were included.

1905	60	1920	310
1910	61	1925	175
1915	76	1929	155

The large increase in 1920 reflects both increased membership in North America and an effort to restaff areas from which personnel had been withdrawn during the war.

Clearly, the missionary emphasis of the church was now firmly established, and while the secularized and urbanized societies of the United States and Europe were increasingly hard to penetrate, the leaders could look for the church to grow most rapidly in the un-developed or developing nations in Asia, Africa, and Latin America. North America, however, continued to supply most of the leaders and financial support for what was now, in terms of membership, a worldwide church. To increase this financial support, the denomination searched for new sources of income. The leaders encouraged members to give ten cents a week for missions and established special funds for which they asked donations, as with the $150,000 fund begun in 1906. Reports of donations to these funds appeared weekly in the *Review and Herald*. In 1909 the General Conference session decided that all Sabbath school offerings were to go to support of missions. As a result, mission offerings increased from approximately $350,000 in 1910 to more than $2.5 million in 1930. In addition, a special program in which members solicited donations from the general public began in 1908: entitled the "Harvest Ingathering Plan" in 1909, the effort proved quite successful, raising $4 million be-tween 1913 and 1924, for example, much of which went to missions.[49]

Although more income was always needed, under A. G. Dan-iells the denominational leadership developed both the resources and organization that made the missionary spirit effective. The ef-ficiency of this structure is virtually impossible to measure, of course, but its overall performance attested to the sincerity of the missionary zeal that motivated it.

JONES VERSUS DANIELLS

The development of this organization, however, did not please everyone. Objections could be heard from the very beginning in 1901. The debate over what organizational form the church should take, although it involved a political struggle at first, led to some serious theological questions, particularly questions of the inspiration and authority of Ellen White. The opposition to reorganization involved only a few people, individuals who lived in Battle Creek and were associated with John Harvey Kellogg. Alonzo T. Jones, in turn a local conference and then a General Conference administrator, became the spokesman for the discontented. On March 4, 1906, in the Battle Creek Tabernacle, he made a speech that he published later as a pamphlet entitled *Some History, Some Experiences, and Some Facts.* Jones argued that, in response to Ellen White's 1901 call for reorganization, the General Conference delegates had adopted a constitution establishing decentralization. He focused specifically on the fact that "no president of the General Conference was chosen; nor was any provided for. The presidency of the General Conference was eliminated to escape a centralized power, a one-man power, a kingship, a monarchy."[50]

Despite the attempt at decentralization, Jones asserted, before the 1903 session the General Conference executive committee had designated Daniells as president rather than simply as the chairman provided for in the constitution. Then at the General Conference session of that year, Jones charged, a new constitution was brought in to justify making Daniells president; it passed by five votes while the opposition delegates were downstairs from the meeting hall. Thus "a Czardom was enthroned." Jones went on to argue that Christianity and bureaucracy are incompatible, that "at least somebody *in* this denomination should be Protestant enough to oppose the arbitrary authority of the church," and that he would never believe that "the church must have a visible head."[51]

These charges sent shock waves through the General Conference administration. About one month after Jones spoke, the General Conference issued *A Statement Refuting Charges Made by A. T. Jones.* The pamphlet argued that the reorganization of 1901 had aimed at certain practical problems rather than "the form of organization itself." If the General Conference executive committee were to follow Jones's ideas, it claimed, and choose a chairman constantly subject to change, disorganization would result. The pamphlet disputed Jones's reading of the events leading up to the 1903 constitutional change and charged that Jones was allied with the Kellogg faction.[52]

> Elder Jones had identified himself with a movement, and has become the champion of a movement, that for years has sought either to dominate, or, if it could not dominate, to overthrow, all properly constituted order, organization, and united effort in this denomination, and which, in not a little of its doings, has truly been "arbitrary," "papal," and "bureaucratic." And now that the Testimonies have rebuked that wrong, ambitious

thing, and the Officers of the General Conference have stood by the Testimonies in seeking to correct that wrong, Elder Jones styles the whole General Conference organization papal, arbitrary, and bureaucratic.[53]

Jones, of course, published his own reply to this General Conference statement. In *The Final Word and Confession* he presented evidence that Daniells had "assumed" the presidency of the General Conference in 1902 and that the constitutional change of 1903 had been instituted by the leaders rather than the delegates on behalf of the people.[54] Jones had the better of the argument concerning the history of the 1903 constitutional change, but the motives behind his criticisms were mixed at best. He had spoken vaguely at the 1901 General Conference session about reorganization as meaning that Christ is at the head, counseling the delegates to "never forget that the ultimate of every organization that ever man accomplished is kingship. Monarchy. And that among men is despotism — and that is ruin."[55]

Jones never presented too clear an alternative, however, either in 1901 or during his period of active criticism in the ensuing years. In his most specific statement, he contended that "each Conference must be a self-governing local Conference, and each church must be a local self-governing church, and *each individual* must be a *local self-governing individual.*" Furthermore, he concluded, "no man in this world can be a self-governing individual except as God in Jesus Christ is his Head, and the man is governed by the power of God."[56]

The ideas Jones expressed in 1901 reveal that he had a philosophical basis, however vague, for his public criticisms of 1906 and thereafter. Political struggle, though, played an important role in his actions. In 1902 some of Kellogg's supporters had attempted to make Jones chairman of the executive committee, because they believed that he would view Kellogg more favorably than Daniells did. This attempt having failed, early in 1903 — before the General Conference meeting — Jones, Kellogg, and their allies again tried to gain support for the unseating of Daniells; again they failed.[57] These attempts indicate that Jones's thinking after 1901 developed in the context of the power struggle between Kellogg and Daniells, with Jones on the losing side. This situation in itself would explain why Jones went public with his criticisms in 1906, whether or not he was envious of the General Conference president, as one recent student has argued.[58]

The results of Jones's criticisms were few. In 1907 the General Conference executive committee voted to ask him to return his ministerial credentials.[59] Eventually he left the official church, although he did remain a believer of its doctrines. The effects of his criticisms appeared in the *Review and Herald* over the next several years, as it often defended the structure of the Seventh-day Adventist world organization, putting emphasis on its crucial role in spreading the gospel and its correspondence to biblical principles. As Spicer wrote in 1909, God "has been the leader in this advent movement, and by the counsels of his Word and through the spirit of prophecy the divine principles of order and organization have been applied to present-day needs and conditions."[60]

ELLEN WHITE'S DIVINE INSPIRATION QUESTIONED

Although Jones's criticism of the church organization did little more than estrange the Kellogg circle from the leaders, it led to another criticism of far greater significance. As first Kellogg and then Jones became more openly critical of the General Conference leaders, they drew criticism from Ellen White, the accepted "messenger of the Lord." Furthermore, church leaders, particularly Daniells, seem to have used the "Testimonies" of Mrs. White as a forceful weapon in their efforts to retain power. Thus the political situation that led to public criticism of the organization also led to public questioning of Ellen White's inspiration and authority. The questions raised had been around for some time, but the poisoned political atmosphere brought them out into the open.

The first published criticisms appeared in Jones's pamphlet *Some History, Some Experiences, and Some Facts.* He attacked the testimonies on two grounds: inconsistencies and mistakes in the testimonies themselves and the use that church leaders were making of the testimonies. To support his first charge, Jones presented three illustrations: 1) that Ellen White had written a testimony that the 1903 General Conference meeting should be held at Healdsburg, California, but later changed this to Oakland; 2) that she had once presented a testimony that a certain person had drawn three hundred dollars on a church account, but that this had never happened; and 3) that certain contents in volume seven of the published work *Testimonies to the Church* had been substantially changed after the book had gone to press. The only conclusion that he could draw, Jones said, was that "these and many other like things, are facts which unquestionably vitiate the claim that 'everything that she [Ellen White] writes is from the Lord.' "[61]

In explaining his own use of the testimonies, Jones criticized the way he felt church leaders were using them:

> I use the Testimonies and the other writings of Sister White
> for my own private study, in the study of the Bible, and in my
> family worship. But to use them on other people as a test of
> *their* orthodoxy or heresy, or as a club to bring them under or
> drive them out, I do not, and I will not. . . . But the Bible is
> the *supreme thing*; and I shall preach only the Bible.[62]

Jones concluded by saying that not everything that Ellen White had
sent out was of the Lord. "I am sorry that it is so. But I can not
help it."[63]

Jones expressed similar feelings privately to Mrs. White. He
wrote to her calling attention to several instances in which "instructions" given to her "in vision" were later changed. One instance
pertained to a vision in which God had told her to ask her critics to
present their problems about the testimonies to her for explanation.
After she had followed these instructions, Jones said, and some criticisms had arrived, Ellen had had another "vision" instructing her
not to answer these criticisms. Jones was even more troubled by the
fact that testimonies critical of particular individuals were sent to
other persons and then used in public. This practice, he felt, was
contrary to biblical counsel that such matters should be dealt with
on a personal, one-to-one basis. Then he brought up several instances in which it appeared that William White, Mrs. White's son,
had either influenced or interfered with her work, particularly when
he had withheld from William W. Prescott a testimony advising
Prescott not to discuss the pantheism question at the Lake Union
Conference meeting at Berrien Springs, Michigan, in 1904. Am-
plifying the position taken in his 1906 pamphlet, Jones concluded:

> I do not deny that you have divine enlightenment. I do not
> deny that you have the Spirit of Prophecy. But I do *deny that
> everything that you have ever written* is of the divine inspiration
> of the Spirit of Prophecy. I do deny that you are infallible, and
> I do deny that everything you have written is the infallible
> word of God.[64]

Jones repeated these assertions during the next few years, claiming
that "it is for the freedom of the individual conscience, even under
the Testimonies that I plead."[65]

Jones was not the only one voicing these criticisms; others in
the Kellogg circle asked similar questions. In response to Ellen White's
request that her critics send in their problems, Dr. William S. Sadler
wrote a lengthy letter. His basic question was whether all communications from Ellen White were "testimonies" or whether some
were only letters, not written under inspiration. He raised several

questions regarding: William White's influence; statements by Ellen White that seemed not to be true; contradictions between one testimony and another; and the propriety of using testimonies as a test of fellowship. Unlike Jones, he did not yet proclaim disbelief in any testimonies:

> I have kept still for many years, for *I believe the Testimonies;* and the only reason I am making a diligent effort to get to the bottom of these things, and get to the bottom *now,* is *that I am pressed on all sides to define my attitude concerning the Testimonies, and these difficulties that have arisen.* [66]

Another Kellogg associate, Dr. Charles E. Stewart (apparently along with Dr. Rowland H. Harris), also wrote Mrs. White a personal letter that was published a short time later. [67] He raised questions similar to those of Jones and Sadler; but he dramatized the problems by printing in parallel columns testimonies and other writings of Ellen White that had been changed between one printing and another, that contradicted one another, or that showed evidences of being plagiarized from other authors. He also drew on personal experiences, especially those pertaining to Ellen White's dealings with Kellogg and the Battle Creek Sanitarium, to support his contention that her "counsels" were often misinformed, unfair, and misused. As a result he wondered whether there was "a human side to the Testimonies":

> Ever since my first acquaintance with your work I have considered you as a fallible messenger of the Lord, and still continue to do so. . . . I have received great benefit from your instructions and advice, and trust my confidence in you and your work shall not be shaken by the determined efforts of some of the leading men of the denomination to make myself and associates accept their interpretation of your writings. . . . The Seventh-day Adventist denomination as a whole has placed you in such a position that they must accept everything you write or say as being equivalent to the Bible, and for this reason should you make a mistake, you can readily see how far-reaching and terribly unjust the results might be, especially if there be individuals in places of authority who are of a designing nature. [68]

Although all of these men were associated with Kellogg, the doctor himself disclaimed any responsibility for their opinions and their publications. Nevertheless, he agreed with them. Beginning in about 1899, Kellogg had changed his attitude toward Ellen White. Whereas he had previously believed in her divine inspiration, by the time of his break with the church he had come to a different view. This change had resulted in part from Mrs. White's criticisms of him, from the duplicates of her testimonies being sent to others, and from her vision of a nonexistent Chicago medical building.[69] In a private interview in 1907 with two members of the Battle Creek Tabernacle, Kellogg charged that the Adventist church leaders, especially Daniells and William White, had manipulated God's messenger:

> If they would let her alone to deal with the great principles of truth, righteousness, temperance and reform, it would have been a wonderful thing; but they have got her tangled up with all the little personal affairs of business and a lot of other things that the Lord has not given her any information about or any light about, and have made her to do business with the sale of books or to settle church quarrels and such things. And the Lord has never authorized any such use at all of the wonderful gifts He gave her.[70]

Kellogg professed not to be troubled by Ellen White's mistakes, inconsistencies, and plagiarisms. He believed that he had established principles for distinguishing her inspired from her uninspired writings: "A lot of the things she writes have got to be accepted and taken, and what you cannot act upon in the fear of the Lord, ask the Lord to show you what your duty is, and do the very best you can to be square and straight with yourself and with every principle of light and truth you see." Furthermore, he said, "the proper way to hold it [the work of Ellen White] up is to let the truth stand on its merits. Whatever is truth will stand."[71]

However much denominational politics brought these ideas into the open, Jones, Sadler, Stewart, and Kellogg raised serious questions that challenged Seventh-day Adventist theology. In essence, they held that the inspiration and authority of any particular writing by Ellen White had to be judged individually. Rather than accept all her messages as infallible communications based on God's revelation, they argued, the church could make no general affirmation of her inspiration. As they saw it, the problem was not a matter of degree of inspiration; something was either inspired or not; and if it contained mistakes, it was of human rather than divine origin.

It was probably the criticisms of Ellen White's writings rather than those of the organizational structure that prompted church leaders to respond so quickly to Jones's pamphlet with their own. In their response the leaders touched on the principal themes of the defense that was to be articulated during the next several years. First of all, the pamphlet asserted that belief in the spirit of prophecy was "a fundamental part of [the Adventist] message."[72] After refuting Jones's examples of Mrs. White's errors, the pamphlet said:

> Since the rise of this message this denomination has believed in the spirit of prophecy. We have preached it as widely as we have the Sabbath and other kindred truths, and believed it as thoroughly. It is an integral part of the beautiful system of truth which we call the third angel's message; so much is this so that those who have given up their faith in this part of the truth have invariably lost their spiritual perception, and eventually given up the whole message.[73]

After arguing the great significance of Ellen White's writings to the church, the pamphlet entered the second major line of argument, namely, that Jones's position as to the need to distinguish between inspired and uninspired testimony was the same attitude as that taken by "higher critics" of the Bible. "They single out certain parts of the Bible, and assert that these are not inspired. But no more subtle nor effective method can be employed than this to break down all faith in all inspired writing."[74]

The church leaders believed that modernism—evolution, pantheism,[75] and higher criticism—was destroying the Protestant churches. Evolution, the *Review and Herald* editorialized, "breaks down all distinction between the original work in the creation of all things and the continuous work of upholding all things. . . . The whole evolutionary conception of the universe, when logically carried out in its application to religion, ends in the claim that all men are holy, that 'God is in all humanity,' and that it only needs proper environment to develop the godlike in every man."[76] Satan had attempted to infiltrate the Adventist cause, God's last bastion of truth, with this doctrine of evolutionary pantheism, they believed, through Kellogg and his book *The Living Temple*. But the Spirit of God has "raised up a standard against the evil thing."[77]

Having just barely escaped the pantheistic threat, the leaders believed, the Adventist church was now under Satan's attack through "higher criticism." Higher criticism was attempting "to destroy faith in the Bible as the Word of God, and to destroy confidence in Jesus Christ as the Redeemer of mankind."[78] Christians must be "instructed and guided by the written word."[79] "When therefore we wish to know concerning these things [the plan of salvation], we must go to the word of God. . . . Men are not writing Bibles in these days. God is not inspiring men today to write what contradicts the revelation given through Moses and the prophets."[80] Believing that Seventh-day Adventists were God's last stronghold and army to fight against "last-day delusions," writers for the *Review* called on church members to stand by their faith in the infallible word of God.[81] A former skeptic, Earle Albert Rowell, wrote that "higher criticism is the only refuge from our faith. The Higher Critics themselves being the judge, the only alternative is to cast aside the Holy Book and be a Higher Critic, or take it as it reads and be a Seventh-day Adventist."[82] The *Review* editorialized that "to meet Satan's last move God has developed the third angel's message, and has committed that message to the Seventh-day Adventist people. Let us hold to it, and publish it in all the earth."[83]

It was in this context that the Adventist leaders reacted to Jones's approach to Ellen White's writings. Pantheism and higher criticism were destroying the Protestant churches; pantheism in the Adventist church had threatened but had been destroyed; now higher criticism was rearing its head. At least that was how they saw the situation.

In addition to what was said in the General Conference pamphlet, several other writers compared Jones's approach to higher criticism. The *Review* commented:

> No man can assail some of the Testimonies and prove them to be unreliable without discrediting the Testimonies as a whole, and without inviting others to reject such Testimonies as do not harmonize with their views of things. We are opposed to the principle of the higher criticism, whether advocated within or without the denomination.[84]

Likewise, H. E. Phelps argued that the church must reject higher criticism of both the Bible and the testimonies.[85] And Stephen N. Haskell advocated:

> We should be very careful not to criticize any prophet of the Lord; second, . . . the principles enunciated by the prophets should be studied that we may be able to understand how God works with the human mind; third, . . . we should never judge of the workings of God's Holy-Spirit from a human standpoint.[86]

Besides criticizing the ideas of Jones and the Kellogg circle, church leaders over the next few years began to instruct readers through the pages of the *Review* about Ellen White's role in the church. Comparing Jones's criticism of Mrs. White with "higher criticism of the Bible" implied equating White's writings with the Bible. Church leaders fought against this implication; yet their fear that the testimonies might be taken lightly moved them, however unconsciously, toward regarding the statements of the Bible and those of Ellen White as of equal force. The protests that Seventh-day Adventists did not regard Ellen White's writings as equal to the Bible were many. In replying to Jones, the *Review* stated that "we do not place the Testimonies above the Bible."[87] To explain the phenomenon of this modern prophet more clearly, Daniel H. Kress compared the work and message of Ellen White with that of John the Baptist.[88] Other writers said much the same thing: that Ellen White only "magnifies the truths of the Bible"[89] and confirms "believers in conclusions they had already reached from a study of scripture."[90]

Francis M. Wilcox played a significant role in defining the Adventist position on Ellen White. During his *Review and Herald* editorship of thirty-three years, he wrote many articles and editorials affirming the prophet's inspiration and role in the church. Wilcox argued that White served God the way Samuel, Elijah, and John the Baptist did.[91] She was a woman, he said, whose "work has been to point mankind to Christ, the Saviour of men, to lead them to search the Scriptures of Truth with greater diligence."[92] Furthermore, her writings "constitute a spiritual commentary upon the Scripture, a divine illumination of the word."[93]

Despite the protests against equating Mrs. White's writings with the Bible, many statements implied otherwise—or said otherwise straight out. Roscoe Porter wrote that "the Testimonies sent are God's word."[94] Many published statements admonished church members "to study the written word and the spirit of prophecy."[95] Next to the Bible, George I. Butler declared, the *Testimonies* were the most precious books in the world.[96] Even more significant than these statements were articles arguing that Seventh-day Adventism could not survive without Ellen White's writings. George O. States, a minister who had been acquainted with her work for many years, wrote several articles emphasizing the imperative need for her writings and arguing that opposition to the prophet's work always resulted in the rejection of Adventism.[97] "All along through our history," he wrote, "different ones have fallen out by the way, and our only safety from going in the same way is to heed the timely counsel the Lord is sending."[98] George A. Irwin argued that "the gift of prophecy will not only be within the church, but the church's reception of the other gifts will turn upon its reception of this gift."[99]

Although these writers probably did not realize it, they implied by their arguments that the Bible alone is insufficient to guide the believer into all truth. In their effort to defend Ellen White's work from criticism, they began to emphasize her work to a degree considerably greater than in previous years. Although it is difficult to document precisely, the years after 1906—as reflected in the contents of the *Review* —show a rapid increase not only in the number of articles about the spirit of prophecy but also in the number of times the magazine's writers referred to White for support of their arguments on theological issues of all kinds.[100]

When Ellen White died in 1915, it appears that many church members wondered whether God would choose another prophet for his people. Wilcox left that question up to God and expressed his belief that the church would go on despite the fact that its prophet had fallen.[101] That such editorials needed to be written is another indication of the widespread feeling that Ellen White, or another such as she, was indispensable to the Adventist church. In her absence, Wilcox advised, the church should continue to follow the Bible and her writings.[102]

Four years after her death, the debate begun publicly by Alonzo T. Jones in 1906 came to a close. In the summer of 1919, the church called its leading ministers and college teachers together for a Bible conference, to be followed by a Bible and History Teachers Council. Although Ellen White's authority was not one of the announced subjects,[103] a number of participants in the Teachers Council questioned the accuracy of her writings on history, health, and theology and her borrowings from other writers. As the participants struggled with the problem of how to handle these questions in the classroom and better understand Ellen White's function in the church, there was a growing consensus during the first day of discussion that the church needed to be educated in these things.[104] On the second day, however, despite their apparent agreement in rejecting both the verbal inspiration and infallibility of Ellen White, the participants backed off from taking any concerted action. Fearing that the membership would be shaken, they concluded that caution was advisable. As A. G. Daniells put it in his closing remarks,

> We must use good sense in dealing with this whole question, brethren. Do not be careless with your words. Do not be careless in reporting or representing men's views. . . . We can not correct that in a day. We must use great judgment and caution. I hope you Bible teachers will be exceedingly careful. . . . I believe the Lord will help us to take care of this if we will be careful and use good sense. I think that is all I can say in this sort of discussion.[105]

As a result, the discussion remained essentially unknown. Although the church leaders had initially intended to hold Bible conferences on a regular basis in the future, none took place until 1952.

Thus the 1919 conference ended the public discussion that

Jones had initiated. The debate closed ambiguously, however, and Jones's questions were left dangling, unsatisfactorily answered. Nevertheless, Adventist leaders affirmed their belief in Ellen White's prophetic gift and placed increasing emphasis on her writings. Although they made the *Testimonies* and other White books theoretically subordinate to the Bible, they also considered them indispensable to Seventh-day Adventists. As a result, Ellen White continued to gain greater theological authority within the church.

END OF THE DANIELLS ERA

Daniells faced another controversy three years later. Although he had presided over the denomination's progress since 1901, opposition to his leadership arose as the 1922 General Conference session approached. Many delegates felt that he ruled with too firm a hand and had not defended Ellen White strongly enough. Thinking that it was time for a change, they blocked Daniells's renomination when the conference took place in San Francisco in May. Emotions ran high while the nominating committee deadlocked at twenty votes for continuing Daniells as president and twenty-nine votes for naming William A. Spicer. The latter refused to accept the nomination because of the political conflict; instead, he asked the committee to find a younger man who could unite both factions. But Spicer's popularity prevented that alternative. [106]

The deadlock broke when Daniells, addressing a secret four-hour session on Sunday afternoon, "denounced the electioneering, the gossiping and spreading of rumors in the corridors, and the backbiting," although he named no names. He then withdrew his name from nomination. Several leaders deplored the "politics" and suggested that the convention administer a rebuke. The meeting concluded with a prayer service. [107]

After this meeting the nominating committee named Spicer president and Daniells secretary. Although men such as W. C. White and Dr. George A. Harding, a medical missionary and brother of Warren G. Harding, the president of the United States at the time, agreed that the "dirty politics" were deplorable, they also argued that delegates had a right to voice their own convictions. Despite their comments, the conference passed a resolution pronouncing "our decided rebuke upon and repudiation of all un-Christian propaganda, insinuation, villification and all false charges whatsoever, either for or against any brother, prior to or in connection with this general conference. . . ." [108]

"SIGNS OF THE END"

The long controversy over Ellen White and the brief one over Daniells's leadership did not entirely dominate the denomination's attention. Between 1909 and 1915, anti-Catholic prejudice, which had a long history in both American society and Adventism, burst forth. Publicized most forcefully by the Adventist *Protestant Magazine*, an explicitly anti-Catholic journal, this phobia also found expression in the *Review and Herald*. While Seventh-day Adventists criticized Catholic doctrines, they also emphasized the papal threat to the American republic. The pope's appointment of three American cardinals in 1911[109] seems to have aroused the Adventist church to a concern that the growth of the Catholic church in the United States, largely a product of the "new immigration" of the 1890s and early 1900s, presented a "peril to American institutions."[110] Over the next several years, writers in the *Review* often claimed that "Rome never changes,"[111] and that Rome was challenging America.[112] As a typical example, one editor wrote:

> The Roman Catholic Church claims America as hers by right
> of discovery; and claiming America as her rightful possession
> she is throwing every power of her mighty organization into
> the work of making it hers in fact, by occupation and control.[113]

Such comments were part of a general wave of anti-Catholicism that pervaded American society at this time, although Adventists had their own peculiar eschatology and were closer to the politically conservative, fundamentalist version of the phobia than they were to the liberal, progressive one.[114]

Adventists opposed progressivism because their apocalyptic outlook led them to view the political events of the day with pessimism. The *Review* argued, for example, that "Christians ought to rid their minds of the chimerical idea of a coming time when the saints will be able in this world to outvote the sinners, and place righteousness in political ascendancy." Instead, Christians should work to save individuals, not governments.[115] Similar pessimism appeared in attitudes toward labor unions, church federation, socialism, and bolshevism. These subjects, however, received a special "Adventist" thrust, for Adventists not only viewed attempts to improve world conditions as hopeless but also regarded such efforts as "signs of the end." Referring to the movement for church unity, for example, the *Review* stated that "when we see plans actually being laid for such an organization as the prophecy demands, we know that we are not far from the culmination of this work."[116]

This apocalyptic note hit its highest peak during World War I, as Adventists sought to interpret the war in the light of the biblical message. Basing their ideas on Daniel 11 and Revelation 16, they believed that Turkey, the "king of the north," would be driven from Europe and would plant its capital temporarily at Jerusalem, the holy mountain. After Turkey's final overthrow at Jerusalem, they thought, there would be a great "time of trouble" for the nations, and that this would end in the "sixth plague" (Revelation 9) and the battle of Armageddon.[117] Adventists watched the movement of events closely, many of them believing, as the *Watchman Magazine* set forth, that "the intense preparations for war, which now constitutes the chief rivalry of the nations, are a prelude of Armageddon."[118]

When war did break forth, the evangelistic magazines — *Signs of the Times*, *Signs of the Times Magazine*, and *Watchman Magazine* — took the position that, although the war itself was not Armageddon, it would be a prelude to that great battle.[119] By 1915, however, the writers for these magazines came ever closer to declaring that the prophecies of Daniel and Revelation would be fulfilled in this war. As one writer said, "*Mene, Mene* is written across the lintel of the Turkish house."[120] According to another publication, "The prophecy declares that the fall of Turkish power ushers in the end. And everywhere the newspapers can see nothing but the hastening of Turkey's end in the turn events have taken."[121]

Meanwhile, Wilcox, editor of the *Review and Herald*, warned readers not to make sensational claims about the war. Over and over he argued that, although the war was certainly contributing to the movement toward Armageddon, "we know not what a day may bring forth. We know not what may be the outcome of the war which has begun."[122] By 1917 the *Review's* position began receiving vindication. First, the United States entered the war; second, Turkey began to retreat from Palestine. By the time war ended, Turkey had lost Palestine and was confined to Asia Minor and a small part of Europe — the opposite of what many Adventists had believed would happen. As a result, people began to question whether Adventist interpretation of the prophecies was correct. But the church did not change its position. Said editor Wilcox:

> We have seen no new interpretation which in our judgment is superior to the old. We believe that the conclusions held by us from the beginning of this movement, that Turkey is represented by the term "king of the north" in the prophecy is correct. And because just at this present juncture in the affairs of this world there seems to be no prospect that Turkey will plant her palaces at Jerusalem, is no reason why we should

change our view of the question. If we cannot see, then it is
best to wait and bide God's time for fuller light, and watch
him work things around us as we believe his Word reveals that
he will.[123]

RIGHTEOUSNESS BY FAITH

Of more lasting significance than this continuation of apocalyptic
thinking, however, was the growing emphasis that Adventists placed
on the doctrine of righteousness by faith. Although the big crisis
over this doctrine had occurred at the 1888 General Conference,
the Adventist concern for God's law prevented righteousness by faith
from becoming fully accepted. Furthermore, as LeRoy E. Froom
observed, the critical problems of the decade 1900 to 1910—particularly the key questions raised by Kellogg and Jones—crowded the
righteousness-by-faith doctrine into the background.[124] This situation continued while the heightened interest in the fate of Turkey
prevailed during World War I. Despite the fact that the doctrine
remained in the background, a number of leading Adventist ministers during these years continued to teach it, including Irwin H.
Evans, William W. Prescott, Elmer E. Andross, and Francis M.
Wilcox.[125] Therefore, when conflict and sensationalism had run
their course, these men were prepared to bring righteousness by faith
once again to the fore.

Prescott, the leading Adventist authority on doctrine and former editor of the *Review* (1901–9), felt that the traditional Seventh-
day Adventist approach to doctrine resulted in a rigid, compart-
mentalized system that did not integrate beliefs with the person of
Christ. To correct this problem, he published a textbook in 1920
entitled *The Doctrine of Christ*.[126] This book, Froom believed, constituted "a bridge, a major connection, between what had been and
what must be. It was the message of 1888 restated in textbook
form."[127] In it Prescott attempted to emphasize "the meaning of the
Revelation of Christ as an experience in the life."[128] To do this, he
presented studies of such subjects as repentance, faith, conversion,
and justification by faith. Justification he defined as "the acceptance
of guilty sinners, before God, by faith." According to Prescott, justification had to do directly with deliverance from guilt and the
power of sin in one's life.[129]

Following up this latter concept, Prescott closed the first volume of his work with a study of "the victorious life," the gaining of
victory over the power of sin. Neither the concept nor the term
"victorious life" was original with him. Prescott appears to have been

influenced by Robert C. McQuilken's *Victorious Life Studies*, a volume strongly shaped by the ideas of the British Keswick Convention. This book grew out of the Victorious Life movement, which emerged in the United States before and during World War I, and which found expression in the *Sunday School Times* and sparked controversy among conservative religious groups over the meaning and possibility of perfection in human life.[130]

In any case, the concept caught on among Seventh-day Adventists, for it provided a means of reconciling their traditional concern for the law with the newer emphasis on Christian experience. Although not everyone liked it, a number of speakers expounded on "the victorious life" at the 1922 General Conference session. In the belief that the spiritual tone of the church was low, leading Adventist ministers continued to emphasize the notion throughout the decade, often making it synonymous with righteousness by faith.[131] As in 1922, nine major speakers at the 1926 General Conference meeting addressed the subject of "victory over sin."[132]

After he left the General Conference presidency in 1922, Daniells continued to play a leading role in bringing Adventist ministers to a consciousness of the importance of righteousness by faith. As secretary of the Ministerial Association, he held ministers' institutes between 1923 and 1925 in the Southwest, Northwest, and Pacific coast conferences. At these institutes he influenced such men as Meade MacGuire, Taylor G. Bunch, and Carlyle B. Haynes.[133] Froom, then editor of the *Watchman Magazine*, recalled many years later the effect that Daniells's Nashville institute had had on him:

> It was the turning point in my life and ministry. Christianity, I soon clearly saw, was basically *a personal relationship to a person — Jesus Christ my Lord. . . .* But I saw that I had too often been believing and trusting in a *message* rather than a *person*. I had propagated a message rather than truly proclaiming a Gospel. I had placed my affection and my allegiance in a Movement ordained of God, rather than in the living Christ of the Movement.[134]

That the efforts of these men were successful in making righteousness by faith prominent in Adventist thinking was reflected also by the publications of the church. The *Sabbath School Lesson Quarterly*, which probably reached more members of the church than did any other publication, touched on righteousness by faith in eighteen of its quarterly issues — the equivalent of four and one-half years — between 1921 and 1930.[135] In addition, a flurry of books elucidated and emphasized the doctrine. Among these were John L.

Shuler's *Christ the Divine One* (1922); Meade MacGuire's *The Life of Victory* (1924) and *His Cross and Mine* (1927); Daniells's *Christ Our Righteousness* (1926); William H. Branson's *The Way to Christ* (1928); LeRoy E. Froom's *The Coming of the Comforter* (1928); Prescott's *The Saviour of the World* (1929); and Milton C. Wilcox's *Studies in Romans* (1930).[136]

Although these Adventist writers saw the victorious life and righteousness by faith as similar, if not synonymous, it has been argued recently that the victorious life is not the same as righteousness by faith, but is, in fact, an unbiblical concept. The exponents of this view, Robert J. Wieland and Donald K. Short, say that the Victorious Life movement introduced to Adventism the idea that Christians need an experience supplemental to conversion — or justification — if they are to gain victory over the power of sin in their lives. Instead of this "second blessing," say Wieland and Short, righteousness by faith brings both justification and victory in the conversion experience.[137]

The eight books published between 1922 and 1930 reveal that Adventist thinking on the subjects of righteousness by faith and the victorious life was not completely unified. A number of authors presented justification and victory as one experience. Prescott wrote that "the experience of justification and of sanctification means receiving Jesus Christ the justifier and the sanctifier, who is Himself our justification and our sanctification."[138] "Righteousness comes by faith," wrote Branson, "and when it is received, it produces commandment keeping in the life."[139] Daniells asserted that righteousness by faith "is a change of standing before God and His law. It is a regeneration, a new birth."[140]

Two writers, however, did propose the idea of victory as constituting a supplemental experience, although neither used the traditional "second blessing" terminology. In his two books, evangelist MacGuire implied a two-step approach in the Christian life: "It is evident that the man who has been justified needs yet another deliverance from the law of sin and death which is in his members."[141] In a later work he wrote that after pardon from our sins, "there is an additional work to be done."[142] Froom expressed the idea most clearly, though, when he said that "there must be an experience beyond the new birth. And that is this filling by and with the Comforter."[143]

This second-experience idea was clearly a minority view. A careful examination of the eight 1922–30 books reveals only three — those by MacGuire and Froom — that speak of the victorious life as an experience separate from conversion. Although the biblical exegesis and the theological understanding might not have been thorough and precise, all the writers were united in their conviction that the individual relationship with Christ is the central theme of Christianity. By this unanimity they sought to establish firmly the doctrine of righteousness by faith in Adventist thinking.[144]

LIBERALISM AND FUNDAMENTALISM

Beyond propounding these doctrinal developments, the church also had to define its theological position in relationship to the other Protestant churches, because the religious liberalism that was pervading much of Protestantism had prompted a reaction—the Fundamentalist movement.[145] As has already become clear in the debates over pantheism and Ellen White, Seventh-day Adventists gave short shrift to modernism, as they called liberal Christianity. When Fundamentalism came to the forefront in the 1920s as the champion of orthodoxy, the Adventists had to define and justify their particular position once again. Seventh-day Adventists agreed with the Fundamentalists on several points. First of all, they rejected the theory of evolution on moral, doctrinal, and scientific grounds.[146] As one Adventist science teacher wrote, "Human minds are too puny to solve these great questions, and would better be employed in something more profitable than in trying to set up their theories in the place of divine revelation."[147] Likewise, Adventists saw "the empty pew, the dry sermon, and the decay of spirituality in the churches" as the result of acceptance of the evolutionary theory.[148]

Similarly, Adventists rejected higher criticism. Francis Wilcox wrote in 1911 that the result of higher criticism and liberal theology would "be the rejection of Jesus Christ as the Saviour of men, the discarding of the Scriptures of truth as the revelation of God, final destruction in the overwhelming flood at the last great day."[149] Rather than accept higher criticism, Adventists affirmed strongly the inspiration and infallibility of the Bible. In 1914 one *Review* writer said that "the inspiration of the Bible is one of the most vital doctrines of Christianity."[150] In addition to arguing the inspiration of the Bible, Adventists also defended its infallibility. As an editor of the *Review* put it:

> When we stop to consider it, it is a terrible charge which the critics have brought against God in the declaration that his Word is "inspired, but not infallible." That would make God the inspirer of that which is fallible, faulty, false, for it is only the infallible that is certain and true.[151]

Seventh-day Adventists also allied themselves with Fundamentalism on a nontheological issue—prohibition. Although prohibition arose partly out of the progressive movement, it received much support from Fundamentalist circles also. Like the Fundamentalists, Adventists supported prohibition for moral and religious reasons. A *Review* editor declared in 1918: "God grant that the closing message of his grace may be heard by a sane and sober world, and that the second advent of our Lord and Master may be hastened."[152] Thus, when the Eighteenth Amendment passed, the *Review* praised it, saying that God was in the movement.[153] Despite the problems of prohibition enforcement, Adventists, like other Fundamentalists, continued to support prohibition throughout the 1920s. As late as 1928 a *Review* writer affirmed that "there is no lack of testimony as to the real benefits of prohibition, even though the results are not all that sober, honest men have hoped and prayed for."[154]

Despite their agreement on such issues as the inspiration of the Bible, evolution, and prohibition, however, when it came to the Fundamentalist movement itself, Adventists spoke both approvingly and critically. On the one hand, the church affirmed that it was fundamentalist,[155] with Francis Wilcox saying that Adventists "should count themselves the chief of Fundamentalists today."[156] Adventists also gave the Fundamentalist movement one of its leading antievolution writers in the person of George McCready Price, who, according to one scholar, moved Fundamentalists toward affirmation of the six-day creation, universal deluge, and six-thousand-year-old earth.[157] Price's contacts with religious leaders of various faiths led him to have considerable sympathy with their work. As a result, Price defined Fundamentalism in Adventist terms:

> Fundamentalism is actually a work of proclaiming the true claims of the Creator; a call for the present generation of evolutionary heathen to "worship Him that made heaven, and earth, and the sea, and the fountains of waters." This language, of course, sounds very familiar to us, as Seventh-day Adventists; but what I have said only goes to show that Fundamentalism is helping to do a work that we have long thought to be peculiarly our own.[158]

On the other hand, although it could speak approvingly of much of Fundamentalism, the Adventist church also had to distinguish itself clearly from the Fundamentalist movement in order to maintain its identity. Therefore, Adventist writers attacked Fundamentalism on the issue of God's law, challenging those who were defending the infallibility of God's word to follow the Lord's will all the way. Writing in the *Review* in 1919, Calvin P. Bollman criticized a list of fundamental doctrines prepared by Reuben A. Torrey, a leading Fundamentalist spokesman, for not including the law.[159] A few years later, Milton Wilcox wrote: "Fundamentalists must face the fact of the law or fail. The decision means death, or by the grace of Christ, life."[160] At about the same time, another *Review* writer defined "true Protestantism" in terms that could only include Seventh-day Adventists:

> While apostate and apostatizing Protestantism in our day is seeking to destroy Protestantism by destroying faith in the Bible as the infallible word of the living God, true Protestantism is calling the people back to the first principles of the Reformation; back to the original protest against the inventions of Rome; back to loyal obedience to the holy Author of our religion; back to the old-fashioned reverence for the Word of God; back to the Sabbath, which He ordained and which has been so long desecrated; back to our Saviour as the only one who can save us from our sins and open heaven to us; back to the law of God, unaltered, as the expression of His divine will and epitome of His character.[161]

By aligning themselves with Fundamentalism, yet maintaining their individuality through their emphasis on the Sabbath, Seventh-day Adventists continued to believe that they had indeed a unique purpose in God's plan.

As the 1920s drew to a close, the Seventh-day Adventist Church appeared to be in a strong condition. During the previous three decades Adventists had established a denominational structure and instituted worldwide missionary enterprises to carry out the gospel commission. They had withstood, though not resolved, attacks on the prophetic ministry of Ellen White as an integral part of their message. They had made righteousness by faith a prominent element in their theological discussions. They had put their denomination in perspective with regard to other Protestant churches. Both theologically and institutionally, the Seventh-day Adventist Church had taken on its modern form.

6 | The Church under Stress 1931–1960

KELD J. REYNOLDS

After years of internal dissension and reorganization, the Seventh-day Adventist Church enjoyed relative calm during the 1920s. With greater institutional and theological unity than it had experienced for some time, the denomination continued to expand, especially through its overseas missionary work. The decade gave Seventh-day Adventists a chance to revitalize themselves before facing stresses of a different kind in the ensuing years.

Whereas the troubles of earlier days had been primarily internal, the ones the denomination faced after 1930 were largely external. International economic depression, a truly worldwide war, and a rapidly changing postwar world strained Seventh-day Adventism to the utmost—as those factors did most other institutions. But the reorganization adopted earlier in the century, together with the creativity of a new generation of leaders, enabled the church to sail successfully the troubled seas. Although not all the problems were resolved, the events of these years broadened the Seventh-day Adventist conception of mission in a more humanitarian direction and to some degree broke down its sectarian exclusiveness. The years of stress were also years of growth—institutionally, theologically, and morally.

DEPRESSION AND WAR

The first major problem the denomination faced was the Great Depression, which began in the United States late in 1929 and soon spread to Europe. The resulting dramatic drop in church income made necessary drastic measures in management of the church's financial affairs. Between 1930 and 1932 the General Conference administrators cut 6 percent from home and foreign appropriations, reduced wages for all North American executives and personnel,[1] cut another 8 percent from foreign-base appropriations, streamlined administration for the sake of economy, and appealed for increased giving by members.[2] In order to cope with runaway inflation and fluctuating national currencies, church officials maintained reserves in strategic overseas locations, moving these reserves from place to place on the advice of international banking consultants, sometimes for profit, always for reasons of safety. By 1936, Charles H. Watson, president of the General Conference (1930– 36), could report to the quadrennial session that, without borrowing and by a gigantic re-duction of expenditure, the church organization had weathered the Depression. In the face of an income reduction from $52 million in 1930 to $34 million in 1934, the Seventh-day Adventists had a balanced budget. Furthermore, in those years the church added ninety thousand new members, established forty-four new institu-tions, entered 184 new countries and islands, and increased its work-ing force by 654 persons.[3]

Problems of a different sort followed the 1933– 35 rise of Adolf Hitler and the German Nazi party. The Nazi concept of totalitarian power endangered Catholic and Protestant communions alike, as the Third Reich sought to establish a new cult of nationalism and to possess the minds and bodies of its youth.[4] Wider in its impact was Hitler's cunningly contrived war, begun with the occupation of the Sudetenland and the conquest of Austria. The work of the church was seriously crippled in the warring countries and in those mobilizing for war. Ministers and institutional personnel were con-scripted; entire congregations were evacuated and scattered, and church records were lost or destroyed. And so many people were called to military service on subsistence wages that the income of the church dwindled to almost nothing. Military governments in occupied territories showed little concern for human rights.[5] From central Europe came reports that in some countries it was impossible to hold meetings that could be attended by any but church members, that church publishing houses and schools were closed, and that the mortality rate among Adventists was very high because most lived in industrial areas, where bomb destruction was greatest. Among survivors, whole families faced problems of Sabbath observance, as women and children were conscripted to replace men in war industries.[6]

On the eve of the 1940 annual International Autumn Council of the church, Frederick Lee editorialized in the *Review and Herald*: "No council of this people ever met under such serious circumstances nor had to wrestle with such tremendous problems."[7] But the problems intensified. In 1941, with the attack on Pearl Harbor, Japanese militarists began an invasion that was to cut off every church, church institution, mission center, and thirty-five thousand Adventist church members in the Far Eastern Division from connection with the world headquarters office in Washington, D.C.[8] Eventually, all American and European mission church officials were placed under house arrest, evacuated, or sent to detention camps. This was especially crippling because in the Orient, unlike in other parts of the world, few nationals were in church administrative posts on the local mission level, and none on the union or division conference levels. With the evacuation or internment of foreigners, full responsibility was suddenly thrust on the nationals.

Internal strife in China further complicated matters. Immediately after World War II, the General Conference appropriated almost $2 million to restore the properties of the church in China and arranged for the return of missionaries who had been evacuated because of the war. By the time the Communists swept into power in 1949, the medical and educational institutions of the church were functioning again and many of the damaged and destroyed church buildings had been restored.[9] The 1949 autumn council of the worldwide church, bowing to necessity, appointed a complete division staff of national officials to take office on January 1, 1950.[10] Seven of these, including the president, Hsu Hwa, were able to attend the 1950 General Conference session held in San Francisco.

But even while the Chinese leaders were in the United States, the Communist campaign against the Christian church was beginning. The "Christian Manifesto" of May 1950 called on Chinese Christians to renounce imperialism, support the revolution, and participate in agrarian reform. This manifesto marked the beginning of the "Three-Self Movement" (self-support, self-administration, self-propagation), on the surface a union of all Protestant bodies, but actually the agency for the destruction of corporate Christianity in China.[11] There followed the "accusation meetings" of 1951 and the organization of "reform churches," of which the Seventh-day Adventist may have been the first to be cleared by the government.[12] The churches had now become tools of the government. Finally, the "Great Proletarian Cultural Revolution" of 1966 turned on the tattered remains of organized Christianity until it burned out its fury. After this, there was little communication with the West.[13]

Out of this ordeal came two constructively critical appraisals of mission organization, polity, and performance in China. The first was written by David Lin Yao Hsi, the 1950 secretary of the China

Division of Seventh-day Adventists, in December 1956, about six months before his arrest; the other was written by S. J. Lee, division treasurer, in 1957, after his arrival in Singapore.[14] To date, the government of the People's Republic of China has not permitted the church to profit from the counsel of its Chinese leaders to emphasize the nurturing of local churches rather than building large institutions.

CONSCIENTIOUS OBJECTION

World War II also inevitably brought to the fore the question of the relationship of Adventists to war. In the United States, as far back as the Civil War, the church had established its official position on war service as one of a cooperating noncombatant status: that is, willingness for its young men, when drafted, to serve their country in ways not requiring the use of firearms. When the United States was drawn into World War II, American Adventists were advised by their church leaders not to enlist, but to await the draft, then to claim 1-A-0 rating, as provided in the Selective Service Act.[15] Enlistment, however, was not made a matter for church discipline. In other countries, especially those under totalitarian rule, the Adventist soldier was faced with a hard choice—one that sometimes included execution as the result of the decision.

The right of the American citizen to decide whether or not to bear arms was given judicial support by the United States Supreme Court in a suit brought by attorneys for the General Conference of Seventh-day Adventists. This was the historic *Girouard v. United States* case (April 22, 1946). James Girouard, a Seventh-day Adventist, had been denied citizenship because of his refusal to obligate himself to bear arms. The Supreme Court decision made it illegal for immigration officers or others to apply this test, which heretofore had been standard practice.[16] Implicit in the decision was the principle that an applicant for citizenship cannot be held to requirements that do not apply to citizens.

The Medical Corps was a logical avenue for military service by Adventists during wartime. As war clouds gathered, Union College (Nebraska) began a training program for medical corpsmen in January 1934, and the first group completed it during that spring semester. This program was begun at the initiative of faculty veterans of World War I, whom President Milian L. Andreasen had asked to serve as a recommending committee, and was led by Everett N. Dick, the history department chairman. Major Emile H. Burgher (a regular Army doctor then in charge of training the Nebraska National Guard), offered his help and the college trustees accepted and endorsed the plan. Dick, the organizer and director of the college corpsmen program, was later asked by the General Conference to be nationwide director of the Medical Cadet Corps (as it came to be named). By that time (1940 – 42), four cadet captains trained by Dick were directing the programs at four Adventist colleges.

A similar program stemming from different roots was organized at the College of Medical Evangelists in California in 1936. An inactive base hospital organization had been sponsored by the medical school at the request of the U.S. Surgeon General since the early 1920s, beginning under the leadership of then college president Newton G. Evans, who had been appointed a lieutenant colonel in the medical reserves. When this Forty-seventh General Hospital was reorganized and staffed with physician faculty members in the 1930s, neurology professor Cyril B. Courville was appointed unit training officer. Under his direction a medical cadet program was offered for young Adventists of the region, and the first class of fifty-nine completed training in the spring of 1937.

Another training program was begun about two years later by Washington Missionary College in Maryland under Captain C. R. Hyatt of the U.S. Navy. Additional programs sprang up spontaneously in other parts of the nation, usually centered at Adventist schools. Even the Adventist Theological Seminary was authorized to offer cadet training.[17] Medical cadet training received official status from representatives of the church at the autumn council of 1939.[18]

Perhaps the brightest hour of the Adventist noncombatant soldier was the rescue by Corpsman Desmond Thomas Doss of approximately seventy-five U.S. infantrymen caught by Japanese fire on an escarpment on Okinawa between April 29 and May 21, 1945. For that valorous act Doss was presented the Congressional Medal of Honor by President Harry S. Truman on October 12 of that year.[19]

Having proved useful in wartime, the medical cadet program was continued in the postwar period, both in the United States and in other countries. The program was placed under the General Conference Commission on National Service and Medical Cadet Training in 1940. In 1950 the General Conference asked Dick to direct and coordinate the sectional training programs in order to regularize the variations of organization, ranking, uniform, and insignia that had developed in the various localities. The General Conference changed the overall program name to War Service Commission in 1942; later it became the National Service Organization, and in

1958 it was made a section of the General Conference Youth Department of Missionary Volunteers.[20]

Another avenue of military service that opened up for Adventists was the chaplaincy. William H. Bergherm, at that time the pastor of the Blythedale congregation in the Washington, D.C., area, was the first to enter the chaplaincy with denominational endorsement in 1943. Bergherm appeared in the pulpit one Sabbath morning clad in the uniform of a U.S. Army chaplain; and before he preached the sermon of the day, he announced that he had accepted a commission in the U.S. Army.[21] This created a stir at the Adventist headquarters, where opinions were divided and it was uncertain just how Bergherm had received his endorsement. Not until seven years later—when it was clear that the victorious Allies would continue to maintain large military establishments and therefore would continue to call up young Adventists—did the church at its 1950 autumn council give clearance for ministers of maturity to continue holding ministerial credentials if they chose to accept commissions as military chaplains.[22] More than twenty-five Adventist military chaplains have served in the armed forces of the United States. In other countries the only person reported to have become a military chaplain was Daniel Pfeiffer, who served in the Belgian army but withdrew from the church while a chaplain.[23] The Adventist church has assigned ministers to serve as civilian chaplains in locations with a concentration of Adventists in military service. The church has also maintained servicemen's centers at American homeland and foreign points of concentration—until the draft was discontinued in 1973.

UNIONS AND BLACKS

World War II also brought about nonmilitary concerns. The wartime acceleration of American industry, and the consequent increase in the power and influence of labor unions, forced the leaders of the church to take a fresh look at its official position: namely, to discourage members from joining the unions because these organizations required their members to surrender personal freedoms deemed essential by the Adventists and because violence sometimes accompanied union activities. In 1945 the church created the Council on Industrial Relations to negotiate with national labor leaders, with Carlyle B. Haynes and others providing the liason. Agreements were reached permitting the Adventist to work on a union job or in a closed shop without being required to join the union or attend union meetings. In return, the Adventist would donate to the union or some charity an amount up to the total of the fees, dues, and assessments imposed by the union; would refrain from interfering with or resisting union activities; and would abide by shop and union regulations as to wages, working conditions, and hours (except as the hours would encroach on the Sabbath).[24] But because of the autonomy enjoyed by local unions, the agreements negotiated with national union leaders fell short of the expected results.

The same conditions that speeded industrialization and urbanization of the American people also brought to a head the questions of race relations and human rights that had been with the church for many years. The Adventist black—smarting under grievances, feeling the power of urban numbers, and experiencing improved educational opportunities for himself and his children whether he lived in the North or the South—raised his voice to better advantage than on former occasions. In 1944 a group of black laymen drew up a list of grievances and recommendations and urged fairness in church hiring practices, nondiscriminatory admission to Adventist educational and medical institutions, and the establishment of black conferences staffed by black officials. The General Conference promptly scheduled meetings to be held with black leaders at the spring council of 1944.[25]

But the black leaders were divided. Some favored separate conferences as the best means of achieving identity, developing leaders, and establishing such institutions as they would need; others favored complete integration at all levels and thought that separate conferences would defeat their goals. This dichotomy reflected the contemporary national debate in the black community between the integration and the separate-but-equal concepts. With the support of the president of the General Conference, J. Lamar McElhany (1936–50), the separate-conference plan prevailed and was approved by the council. Before the end of the year, the first "Negro conferences" were organized, later to be called "regional conferences."[26]

This was not, however, the end of the matter of race relations. In the 1940s and 1950s the social climate of the nation was building toward civil rights for blacks and other ethnic minorities. Black Adventists felt that their church was moving too slowly. Under the administration of Reuben R. Figuhr, who was president of the General Conference from 1954 to 1966, they succeeded in obtaining the appointment of a committee on race relations, which drafted a statement that was passed at the 1961 autumn council of the General Conference. In summary, it stated that inasmuch as the church believes all men are of one blood and equally destined for eternity in the kingdom of God, the church recognizes no distinction of race, color, or nationality.[27] The status of minority Adventists was showing some improvement.

RELIEF WORK

When the tumult of World War II had ceased, the world could assess the awful cost in lives and property, and the Adventist church joined hands with other organizations to repair the damage — insofar as this was possible — and bring assistance to survivors. Adventist relief work, small before the war, was greatly expanded to meet postwar needs. Clothing depots were set up on the Atlantic and Pacific coasts during 1944 and 1945; by 1946 the treasurer of the General Conference could report that 500 tons of clothing had been sent overseas, largely through the efforts of the auxiliary arm of local churches known as the Dorcas Society. He also reported that 2,000 blankets, 1,000 comforters, 1,000 pairs of new shoes, 2,000 pairs of repaired shoes, 10,000 pairs of socks, and 10,000 suits of winter underwear had been bought from war surplus and shipped overseas. In addition, congregations and individuals had sent 236,000 pounds of clothing in 26,000 packages to addresses furnished by European and Far Eastern church organizations.

The magnitude of the effort required systemization. In the summer of 1946, the president and the secretary of the General Conference sent John J. Strahle and James J. Aitken to Europe to organize the relief program — Strahle to Denmark and Aitken to Switzerland. Strahle was provided with $125,000 and Aitken with $120,000 to begin the purchase of supplies of food. Both men quickly teamed up with the International Red Cross, the Evangelical Church for German distribution, and the military authorities in occupied zones. The denomination believed that it would have been inhumane to limit the assistance of the church to its own destitute members.[28]

Butter, beans, peas, cheese, powdered milk, and other staples were bought by the hundreds of tons in Scandinavia and Switzerland and shipped by truck convoy to Poland and Czechoslovakia and by railroad car lots to Germany and Austria. Because the Russians limited to one pound the packages to be sent into their occupation zone, only chocolate bars were sent there — to provide the most nutrition for the least weight. The providers found it possible to send some supplies directly to Adventists through the conference organizations, from five hundred to one thousand packages to each conference in proportion to membership. Each package contained two pounds of butter, two pounds of cheese, malt syrup, barley, dried peas, and beans. These were in addition to the shipments for general distribution. In all, between 1946 and 1949, the General Conference relief organizations in Europe provided more than 3,300,000 pounds of food and 1,100,000 pounds of clothing. [29]

Having enlarged its concept of brotherly love and concern, the church found welfare needs extending into the uneasy peace. When the fear of sudden attack on vulnerable urban centers led to elaborate preparations for civil defense in the United States, William H. Branson, president of the General Conference (1950 – 54), announced a policy of cooperation. In an article entitled "If Bombs Fall," Branson urged church officials, clergy, and laypeople to be foremost in responding to the call of civil authorities in efforts to save life. [30] At the 1956 autumn council the General Conference urged local pastors to offer civil defense units the services of their congregations. [31]

As it was expanding its social concern, the denomination also had to reconstruct its own worldwide organization. President McElhany's opening address to the 1945 autumn council of the General Conference warned the church against militant nationalism and reminded his associate leaders of their obligation of universal love and the church at large of its global mission. [32] As early as 1943, McElhany had directed the attention of the church to postwar problems: the restoration of communication with scattered congregations and members, the rebuilding of church organization, immediate massive relief, and provision for training a new generation of national workers and leaders. [33]

RESTORING ORDER

The first task facing the church after the collapse of the Axis Powers and the restoration of a degree of order on the international scene was the resumption of communication and the reconstruction of organization. By 1947, the year that the General Conference sanctioned the expense of travel on commercial airlines by its personnel, the officers and department secretaries from the Washington headquarters of the church met with national church leaders in countries where government regulations permitted (many of these leaders had been out of touch for a number of years); they appraised progress and deterioration. They had to recognize with peer status the self-sufficiency that necessity and isolation had developed in the stronger overseas divisions of the church. They found that the prewar organizational pattern of divisions, union conferences, and local conferences was flexible enough to serve postwar needs. It was also clear that the church needed to strengthen its school system for the educating and training of a new generation of leaders. Imperative was the need for more uniform church polity, firmer agreement on theology and concepts of Christian conduct, and more extensive international representation in the councils of the church leaders.

To restore communication in Europe, the General Conference established the direction of holding various conferences: educational councils by the Department of Education; youth congresses by the Young People's Missionary Volunteer Department; and ministerial institutes by the Ministerial Association.[34] The educational councils and inspections of the higher schools in many lands served not only to restore communication between the General Conference and the school personnel, but also to facilitate reappraisal. Except in the North American Division, before World War II, Adventists operated few elementary schools in the developed countries and few advanced schools in the less developed countries. They usually regarded higher education in these foreign countries as training for those aspiring to the ministry. Now the representatives from the General Conference education department urged curriculum changes in the stronger advanced schools to permit their graduates to pass the official examinations of their country at the end of the secondary level, or for university matriculation, which could be done without sacrifice of the essential features of Christian education as conceived in the Seventh-day Adventist Church. This strengthening gave status to Adventist advanced schools in those countries where the plan was adopted, and the church benefited through improved recognition and support of its schools, increased attendance, better-educated members, and an enlarged pool from which church workers could be drawn. Ministerial education, of course, was retained and upgraded.[35]

The Paris Youth Congress of July 24-28, 1951, was cited in the *Review and Herald* as a precedent in building European unity.[36] More than five thousand youths attended the congress, many of whom grew up isolated from other Adventist young people, even from those of their own nationality, in countries and communities where wartime resentments and frustrations still smoldered. It was a heady experience for young Christians to meet in this international gathering in which fellowship and sharing went on from morning to night—with simultaneous translations into English, French, Dutch, Portuguese, German, Italian, Danish-Norwegian, and Finnish.[37] A number of these congresses were held before and after the major one at Paris, all of them building bridges of understanding and love.

PUBLICATION OF BELIEFS

The restoration of communication between the church and its ministers clearly indicated the need for a statement of beliefs more readily defined and transmitted than presently existed and a clearer
definition of the lifestyle of the Adventist communicant. To some
extent these needs had been anticipated. The *Church Manual* had
been prepared in 1932 by McElhany when he was the North American vice president. This manual described the plan of organization
for the individual church, responsibilities of church officers, regulations for holding church property, the systemization of finance,
the order of services, acceptable concepts of Sabbath observation,
practices pertaining to the Christian marriage, and a previously published statement of "fundamental beliefs."[38]

In December 1929 the General Conference executive committee had asked the chairman, President Watson, to appoint a
committee (to include himself) that would draft a statement of the
beliefs of Seventh-day Adventists for inclusion in the church yearbook. Watson appointed Milton E. Kern, a department secretary,
Francis M. Wilcox, senior editor of the *Review*, and Edwin R. Palmer, manager of the Review and Herald Publishing Association.
The committee accepted a statement drafted by Wilcox, and without
further processing, this statement appeared first in the *Seventh-day
Adventist Yearbook* for 1931; again in the first official *Church Manual* (published in 1932); and in subsequent editions of both. The
General Conference session of 1946 gave a sort of offhand impri-
matur to the statement by voting that changes could be made only
by the General Conference delegates in official session.[39] This initial
"fundamental beliefs" statement thus became the official statement
of Seventh-day Adventist doctrine.

A logical next step was the adoption of a uniform baptismal
covenant—or vow. Because some administrative units of the
church—and certain prominent evangelists—had adopted their own
"catechisms" and devised their own baptismal certificates, the existing understandings and requirements varied from place to place.
In an effort to ensure that incoming communicants would hold
common denominators of belief, the General Conference adopted
a recommendation at its 1941 autumn council that included an
expanded statement of belief, a baptismal vow, and a standard baptismal certificate. These were formulated by a committee headed by
William H. Branson, then the vice president of the General
Conference.

The candidate for baptism and church membership was expected from then on to assent to eleven propositions, among them those dealing with the following: the Trinity; the atoning sacrifice of Christ on the Cross; the Bible as God's inspired word; the imminent Second Coming of Christ as King; the intercessory ministry of Christ in the heavenly sanctuary; Christ as a personal Savior accepted through faith in his promises; the obligation to keep the law of God, thus ordering one's life—by God's grace—according to the Bible principles taught by the Seventh-day Adventist Church; the personal support of the church by the financial system devised for it; and public baptism by immersion as the mode of signifying one's faith in the forgiveness of sins and in his acceptance by Christ.[40]

Ten years after publication of the first *Church Manual*, the church issued a revised *Manual for Ministers*. This outlined the procedures for organizing a new congregation and dedicating its place of worship; it also recommended the order of services for divine worship, baptism, communion, marriage, and burial; and ministers were urged to observe unity in conducting these services.[41] Then a lengthy statement on "Standards of Christian Living" was presented at the 1946 General Conference session and approved for publication. This statement covered such topics as community relations; Christian principles pertaining to entertainment, amusement, and recreation; simplicity of lifestyle; intelligent regard for health, without fanaticism; and Christian courtship, marriage, and divorce. The obvious intention was to define and preserve the Adventist lifestyle.[42] The next step, even more significant than those preceding it, was to bring the teachings of the church under the discipline of contemporary Adventist theology.

The two decades following the publication of "fundamental beliefs" brought significant developments in Adventist theological affirmations. Among the pressures were requests for information about Adventism from editors of encyclopedias and writers of books about the contemporary church; the appearance in increasing numbers of professional Adventist theologians, creationist scientists, and biblical archaeologists; the establishment in 1937 of the Seventh-day Adventist Theological Seminary; and the need to give cohesion and efficacy to the teaching of religion in the schools and colleges of the church. The most significant events were the Bible conference of 1952; the beginning of the publication of the monumental *Seventh-day Adventist Bible Commentary* in 1953; and the issuance in 1957 of the definitive publication entitled *Seventh-day Adventists Answer Questions on Doctrine*, which was the product of a series of dialogues between Adventist theologians and leading evangelicals of other communions.

At its 1951 autumn council the General Conference officially called a Bible conference to convene in September 1952. The reasons for the conference, as announced to the clergy by the General Conference president, were principally three: a new generation of clergymen had come on the scene since the Bible conference of 1919; the church needed to maximize the effectiveness of timeless truth in changing times; present truth needed to be plumbed so that deeper truths could be identified and defined.[43]

There were other reasons. Like the 1919 conference, this one was called in the aftermath of international upheaval. In 1952 it was just beginning to be possible to assemble worldwide representation for high-level church leadership meetings. The church officialdom wanted to find out what the warring armies and ideologies had done to the attitudes and beliefs of Adventists isolated for years from the mainstream. The educational level of laity and clergy had risen greatly in recent years. The Adventist colleges were now staffed by teachers of religion with seminary and university preparation in theology and biblical studies. The church administrators had to know what the thinking was at these levels. And finally, the five-year commentary project—long in planning by the Review and Herald Publishing Association, with the knowledge of the General Conference, but as an enterprise of the publishing house—was drawing contributors representing a wide spectrum of Adventist scholarship. Would the commentary be a means of enabling the communicants to hold views in common and the public to obtain a clear understanding of Adventist belief? Would it cause confusion? The church leaders were eager to know.

One incident in 1950 may well have had a bearing on the decision to hold the conference. In the early 1940s the faculty of religion and biblical languages at Pacific Union College (Angwin, California) had begun dialogues about doctrine in which they prepared position papers for discussion. The Bible Research Fellowship took shape when teachers on other Adventist college campuses joined in this time-honored custom of examining consensus and dissent. Rumors began to fly among church administrators. Then in 1950 the religion faculties of the North American Adventist colleges met at Pacific Union College for what had become a regular quadrennial session; the dean of the Seventh-day Adventist Theological Seminary was chairman. Since the forty-sixth session of the General Conference was to convene in San Francisco at the same time, it was natural that visitors would attend the meeting of the religion faculties as well. One such visitor, an Australian named Louis F. Were, was at odds with the church officials in his home country because his interpretations of prophecy were considered erroneous and he would not be convinced to accept other views. The theological discussions—at least in his perception of them—seemed to endorse his views, and in due time he reported back home that the American theologians were in agreement with him. When this word reached Washington, the newly elected president of the General Conference, William H. Branson, issued a general letter of warning.[44]

This turn of events shocked academic Adventist theologians, who saw themselves thus becoming the targets of unjustified suspicion and misunderstanding; this they expressed in spirited letters to the General Conference president. The theologians and the official leaders of the church saw in this incident an imperative for dialogue. Dialogue could best be accomplished in a conference at which there could be general participation.[45] President Branson was aware of all this when he stood before the assembled delegates at the opening session of the theological conference on September 1, 1952. Said he: "This is the hardest job I know of that has ever been given to preachers; to stand before theologians, brethren from all over the earth, Bible teachers from our colleges, evangelists, and men who are mighty in the Scriptures, and undertake to set before you anew the great verities of this message."[46]

In the introduction to the printed report appeared the statement that the conference "was an outstanding example of order and careful planning."[47] Ground rules had been laid down by the planning committee of twenty-three members (with Branson as chairman). Certain "great fundamental" subjects had been preselected for study and assigned by the committee to able scholars. The planning committee had appointed a committee of counselors to be responsible for reading the papers before they were presented, and editing them afterward for publication. Several counseling committee members themselves presented papers. Although the planning committee ruled out open-forum discussion, they did schedule "discussion" periods, at which written questions—submitted in advance by the delegates and given the approbation of the "committee of chairmen"—were answered from the pulpit. This last committee was composed of the president and the four vice presidents of the General Conference.[48]

The pattern of worldwide representation at the conference had been set by the 1951 autumn council. Actual attendance totaled 512 delegates and special guests, not counting wives of delegates. The distribution of delegates was as follows: General Conference—78; North American Division—170; overseas divisions—194; North American institutions—59; invited guests—11. The North American strength totaled 307, the overseas 194.[49] Compared with the one in 1919, this conference put greater emphasis on the doctrines of salvation and the nature and work of God's "remnant" and less emphasis on the specifics of prophetic interpretations of history.[50]

At the close of the conference, *Review* editor Francis D. Nichol made these statements of evaluation: "It is an impressive fact that we have not changed our theology. . . . Our primary doctrines are interlocked. . . . Our prime doctrines are a tapestry. . . . We realized with new force that Christ is the heart and center of all our teaching."[51]

The General Conference afterward appointed a standing committee for biblical study and research—"to encourage, organize and coordinate . . . Biblical exegesis and research and then to function as a body of counsel to give guidance to those who in any part of the world field make what appears to them to be significant discoveries of truth."[52] This action was taken at the suggestion of scholars who held the opinion that the events preceding the Bible conference had thrown a cloud over the college-based Bible Research Fellowship. They hoped that such a committee would provide needed protection for theologians working on the "growing edge" of truth, seeking deeper insights into the basic and accepted doctrines.

Receiving more attention was the *Seventh-day Adventist Bible Commentary*, which consisted of seven volumes and some seven thousand pages. Produced by the Review and Herald Publishing Association between 1953 and 1957, it was the largest single publishing project in the history of the church. Each volume was divided into three parts: general articles, commentary, and supplementary material. Throughout, the commentary sought to set forth only those interpretations of Scripture (the King James text was followed) that were in harmony with Adventist beliefs and standards of life.[53] The editor was Francis D. Nichol, the associates Raymond F. Cottrell and Don F. Neufeld, all editors of the *Review and Herald*. The basic seven commentary volumes were followed by the *Supplement* (1957, volume 7-A), the *Seventh-day Adventist Bible Dictionary* (1960), the *Seventh-day Adventist Bible Students' Source Book* (1962), and the one-volume *Seventh-day Adventist Encyclopedia* (1966)—eleven volumes in all. Although this work has been invaluable for the Adventist scholar and student, it was not in a form useful to interested individuals of other faiths who may have wanted a compact handbook from which to learn about the Seventh-day Adventist Church. Such a handbook came from the presses in 1957, however, as a result of a series of dialogues.

DIALOGUES WITH EVANGELICALS

Donald Grey Barnhouse, a Presbyterian minister from Philadelphia and editor of *Eternity*, the influential Evangelical journal, delivered a series of radio studies on the Book of Romans in 1949. T. Edgar Unruh, a Seventh-day Adventist minister and church administrator, wrote to Barnhouse commending him for his radio presentation of the doctrine of righteousness by faith.[54] In reply, Barnhouse expressed his astonishment that an Adventist would commend him for his studies on Romans, since, according to Barnhouse, it was well known that Adventists believed in righteousness by works. Barnhouse went on to say that he was thoroughly familiar with Adventist teaching and that their concept of the nature of Christ was dangerous and Satanic. Yet he expressed a desire to have lunch with so strange an Adventist.[55] Unruh returned a soft answer, agreed that discussion over a lunch would be interesting, and sent a copy of *Steps to Christ*, which he calculated might alter the misconceptions of his correspondent. A few months later, however, Barnhouse sharply criticized *Steps to Christ* and its author in *Eternity*.[56] Unruh, who thought he had Barnhouse's word that he would publish nothing more against Adventists before their conference, lost both confidence and interest.

Meanwhile, Barnhouse had given Unruh's name to Walter R. Martin, the director of cult apologetics for Zondervan Publishing Company and a contributing editor of *Eternity*, so that Martin could gather firsthand material for a book he had been commissioned to write against the Adventists. Martin asked Unruh for representative books and an opportunity to interview Adventists qualified to answer questions that he would raise. Unruh supplied the books and arranged the conference to take place in Washington, D.C. Martin brought with him George E. Cannon, a professor of New Testament Greek in a Bible college; they met with Adventists R. Allan Anderson, LeRoy E. Froom, Walter E. Read, and Unruh, the last serving as chairman at the initial meeting.

After the conferences had been going on for some weeks, Martin was convinced that he had been wrong about the Adventists; whereupon, he told Barnhouse that he had been meeting with the Adventists and that his and Barnhouse's position on Adventism had been wrong—and that Unruh was hurt by what he considered a breach of faith on the part of Barnhouse. Greatly distressed, Barnhouse promptly invited the conferees to meet at his home in Doylestown, Pennsylvania. Here he apologized to Unruh, and at the opening of the discussion he prayed for light and brotherhood. Also present were his son, Donald Grey Barnhouse, Jr., a theological adviser on the staff of Billy Graham, and Russell Hitt, the managing editor of *Eternity*.

The Doylestown meetings were crucial, for here the Barnhouses, father and son, reached agreement with Martin that the Adventists were Christian brethren rather than a non-Christian cult, which Evangelicals generally believed. Here also, Donald Barnhouse, Jr., persuaded his father that their conclusions should be reported in the columns of *Eternity*, even if it meant losing some startled subscribers. In these conferences the Evangelical theologians had their first exposure to the one distinctive doctrine in Adventist theology — the work of Christ in the heavenly sanctuary. Read dealt with the Adventist interpretation of the work of the Old Testament priest, and Anderson took up the priesthood of Christ as presented in the New Testament.[57]

These 1955 — 56 dialogues were of considerable historical importance, because they forced the Adventists to sort out their beliefs: a first basic category that they shared with conservative Christians of all ages, a second category in which Adventists stand with some Christian bodies but not with others, and a third category representing Seventh-day Adventists alone and justifying their separate denominational existence. The dialogues drew from the participating Evangelicals an unreserved acknowledgment that Adventists who believed as those with whom they had talked were indeed Christians.[58] In addition, the Evangelicals urged the Adventists to answer publicly the allegations of their critics and thus improve their image in the Christian world. Finally, as a result of the dialogues, both Evangelicals and Adventists published noteworthy books about those discussions.

In the conferences the Evangelicals presented formal questions for the Adventists to answer. At first these questions reflected the views of defectors such as Dudley M. Canright, Edward S. Ballenger, Louis R. Conradi, and Ernest B. Jones, about which views the Evangelicals wanted both historical and current answers. But as the dialogue progressed, the Martin-Barnhouse group joined forces with the Adventists in formulating written questions and answers designed to bring out the actual teachings of Adventism with the greatest clarity. In some instances this required translation of the inbred vocabulary of the church into language common among theologians of other communions. The questions and answers, after passing through a committee of leading Adventist clergymen, including officials of the General Conference, were submitted to more than 250 representative Adventist leaders throughout the world for criticism and suggestions. When the results had been given due consideration in Washington, the General Conference officers authorized the pub-lication of the 1957 compendium entitled *Seventh-day Adventists Answer Questions on Doctrine*.[59]

This detailed statement had a double impact. It was published to give an accurate and comprehensive analysis of belief for the benefit of the seeker after truth—including the priest, the rabbi, and the Protestant clergyman—who was interested in learning what Ad-ventists say about their own faith. But it also had a unifying and stabilizing influence on the Adventist clergy and seminarians throughout the world. A second book growing directly out of the conference was Martin's *The Truth About Seventh-day Adventism*. The author declared in the preface that the book resulted from seven years of his study of Adventism, in which he used primary sources and conferred with Adventist leaders.[60] He consistently referred to *Questions on Doctrine* as an authoritative source of Adventist ten-ets—suggesting that the Adventist book was circulated prior to publication.

Martin's book is the work of an honest investigator and a com-petent theologian. He understood and reported accurately what Ad-ventists told him they believed, and he cited their proofs exhaustively. He pointed out areas of agreement, and he also identified Adventist beliefs with which the Evangelicals could not agree. The former included all elements of the Christian faith necessary for salvation. The latter, the points of disagreement, were the Adventist teachings concerning conditional immortality; the seventh-day Sabbath; the investigative judgment and priestly work of Christ in the heavenly sanctuary; and, finally, the concept of a special people for a special message for a special time, which Martin saw as spiritual exclusive-ness.[61] He was unconvinced that Ellen G. White was a divinely appointed messenger of God. But he pointed out that most religious movements have one extraordinary and gifted personality who dom-inates the scene and that Ellen White was such a person. Also, he conceded that everything Mrs. White wrote on salvation and Chris-tian living characterized her as a Christian in every sense of the term.[62]

In his concluding chapter Martin wrote: "In the providence of God and in His own good time, we trust that evangelical Chris-tianity as a whole will extend the hand of fellowship to a group of sincere, earnest fellow Christians, distinguished though they are by some peculiar views, but members of the Body of Christ and pos-sessors of the faith that saves."[63]

The Barnhouse and Martin plea that Adventists be recognized as a Christian denomination did not receive instant or full accep-

tance from Evangelicals. Harold Lindsell, dean of the faculty of
Fuller Theological Seminary, though admitting that the situation
was changing, still charged Adventists with mixing grace and works
and with being more like the Roman Catholic Church than like the
Evangelicals on that crucial point.[64] Frank A. Laurence, a Presbyterian clergyman who reviewed Martin's book, thought it strange
that Martin was ready to accept the Adventists as brethren despite
their "dogmatic adherence to speculative interpretation and their
inflexibility concerning the remnant church." Laurence predicted
that the Martin volume would cause "consternation and bitterness,"
and said further: "This is a book which will be 'kicked around' in
evangelical and Adventist circles until the Southern Baptists appoint
an envoy to the Vatican."[65]

* * *

The Seventh-day Adventist Church emerged from the 1950s with
a sharply defined, but still open-ended, body of belief. The dialogues
had much to do with both the focus and the defense. Benefited by
knowing where it stood with the Evangelicals, the Adventist church
went forward with efforts to purge from its older literature the fact
or appearance of error—which earlier it had already undertaken,
beginning with Uriah Smith's *Thoughts on Daniel and the Revelation.*[66] In addition, the Adventist church added to its achievements
a considerable body of denominational literature on theology and
related subjects written by its scholars. These developments, together
with the establishment of a theological seminary in Washington,
D.C., in 1937, were helping create a more professional clergy.

MEDIA EVANGELISM

One of the traditional tasks of the Adventist minister had been evangelism. Beginning in the 1930s, Seventh-day Adventists approached
evangelism in an experimental mood, creating a specialized activity
that for many ministers would be a career. The evangelist now
emerged in the role of a lecturer dealing in biblical terms with social
needs and spiritual goals: he learned how to reach urban society; he
learned how to use the city newspaper, radio, and television to gain
admittance to the homes of people who would never go near a gospel
tent; he experimented successfully with health evangelism; he learned
to make improved use of lay persons and to have confidence in
them. And he shortened the length of his campaign.

Because the evangelists were innovators, they became the targets for criticism within the church. If there was apostasy, it was

blamed on their eagerness to set baptismal records. If they hid their church identity because of a real or imagined public hostility toward Adventism, they were accused of advertising themselves more than their message. In a General Conference action of 1931, this concern surfaced with the church's asserting official jurisdiction over evangelistic endeavors and reminding the evangelist that he or she was a spokesman for the church as an institution as well as for the Lord. The church action called on Adventist evangelists:

> (1) to avoid all efforts to enlarge their own prestige by the use of titles such as "Reverend," "Bishop," "Doctor," and "Professor," to which they are not entitled. . . . (2) to eliminate from their advertisements . . . all blatant and unsupported claims, all unfair and unsupported reflections upon other organizations. . . . (3) to discard all sensationalism and theatrical methods in preaching this message. . . . (4) to seek to keep within the . . . message itself in the selection of topics, not wasting time with things foreign to this.[67]

The Great Depression of the early 1930s and the ominous rumblings of political and social change in Europe and other parts of the globe had a sobering effect on the English-speaking world and tended to increase public interest in the preacher and his message. This was the period of the "star" evangelists in the Seventh-day Adventist Church, with such men in ascendance as R. Allan Anderson, John E. Ford, John L. Shuler, Robert L. Boothby, H. M. S. Richards, Philip Knox, and others of like stature, most of them virtuosos willing to experiment with their material and methodology.[68]

One of the most successful of the new evangelists was John Ford, whose campaigns in the West and in the Middle Atlantic states netted from two hundred to four hundred converts in each series of meetings. The first General Conference radio commission was established in 1935 primarily for the support of Ford's "chain broadcasting." In the same year, the church leaders appointed him as their first sponsored radio speaker.[69] But this pioneer effort to adapt radio broadcasting to evangelism was deemed too costly and came under attack at the General Conference. The church seemed reluctant to use the new medium of radio. But while attention was still focused on Ford, H. M. S. Richards, who had been broadcasting since 1928, launched his "Adventist Hour and Tabernacle of the Air" over California stations KGER Long Beach and KTN Los Angeles. By 1936, Richards was on nine California stations, and five years later he was on seventeen Mutual Network stations in California and Arizona. And in 1940, Richards received an award for the best religious broadcast in North America—for his brief, low-key, Bible-study kind of radio sermon, with supporting music, which had become the hallmark of the "Voice of Prophecy."[70]

Now officialdom paid attention. The 1941 autumn council of the General Conference voted to begin a national broadcasting campaign.[71] Nationwide network broadcasting began on January 4, 1942, and by 1944 the program was on 363 stations in North America and 105 foreign stations in English, Portuguese, and Spanish. Bible correspondence course lessons were offered in English, German, Italian, Chinese, and Braille; and newspaper columns with questions and answers on Bible topics were published in 725 newspapers.[72] Radio evangelism brought converts to the church.

Some of the "star" evangelists became teachers in an effort to prepare additional pastors and ministerial students for effective evangelism. In 1937, Shuler directed an evangelism field school in North Carolina that became a model for training young ministers. In 1938, Anderson's appointment to the religion department of La Sierra College (California) was an example of the efforts of the Adventist colleges to bring the best in instruction to ministerial students. At the same time, George E. Vandeman was demonstrating to the college students at Emmanuel Missionary College (Michigan) the value of the field school method. The Seventh-day Adventist Theological Seminary (then in Washington, D.C.) invited Shuler to develop courses in the philosophy and methodology of evangelism, which program was first offered in 1939.[73]

In these years it was customary for General Conference sessions of the church to call for the intensification of evangelism. The 1938 autumn council, for example, appealed for total commitment to evangelism by the church.[74] Responding, the Columbia Union Conference in 1939 offered a pilot evangelistic institute, which was attended by several hundred clergymen from the Middle Atlantic states. A number of the other North American union conferences followed with their own institutes (1939 through 1941), at which Shuler served as coordinator and principal instructor. Concurrently, laymen were recruited and trained in lay preacher's councils, begun in 1941 by the General Conference home missionary department.[75] A high point was the North American Layman's Congress, held August 29 to September 3, 1951, at Grand Ledge, Michigan, where the delegates explored the possible range of lay involvement.[76]

An important step in the institutionalization of evangelism came when the 1941 General Conference session appointed R. Allan Anderson associate secretary of the Ministerial Association, with the specific responsibility of promoting evangelism. In addition, Louise C. Kleuser's appointment as an assistant secretary to promote the role of the Bible instructor attached to an evangelistic team or on the staff of a local conference gave emphasis to individual and family Bible studies.[77]

The new teaching program for evangelism demanded textbooks. The first were duplicated manuals prepared by Ford, Shuler, and Fordyce Detamore. A work by Carlyle B. Haynes appeared in 1937 under the title *Living Evangelism;* and Shuler's *Public Evangelism* (1939) became a standard text for ministerial students in Adventist colleges. A field school of evangelism conducted by Anderson in Cleveland in 1943 pointed up a need for the compilation of statements on the subject from the works of Ellen White; the result was the publication in 1946 of *Evangelism*, a book destined to serve as the standard reference on the philosophy of Adventist evangelism. The next of the books on the subject, Anderson's *The Shepherd-Evangelist* (1950), dealt with the total commitment of the church at large, with the pastor of a congregation in the role of evangelist.

Evangelism entered a new field in the 1950s. In contrast to their initial response to radio, Adventists were quick to see the advantages of the television medium with the coming of home TV sets. In fact, the church was the first to go on network television.[78] Julius L. Tucker, Raymond H. Libby, and William A. Fagal were among the first to experiment in this field. In 1950, Fagal began a weekly telecast in New York City called "Faith For Today." At the autumn council that year, church representatives approved a budget to put "Faith For Today" on two networks in 1951, one in the East under the direction of Fagal, another in the West under Richards.[79] Excessive costs, however, led to the discontinuation of the program in the West, leaving Fagal to carry "Faith For Today" from the East, distributing to network stations by means of kinescopes.

About this time—and with the support of two successive General Conference presidents—Vandeman had on his drawing board an ambitious plan for a forceful television evangelistic campaign: it would combine a build-up by mass media with house-to-house calls, followed by house-to-house personal instruction. Just as Vandeman was ready to go, however, the General Conference Radio-Television Department secretary persuaded the officers to support "Faith For Today."[80] Vandeman was then invited to England, where he conducted public evangelism in large theaters with great success. He returned to the United States in 1954 to resume work on his pilot films and a program designed to coordinate television and "fine-tooth" evangelism. The initial run of what was to become the "It is Written" program began in Fresno, California, in 1958 with the encouragement and support of Morris L. Venden, president of the

Central California Conference. Mary Walsh, Bible instructor, co-ordinated the house-to-house follow-up by laypeople.[81]

Another approach got started when the 1947 autumn council of General Conference representatives adopted a resolution calling for permanent evangelistic centers.[82] Trial runs were made in 1950 and 1951 by Robert M. Whitsett in Chicago's Lyric Theater, by Anderson in New York's Carnegie Hall, and by Vandeman in London's Coliseum Theatre. By this time the General Conference leaders were insisting that the evangelists identify themselves as Seventh-day Adventists, which the major evangelists were already doing.[83] On the strength of these pilot programs, the General Conference officially appropriated funds to assist the Northern European Division and the Greater New York Conference to develop permanent evangelistic centers. They acquired the famous and well-located New Gallery Theatre, on Regent Street just off Picadilly Circus in London, for this purpose. The New York center was developed from a remodeled hotel on West Forty-sixth Street, near Times Square in the heart of the theater district. Although the principal thrust in these centers was evangelism, ancillary activities included counseling, concerts, lectures, nutrition "schools," and the provision of reading and prayer rooms. These New York and London projects provided the basic design for permanent centers in other parts of the world.

As the Adventist evangelists became aware of their church's better public image, and as experience gave them confidence in the support of church members in general, they tended to change over from the conventional three-to-six-month campaigns to short, intensive series of about three weeks. This has been called the most significant Adventist innovation in evangelism of the mid-century.[84] Veteran evangelist Fordyce Detamore, more than any other, was the father of the short campaign. He hit upon it by accident in 1952 in Indonesia, where he had been invited with singing assistant Ray Turner to conduct evangelistic training institutes for the nationals. He was very successful in reclaiming former Adventist communicants and converting Bible correspondence school "graduates." Imported to North America, the short campaign proved equally successful. It had timely advantages that could be used by the local pastor, supported by his congregation. It was aimed generally at people who had already been partially informed and were already favorably impressed by other means. It was useful in pressing for commitment to Christ in the manner of the traditional revival. And it lent itself well to "harvesting" those whose interest had been awakened by Adventist programs on radio and television or by printed matter that colporteurs disseminated. "The coordinate use of mass media, laymen's action, and short series of public or semipublic decision meetings," writes Howard B. Weeks, "seemed to the younger generation of Adventist evangelists in the 1960s to be the wave of the future."[85]

THE HEALTH MINISTRY

Seventh-day Adventist evangelism also increasingly emphasized healthful living. Very early in Adventist history, Ellen White had affirmed the inseparability of the gospel and the health ministry, citing Christ's example. Pioneers such as Drs. David Paulson, John Harvey Kellogg, Daniel H. Kress, and Lauretta E. Kress sought working formulas for what Cotton Mather had called the "Angelic Conjunction"—which Adventists came to call the "double ministry." The search for methodology was continued in the 1920s by physicians Archie W. Truman, Julia A. White, and Mary Cornell McReynolds, and clergyman John H. N. Tindall. For many years, extending into the 1930s, Tindall conducted a medical evangelism field school at which ministers, physicians, and nurses took courses in gospel preaching for large audiences and in ancillary teaching of nutrition, cookery, physiology, and simple treatments, within the concept of a whole gospel for the whole person.[86]

A public service emphasis in medical ministry was initiated in the 1950s by Clifford R. Anderson in "Your Radio Doctor," which was identified as a Seventh-day Adventist program. This series of health topics was released on tape in many countries of the world and was an effective instrument for creating good will for the church among government officials and leaders of other faiths.[87] Medical evangelism was used effectively on the Atlantic seaboard in 1962 in a series of congregational revivals under the direction of Willis J. Hackett, president of the Atlantic Union Conference, with Dr. J. Wayne McFarland. In the same year Elman J. Folkenberg joined McFarland and Dr. and Mrs. Henry W. Vollmer in medical evangelism in a new design. It was this team that developed the techniques that later became known as the "Five-day Plan to Stop Smoking." The plan was reported at a ministerial institute preceding the General Conference session of 1962.[88]

The evangelistic thrust of the Seventh-day Adventist Church in the so-called undeveloped lands had many of the same characteristics as that in the United States, perhaps with greater emphasis on healthful living, sanitation, nutrition, and medicine as components secondary to, but intermingled with, gospel preaching. Gone were the days of the helmeted "bush missionary" or the missionary doctor making do with primitive facilities. The mission launch had replaced the canoe, the airplane the mule, and the well-appointed hospital and clinic the itinerant black bag. Moreover, mission service ceased to be mainly the responsibility of the white North American. Australia and New Zealand supplied missionaries for the islands of the Pacific, and Europe for Africa. Having learned a hard lesson from the experience of the church in Asia, the General Conference increasingly prepared nationals and advanced them to positions of responsibility in their own lands and some to the top levels of the hierarchy of the church. The role of the "foreigner" was becoming that of counselor rather than administrator.

The American black Adventist community, seeking a mission outlet, found Liberia (West Africa) a suitable location for evangelism because of the country's Afro-American historical background. In 1945, pioneers G. Nathaniel Banks, C. D. Henri, and Philip Giddings, Jr., went to Liberia with their families.[89] They were received well and succeeded as evangelists and educators. Banks, the president of the mission, gave Bible instruction in the official Liberian presidential residence to William V. S. Tubman, the president of the republic, at the latter's request.[90] In contrast, when the suggestion was first made to introduce black American evangelists in Ghana (then the Gold Coast), the Ashanti Adventist leaders demurred. The Ashanti remembered that their ancestors had captured members of weaker neighboring tribes to sell on the coast as slaves for American plantations—and that these slaves were the ancestors of the evangelists the Ashanti were now being asked to accept as their leaders. This reversal of role seemed unacceptable.[91] Time and diplomacy have tended to alter such attitudes, and some North American black evangelists have had marked success in black Africa.

The medical missionary program of the church was profoundly influenced by postwar trends in the developing countries. The missionary with a smattering of medical knowledge was replaced by the white-coated specialist practicing in a modern, well-equipped hospital much as he would back home. But there were danger signs ahead. It was increasingly difficult to finance the operation from the small fees the nationals were able to pay, particularly in locations where the mission hospital had to compete with subsidized government hospitals staffed by national doctors with expertise approaching or equaling that of the foreign missionary doctor. Sometimes nationalization took place; but with the loss of church control went the Adventist missionary character of the hospital. If the church wished to continue its medical mission, it would have to develop resourceful ideas.

Leo B. Halliwell began a medical river launch ministry in the Amazon Basin between 1929 and 1931. By 1956 the first of the *Luceiro* fleet had grown to five power boats. Halliwell was named fleet commander and his base of operation moved to Rio de Janeiro. By 1960 there were nine medical launches in Brazil, and the same kind of service was spreading to other parts of the world. Leo and Jessie Halliwell, honored and assisted by the grateful Brazilian government, were acclaimed as the couple who had brought physical healing and spiritual light to thousands of river people and had given structure and meaning to a new kind of medical missionary program.[92] Near Campo Grande, Mato Grosso, Brazil, Adventist medical scientists established an experimental clinic for the treatment of the dreaded tropical disease *penfigo* (or "savage fire") in the 1950s. Within a few years the staff was able to report 40 percent cure and a good record of arrest of the otherwise generally fatal disease.[93]

A health evangelism committee of the College of Medical Evangelists in California—soon to be Loma Linda University—in 1958 initiated college-sponsored field trips for medical evangelism and health education. The first of these summer trips was to the state of Chiapas in southern Mexico. Faculty members and students of medicine, dentistry, nursing, dietetics, and physical therapy participated under the direction of Howard L. Marin of the prosthodontics department faculty of the School of Dentistry.[94] Other field trips followed to Chiapas, as well as to Navojoa in Mexico, and to Adventist hospitals in InterAmerica, where the School of Medicine conducted externships for its students under the direction of then Associate Dean John E. Peterson. This was the first exposure for many of the participants to people of cultures not their own, their first view of the great need among underprivileged nationals of other countries, and their first attempt to communicate and render service.

Still another 1958 development was the inauguration of a "research and assistance program" of the School of Tropical and Preventive Medicine (forerunner of the School of Health)—also part of the coming Loma Linda University—after a comprehensive 1957 survey of the Waha tribe of Tanganyika (later Tanzania). The program was put together by Drs. Harold N. Mozar (physician) and Saleem A. Farag (health educator), with assistance from staff member Karl C. Fischer (builder and sanitarian), who was in charge of construction. Under the direction of the Loma Linda representatives, selected Adventist nationals (most of them destined to enter the ministry) built a model sanitary village at the Heri Mission Hospital, where they would live for one year while taking instruction and training in healthful living, sanitation, and diet; in the growing of good crops suitable to the region for adequate nutrition; and in a range of subject matter that would enable them to work as quasi health educators under the supervision of a physician or the district medical officer. After a few annual rotations of national trainees, the program was to become self-sustaining and to be supported by the local mission organization rather than the American group.[95] A somewhat similar program was subsequently developed by Farag in New Guinea.

The observance of the seventh-day Sabbath made it difficult for Adventist young people in some countries to obtain higher education for the professions. This was particularly troublesome in countries where national physicians were few in number and the need was great. A pilot effort to solve this problem was the 1945 affiliation of the Seventh-day Adventist Church with the Christian Medical College in Vellore, South India, an interdenominational school founded by Ida Scudder, the widely known missionary physician. The church contracted to give financial assistance and to help supply capable medical teaching staff to augment the existing faculty. In return, qualified Adventist students would be allowed to take medical education there without embarassment concerning their Sabbath.[96]

SUBSTANTIAL GROWTH

The combination of internal growth factors with the international evangelistic thrust by clergymen and lay members resulted in a substantial growth in the membership of the church during the three decades between 1930 and 1960. Baptized communicants in the United States increased from 120,560 to 332,364, and in the rest of the world from 193,693 to 921,761; proportionately, the "foreign" communicants increased from 62 percent of the total to 74 percent.[97] As this trend has continued, questions have been raised regarding the proportion of foreign representation at the worldwide administrative level. Ordained clergy serving the international church numbered 2,062 in 1930 and 6,515 in 1960.[98]

During this same period, the publishing houses of the church performed a major role in supporting this growth by providing textbooks for Adventist schools, books for Adventist homes, and materials for dissemination by Adventist lay evangelists. Book and periodical sales reflected the increased activity of the "literature evangelist," or colporteur. In 1930 book sales by North American

Adventist publishing houses totaled 1,291,815 units, and 1,450,341 from publishing houses in other lands; in 1960 the corresponding figures were 9,880,305 and 5,107,634.[99] Periodicals sold around the world totaled 1,973,552 units in 1930 and 8,555,193 in 1960.[100] The total value of sales was $4,715,709 in 1930 and $23,543,132 in 1960.[101]

EDUCATION

As evangelism and the health ministry became broader in concept and more professional and specialized in conduct, the Seventh-day Adventist Church also expanded its educational program on all fronts. On the college and graduate levels, the increase was 400 percent; on the secondary level 442 percent; and on the elementary and intermediate level 1,987 percent.[102] Among the significant achievements of this period were the accreditation of the North American colleges and secondary schools, the establishment of a theological seminary, and the emergence of two universities. In 1929 church leaders decided to establish a Seventh-day Adventist accrediting agency in order to ensure the continuation of the Adventist concept of Christian education. The formation of the Association of Seventh-day Adventist Colleges and Secondary Schools that ensued was modeled after existing regional associations: membership in it was to be by the accreditation of that association's board of regents.[103] It was quickly obvious to those responsible for medical and premedical education that this plan would not work for special purpose education and that regional and professional accreditation would have to be sought.

After much debate, General Conference representatives at the 1931 autumn council voted to permit the four-year colleges to seek secular accreditation as a temporary measure until the Adventist board of regents could become established as an accrediting agency.[104] In this initial group were Emmanuel Missionary College (Michigan), Pacific Union College (California), Union College (Nebraska), Washington Missionary College (Maryland—later Columbia Union College), and Walla Walla College (Washington), plus three junior colleges: Canadian Junior College (Alberta—later Canadian Union College), Southern Junior College (Tennessee—later Southern Missionary College), and Atlantic Union College (Massachusetts—at that time reduced temporarily from senior to junior status). The Adventist church leaders indicated their misgivings by the additional actions they took at the same meeting in 1931. They advised colleges to give hiring preference to selected teachers authorized by their respective institutional trustees to attend universities in pursuit of advanced degrees. College catalogues or bulletins were not to show the academic degrees held by faculty members, and teachers who had achieved doctoral status were not to be addressed as "Doctor."[105] Brave indeed were the teachers who earned doctoral degrees in those days in the face of the uneasy and chilly attitudes of some church leaders who feared the rise of an intellectual elite in the church.

Pacific Union College was the first to achieve accreditation from the Adventist board of regents (1932) and likewise from the regional Northwest Association of Secondary and Higher Schools (1933), thus becoming the first Adventist college to be granted regional accreditation.[106] Approval of Adventist colleges and secondary schools by secular agencies, however, became a permanent necessity, mainly because the medical school, to keep its accreditation, could not accept graduates of unaccredited institutions. Regional agencies actually judged the institutions of the church in terms of the stated objectives: they were tough only in the areas of competent teaching, adequate equipment, sound financing, and efficient administration. Thus, in the accreditation process, Adventism's advanced schools were raised from the uneasy status of Bible colleges, serving a narrow clientele, to multitrack institutions of learning from which many thousands were graduated each year for a growing diversity of occupations, vocations, and professions. If this created an "elite," then the church benefited. A mid-century survey showed that Adventists in the United States surpassed the general population in percentage of college graduates by three to one.[107]

Similar directions developed in the Adventist training schools in other lands, especially in the more advanced countries, where status recognition was based on the ability of the schools to produce graduates capable of passing state-approved external examinations. In some countries it was possible for the advanced schools of the church to offer degree programs in their own right. In others, notably the British Commonwealth nations, they found it advantageous to work through affiliations. The first such affiliation was arranged between the Australasian Missionary College (now Avondale College in New South Wales), and Pacific Union College. The agreement permitted graduates from the Australasian college to obtain degrees conferred by Pacific Union College in education and in ministerial training. With the acceptance of the plan by the trustees of the Australasian college and the endorsement by those of Pacific Union College in the spring of 1953, the affiliation became effective in Australia for the 1954 school year. The understanding was that it was a temporary measure until Avondale could secure its own national accreditation. [108] This arrangement was the prototype for later similar affiliations. One began in 1955– 56 between Newbold College (England) and Washington Missionary College (later Columbia Union College in Maryland), and another was made between Middle East College (Lebanon) and Loma Linda University beginning in 1965. [109]

Another area of educational concern was the Adventist ministry. The Seventh-day Adventist Church required a number of years to develop its own theological seminary. Initially, conference officials were not easily convinced that lengthening the training period for young pulpit ministers was worthwhile. There was also some misgiving that exposure to theological studies might produce more theologians than pastors and evangelists. Added to these reservations was the concern that a shift from biblical to systematic theology would have a liberalizing influence on Adventist religion teachers, as it had in many leading seminaries and divinity schools. Conservative Evangelicals saw this influence as a mortal danger. Even stronger than these apprehensions, however, was the need for the colleges of the church to have professionally prepared theologians and teachers of religion who would be just as academically qualified as faculty members in the arts and sciences were required to be in their respective fields — under the standards of accreditation.

The seeds of a seminary were sown in summer Bible schools conducted for ministers and publishing house editors in the early 1930s at Pacific Union College, with Milton E. Kern as dean. [110] In 1936 church leaders decided that advanced Bible studies could best be pursued in a separate institution and that such instruction should be under the direct scrutiny of the General Conference rather than that of the union conference, as it is the case in the regionally supported and controlled Adventist colleges. Accordingly, the Seventh-day Adventist Theological Seminary opened in Washington, D.C., in 1937, with Kern as the first president. A bachelor of divinity degree was announced in 1945, and the first master of theology degree was conferred in 1959. [111]

In 1956, when Ernest D. Dick was president of the seminary, the General Conference autumn council voted to add a school of graduate studies; this combination with the seminary was to be called Potomac University and was to be affiliated with Washington Missionary College. [112] But the plan did not materialize. No adequate campus site was found. In addition, complications in administration could be expected to develop, because the college would be governed by the Columbia Union Conference, but Potomac University would be governed by the General Conference. Two years later, the General

Conference delegates voted at the autumn council to move the seminary and graduate school to Berrien Springs, Michigan, and affiliate them with Emmanuel Missionary College. The move was completed in 1960, and in that year the entire complex became Andrews University and was placed under General Conference control and support, with Floyd O. Rittenhouse as president.[113].

The second Seventh-day Adventist university came into being in California on July 1, 1961, when the College of Medical Evangelists was legally renamed Loma Linda University. In some part, this change came as a natural result of the postwar upgrading of professional curricula of the complex of schools constituting the college on its two campuses at Loma Linda and Los Angeles. Although instruction had begun primarily in nursing (1905) and medicine (1909), with particular emphasis on an evangelical purpose, other allied health curricula had emerged periodically in the institution from 1922 on into the 1950s. By the 1940s and 1950s, these had become primarily baccalaureate degree programs (instead of the shorter certificate programs begun earlier) that increasingly called for general undergraduate arts and science courses and environment. The establishment of the dental school in 1953, plus the surge of demand for postdoctoral courses in medicine and for graduate-level programs in the basic sciences, indicated the need for an institutional name commensurate with the scope and quality of offerings that existed and were developing.[114]

A church-appointed committee on graduate work in the West had laid the groundwork in 1959 for the involvement of the three California Adventist colleges — Pacific Union, La Sierra, and CME — in a composite graduate program to be part of the university. Godfrey T. Anderson, the president of the College of Medical Evangelists from 1954 on, was named president of Loma Linda University.[115] By the time of the presentation of the first diplomas under the name of Loma Linda University in June 1962, however, it was clear that Pacific Union College would not be a partner in the cooperative graduate program. Thus La Sierra College and Loma Linda University were left to continue the dialogue.

The accrediting agency, the Western Association of Schools and Colleges, indicated that the university might risk the loss of its *general* accreditation unless it provided an undergraduate liberal arts base — which its administration had, in fact, proposed and endeavored to do, but without success in convincing the trustees. Sentiment generated within the faculty at La Sierra College (the Adventist liberal arts institution twenty miles from Loma Linda on the west edge of Riverside) meanwhile favored becoming part of the university system. The combination of these factors thus paved the way for a decision based on a proposal by a General Conference commission on unification presented on March 30, 1967: in quick succession, the General Conference officers, plus the faculty, trustees, and constituency of La Sierra College and the trustees and constituency of Loma Linda University (its faculty having dissented) approved the joining of the two institutions to constitute Loma Linda University.[116] Since Anderson had tendered his resignation, the university trustees named David J. Bieber, then the head of La Sierra College, university president. Thus the church found itself responsible for nurturing two infant universities—Andrews and Loma Linda—to respectable maturity.

Even before the question of a western Adventist university was being seriously considered throughout the 1950s, however, another longstanding problem was being debated—a problem regarded by some as more fateful than the later question: the location of Loma Linda University. Although this question involved all the institutional programs except those of the school of dentistry, the focus of conflict was the school of medicine. Should it all be at Loma Linda? Or should it all be at Los Angeles, where the White Memorial Hospital and Clinic had been developed? Or should it be continued as it was, part on each campus? Dialogue on the matter went on for some years, with a great deal of "solid" logic on all sides. But there was at work pervasive and persevering conviction that divine guidance had led to the founding of the institution at Loma Linda, with specific aims and characteristics and an indicated location, and that the quality of the educational programs would be immeasurably enhanced by centralization.

The phenomenal growth of population in the inland valley and the success of the school of dentistry in attracting clinic patients from the Loma Linda environs were strong factors in support of the conviction favoring Loma Linda. The decision to consolidate the school of medicine there was reached by the trustees in September 1962, and the process of transfer continued into the sixties as the school prepared adequate clinical facilities there.[117] In the new design, the White Memorial Hospital was initially to provide postdoctoral education in medicine. Lest this distinguished medical center become a "stepchild" of Loma Linda, as some feared, provision was made for "the White" to come under the control of the Southern California Conference of Seventh-day Adventists, the changeover to be effective in January 1964.[118]

In addition to expanding its higher education programs, the denomination also supported its growing elementary and secondary schools by producing English-language textbooks. The usual pattern was the preparation of text material by a group, then editing for publication, and, generally, production by the denominational publishing houses. Of timely significance was the application of new expertise in grading vocabulary and subject matter to the capacity and interest of school age groups, and the inclusion of multiethnic elements in the story materials. A notable departure from this pattern took place when a secular publishing house known for specialization in textbooks collaborated with the General Conference education department. This arrangement produced a series of basic readers in which story material provided by Adventist educators was prepared for publication by specialists on the staff of Scott, Foresman and Company.[119]

MEDICAL INSTITUTIONS

Alongside education, medical institutions absorbed much of the denomination's resources. Changes in the contemporary delivery of health care placed pressures on these institutions that resulted in Adventists' reexamining their practices and goals. The denomination redefined its role in community health care and in preventive medicine and dentistry, and it took its place among the agencies to which people and governments look for health services and education. It also defined the role of the medical chaplain and set up chaplaincy training programs in the medical institutions of the church.

In 1930, Seventh-day Adventists operated 41 sanitariums and hospitals, 24 of them outside the United States and Canada. In addition, internationally there were 35 privately owned but church-affiliated sanitariums, treatment centers, dispensaries, nursing homes, and the like.[120] By 1960 there were 29 sanitariums and hospitals in the United States and Canada, and 82 in the rest of the world that were owned and operated by the church. Independent but church-related institutions had grown in number to 113 dispensaries and clinics and 23 convalescent homes, retirement centers, and orphanages.[121] Behind these figures is a story of resourcefulness and adaptation.

A council of Adventist institutional medical personnel met in 1940 and gave its attention to the expanding health services of the church. Agenda topics included continuing emphasis on the "sanitarium" concept, responsibility of the Adventist medical institution relative to the health of the community, professional training for administrators, and reexamination and redefinition of the role of the medical chaplain. The council recommended that every church conference, local or regional, designate a conference representative (preferably a salaried physician or nurse), and that the medical institutions discontinue the institutional salaried-surgeon system then in use and substitute instead the direct surgeon-patient relationship (with direct billing by the surgeon for professional services) as endorsed by the American College of Surgeons.[122]

At the 1941 autumn council, church leaders accepted the first of these recommendations and referred the second to the respective governing bodies of the various medical institutions for local decision. Most of these institutions in the United States soon found themselves with the entire physician staff engaged in private practice *within* the institution. A further recommendation of the 1941 council was that all ministers and conference officers become informed supporters of the health programs of the church and that the seminary add courses to prepare ministerial trainees in methods of presenting health principles to the public.[123]

In 1949 medical personnel of the church met again, this time chiefly physicians. Discussion topics included the goals of a sanitarium as distinct from those of a hospital; the Adventist medical institution as a spiritual force in the community; the role of medical institutions in improving dietary practices and discouraging harmful habits such as alcohol and tobacco use; the separation of administering medical and business affairs in the institution; the inclusion of medical staff representation on the governing board; and the renewal of emphasis on physical medicine "to regain leadership in our greatest medical heritage—physical therapy."[124] The agenda of the medical councils of 1940 and 1949 were significant straws in the wind.

In a memorable defense of the sanitarium idea, Francis D. Nichol, then editor of the *Review*, identified for the 1949 medical council three major characteristics of the traditional Adventist sanitarium:

> Viewed . . . medically, they are places where a primary emphasis is placed on three therapeutic procedures—mental hygiene, physical medicine, and diet therapy. Viewed educationally, they are places where an earnest endeavor is made, not simply to cure the immediate malady, but to instruct the patient in basic principles of health, and if possible, to generate in his mind an enthusiasm to carry out these principles in his future living. Viewed spiritually, they are places where these health principles are presented in a religious setting, with the hope of furnishing the patient a spiritual incentive to live in harmony with physical laws, and to find release from the tensions of life in a fellowship with God.[125]

This concept fit neatly into the Adventist emphasis on addressing the totality of the human being. But it did not fit as easily into the emerging view of medical theory and practice in which physicians would be more preoccupied with the disease than concerned about the person who had it. Science and technology had made diagnosis impressively swift and accurate, and antibiotics and chemotherapy had begun to revolutionize the treatment of disease. The public, influenced by the literature of popular medicine and the "doctor" serials on radio and television, had developed a childlike confidence in the physician. Aesculapius was a demigod once again. People confidently went to the hospital, no longer to die, but to get a new lease on life—quickly, if possible. The patient could not stay long in the hospital. It was too expensive, even with insurance, and often there was a waiting list for the bed. Even the person who could afford to stay was pushed out so that the bed could be readied for the more acute, waiting patient. And even if the hospital was willing to let the patient stay, those paying the bills wanted him out as soon as he could safely be released. This was not the kind of society in which sanitariums flourish.

At least three internal factors tended to move the church's emphasis from the sanitarium to the hospital. The increasing difficulty of satisfying insurance requirements in a sanitarium, in comparison to a hospital with its beds for the acutely ill, gave encouragement to change the name and orientation of medical institutions. The increased size of health institutions, for reasons of operational economy, often made community support necessary, tending to diminish staff selection—indeed, tending to bring about open staffing and the resulting dilution of Christian atmosphere and influence. Loss of the preponderance of Adventist influence accelerated the change from the salaried staff to the private practice group in the hospital, which, in turn, also tended to weaken the ties of the medical staff to the church and thus weaken the identification of the hospital with the church.

Although much was lost with the passing of the sanitarium, it should be pointed out that nothing in the delivery of health care in modern Adventist hospitals rules out the possibility of the free opportunity for the Christian professional to witness for Christ or to help the patient sense his need for a different lifestyle, supported by a personal Savior. However, the witnessing Christian staff member, given a shorter exposure time, must make better use of his or her opportunities than was necessary in the sanitarium's relaxed and extended exposure of patient to staff. In this context the emerging professionally trained medical chaplain plays a vital role.

Professional pastoral care of the sick emerged in the 1930s. Pioneers were Richard C. Cabot, a medical professor at Harvard Medical School; Anton T. Boisen, a Protestant clergyman; A. Philip Guiles, professor of pastoral care at Andover-Newton Theological Center; and Russell L. Dicks, coauthor with Dr. Cabot of *The Art of Ministering to the Sick*, published in 1936.[126] Adventists were quick to see the advantages of professional chaplain service in their medical institutions and to set up training programs of their own. The professional chaplain moved among the patients as a man of the cloth, accepting referrals from staff members to those who were troubled. He cultivated the art of listening in order to discover the problems that preyed on a patient's mind and delayed his recovery until they were resolved. Where there was patient interest, the chaplain could arrange for ongoing counseling or Bible study in the individual's home. In short, in the context of the hospital, the professional medical chaplain could be a supportive Christian friend and a spiritual counselor.[127]

The Adventist interest in preventing disease through healthful living also expressed itself in increased temperance activity. Adventists established the American Temperance Society in 1932 in an effort to help save the Eighteenth Amendment. Though this effort proved of no avail, the interest of the church had been rewakened; and the 1947 autumn council recommended the organizing of both international and national temperance societies.[128] In this setting, William A. Scharffenberg, an Adventist clergyman, Winton H. Beaven, an Adventist educator, and others—with the blessing of the church—set up a nonsectarian educational organization called the International Commission for the Prevention of Alcoholism. This 1950 corporation, independent of the church in management and financial support, was administered by officers elected by its international membership. The commission, in turn, set up a plan for national committees in 1954. The National Committee for the Prevention of Alcoholism in the United States, the first to be organized, served as a prototype.

Members of the U.S. commission included scientists, educators, statesmen, judges, editors, temperance leaders from other organizations, representatives from medicine and public health, and clergymen representing five denominations. The plan was for each national commission to be an affiliate of its parent international commission. Each national commission, within its own territory, was expected to conduct periodic institutes of scientific studies to which scientists and public officials would be invited as participants and observers.[129] The International Commission for the Prevention of Alcoholism and its affiliates had remarkable success, throughout many countries of the world for a time, in supporting abstinence from the use of alcoholic beverages and of temperance in lifestyle.

WORLD RELIEF

The development of a humane conscience about and concern for the victims of natural disasters wherever they occur (whether from earthquake, drought, or flood), and the will to relieve the suffering of people in the slums and ghettos of our urbanized society, has been called the most significant social movement of modern times.[130] Many of these disaster relief and public health programs got under-way around mid-century. The Seventh-day Adventist Church readily relates to programs of this sort. An example is SAWS (Seventh-day Adventist World Service, incorporated in 1956), which works with AID (the U.S. Agency for International Development) and with the International Red Cross. Begun in the North American division and then diffused to other parts of the world, SAWS now dispatches Adventist community service trucks to disaster areas, and they are among the first to arrive wherever victims need food, warm clothing, or medical attention. Inner-city programs operate in urban centers where health education, family counseling, and medical services are needed. Family health care workers screen public school children to discover what they may need in medical or dental services or in education. Students from Adventist colleges and professional schools — especially attracted to service of this sort — sometimes help train local people to carry on when professional services are discontinued.

Toward the end of the 1950s the seers of medicine were point-ing out that ecology is more than a way of looking at the physical environment — that, indeed, it includes a philosophy of medical practice.[131] In the years ahead, they tell us, lies an era in which medical attention and practice will encompass the whole patient and his community rather than merely a disease entity. They point out that, in historical perspective, by our concentration on disease we have tended to create new diseases. They would have us correct this trend by giving more attention to the person who has not yet reached the sickbed — so that, insofar as it is possible, we may keep him out of it! This is precisely the insight that the Seventh-day Adventist Church has had and promoted for a century as part of its historical legacy, a legacy to which it has given a degree of good stewardship.

* * *

As the 1950s ended it was evident that Seventh-day Adventism had reached its maturity. Although changes would certainly continue to take place, the experiences of the Depression, World War II, and postwar reconstruction had tested its organization and found it both flexible and strong and had significantly broadened the denomination's concept of mission. Sectarian though it still might be, Seventh-day Adventism was now willing to participate with secular organizations in such things as disaster relief, and through its dialogues with Evangelical leaders, it moved somewhat closer to mainstream conservative theology. At the same time that it had begun to participate more fully in the larger society, Adventism reflected trends in that society in its efforts to develop more professional personnel and to emphasize specialization in its varied activities. External pressures brought about many of these changes, but the denomination as a whole benefited and was thereby better able to face the rapidly changing world of the following decades.

7 | Coping with Change 1961–1980

GARY LAND

Seventh-day Adventism came out of the immediate postwar years in a strong condition. With a growing membership, theological unity, and a good financial base, it looked forward to "finishing the work" in the near future. But as with other institutions, religious and secular, it discovered an increasingly complicated and tumultuous world in the 1960s and 1970s. In its American homeland the denomination faced secularization, social unrest, the decline of traditional values, and inflation; abroad it had to deal with nationalism, the relative decline of American prestige and power, and—for a time— the fast sinking value of the dollar. These were problems that required creative thinking that could see where new ideas and flexibility were needed and when the church had to uphold traditional views and practices. As Seventh-day Adventism entered the 1980s, it was faced with the dilemma of maintaining and reinforcing its sectarian tradition or moving toward accommodation with other denominations and society at large. The former could mean increasing isolation from American society, while the latter could possibly mean a loss of identity.

CHURCH GROWTH

A major element working for both strength and change in the church during these years was its growth. Worldwide Seventh-day Adventists were growing in the 1960s and 1970s at an annual rate of 5.5 to 6.5 percent. As early as the 1920s, however, it had become clear that the rate of growth on the continents of Africa, Asia, and Latin America, and in the islands of the Pacific was outstripping that of the United States, Europe, and Australia—New Zealand. As the years passed, that trend accelerated, so that after 1960, in the words of Gottfried Oosterwal, "a shift of gravity" occurred. As the 1980s began, 76 percent of the 3.5 million Adventists lived in the Third World, whereas North America had only 16 percent, Europe 6 percent, and Australia–New Zealand 1 percent. This shift held tremendous potential for changing the denomination, for as Oosterwal writes, "It is also a shift from an older to a younger church; from a tradition-clergy-oriented denomination to a dynamic, lay-centered missionary movement, from a 'second generation' church to a first generation church."[1]

As the foregoing figures imply, the church was growing slowly in the United States in recent years, about 2 to 3 percent annually. The real growth rate was probably smaller, for one study indicates that much of the growth has come from black churches, where there has been more turnover in active members that is not reflected statistically. Geographically, the denomination found—as it had in the past—that its fastest growth took place in areas with mobile populations, particularly the Northwest, West, and Southeast.[2]

In these growth trends Seventh-day Adventism was following much the same pattern as have other small, conservative sects. Mormons, Jehovah's Witnesses, and Pentecostals all have grown much more slowly in the United States than they have abroad, especially in the Third World. Slow as its growth in America might be, however, Adventism was growing—in contrast to the more liberal mainline denominations, which were experiencing declining membership.[3] But slow growth instead of decline was of small comfort to Seventh-day Adventists, who were finding it increasingly difficult to address the secularized West. As Sydney Ahlstrom has said regarding the so-called third force in American Protestantism, "Conservatism in politics and their immense emphasis in foreign missions reflect their alienation from the domestic American scene."[4]

The shift of gravity to the Third World has had a significant impact on the church. Under the leadership of Russell Staples and anthropologist Gottfried Oosterwal, the Department of World Mission at Andrews University developed a Mission Institute, which began in 1966 and took place periodically for missionaries leaving the United States for work abroad. These institutes sought to better prepare missionaries to cope with a different culture and understand the task of an American missionary in a world no longer dominated by the West.[5] But the ratio of American missionaries to those from elsewhere changed. By 1980 nearly half of the denomination's missionaries came from the Third World.[6]

The changing population base also forced the church to take

nationalistic impulses more seriously. Increasingly, the church put national leaders in administrative positions on the mission, union, and division levels. It also made efforts to involve division leaders more directly in the General Conference decision-making process by including them in the annual councils. But the patterns and traditions of the past were hard to break: Seventh-day Adventism was still largely operated by Americans and according to the American perspective. Criticizing this process, Oosterwal writes: "We need to find a way whereby the sorely needed information, wisdom, spirituality and viewpoints from the churches in the Third World can become an integral part of the process of planning and decision making for the whole church based on equality, interdependence, and mutual support."[7]

The role of the North American church was also changing because of economic factors. Although Americans continued to increase their giving for missions, the increase lagged behind the inflation rate and dropped in relationship to the tithe. In short, American Adventists were giving a declining percentage of their total income for missions.[8] The financing of missions was further complicated when the United States devalued the dollar in 1971. As a result, the divisions outside North America had to cut their budgets, and the number of missionaries supported by American dollars was reduced. Although a special offering in 1973 made up about one-half of the currency adjustment, the continuing instability of the dollar was in the long term reducing American influence within the denomination.[9] This trend was perhaps one reason why denominational leaders, fearing that Adventism might split into independent geographical and ethnic churches, became increasingly concerned with unity. Although a Commission on Church Unity was established in 1977, the problem was a continuing one with no easy solution. With America losing its role as a cohesive force, denominational leaders believed that they had to find new ways to keep Adventism's worldwide work bound into a single whole.[10]

CHANGING TIMES

A rapidly changing society also buffeted the church within the United States. Although articles in and letters to the *Review and Herald* indicated a negative reaction to such superficial symbols of cultural change as beards and long hair for men, dress styles, and rock music, the denomination had to respond organizationally to some major social forces. The developing youth culture of the 1960s required relatively little action from the denomination. A significant change from previous policy occurred, however, in response to the requests of Adventist young men for church support in acquiring the 1-0 draft classification, which would allow them to perform a civilian alternative to military service. Traditionally, the church had advised its draft-age men to seek the noncombatant 1-A-0 classification, but the opposition to the Vietnam War among the youth often made any kind of military service unacceptable to them. After considerable discussion, the 1969 autumn council, although continuing to advise the 1-A-0 classification, indicated it would help those whose sincerity was unquestionable to obtain the 1-0 status.[11] About the same time, the denomination came under considerable criticism for co-operating with the army in Project Whitecoat, a program that tested defenses against biological warfare using Adventist noncombatant servicemen.[12]

The effects of the youth culture also appeared in the decision to discontinue the denomination's magazine *The Youth's Instructor* and replace it with *Insight*, a publication more contemporary in style.[13] Because local churches purchased most copies of this magazine for distribution through the Sabbath school, the new publication—though popular with youth—encountered considerable opposition and in time was forced to become more conservative both in appearance and content. Meanwhile, the "Voice of Prophecy" began its "Wayout" evangelistic program, a series of youth-oriented publications advertised through short commercials on rock radio stations.[14] Despite the denomination's strong cultural conservatism, these two efforts indicated that some of its leaders realized that flexibility was required if the church was to keep its own youth and attract young converts.

The emergence of the Association of Adventist Forums was also partially related to the growing activism among young people. As increasing numbers of Seventh-day Adventists began to attend non-Adventist graduate schools, they expressed concern that the church was not meeting their intellectual, spiritual, and social needs. Under the leadership of Roy Branson, a student at Harvard University, and with the help of denominational leaders Reinhold R. Bietz and Neal Wilson, the Association of Adventist Forums was established in 1967 and two years later began producing a quarterly journal called *Spectrum*. The association soon ran into conflict with the church—from which it was organizationally independent—over articles appearing in *Spectrum*, and it experienced tension within its own ranks between those who wanted it to focus on intellectual concerns and those who saw it as a medium to generate broad-based lay activism within the church. By the late 1970s the Association of

Adventist Forums was concentrating on *Spectrum* and the sponsorship of local discussion and study groups. Increasingly, many Adventists believed that the organization represented the liberal wing
of the denomination, a labeling the association sought to avoid.[15]

RACIAL ADAPTATIONS

The continuing discontent among blacks, however, posed a more
serious problem for the denomination's organizational structure. The
problem had two principal dimensions. One aspect raised questions
regarding the church's role in social change. Theologically, Adventism adhered to the position of the conservative Evangelicals that
rejected the "social gospel," arguing instead that social improvement
would come about only as the result of individual conversion.[16]
Through its disaster relief work, however, the denomination gave
aid to Detroit and other riot centers in 1967 and served the Poor
People's encampment at Resurrection City in Washington, D.C.,
the next year. Having had its consciousness of the inner city raised,
the denomination also developed programs that combined education, medical care, and evangelism in a number of cities.[17] Through
these activities Adventism sought to tread a fine line between evangelism and humanitarian concern on the one hand and challenge
to existing political structures on the other.

The second aspect raised questions about the denomination's
treatment of its own black members. Although the problem was a
longstanding one, it became particularly intense in the mid-1960s
and remained a perennial topic of debate. In 1965 the General
Conference committee resolved that no denominational institutions,
most of which had followed prevailing local custom, could practice
racial discrimination. The next year the General Conference session
established a Human Relations Committee and adopted a resolution
stating that "No Wall of Partition" was to exist between the races
within the Seventh-day Adventist Church.[18] Such actions did not
fully satisfy blacks, however, who wanted more black leadership,
more money for inner-city work, and black unions. According to
Christianity Today, some blacks at the 1970 General Conference
session charged the church with a "callous and racist attitude." In
response, the session took a major step by including in the baptismal
vows a statement that ethnic or social background was to have nothing to do with church membership or inclusion in the family of
God.[19]

Rejected at the 1970 General Conference session, black unions
became a major focus of concern during the next decade. In 1969

the North American Regional Department had proposed that the possibility of black unions be studied. These unions, umbrella organizations over the black regional conferences, were thought to be a possible means of obtaining more significant black leadership positions and concentrating more money on black concerns. Blacks themselves were not fully agreed on the viability of black unions; furthermore, the denominational leadership feared that such a move would lead toward further separation of black and white Adventists. In response to the pressure for black unions, the denomination began to appoint more blacks to leadership positions outside the regional conferences, culminating in C. E. Bradford's election as vice president for North America in 1979. And at its 1978 annual council, where black unions were again discussed, the denomination established an Office of Ethnic Affairs (replacing the Office of Regional Affairs, later renamed the Office of Human Relations) assigned to promote cultural interaction; adopted a statement on Human and Race Relations to be included in the *Church Manual*; pledged itself to promote workshops, literature, and textbooks on race relations; and asserted that all ethnic groups would be considered in hiring personnel.[20] With the proportion of blacks in American Adventism growing, it was clear that pressure for greater power and visibility would continue. Thus far the church had been relatively successful in accommodating itself to the pressure for change.

THE WOMEN'S ISSUE

The denomination was less successful in adapting to the women's movement. Ironically, considering the major role played by Ellen White in shaping the church, Seventh-day Adventists had not ordained women to either local church offices or the ministry and had given them few leadership positions. Some sentiment developed for the ordination of women, but the denominational leadership, though seeing no biblical obstacle to the practice, felt that cultural factors in various parts of the world made it impossible for the time being. Women were licensed as ministers, however, and served as associate pastors in a few American churches. When M. Carol Hetzell became director of the General Conference Communication Department in 1975, she became the first woman to hold a major office in more than thirty years.[21]

Alongside these small improvements, however, the women's issue caught the denomination in a group of lengthy, costly, and embarrassing court cases involving discriminatory pay practices. In January 1973, eight months after being turned down for head of household status (which would have made her eligible for higher pay), Merikay Silver, an editorial assistant at Pacific Press, filed a class-action suit against her employer that charged it with violating Title VII of the Civil Rights Act. In time, this led to two other suits: *EEOC v. PPA* charging retaliation, and *Department of Labor v. PPA* charging violations of the Equal Pay Act. The General Conference took over the defense, essentially arguing that, because of the First Amendment, the government had no right to get involved in internal church affairs. Its brief, which stated that the church was hierarchical in structure and referred to the General Conference president as the "First Minister," drew considerable criticism from some sectors of the denomination. In the end, the Silver case was settled out of court, but as of the mid-1980s, the press was still considering whether to appeal a second EEOC suit (the first one having been overturned on a technicality) to the Supreme Court; and the Labor Department suit was still outstanding.[22]

To further complicate matters, the General Conference session of 1975 passed an action stating that the instigation or continuation of legal action against the church were grounds for disfellowshiping. The same year's autumn council then backtracked, for it added a footnote to the *Church Manual* advising a church to seek counsel from a conference or mission president before taking such action. Apparently no one was disfellowshiped for this reason, and the issue was closed when the 1980 General Conference session rescinded its earlier action, stating that after exhausting the "Biblically outlined procedure for the settlement of difference," the church member should then follow his or her conscience.[23]

The long-term significance of this complex episode is difficult to assess. It forced the denomination to adjust its pay practices to the requirements of federal law, and it indicated the difficulty a conservative and independent-minded denomination experienced when faced with social trends it could not understand. Although a strong defender of God's law and an upholder of personal morality, Adventism was being forced, despite its wishes, to address larger questions of social justice.

* * *

Changes with controversial implications were also taking place within the denomination's medical work. Beginning in 1972, Seventh-day Adventist hospitals joined together into union-wide corporations for improved cost effectiveness. Within a few years these corporations began crossing union boundaries until, by 1981, four regional corporations had emerged: Adventist Health Systems/Sunbelt, Adventist

Health Systems — West, Adventist Health Systems/Eastern and Middle America, and Adventist Health Systems — North. It appeared that a national corporation would be the next step. These corporations raised several questions. Many denominational leaders believed that there was not enough of a church "presence" in the hospitals operated by the health systems; they wanted the Adventist element to be clarified, perhaps by stipulating a minimum percentage of employees that had to be Adventists. Further, some hospital administrators objected to the growing centralization that was taking away their independence. And when the autumn council of 1978 allowed the hospitals to pay salaries higher than the standard "sacrificial" or "living" denominational wage, it enabled them to more easily attract qualified employees from other denominational institutions. Step by rapid step, the denomination was moving into big business, operating sixty-five hospitals with over $661 million in combined assets. Although Adventism saw itself as separate from the world and unique, its development of a centralized health care system was part of a national trend.[24]

THEOLOGICAL DEBATES

While these social forces were gradually reshaping American Adventism, the church was also experiencing theological controversy. The key issues were the perennial problem of righteousness by faith, Ellen G. White, the alleged inroads of liberalism, and — near the end of the 1970s — the doctrines of the heavenly sanctuary and the investigative judgment. Throughout the debates on these issues the key question seemed to be Adventism's uniqueness: would Seventh-day Adventism retain its self-understanding as God's remnant church destined to play the key role in the closing events of history, or would it simply become one of many Protestant denominations?

To some degree the issue of righteousness by faith stemmed from the theme that General Conference president Robert H. Pierson sounded from the time of his election in 1966. Although Seventh-day Adventists had set no dates for Christ's Second Coming, their unfulfilled expectation of that event's imminence cried out for an explanation as the years passed. Drawing largely on the writings of Ellen White, Pierson addressed the problem by holding the church responsible for the "delay." He repeatedly called for "revival and reformation"; only when such a transformation took place could the Lord return.[25] The major councils of the church responded by issuing calls for revival and reformation,[26] and in 1976 they redefined the priorities of the church in terms of evangelism. Pointing out the need to overcome the denomination's inertia, the 1976 annual council declared:

> The finishing of the Work means one thing: communicating God's message through the power and ministry of the Holy Spirit to all of earth's population so that God can proclaim His work finished. When this happens Jesus will come.[27]

The *Review and Herald*, particularly through its associate editor, Herbert Douglass, worked out a theological basis for this revival and reformation theme. The key element in this theology was Christology, according to both Douglass and Kenneth Wood, editor of the *Review*: Jesus, with all the genetic human disadvantages,[28] had given an example of how to live the sanctified life. As Douglass put it,

> The last generation of Adventists will demonstrate the all-sufficiency of the grace and power of God as Jesus did in His day. They will confirm the triumph of Jesus—that men, partaking of the divine nature through the Holy Spirit, can overcome all sin in this life.[29]

In short, such people could "be trusted with everlasting life."[30]

As Wood pointed out, this theology restored traditional Adventist thinking, most recently formulated by M. L. Andreasen in the 1940s, which had faded from view at about the time that *Questions on Doctrine* had appeared.[31] That book, strongly shaped by LeRoy Edwin Froom and R. Allen Anderson, who wanted to show that Adventism was truly within the Christian tradition, had abandoned the notion of Christ having a sinful human nature. Led by Edward Heppenstall, several Adventist theologians in the 1960s moved one step further in denying the possibility of perfection. By the end of the decade it was clear that two streams of thought were emerging within Adventism regarding the nature of Christ and its implications for salvation and eschatology; and by the mid-1970s these questions had become issues in an intense debate. Robert Brinsmead, a controversial Australian who had been actively pushing a form of perfectionism, decided in about 1970 that not only was perfectionism wrong but that the Adventist understanding of righteousness by faith as including both justification and sanctification needed correction as well. Seventh-day Adventists, he argued, should take the Reformation principle that salvation could come only through faith that the believer's life is covered by Christ's righteousness. Sanctification is not the basis of salvation.

As Brinsmead publicized his ideas, particularly through a magazine entitled *Present Truth*, he stirred up new controversy among

Adventists in Australia. Soon Desmond Ford, chairman of the theology department at Avondale College (an Adventist institution in Australia), became a central figure in the Australian debate, partly because of his wife's book *The Soteriological Implications of the Human Nature of Christ.* Even before the book was published, the discussion had become so intense that General Conference and Australian denominational administrators had planned a conference to resolve the issue. This meeting, involving both administrators and theologians, took place April 23-30, 1976, in Palmdale, California. The statement that came out of the meeting asserted that by his life and death Christ made it possible for us to be justified by faith and that faith also brings changes in character. Obedience, it concluded, is the evidence of our saving faith.[32]

Although Ford believed that the "Palmdale statement" had adopted his (and Brinsmead's) view that righteousness by faith includes only justification, Kenneth Wood, in commenting on the statement in the *Review,* interpreted it as reaffirming the historic Seventh-day Adventist position.[33] Obviously, nothing had been settled. In fact, the debate spread to America, intensified by Herbert Douglass's adult Sabbath school lesson quarterly of 1977 entitled *Jesus, the Model Man*; the publication by an Australian Anglican minister, Geoffrey J. Paxton, of *The Shaking of Adventism*, which examined Adventist teaching on righteousness by faith from a perspective similar to that of Brinsmead and Ford; and Ford's move to Pacific Union College to serve as a visiting professor.

The support for the Ford-Brinsmead-Paxton position on righteousness by faith seems to have come primarily from students and laypeople. The denomination's theologians, while largely opposing the perfectionist view of Herbert Douglass, continued to argue that righteousness by faith included both justification and sanctification. Hans K. La Rondelle of the SDA Theological Seminary, for example, said:

> There is an indissoluble union of law and gospel, of justification and sanctification, without confusing the two. Thus the Christian will trust exclusively in Christ's righteousness for his present and future salvation, while his character is daily more reformed according to the divine similitude in Jesus Christ, the perfectly obedient man.[34]

But debate continued. During a speaking tour at Adventist centers in the United States in 1978, Paxton, largely as a result of General Conference pressure, was prevented from speaking at Andrews University. High-level consultations on righteousness by faith took place in 1978 and 1979. Finally, Neal Wilson, shortly after becoming General Conference president, called for an end to public discussion of the "fine points" of righteousness by faith and appointed an official committee to study the problem.[35]

Several months later, the committee issued a statement on "the dynamics of salvation." Because humanity is desperately in need of salvation, it said, God has taken the initiative to provide it. When the individual human being, with the Holy Spirit's help, decides to accept reconciliation with God, he receives a new status in Christ, encompassed by such terms as justification, reconciliation, forgiveness, adoption, and sanctification. This new status involves a new life in Christ characterized by new birth, restoration, growth, grace and faith, assurance, and praise. Consummation is achieved with Christ's Second Coming, which will restore the universe to a "perfect, sinless state."[36]

In essence, the statement addressed the righteousness by faith debate by analyzing the theological terms involved, attempting to bring together all elements of the subject, and placing the whole within an Adventist eschatological context. Although it included an emphasis on sanctification, that concept was now one of several elements. By offering an enlarged understanding of salvation, the statement appeared to provide room for both sides of the debate.

It appears on the surface that the righteousness by faith debate pivoted on the technical issue of a definition. But the fact that so many people could get so disturbed over the question indicates that it hit a raw nerve within Adventism. The Ford-Brinsmead-Paxton position seems to have appealed to a large number of Adventists because it offered an assurance of salvation that they felt the traditional emphasis on sanctification had not allowed. On the other hand, many of those who opposed the new teaching feared that it might open the door to an antinomianism that would undermine the Adventist concern with God's law. Thus, by implication, the debate again raised the question of Adventism's uniqueness. Responding to Paxton's argument that Adventists must accept the Reformation teaching on righteousness by faith, La Rondelle said that, although recognizing the reformers as God's instruments, Adventists could not "accept the reformation gospel as the canon for their understanding of the apostolic gospel. Only the original apostles possessed the gospel in its fullness and accepted it as the norm 'for all future ages.' "[37] Or as Fritz Guy, also of the SDA Seminary, put it:

> One of the most important elements in our Adventist heritage
> is the notion of "present truth"—truth that has come newly
> alive and has become newly understood and significant be-

cause of a new experience, a present situation. What is important, then, theologically and experientially, is not whether our understanding is just like that of the Reformers; what is important is whether our beliefs are *true*. [38]

In the view of most denominational theologians, Seventh-day Adventists had the unique problem and unique opportunity of understanding the relationship of justification and sanctification, or law and gospel, in a way that did justice to both. Whether in doing so Adventist thinkers could be true to their sectarian heritage and at the same time offer assurance to the believer remained to be seen.

DEBATE OVER ELLEN WHITE

Although the debate over righteousness by faith raised the question of Adventism's uniqueness only by implication, an emerging discussion of the nature and authority of Ellen White's writings addressed directly one of the "pillars" of the faith. Ever since the 1919 Bible Conference, the denomination had promoted Ellen White's writings and published several works defending them against their critics. These efforts continued into the 1960s and 1970s through such programs as "Testimony Countdown" and the establishment of Ellen G. White research centers abroad. [39] The creation of these research centers probably reflected the larger concern for denominational unity, for Ellen White had never had the impact on Adventists in some areas of the world that she had had on the Americans.

On the other hand, the appearance of *Spectrum*, published outside the control of denominational administrators, gave an outlet to renewed examination of the questions shelved by the 1919 Bible Conference. The discussion began when *Spectrum* (in its autumn 1970 issue) offered several articles on Ellen White. Two theologians, Harold Weiss and Roy Branson, called for a reexamination of Mrs. White's writings in terms of her relationship to other authors, her intellectual and social milieu, and her own intellectual development. [40] As if in answer to this proposal William S. Peterson, an English professor at Andrews University, argued that Ellen White's account of the French Revolution in *The Great Controversy* was drawn primarily from books by Sir Walter Scott and James A. Wylie. "It simply will not suffice to say that God showed her the broad outline of events," he concluded, "and she then filled in the gap with her readings. In the case of the French Revolution, there was no 'broad outline' until she had read the historians." [41]

Two other articles about Ellen White appeared in the same issue of *Spectrum*, though those by Weiss, Branson, and Peterson caused the most discussion. W. Paul Bradley, speaking for the White Estate — custodian of the prophetic writings — saw no need for critical scholarship, declaring that "no reinterpretation is required to make us know God's messages for us." He further rejected the suggestion that Mrs. White had obtained her ideas from other authors, and he concluded that,

> in forming one's personal judgement about the validity of the gift that resulted in the work of Ellen G. White . . ., one must doubt whether historical criticism will have a preponderance of weight. There will always have to be present a strong element of faith.[42]

The discussion of Peterson's article continued until Ronald Graybill, a research assistant at the White Estate, showed that Ellen White drew her material from Uriah Smith, who had, in turn, obtained it from the historians.[43]

The subject of this debate may seem a minor one, but the issues involved — the validity of historical criticism and the relationship of its findings to an understanding of Ellen White — were large. And it was not only the findings of scholarship but also suggestions that the prophet had borrowed and even mishandled information that threatened the authoritative role Ellen White had come to play in the church.

The next major contribution came from historian Ronald L. Numbers, whose *Prophetess of Health* (1976) reexamined the development of Mrs. White as a health reformer. Numbers noted that he was departing from traditional Adventist scholarship in not presupposing inspiration or ignoring witnesses who rejected Ellen White as inspired. The volume developed two major themes: that Ellen White had drawn upon the ideas of contemporary health reformers, and that she had changed her ideas on a number of health subjects. Numbers concluded that Ellen White's historical function had been to make a religion out of health reform.[44]

Even before publication, Numbers's book aroused a storm of controversy when clandestinely obtained copies of his first-draft typescript circulated within the church community. In response, the denomination published in early 1976 a paperback edition of D. E. Robinson's *Story of Our Health Message*, originally published in 1943, together with a study guide for use in the churches. The White Estate sent speakers to Adventist centers to present the official church position, and letters went out to ministers warning against those who questioned Ellen White's inspiration. After *Prophetess of Health* was published, the controversy caught the attention of *Time* magazine, which, in turn, inspired a *Review and Herald* editorial that claimed the book really presented no challenge to the faith of a knowledgeable Adventist. The White Estate prepared a twenty-three page response to Numbers's book that was made immediately available, and a larger printed critique that appeared in the fall.[45]

The White Estate response followed Bradley's earlier argument. "If divine inspiration is excluded *a priori*," the estate argued, "then one is left with nothing but a secularist-historicist interpretation of Ellen White's life and with implicit denial of the validity or truthfulness of her claim to divine inspiration." The estate then provided a chapter-by-chapter critique of *Prophetess of Health*, asserting that Numbers had misread his sources on crucial points and had left out important evidence. Although admitting some problems and some borrowing in Ellen White's writings, the estate concluded, "This late-hour attack upon the validity of her messages does not stand the test of history nor the judgement through the years of the church's trusted spiritual leaders."[46] After *Spectrum* presented several articles on the book in early 1977, among which two Adventist historians pointed to the need for a reexamination of the denomination's understanding of Ellen White, the controversy faded.[47]

While the discussion of Numbers's book took place publicly, more work was going on behind the scenes. Donald R. McAdams, a professor of history at Andrews University before assuming the presidency at Southwestern Adventist College, carefully examined Ellen White's use of secondary sources in writing her chapter on John Hus in *The Great Controversy*. Tracing the volume's evolution from first draft to publication, he concluded:

> . . . the historical portions of *The Great Controversy* that I have examined are selective abridgements and adaptation of historians. Ellen White was not just borrowing paragraphs here and there that she ran across in her reading, but in fact following the historians page after page, leaving out much material, but using their sequence, some of their ideas, and often their words.[48]

He later found that Ellen White's literary assistants had significantly altered the manuscript before publication.

McAdams presented his paper to the White Estate, which pursued its own investigation, this time of the chapter on Luther, coming to essentially the same conclusions that McAdams had. In its official response to the McAdams paper, the estate acknowledged that Ellen White had used historians as sources of information and allowed the possibility of historical error in her writings.[49]

Although McAdams reported his finding to only a restricted audience, another researcher, California minister Walter Rea, was spreading widely his conclusion that other Ellen White books, particularly *Prophets and Kings* and *The Desire of Ages*, were based on works by a contemporaneous writer, Alfred Edersheim. This seems to have prompted a series of articles in the *Adventist Review* in 1978 entitled "Toward an Adventist Concept of Inspiration." In this series, Arthur White, secretary of the White Estate, although not mentioning any of the research taking place, said that Ellen White could have obtained minor details from sources other than her visions. In 1979, Arthur White wrote another series, this time making a general acknowledgment that others were doing research. He indicated that *The Great Controversy* contained extensive borrowing from historians and some historical errors. In discussing *The Desire of Ages*, Arthur White seems to have drawn on two studies commissioned by the White Estate that examined the relationship of that book to another contemporaneous writer, William Hanna. The authors of these studies, Raymond Cottrell and Walter F. Specht, had concluded that Ellen White had used Hanna only sparingly and creatively.[50]

Meanwhile, Walter Rea was expanding his search for Ellen White's literary sources, arguing that an alarmingly large portion of her work was borrowed. In response to Rea's assertions, Neal Wilson, the General Conference president, appointed a committee of scholars and administrators to meet with Rea and examine his evidence on January 28 and 29, 1980. Although several members objected to Rea's "sloppy" methodology, the committee voted "that we recognize that Ellen White, in her writing, used various sources more extensively than we had previously believed." They further recommended that the General Conference both encourage further study and develop a plan to communicate the findings of recent Ellen White scholarship to the laity.[51] In the March 20, 1980 *Adventist Review*, Neal Wilson reported to the church the work of the "Rea Committee" and pointed out that "God inspired people, not words."[52] Before the year ended, however, Rea's views appeared in a *Los Angeles Times* article that received wide dissemination. As a result, the denomination revoked Rea's ministerial credentials.[53]

Although the bulk of the research on Ellen White during the 1970s concerned her sources, a few other studies examined larger questions. New Testament scholar Joseph J. Battistone, for instance, suggested that Ellen White's writings tended to be homiletical rather than exegetical and therefore could not be taken as authoritative biblical commentary. And historian Jonathan Butler argued that her writings on eschatology reflected the religious and political situation of nineteenth-century America and were not unchangeable predictions of the future.[54] These two articles pointed the direction that future scholarship on Ellen White would probably take, but, as Donald McAdams has pointed out, the research of the 1970s established three points: Ellen White borrowed much material from others; she was a part of late-nineteenth-century culture; and she was not inerrant.[55] From the furor of opposition to Ronald Numbers's study in the mid-1970s, the denomination—though obviously uncomfortable with public discussion of the issue—had by the end of the decade moved toward accepting the general points that the entire body of research had established. The application of these findings to practice and belief, however, remained to be determined.

THE SANCTUARY DOCTRINE

One step in making this determination took place in the context of another controversy late in 1979. The doctrines of the heavenly sanctuary and the investigative judgment, which had their origins in Hiram Edson's explanation of the 1844 disappointment, had long been a trouble spot in Seventh-day Adventist theology. Not only did Adventism's Evangelical critics find these doctrines unbiblical, but over the years several prominent ministers, Albion Ballenger and L. R. Conradi among them, had left the church partly because of their objections to them. In the 1960s the General Conference appointed a committee to study problems concerning the interpretation of Daniel 8:14, a text basic to the doctrines. But the "Daniel Committee," as it came to be called, was unable to reach a consensus and never issued a report.[56] Meanwhile, denominational publications continued to present articles on the heavenly sanctuary and investigative judgment, often identifying the belief as absolutely essential to Adventism's identity.[57]

The doctrine became a public issue when the already controversial Desmond Ford rejected its traditional formulation in a lecture to the Adventist Forum at Pacific Union College on October 27, 1979. Ford argued that the Bible did not support such notions as the literal heavenly sanctuary and Christ's confinement to the Holy Place until 1844. Although he accepted the idea of a pre-Advent judgment, he said that the traditional Adventist understanding of it was wrong. Because Ellen White's writings had played such a major role in confirming this doctrine, Ford also addressed the question of the nature of her inspiration and function. While her inspired messages were absolutely indispensable to the development and survival of Seventh-day Adventism, he said, Ellen White's legacy was "pastoral" rather than "canonical."[58]

Local opposition arose almost immediately. J. W. Cassell and Gordon Madgwick, the president and academic dean respectively of Pacific Union College—where Ford was still a visiting professor— went to Washington, D.C., to discuss the matter with the General Conference officers.[59] This discussion resulted in the decision to give Ford a six-month "leave of absence with salary to provide him an opportunity to devote his full time to continued research and preparation of a documented statement on the topic of the sanctuary and related issues." Ford received accommodations in Washington during this period so that he could be close to the resources of the Ellen G. White Estate and the General Conference archives. He was also assigned a small group of biblical scholars who would offer him ongoing criticism as he developed his study. On completion of this work, Ford was to present it to a large committee of more than a hundred theologians, biblical scholars, and church administrators.[60]

While Ford worked on his manuscript, the *Adventist Review* made it clear in numerous articles and editorials that the sanctuary doctrine was absolutely essential to Adventism's raison d'etre. It said, for example:

> These landmark doctrines are to be received and held
> fast, not in formal fashion but in the light of divine guidance
> given at the beginning of the movement and made our own.
> Thus we become part and parcel with the movement, and the
> beliefs that made the original Seventh-day Adventists make us
> Seventh-day Adventists too.[61]

Ford completed his manuscript entitled "Daniel 8:14, The Day of Atonement, and the Investigative Judgment" in the summer. This lengthy document argued, among other things, that Christ has been interceding for his people as their High Priest in the Most Holy Place of the heavenly sanctuary since his ascension. This position denied the traditional Adventist teaching that Christ entered the Most Holy Place in 1844 to begin his work of investigative judgment. On the basis that prophecies have multiple fulfillments, Ford reinterpreted the significance of 1844 "as marking the time when God, in heaven and on earth, raised up a people to whom He entrusted His last, everlasting gospel of righteousness by faith in Christ, for the world."[62]

Copies of Ford's document went out to the members of the "Sanctuary Review Committee," about 115 of whom met at Glacier

View Ranch (a denominational youth campground) in Colorado during the week of August 10-15, 1980. Called upon by President Neal Wilson to develop a consensus, the committee adopted two statements. The first, "Christ in the Heavenly Sanctuary," commented on a number of technical problems raised by Ford, affirmed that 1844 marked the beginning of a pre-Advent judgment, and emphasized throughout the assurance that the Christian may have because of Christ's intercession. In this emphasis the statement moved beyond traditional Adventist teaching. The second statement, "The Role of the Ellen G. White Writings in Doctrinal Matters," affirmed that her authority "transcends that of all noninspired interpreters." A participant, Raymond Cottrell, commented on these actions: "In the thinking of the majority at Glacier View, Adventist tradition was the norm for interpreting the Bible, rather than the Bible for tradition."[63]

Although many of those who met at Glacier View felt that the consensus statement on the sanctuary doctrine was broad enough to include both Ford and his opponents, the *Review* announced: "Ford document studied; variant views rejected." And a few weeks later, on a recommendation from the General Conference, the Australasian Division removed Ford's ministerial credentials. This action raised considerable controversy. Several "Evangelical Adventist" churches were formed, a number of ministers either left their positions or were fired after publicly opposing the Ford decision, and a new magazine—*Evangelica*—emerged that defended Ford's theology.[64] Adventism was obviously theologically fragmented; only time would tell how significant that fragmentation would become.

ADVENTISM IN TRANSITION

The denomination dismissed Ford partly on the grounds that he did not agree with the statement of fundamental beliefs voted by the General Conference session in the spring of 1980. This official action seems to have been related to an effort that had been going on for several years to define more fully Seventh-day Adventist doctrine. Concerned that a number of denominational positions were being questioned by church employees, particularly educators, some members of the Robert Pierson administration sought written definitions of "landmark" doctrines.

This movement arose for a number of reasons. President Pierson had served as an overseas missionary for many years, and at the time he took office he was probably out of touch with intellectual developments on Seventh-day Adventist campuses. As he became

aware of contemporary Adventist thought, he found aspects of it —
particularly with regard to creationism and Ellen White — rather
different from the Adventism in which he had been schooled. Second, the appearance of *Spectrum* provided a previously unavailable
outlet for critical analysis of traditional Adventist views. Third, a
Newsweek magazine article in 1971 suggested that liberalism was
creeping into the SDA Theological Seminary at Andrews University,
an assertion that, although publicly denied, probably confirmed sus-
picions held by some church administrators.[65] And fourth, in the
background lay the upheavals in the evangelical world: the inerrancy
movement so highly publicized by Harold Lindsell's *Battle for the
Bible* and the division in the Lutheran Church — Missouri Synod.[66]
Some Adventists felt that liberalism had to be rooted out of Adventist
colleges before it grew significant enough to force a similar split in
Seventh-day Adventism. More generally, the denomination, in putting great emphasis on education, had inadvertently produced intellectuals who, on the basis of new experiences and new information,
were in various ways reformulating Adventism. The real question
was, how much theological pluralism could or would the denomination tolerate?

Although Pierson and others in his administration had previously voiced objections to attempts to "modernize" Adventism,[67]
their concern did not achieve focus until 1977, when they began to
develop statements of key Adventist beliefs that would be normative
for church employees. In a *Review* editorial announcing this move,
Vice President Willis J. Hackett explained that early in its history
the denomination had "fixed certain landmarks of truth that, ever
since, it has held to be nonnegotiable." Because of the church's
growth and the advanced education of some of its members, however, an erosion of faith was possible. Therefore, these statements
of belief would be used to "evaluate persons already serving the
church, and those hereafter appointed, as to their commitment to
what is considered basic Adventism. Thus the church will be protected against the subtle influence of those who have become unclear
and doubtful as to God's self-revelation in His Word and in the
counsels of the Holy Spirit."[68]

The first two statements to appear addressed the subjects of
"inspiration and revelation" and "creation," the former intending to
establish a high view of scriptural (and Ellen G. White's) authority,
the latter seeking to hold the denomination to belief in a literal six-
day creation that took place a few thousand years ago.[69] The content
of the statements received little attention, however, for almost immediately the Adventist academic community concentrated on the

use to which the statements would be put and the implied threat to academic freedom.

Before putting the statements in their final form, the General Conference officials intended to meet with the college and university religion and science teachers. Their meeting with religion teachers from Pacific Union College, Loma Linda University, and Walla Walla College precipitated some formal protests. Before the joint meeting of these West Coast teachers (and before the appearance of Hackett's editorial), the PUC religion department circulated a letter questioning the potential use of the statements and pointing out that they would enhance church rather than biblical authority. The meeting itself seems to have been somewhat stormy, with the teachers expressing fear that a creed was developing—opposition to which went back to the days of William Miller—while the officials largely tried to dismiss these fears and pleaded for doctrinal unity. Although one of these officials, Duncan Eva, said that the administrators should further consider and clarify the use of the statements, the appearance of Hackett's editorial a few days later prompted the chairmen of the three religion departments to send a joint letter to several General Conference and college administrators questioning whether the statements would assume a "creedal function" and whether they would "be more divisive than whatever heretical tendencies may currently exist among church members."[70]

Basic to the teachers' viewpoint was their understanding of the nature of truth. In a Friday evening devotional talk to this West Coast convocation, Fred Veltman of the PUC religion department said that "faithfulness to God demands a dynamic, changing involvement with God's sovereign role in history, a sensitiveness to our place and condition in the last quarter of the twentieth century, an openness to the ongoing revelation of God in our experience, in nature, in His Word." Along these same lines, the joint letter asked whether the statements would "harmonize with the historic Seventh-day Adventist commitment to a progressive understanding of truth."[71] Furthermore, the teachers were questioning the role of administrators in determining truth. As Richard Rice has pointed out, both the publishing house defense briefs in the Merikay Silver case, with their emphasis on "spiritual leaders," and the hierarchical church organization and the statements of belief drawn up by administrators raised similar questions. "To some," he writes, "the attempt to establish doctrinal consensus by administrative action is a disturbing departure from historic Adventism, with its commitment to the ongoing discovery of truth, and its belief that the development of doctrine is the responsibility of church members in general and not the special province of official leaders."[72]

A few other meetings between General Conference officials and the science and religion teachers took place, and the doctrinal statements themselves went through a number of changes. But opposition both from teachers and within the General Conference itself appears to have derailed the doctrinal loyalty effort. Partly in response to the controversies of the past decade, however, the 1980 General Conference session adopted — for the first time as a General Conference action — a statement of fundamental beliefs. This included very brief summations of Adventist doctrine — in contrast to the extended statements being pushed earlier — which revised the wording of the fundamental beliefs that had held semiofficial status since the 1930s. But the debate over the extended statements, and the whole range of theological discussion in the 1970s, affected the 1980 action. After long discussion over details of the fundamental beliefs statement, the General Conference session adopted a preamble proposed by Ronald Graybill of the White Estate, which said:

> Seventh-day Adventists accept the Bible as their only creed and hold certain fundamental beliefs to be the teaching of the Holy Scriptures. These beliefs, as set forth here, constitute the church's understanding and expression of the teaching of Scripture. Revision of these statements may be expected at a General Conference session when the Church is led by the Holy Spirit to a fuller understanding of Bible truth or finds better language in which to express the teachings of God's Holy Word.[73]

One result of a decade of theological controversy was, therefore, a theoretical commitment to flexibility, a recognition that human understanding and knowledge at any particular time is but a reflection of the truth grounded in God. On the other hand, as the Ford case revealed, there existed an even stronger commitment to hold to tradition.

FROM SECT TO CHURCH

Although the theological debates caught most of the attention, and their ultimate significance was unclear, Seventh-day Adventist theology was, in some important ways, becoming more sophisticated. Works by such theologians as Jack Provonsha and Edward W. H. Vick interacted with the contemporary theological world to a much greater degree than had most books coming from Adventist presses. Perhaps because of this greater awareness of thought outside Adventism, scholars extended significant efforts to rethink the two key

Adventist concerns. The Second Advent, according to Provonsha and Sakae Kubo, is as important for the present life as it is for the future. This interest in showing the contemporary relevance of religious belief revealed itself even more significantly in treatments of the Sabbath doctrine, in which various writers began to unravel its symbolic significance. Suggestions that the Sabbath might lead to a deeper understanding of God, humans, salvation, church, and human destiny led Richard Rice to conclude that "far more than just one of Adventism's distinctive doctrines, then, the Sabbath may represent its most profound theological and experiential resource."[74]

This theological sophistication was appearing in other ways as well. The Seventh-day Adventist Theological Seminary at Andrews University received accreditation from the American Association of Theological Schools in 1970 and a short time later began offering D. Min. and Th.D. graduate programs.[75] Also, beginning in 1968, the Old Testament Department of the seminary sponsored an archaeological excavation of Tell Hesban, Jordan, under the direction of Siegfried Horn and later Lawrence T. Geraty.[76] And the publications of Andrews University Press offered continuing expressions of Adventist biblical scholarship.

When Robert Pierson announced to the 1978 General Conference annual council his retirement because of ill health, he observed that other denominations had moved from sect to church. His appeal was: "Brethren and Sisters, this must never happen to the Seventh-day Adventist Church! This will not happen to the Seventh-day Adventist Church. This is not just another church—it is God's Church!"[77] Yet, as Donald McAdams has commented, the primary attention of that very council to matters of administration indicated that much of the change from sect to church had already occurred.[78] Furthermore, many of the recent developments in theology and biblical studies were indicating that Seventh-day Adventism was moving closer to conservative Protestant theology and to a limited participation in the larger scholarly world.

These signs that the "sectarian" mentality was declining, though not without resistance, take on significance when placed in conjunction with other, more obvious, events. Beginning in 1965, for instance, Seventh-day Adventists held annual conversations with the World Council of Churches' Faith and Order Commission. Although the Adventists, believing that they had a special purpose, had no intention of joining the WCC, the "conversations" provided a previously nonexistent communication link with the Christian community.[79] Other less important events were Don F. Neufeld's attendance as an observor at the Evangelical-sponsored Jerusalem

Conference on Bible Prophecy in 1971 — where he seems to have been surprised to find that the historicist position had been abandoned in favor of the futurist and preterist[80] — and D. A. Roth's visit to the Seventh-day Baptist General Conference session in 1976.[81] Beginning in 1976, in an effort that sought better understanding with other Christian groups and offered a means of evangelism, the denomination sent *Ministry*, its professional ministerial journal, to virtually all Christian ministers, first in the Columbia Union Conference and later to all of North America.[82] Finally, though it has nothing to do with denominational structure, in 1968 Jerry L. Pettis became the first Adventist to be elected to the United States Congress.[83] For a denomination that still found it necessary to publish articles discussing whether or not Adventists should vote,[84] Pettis's election appears to have been a major signal that Adventists were integrating themselves into American society. The social alienation that had characterized its origins, though still alive, was no longer as all-inclusive and dominant in Adventist faith and practice as it had been.

* * *

As Seventh-day Adventism moved into the decade of the 1980s, it appeared to be in the midst of significant change. What had been an American-dominated church was becoming a Third World — dominated church, though what this might mean for the shape and character of Adventism in the future was not yet clear. What had been a sectarian and in many ways fundamentalist theology appeared to be moving toward conservative Protestantism, though that movement was facing a strong reaction. Both areas of change challenged the denominational leadership to be flexible and creative and at the same time to be firmly committed to the Adventist tradition. As the 1980s dawned, tradition appeared to be outweighing flexibility; but the forces of change have been running too deep for that imbalance to continue.

If, as seems to be the case, Seventh-day Adventism is a sect that has moved a long way toward becoming a church, its fundamental struggle in the coming years will be, as Donald McAdams has put it, "to retain the spark, commitment and message that gave the sect its original power, while accepting the institutional, structural and cultural changes that are the inevitable concomitant of growth in the real world."[85] Though holding fast to its belief in the imminent Second Coming of Christ, Adventism will have to face resolutely the implications of the command given by the nobleman of Christ's parable, "Occupy till I come."[86]

APPENDIX 1

Seventh-day Adventist Statements of Beliefs

APPENDIX 1 A

1872

In presenting to the public this synopsis of our faith, we wish to have it distinctly understood that we have no articles of faith, creed, or discipline, aside from the Bible. We do not put forth this as having any authority with our people, nor is it designed to secure uniformity among them, as a system of faith, but is a brief statement of what is and has been, with great unanimity, held by them. We often find it necessary to meet inquiries on this subject, and sometimes to correct false statements circulated against us, and to remove erroneous impressions which have obtained with those who have not had an opportunity to become acquainted with our faith and practice. Our only object is to meet this necessity.

As Seventh-day Adventists, we desire simply that our position shall be understood; and we are the more solicitous for this because there are many who call themselves Adventists, who hold views with which we can have no sympathy, some of which, we think, are subversive of the plainest and most important principles set forth in the word of God.

As compared with other Adventists, Seventh-day Adventists differ from one class in believing in the unconscious state of the dead, and the final destruction of the unrepentant wicked; from another, in believing in the perpetuity of the law of God, as summarily contained in the ten commandments, in the operation of the Holy Spirit in the church, and in setting no times for the advent to occur; from all, in the observance of the seventh day of the week as the Sabbath of the Lord, and in many applications of the prophetic scriptures.

With these remarks, we ask the attention of the reader to the following propositions which aim to be a concise statement of the more prominent features of our faith.

I

That there is one God, a personal, spiritual being, the creator of all things, omnipotent, omniscient, and eternal, infinite in wisdom, holiness, justice, goodness, truth, and mercy; unchangeable, and everywhere present by his representative, the Holy Spirit. Ps. 139:7.

II

That there is one Lord Jesus Christ, the Son of the Eternal Father, the one by whom God created all things, and by whom they do consist; that he took on him the nature of the seed of Abraham for the redemption of our fallen race; that he dwelt among men, full of grace and truth, lived our example, died our sacrifice, was raised for our justification, ascended on high to be our only mediator in the sanctuary in Heaven, where, with his own blood he makes atonement for our sins; which atonement, so far from being made on the cross, which was but the offering of the sacrifice, is the very last portion of his work as priest, according to the example of the Levitical priesthood, which foreshadowed and prefigured the ministry of our Lord in Heaven. See Lev. 16; Heb. 8:4, 5; 9:6, 7; &c.

III

That the Holy Scriptures, of the Old and New Testaments, were given by inspiration of God, contain a full revelation of his will to man, and are the only infallible rule of faith and practice.

IV

That baptism is an ordinance of the Christian church, to follow faith and repentance, an ordinance by which we commemorate the resurrection of Christ, as by this act we show our faith in his burial and resurrection, and, through that, of the resurrection of all the saints at the last day; and that no other mode fitly represents these facts than that which the Scriptures prescribe, namely, immersion. Rom. 6:3-5; Col. 2:12.

V

That the new birth comprises the entire change necessary to fit us for the kingdom of God and consists of two parts: First, a moral change wrought by conversion and a Christian life; second, a physical change at the second coming of Christ, whereby, if dead, we are raised incorruptible, and, if living, are changed to immortality in a moment, in the twinkling of an eye. John 3:3, 5; Luke 20:36.

VI

We believe that prophecy is a part of God's revelation to man; that it is included in that scripture which is profitable for instruction; 2 Tim. 3:16;

that it is designed for us and our children; Deut. 29:29; that so far from being enshrouded in impenetrable mystery, it is that which especially constitutes the word of God a lamp to our feet and a light to our path; Ps. 119:105; 2 Pet. 2:19; that a blessing is pronounced upon those who study it; Rev. 1:1-3; and that, consequently, it is to be understood by the people of God, sufficiently to show them their position in the world's history, and the special duties required at their hands.

VII

That the world's history from specified dates in the past, the rise and fall of empires, and chronological succession of events down to the setting up of God's everlasting kingdom, are outlined in numerous great chains of prophecy; and that these prophecies are now all fulfilled except the closing scenes.

VIII

That the doctrine of the world's conversion and temporal millennium is a fable of these last days, calculated to lull men into a state of carnal security, and cause them to be overtaken by the great day of the Lord as by a thief in the night; that the second coming of Christ is to precede, not follow, the millennium; for until the Lord appears, the papal power, with all its abominations, is to continue, the wheat and tares grow together, and evil men and seducers wax worse and worse, as the word of God declares.

IX

That the mistake of Adventists in 1844 pertained to the nature of the event then to transpire, not to the time; that no prophetic period is given to reach to the second advent, but that the longest one, the two thousand and three hundred days of Dan. 8:14, terminated in that year, and brought us to an event called the cleansing of the sanctuary.

X

That the sanctuary of the new covenant is the tabernacle of God in Heaven, of which Paul speaks in Hebrews 8, and onward, of which our Lord, as great High Priest, is minister; that this sanctuary is the antitype of the Mosaic tabernacle, and that the priestly work of our Lord, connected therewith, is the antitype of the work of the Jewish priests of the former dispensation; Heb. 8:1-5, &c.; that this is the sanctuary to be cleansed at the end of the 2300 days, what is termed its cleansing being in this case, as in the type, simply the entrance of the high priest into the most holy place, to finish the round of service connected therewith, by blotting out and removing from the sanctuary the sins which had been transferred to it by means of the ministration in the first apartment; Heb. 9:22, 23; and that this work, in the antitype, commencing in 1844, occupies a brief but indefinite space, at the conclusion of which the work of mercy for the world is finished.

XI

That God's moral requirements are the same upon all men in all dispensations; that these are summarily contained in the commandments spoken by Jehovah from Sinai, engraven on the tables of stone, and deposited in the ark, which was in consequence called the "ark of the covenant," or testament; Num. 10:33; Heb. 9:4; &c.; that this law is immutable and perpetual, being a transcript of the tables deposited in the ark in the true sanctuary on high, which is also, for the same reason, called the ark of God's testament; for under the sounding of the seventh trumpet we are told that "the temple of God was opened in Heaven, and there was seen in his temple the ark of his testament." Rev. 11:19.

XII

That the fourth commandment of this law requires that we devote the seventh day of each week, commonly called Saturday, to abstinence from our own labor, and to the performance of sacred and religious duties; that this is the only weekly Sabbath known to the Bible, being the day that was set apart before paradise was lost, Gen. 2:2, 3, and which will be observed in paradise restored, Isa. 66:22, 23; that the facts upon which the Sabbath institution is based confine it to the seventh day, as they are not true of any other day; and that the terms, Jewish Sabbath and Christian Sabbath, as applied to the weekly rest-days are names of human invention, unscriptural in fact, and false in meaning.

XIII

That, as the man of sin, the papacy, has thought to change times and laws (the laws of God), Dan. 7:25, and has misled almost all Christendom in regard to the fourth commandment, we find a prophecy of a reform in this respect to be wrought among believers just before the coming of Christ. Isa. 56:1, 2; 1 Pet. 1:5; Rev. 14:12, &c.

XIV

That, as the natural or carnal heart is at enmity with God and his law, this enmity can be subdued only by a radical transformation of the affections, the exchange of unholy for holy principles; that this transformation follows repentance and faith, is the special work of the Holy Spirit, and constitutes regeneration or conversion.

XV

That, as all have violated the law of God and cannot of themselves render obedience to his just requirements, we are dependent on Christ, first for justification from our past offenses, and secondly, for grace whereby to render acceptable obedience to his holy law in time to come.

XVI

That the Spirit of God was promised to manifest itself in the church through certain gifts, enumerated especially in 1 Cor. 12 and Eph. 4, that these gifts are not designed to supersede, or take the place of, the Bible, which is sufficient to make us wise unto salvation, any more than the Bible can take the place of the Holy Spirit; that in specifying the various channels of its operation, that Spirit has simply made provision for its own existence and presence with the people of God to the end of time, to lead to an understanding of that word which it had inspired, to convince of sin, and work a transformation in the heart and life; and that those who deny to the Spirit its place and operation do plainly deny that part of the Bible which assigns to it this work and position.

XVII

That God, in accordance with his uniform dealings with the race, sends forth a proclamation of the approach of the second advent of Christ, that this work is symbolized by the three messages of Rev. 14, the last one bringing to view the work of reform on the law of God, that his people may acquire a complete readiness for that event.

XVIII

That the time of the cleansing of the sanctuary (as proposition X), synchronizing with the time of the proclamation of the third message, is a time of investigative judgment, first, with reference to the dead, and, at the close of probation, with reference to the living, to determine who of the myriads now sleeping in the dust of the earth are worthy of a part in the first resurrection, and who of its living multitudes are worthy of translation— points which must be determined before the Lord appears.

XIX

That the grave, whither we all tend, expressed by the Hebrew *sheol* and the Greek *hades*, is a place of darkness in which there is no work, device, wisdom, or knowledge. Eccles. 9:10.

XX

That the state to which we are reduced by death is one of silence, inactivity, and entire unconsciousness. Ps. 146:4; Eccles. 9:5, 6; Dan. 12:2, &c.

XXI

That out of this prison house of the grave mankind are to be brought by a bodily resurrection: the righteous having part in the first resurrection, which takes place at the second advent of Christ; the wicked, in the second resurrection, which takes place a thousand years thereafter. Rev. 20:4-6.

XXII

That at the last trump, the living righteous are to be changed in a moment, in the twinkling of an eye, and with the resurrected righteous are to be caught up to meet the Lord in the air, so forever to be with the Lord.

XXIII

That these immortalized ones are then taken to Heaven, to the New Jerusalem, the Father's house in which there are many mansions, John 14:1-3, where they reign with Christ a thousand years, judging the world and fallen angels, that is, apportioning the punishment to be executed upon them at the close of the one thousand years; Rev. 20:4; 1 Cor. 6:2, 3; that during this time the earth lies in a desolate and chaotic condition, Jer. 4:20-27, described, as in the beginning, by the Greek term *abussos* (. . .) bottomless pit (Septuagint of Gen. 1:2); and that here Satan is confined during the thousand years, Rev. 20:1, 2, and here finally destroyed; Rev. 20:10; Mal. 4:1; the theater of the ruin he has wrought in the universe, being appropriately made for a time his gloomy prison house, and then the place of his final execution.

XXIV

That at the end of the thousand years, the Lord descends with his people and the New Jerusalem, Rev. 21:2, the wicked dead are raised and come up upon the surface of the yet unrenewed earth, and gather about the city, the camp of the saints, Rev. 20:9, and fire comes down from God out of heaven and devours them. They are then consumed root and branch, Mal. 4:1, becoming as though they had not been. Obad. 15, 16. In this everlasting destruction from the presence of the Lord, 2 Thess. 1:9, the wicked meet the everlasting punishment threatened against them. Matt. 25:46. This is the perdition of ungodly men, the fire which consumes them being the fire for which "the heavens and the earth which are now" are kept in store, which shall melt even the elements with its intensity, and purge the earth from the deepest stains of the curse of sin. 2 Pet. 3:7-12.

XXV

That a new heavens and earth shall spring by the power of God from the ashes of the old, to be, with the New Jerusalem for its metropolis and capital, the eternal inheritance of the saints, the place where the righteous shall evermore dwell. 2 Pet. 3:13; Ps. 47:11, 29; Matt. 5:5.

APPENDIX 1 B

1931

Seventh-day Adventists hold certain fundamental beliefs, the principal features of which, together with a portion of the scriptural references upon which they are based, may be summarized as follows:

1

That the Holy Scriptures of the Old and New Testaments were given by inspiration of God, contain an all-sufficient revelation of His will to men, and are the only unerring rule of faith and practice. 2 Tim. 3:15-17.

2

That the Godhead, or Trinity, consists of the Eternal Father, a personal, spiritual Being, omnipotent, omnipresent, omniscient, infinite in wisdom and love; the Lord Jesus Christ, the Son of the Eternal Father, through whom all things were created and through whom the salvation of the redeemed hosts will be accomplished; the Holy Spirit, the third person of the Godhead, the great regenerating power in the work of redemption. Matt. 28:19.

3

That Jesus Christ is very God, being of the same nature and essence as the Eternal Father. While retaining His divine nature He took upon Himself the nature of the human family, lived on the earth as a man, exemplified in His life as our Example the principles of righteousness, attested His relationship to God by many mighty miracles, died for our sins on the cross, was raised from the dead, and ascended to the Father, where He ever lives to make intercession for us. John 1:1, 14; Heb. 2:9-18; 8:1, 2; 4:14-16; 7:25.

4

That every person in order to obtain salvation must experience the new birth; that this comprises an entire transformation of life and character by the recreative power of God through faith in the Lord Jesus Christ. John 3:16; Matt. 18:3; Acts 2:37-39.

5

That baptism is an ordinance of the Christian church and should follow repentance and forgiveness of sins. By its observance faith is shown in the death, burial, and resurrection of Christ. That the proper form of baptism is by immersion. Rom. 6:1-6; Acts 16:30-33.

6

That the will of God as it relates to moral conduct is comprehended in His law of ten commandments; that these are great moral, unchangeable precepts, binding upon all men, in every age. Exod. 20:1-17.

7

That the fourth commandment of this unchangeable law requires the observance of the seventh day Sabbath. This holy institution is at the same time a memorial of creation and a sign of sanctification, a sign of the believer's rest from his own works of sin, and his entrance into the rest of soul which Jesus promises to those who come to Him. Gen. 2:1-3; Exod. 20:8-11; 31:12-17; Heb. 4:1-10.

8

That the law of ten commandments points out sin, the penalty of which is death. The law can not save the transgressor from his sin, nor impart power to keep him from sinning. In infinite love and mercy, God provides a way whereby this may be done. He furnishes a substitute, even Christ the Righteous One, to die in man's stead, making "Him to be sin for us, who knew no sin; that we might be made the righteousness of God in Him." 2 Cor. 5:21. That one is justified, not by obedience to the law, but by the grace that is in Christ Jesus. By accepting Christ, man is reconciled to God, justified by His blood for the sins of the past, and saved from the power of sin by his indwelling life. Thus the gospel becomes "the power of God unto salvation to every one that believeth." This experience is wrought by the divine agency of the Holy Spirit, who convinces of sin and leads to the Sin-Bearer, inducting the believer into the new covenant relationship, where the law of God is written on his heart, and through the enabling power of the indwelling Christ, his life is brought into conformity to the divine precepts. The honor and merit of this wonderful transformation belong wholly to Christ. 1 John 3:4; Rom. 7:7; Rom. 3:20; Eph. 2:8-10; 1 John 2:1, 2; Rom. 5:8-10; Gal. 2:20; Eph. 3:17; Heb. 8:8-12.

9

That God only hath immortality. Mortal man possesses a nature inherently sinful and dying. Immortality and eternal life come only through the gospel, and are bestowed as the free gift of God at the second advent of Jesus Christ our Lord. 1 Tim. 6:15, 16; 1 Cor. 15:51-55.

10

That the condition of man in death is one of unconsciousness. That all men, good and evil alike, remain in the grave from death to the resurrection. Eccles. 9:5, 6; Ps. 146:3, 4; John 5:28, 29.

11

That there shall be a resurrection both of the just and of the unjust. The resurrection of the just will take place at the second coming of Christ; the resurrection of the unjust will take place a thousand years later, at the close of the millennium. John 5:28, 29; 1 Thess. 4:13-18; Rev. 20:5-10.

12

That the finally impenitent, including Satan, the author of sin, will, by the fires of the last day, be reduced to a state of non-existence, becoming as though they had not been, thus purging the universe of God of sin and sinners. Rom. 6:23; Mal. 4:1-3; Rev. 20:9, 10; Obad. 16.

13

That no prophetic period is given in the Bible to reach to the second advent, but that the longest one, the 2300 days of Dan. 8:14, terminated in 1844, and brought us to an event called the cleansing of the sanctuary.

14

That the true sanctuary, of which the tabernacle on earth was a type, is the temple of God in Heaven, of which Paul speaks in Hebrews 8 and onward, and of which the Lord Jesus, as our great high priest, is minister; and that the priestly work of our Lord is the antitype of the work of the Jewish priests of the former dispensation; that this heavenly sanctuary is the one to be cleansed at the end of the 2300 days of Dan. 8:14; its cleansing being, as in the type, a work of judgment, beginning with the entrance of Christ as the high priest upon the judgment phase of His ministry in the heavenly sanctuary foreshadowed in the earthly service of cleansing the sanctuary on the day of atonement. This work of judgment in the heavenly sanctuary began in 1844. Its completion will close human probation.

15

That God, in the time of the judgment and in accordance with His uniform dealing with the human family in warning them of coming events vitally affecting their destiny (Amos 3:6, 7), sends forth a proclamation of the approach of the second advent of Christ; that this work is symbolized by the

three angels of Revelation 14; and that their threefold message brings to
view a work of reform to prepare a people to meet Him at His coming.

16

That the time of the cleansing of the sanctuary, synchronizing with the
period of the proclamation of the message of Revelation 14, is a time of
investigative judgment, first with reference to the dead, and secondly, with
reference to the living. This investigative judgment determines who of the
myriads sleeping in the dust of the earth are worthy of a part in the first
resurrection, and who of its living multitudes are worthy of translation.
1 Pet. 4:17, 18; Dan. 7:9, 10; Rev. 14:6, 7; Luke 20:35.

17

That the followers of Christ should be a godly people, not adopting the
unholy maxims nor conforming to the unrighteous ways of the world, not
loving its sinful pleasures nor countenancing its follies. That the believer
should recognize his body as the temple of the Holy Spirit, and that therefore he should clothe that body in neat, modest dignified apparel. Further,
that in eating and drinking and in his entire course of conduct he should
shape his life as becometh a follower of the meek and lowly Master. Thus
the believer will be led to abstain from all intoxicating drinks, tobacco, and
other narcotics, and the avoidance of every body and soul-defiling habit
and practice. 1 Cor. 3:16, 17; 9:25; 10:31; 1 Tim. 2:9, 10; 1 John 2:6.

18

That the divine principle of tithes and offerings for the support of the gospel
is an acknowledgment of God's ownership in our lives, and that we are
stewards who must render account to Him of all that He has committed to
our possession. Lev. 27:30; Mal. 3:8-12; Matt. 23:23; 1 Cor. 9:9-14; 2 Cor.
9:6-15.

19

That God has placed in His church the gifts of the Holy Spirit, as enumerated in 1 Corinthians 12 and Ephesians 4. That these gifts operate in
harmony with the divine principles of the Bible, and are given for the
perfecting of the saints, the work of the ministry, the edifying of the body
of Christ. Rev. 12:17; 19:10; 1 Cor. 1:5-7.

20

That the second coming of Christ is the great hope of the church, the grand
climax of the gospel and plan of salvation. His coming will be literal,
personal, and visible. Many important events will be associated with His

return, such as the resurrection of the dead, the destruction of the wicked, the purification of the earth, the reward of the righteous, the establishment of His everlasting kingdom. The almost complete fulfillment of various lines of prophecy, particularly those found in the books of Daniel and the Revelation, with existing conditions in the physical, social, industrial, political, and religious worlds, indicates that Christ's coming "is near, eve at the doors." The exact time of that event has not been foretold. Believers are exhorted to be ready, for "in such an hour as ye think not, the Son of man" will be revealed. Luke 21:25-27; 17:26-30; John 14:1-3; Acts 1:9-11; Rev. 1:7; Heb. 9:28; James 5:1-8; Joel 3:9-16; 2 Tim. 3:15; Dan. 7:27; Matt. 24:36, 44.

21

That the millennial reign of Christ covers the period between the first and the second resurrections, during which time the saints of all ages will live with their blessed Redeemer in Heaven. At the end of the millennium, the Holy City with all the saints will descend to the earth. The wicked, raised in the second resurrection, will go up on the breadth of the earth with Satan at their head to compass the camp of the saints, when fire will come down from God out of Heaven and devour them. In the conflagration which destroys Satan and his host, the earth itself will be regenerated and cleansed from the effects of the curse. Thus the universe of God will be purified from the foul blot of sin. Rev. 20; Zech. 14:1-4; 2 Pet. 3:7-10.

22

That God will make all things new. The earth, restored to its pristine beauty, will become forever the abode of the saints of the Lord. The promise to Abraham, that through Christ he and his seed should possess the earth throughout the endless ages of eternity, will be fulfilled. The kingdom and dominion and the greatness of the kingdom under the whole heaven will be given to the people of the saints of the Most High, whose kingdom is an everlasting kingdom, and all dominions shall serve and obey Him. Christ, the Lord, will reign supreme and every creature which is in heaven and on the earth and under the earth, and such as are in the sea will ascribe blessing and honor and glory and power unto Him that sitteth upon the throne and unto the Lamb forever and ever. Gen. 13:14-17; Rom. 4:13; Heb. 11:8-16; Matt. 5:5; Isa. 35; Rev. 21:1-7; Dan. 7:27; Rev. 5:13.

APPENDIX 1 C

1980

Seventh-day Adventists accept the Bible as their only creed and hold certain fundamental beliefs to be the teaching of the Holy Scriptures. These beliefs, as set forth here, constitute the church's understanding and expression of the teaching of Scripture. Revision of these statements may be expected at a General Conference session when the church is led by the Holy Spirit to a fuller understanding of Bible truth or finds better language in which to express the teachings of God's Holy Word.

1

The Holy Scriptures, Old and New Testaments, are the written Word of God, given by divine inspiration through holy men of God who spoke and wrote as they were moved by the Holy Spirit. In this Word, God has committed to man the knowledge necessary for salvation. The Holy Scriptures are the infallible revelation of His will. They are the standard of character, the test of experience, the authoritative revealer of doctrines, and the trustworthy record of God's acts in history. (2 Pet. 1:20, 21; 2 Tim. 3:16, 17; Ps. 119:105; Prov. 30:5, 6; Isa. 8:20; John 10:35; 17:17; 1 Thess. 2:13; Heb. 4:12.)

2

There is one God: Father, Son, and Holy Spirit, a unity of three co-eternal Persons. God is immortal, all-powerful, all-knowing, above all, and ever present. He is infinite and beyond human comprehension, yet known through His self-revelation. He is forever worthy of worship, adoration, and service by the whole creation. (Deut. 6:4; 29:29; Matt. 28:19; 2 Cor. 13:14; Eph. 4:4-6; 1 Pet. 1:2; 1 Tim. 1:17; Rev. 14:6, 7.)

3

God the eternal Father is the Creator, Source, Sustainer, and Sovereign of all creation. He is just and holy, merciful and gracious, slow to anger, and abounding in steadfast love and faithfulness. The qualities and powers exhibited in the Son and the Holy Spirit are also revelations of the Father. (Gen. 1:1; Rev. 4:11; 1 Cor. 15:28; John 3:16; 1 John 4:8; 1 Tim. 1:17; Exod. 34:6, 7; John 14:9.)

4

God the eternal Son became incarnate in Jesus Christ. Through Him all things were created, the character of God is revealed, the salvation of humanity is accomplished, and the world is judged. Forever truly God, He became also truly man, Jesus the Christ. He was conceived of the Holy Spirit and born of the virgin Mary. He lived and experienced temptation as a human being, but perfectly exemplified the righteousness and the love of God. By His miracles He manifested God's power and was attested as God's promised Messiah. He suffered and died voluntarily on the cross for our sins and in our place, was raised from the dead, and ascended to minister in the heavenly sanctuary in our behalf. He will come again in glory for the final deliverance of His people and the restoration of all things. (John 1:1-3, 14; 5:22; Col. 1:15-19; John 10:30; 14:9; Rom. 5:18; 6:23; 2 Cor. 5:17-21; Luke 1:35; Phil. 2:5-11; 1 Cor. 15:3, 4; Heb. 2:9-18; 4:15; 7:25; 8:1, 2; 9:28; John 14:1-3; 1 Pet. 2:21; Rev. 22:20.)

5

God the eternal Spirit was active with the Father and the Son in Creation, incarnation, and redemption. He inspired the writers of Scripture. He filled Christ's life with power. He draws and convicts human beings; and those who respond He renews and transforms into the image of God. Sent by the Father and the Son to be always with His children, He extends spiritual gifts to the church, empowers it to bear witness to Christ, and in harmony with the Scriptures leads it into all truth. (Gen. 1:1, 2; Luke 1:35; 2 Pet. 1:21; Luke 4:18; Acts 10:38; 2 Cor. 3:18; Eph. 4:11, 12; Acts 1:8; John 14:16-18, 26; 15:26, 27; 16:7-13; Rom. 1:1-4.)

6

God is Creator of all things, and has revealed in Scripture the authentic account of His creative activity. In six days the Lord made "the heaven and the earth" and all living things upon the earth, and rested on the seventh day of that week. Thus He established the Sabbath as a perpetual memorial of His completed creative work. The first man and woman were made in the image of God as the crowning work of Creation, given dominion over the world, and charged with responsibility to care for it. When the world was finished it was "very good," declaring the glory of God. (Gen. 1:2; Exod. 20:8-11; Ps. 19:1-6; 33:6, 9; 104; Heb. 11:3; John 1:1-3; Col. 1:16, 17.)

7

Man and woman were made in the image of God with individuality, the power and freedom to think and to do. Though created free beings, each is an indivisible unity of body, mind, and soul, dependent upon God for life and breath and all else. When our first parents disobeyed God, they denied their dependence upon Him and fell from their high position under God. The image of God in them was marred and they became subject to death. Their descendants share this fallen nature and its consequences. They are born with weaknesses and tendencies to evil. But God in Christ reconciled the world to Himself and by His Spirit restores in penitent mortals the image of their Maker. Created for the glory of God, they are called to love Him and one another, and to care for their environment. (Gen. 1:26-28; 2:7; Ps. 8:4-8; Acts 17:24-28; Gen. 3; Ps. 51:5; Rom. 5:12-17; 2 Cor. 5:19, 20.)

8

All humanity is now involved in a great controversy between Christ and Satan regarding the character of God, His law, and His sovereignty over the universe. This conflict originated in heaven when a created being, endowed with freedom of choice, in self-exaltation became Satan, God's adversary, and led into rebellion a portion of the angels. He introduced the spirit of rebellion into this world when he led Adam and Eve into sin. This human sin resulted in the distortion of the image of God in humanity, the disordering of the created world, and its eventual devastation at the time of the worldwide flood. Observed by the whole creation, this world became the arena of the universal conflict, out of which the God of love will ultimately be vindicated. To assist His people in this controversy, Christ sends the Holy Spirit and the loyal angels to guide, protect, and sustain them in the way of salvation. (Rev. 12:4-9; Isa. 14:12-14; Exod. 28:12-18; Gen. 3; Gen. 6-8; 2 Pet. 3:6; Rom. 1:19-32; 3:12-21; 8:19-22; Heb. 1:4-14; 1 Cor. 4:9.)

9

In Christ's life of perfect obedience to God's will, His suffering, death, and resurrection, God provided the only means of atonement for human sin, so that those who by faith accept this atonement may have eternal life, and the whole creation may better understand the infinite and holy love of the Creator. This perfect atonement vindicates the righteousness of God's law and the graciousness of His character; for it both condemns our sin and provides for our forgiveness. The death of Christ is substitutionary and expiatory, reconciling and transforming. The resurrection of Christ proclaims God's triumph over the forces of evil, and for those who accept the atonement assures their final victory over sin and death. It declares the Lordship of Jesus Christ, before whom every knee in heaven and earth will bow. (John 3:16; Isa. 53; 2 Cor. 5:14, 15, 19-21; Rom. 1:4; 3:25; 4:25; 8:3, 4; Phil. 2:6-11; 1 John 2:2; 4:10; Col. 2:15.)

10

In infinite love and mercy God made Christ, who knew no sin, to be sin for us, so that in Him we might be made the righteousness of God. Led by the Holy Spirit we sense our need, acknowledge our sinfulness, repent of our transgressions, and exercise faith in Jesus as Lord and Christ, as Substitute and Example. This faith which receives salvation comes through the divine power of the Word and is the gift of God's grace. Through Christ we are justified, adopted as God's sons and daughters, and delivered from the lordship of sin. Through the Spirit we are born again and sanctified; the Spirit renews our minds, writes God's law of love in our hearts, and we are given the power to live a holy life. Abiding in Him we become partakers of the divine nature and have the assurance of salvation now and in the judgment. (Ps. 27:1; Isa. 12:2; Jonah 2:9; John 3:16; 2 Cor. 5:17-21; Gal.

1:4; 2:19, 20; 3:13; 4:4-7; Rom. 3:24-26; 4:25; 5:6-10; 8:1-4, 14, 15, 26, 27; 10:7; 1 Cor. 2:5; 15:3, 4; 1 John 1:9; 2:1, 2; Eph. 2:5-10; 3:16-19; Gal. 3:26; John 3:3-8; Matt. 18:3; 1 Pet. 1:23; 2:21; Heb. 8:7-12.)

11

The church is the community of believers who confess Jesus Christ as Lord and Saviour. In continuity with the people of God in Old Testament times, we are called out from the world; and we join together for worship, for fellowship, for instruction in the Word, for the celebration of the Lord's Supper, for service to all mankind, and for the worldwide proclamation of the gospel. The church derives its authority from Christ, who is the incarnate Word, and from the Scriptures, which are the written Word. The church is God's family; adopted by Him as children, its members live on the basis of the new covenant. The church is the body of Christ, a community of faith of which Christ Himself is the Head. The church is the bride for whom Christ died that He might sanctify and cleanse her. At His return in triumph, He will present her to Himself a glorious church, the faithful of all the ages, the purchase of His blood, not having spot or wrinkle, but holy and without blemish. (Gen. 12:3; Acts 7:38; Matt. 21:43; 16:13-20; John 20:21, 22; Acts 1:8; Rom. 8:15-17; 1 Cor. 12:13-27; Eph. 1:15, 23; 2:12; 3:8-11, 15; 4:11-15.)

12

The universal church is composed of all who truly believe in Christ, but in the last days, a time of widespread apostasy, a remnant has been called out to keep the commandments of God and the faith of Jesus. This remnant announces the arrival of the judgment hour, proclaims salvation through Christ, and heralds the approach of His second advent. This proclamation is symbolized by the three angels of Revelation 14; it coincides with the work of judgment in heaven and results in a work of repentance and reform on earth. Every believer is called to have a personal part in this worldwide witness. (Mark 16:15; Matt. 28:18-20; 24:14; 2 Cor. 5:10; Rev. 12:17; 14:6-12; 18:1-4; Eph. 5:22-27; Rev. 21:1-14.)

13

The church is one body with many members, called from every nation, kindred, tongue, and people. In Christ we are a new creation; distinctions of race, culture, learning, and nationality, and differences between high and low, rich and poor, male and female, must not be divisive among us. We are all equal in Christ, who by one Spirit has bonded us into one fellowship with Him and with one another; we are to serve and be served without partiality or reservation. Through the revelation of Jesus Christ in the Scriptures we share the same faith and hope, and reach out in one witness to all. This unity has its source in the oneness of the triune God, who has adopted us as His children. (Ps. 133:1; 1 Cor. 12:12-14; Acts 17:26, 27; 2 Cor. 5:16, 17; Gal. 3:27-29; Col. 3:10-15; Eph. 4:1-6; John 17:20-23; James 2:2-9; 1 John 5:1.)

14

By baptism we confess our faith in the death and resurrection of Jesus Christ, and testify of our death to sin and of our purpose to walk in newness of life. Thus we acknowledge Christ as Lord and Saviour, become His people and are received as members by His church. Baptism is a symbol of our union with Christ, the forgiveness of our sins, and our reception of the Holy Spirit. It is by immersion in water and is contingent on an affirmation of faith in Jesus and evidence of repentance of sin. It follows instruction in the Holy Scriptures and acceptance of their teachings. (Matt. 3:13-16; 28:19, 20; Acts 2:38; 16:30-33; 22:16; Rom. 6:1-6; Gal. 3:27; 1 Cor. 12:13; Col. 2:12, 13; 1 Pet. 3:21.)

15

The Lord's Supper is a participation in the emblems of the body and blood of Jesus as an expression of faith in Him, our Lord and Saviour. In this experience of communion Christ is present to meet and strengthen His people. As we partake, we joyfully proclaim the Lord's death until He comes again. Preparation for the Supper includes self-examination, repentance, and confession. The Master ordained the service of foot washing to signify renewed cleansing, to express a willingness to serve one another in Christlike humility, and to unite our hearts in love. The communion service is open to all believing Christians. (Matt. 26:17-30; 1 Cor. 11:23-30; 10:16, 17; John 6:48-63; Rev. 3:20; John 13:1-17.)

16

God bestows upon all members of His church in every age spiritual gifts which each member is to employ in loving ministry for the common good of the church and of humanity. Given by the agency of the Holy Spirit, who apportions to each member as He wills, the gifts provide all abilities and ministries needed by the church to fulfill its divinely ordained functions. According to the Scriptures, these gifts include such ministries as faith, healing, prophecy, proclamation, teaching, administration, reconciliation, compassion, and self-sacrificing service and charity for the help and encouragement of people. Some members are called of God and endowed by the Spirit for functions recognized by the church in pastoral, evangelistic, apostolic, and teaching ministries particularly needed to equip the members for service, to build up the church to spiritual maturity, and to foster unity of the faith and knowledge of God. When members employ these spiritual gifts as faithful stewards of God's varied grace, the church is protected from the destructive influence of false doctrine, grows with a growth that is from God, and is built up in faith and love. (Rom. 12:4-8; 1 Cor. 12:9-11, 27, 28; Eph. 4:8; 11-16; 2 Cor. 5:14-21; Acts 6:1-7; 1 Tim. 2:1-3; 1 Pet. 4:10, 11; Col. 2:19; Matt. 25:31-36.)

17

One of the gifts of the Holy Spirit is prophecy. This gift is an identifying mark of the remnant church and was manifested in the ministry of Ellen G. White. As the Lord's messenger, her writings are a continuing and authoritative source of truth and provide for the church comfort, guidance, instruction, and correction. They also make clear that the Bible is the standard by which all teaching and experience must be tested. (Joel 2:28, 29; Acts 2:14-21; Heb. 1:1-3; Rev. 12:17; 19:10.)

18

The great principles of God's law are embodied in the Ten Commandments and exemplified in the life of Christ. They express God's love, will, and purposes concerning human conduct and relationships and are binding upon all people in every age. These precepts are the basis of God's covenant with His people and the standard in God's judgment. Through the agency of the Holy Spirit they point out sin and awaken a sense of need for a Saviour. Salvation is all of grace and not of works, but its fruitage is obedience to the Commandments. This obedience develops Christian character and results in a sense of well-being. It is an evidence of our love for the Lord and our concern for our fellow men. The obedience of faith demonstrates the power of Christ to transform lives, and therefore strengthens Christian witness. (Exod. 20:1-17; Matt. 5:17; Deut. 28:1-14; Ps. 19:7-13; John 14:15; Rom. 8:1-4; 1 John 5:3; Matt. 22:36-40; Eph. 2:8.)

19

The beneficent Creator, after the six days of Creation, rested on the seventh day and instituted the Sabbath for all people as a memorial of Creation. The fourth commandment of God's unchangeable law requires the observance of this seventh-day Sabbath as the day of rest, worship, and ministry in harmony with the teaching and practice of Jesus, the Lord of the Sabbath. The Sabbath is a day of delightful communion with God and one another. It is a symbol of our redemption in Christ, a sign of our sanctification, a token of our allegiance, and a foretaste of our eternal future in God's kingdom. The Sabbath is God's perpetual sign of His eternal covenant between Him and His people. Joyful observance of this holy time from evening to evening, sunset to sunset, is a celebration of God's creative and redemptive acts. (Gen. 2:1-3; Exod. 20:8-11; 31:12-17; Luke 4:16; Heb. 4:1-11; Deut. 5:12-15; Isa. 56:5, 6; 58:13, 14; Lev. 23:32; Mark 2:27, 28.)

20

We are God's stewards, entrusted by Him with time and opportunities, abilities and possessions, and the blessings of the earth and its resources. We are responsible to Him for their proper use. We acknowledge God's ownership by faithful service to Him and our fellow men, and by returning tithes and giving offerings for the proclamation of His gospel and the support and growth of His church. Stewardship is a privilege given to us by God for nurture in love and the victory over selfishness and covetousness. The steward rejoices in the blessings that come to others as a result of his faithfulness. (Gen. 1:26-28; 2:15; Haggai 1:3-11; Mal. 3:8-12; Matt. 23:23; 1 Cor. 9:9-14.)

21

We are called to be a godly people who think, feel, and act in harmony with the principles of heaven. For the Spirit to recreate in us the character of our Lord we involve ourselves only in those things which will produce Christlike purity, health, and joy in our lives. This means that our amusement and entertainment should meet the highest standards of Christian taste and beauty. While recognizing cultural differences, our dress is to be simple, modest, and neat, befitting those whose true beauty does not consist of outward adornment but in the imperishable ornament of a gentle and quiet spirit. It also means that because our bodies are the temples of the Holy Spirit, we are to care for them intelligently. Along with adequate exercise and rest, we are to adopt the most healthful diet possible and abstain from the unclean foods identified in the Scriptures. Since alcoholic beverages, tobacco, and the irresponsible use of drugs and narcotics are harmful to our bodies, we are to abstain from them as well. Instead, we are to engage in whatever brings our thoughts and bodies into the discipline of Christ, who desires our wholesomeness, joy, and goodness. (1 John 2:6; Eph. 5:1-13; Rom. 12:1, 2; 1 Cor. 6:19, 20; 10:31; 1 Tim. 2:9, 10; Lev. 11:1-47; 2 Cor. 7:1; 1 Pet. 3:1-4; 2 Cor. 10:5; Phil. 4:8.)

22

Marriage was divinely established in Eden and affirmed by Jesus to be a lifelong union between a man and a woman in loving companionship. For the Christian a marriage commitment is to God as well as to the spouse, and should be entered into only between partners who share a common faith. Mutual love, honor, respect, and responsibility are the fabric of this relationship, which is to reflect the love, sanctity, closeness, and permanence of the relationship between Christ and His church. Regarding divorce, Jesus taught that the person who divorces a spouse, except for fornication, and marries another, commits adultery. Although some family relationships may fall short of the ideal, marriage partners who fully commit themselves to each other in Christ may achieve loving unity through the guidance of the

Spirit and the nurture of the church. God blesses the family and intends that its members shall assist each other toward complete maturity. Parents are to bring up their children to love and obey the Lord. By their example and their words they are to teach them that Christ is a loving disciplinarian, ever tender and caring, who wants them to become members of His body, the family of God. Increasing family closeness is one of the earmarks of the final gospel message. (Gen. 2:18-25; Deut. 6:5-9; John 2:1-11; Eph. 5:21-33; Matt. 5:31, 32; 19:3-9; Prov. 22:6; Eph. 6:1-4; Mal. 4:5, 6; Mark 10:11, 12; Luke 16:18; 1 Cor. 7:10, 11.)

23

There is a sanctuary in heaven, the true tabernacle which the Lord set up and not man. In it Christ ministers on our behalf, making available to believers the benefits of His atoning sacrifice offered once for all on the cross. He was inaugurated as our great High Priest and began His intercessory ministry at the time of His ascension. In 1844, at the end of the prophetic period of 2300 days, He entered the second and last phase of His atoning ministry. It is a work of investigative judgment which is part of the ultimate disposition of all sin, typified by the cleansing of the ancient Hebrew sanctuary on the Day of Atonement. In that typical service the sanctuary was cleansed with the blood of animal sacrifices, but the heavenly things are purified with the perfect sacrifice of the blood of Jesus. The investigative judgment reveals to heavenly intelligences who among the dead are asleep in Christ and therefore, in Him, are deemed worthy to have part in the first resurrection. It also makes manifest who, among the living are abiding in Christ, keeping the commandments of God and the faith of Jesus, and in Him, therefore, are ready for translation into His everlasting kingdom. The completion of this ministry of Christ will mark the close of human probation before the Second Advent. (Heb. 1:3; 8:1-5; 9:11-28; Dan. 7:9-27; 8:13, 14; 9:24-27; Num. 14:34; Ezek. 4:6; Mal. 3:1; Lev. 16; Rev. 14:12; 20:12; 22:12.)

24

The second coming of Christ is the blessed hope of the church, the grand climax of the gospel. The Saviour's coming will be literal, personal, visible, and worldwide. When He returns, the righteous dead will be resurrected, and together with the righteous living will be glorified and taken to heaven, but the unrighteous will die. The almost complete fulfillment of most lines of prophecy, together with the present condition of the world, indicates that Christ's coming is imminent. The time of that event has not been revealed, and we are therefore exhorted to be ready at all times. (Titus 2:13; John 14:1-3; Acts 1:9-11; 1 Thess. 4:16, 17; 1 Cor. 15:51-54; 2 Thess. 2:8; Matt. 24; Mark 13; Luke 21; 2 Tim. 3:1-5; Joel 3:9-16; Heb. 9:28.)

25

The wages of sin is death. But God, who alone is immortal, will grant eternal life to His redeemed. Until that day death is an unconscious state for all people. When Christ, who is our life, appears, the resurrected righteous and the living righteous will be glorified and caught up to meet their Lord. The second resurrection, the resurrection of the unrighteous, will take place a thousand years later. (1 Tim. 6:15, 16; Rom. 6:23; 1 Cor. 15:51-54; Eccles. 9:5, 6; Ps. 146:4; 1 Thess. 4:13-17; Rom. 8:35-39; John 5:28, 29; Rev. 20:1-10; John 5:24.)

26

The millennium is the thousand-year reign of Christ with His saints in heaven between the first and second resurrections. During this time the wicked dead will be judged; the earth will be utterly desolate, without living human inhabitants, but occupied by Satan and his angels. At its close Christ with His saints and the Holy City will descend from heaven to earth. The unrighteous dead will then be resurrected, and with Satan and his angels will surround the city, but fire from God will consume them and cleanse the earth. The universe will thus be freed of sin and sinners forever. (Rev. 20; Zech. 14:1-4; Mal. 4:1; Jer. 4:23-26; 1 Cor. 6; 2 Pet. 2:4; Ezek. 28:18; 2 Thess. 1:7-9; Rev. 19:17, 18, 21.)

27

On the new earth, in which righteousness dwells, God will provide an eternal home for the redeemed and a perfect environment for everlasting life, love, joy, and learning in His presence. For here God Himself will dwell with His people, and suffering and death will have passed away. The great controversy will be ended, and sin will be no more. All things, animate and inanimate, will declare that God is love: and He shall reign forever. Amen. (2 Pet. 3:13; Gen. 17:1-8; Isa. 35; 65:17-25; Matt. 5:5; Rev. 21:1-7; 22:1-5; 11:15.)

APPENDIX 2

Seventh-day Adventist Membership Statistics

APPENDIX 2 A:
NORTH AMERICAN MEMBERSHIP BY GEOGRAPHICAL REGION*

	NORTHEAST	MID-ATLANTIC	GREAT LAKES	SOUTHEAST	SOUTHWEST	MIDWEST-MOUNTAIN	PACIFIC	CANADA
1870	1,629	293	2,651			687	130	
1875	1,237	293	3,933			1,929	450	
1879	1,876	355	6,054	198	250	3,936	965	143
1885	2,199	680	7,927	232	300	6,007	2,004	127
1890	2,464	1,530	9,343	555	698	8,883	3,364	194
1895	3,153	2,631	13,500	1,072	1,740	13,633	5,838	384
1900	3,844	3,829	16,821	1,771	2,415	18,331	7,860	1,146
1905	4,733	3,805	15,682	2,781	3,613	17,027	10,163	1,456
1910	4,902	4,356	12,952	3,480	4,697	15,517	13,191	1,813
1915	6,583	5,951	14,362	6,307	4,982	17,917	18,306	3,397
1920	8,741	8,322	16,506	8,552	5,188	21,578	22,085	5,007
1925	9,245	8,779	18,688	10,088	6,186	22,276	28,472	5,213
1930	9,581	9,380	20,791	11,649	7,245	22,400	33,576	5,836
1935	12,035	12,347	27,491	15,268	10,593	27,910	43,794	7,912
1940	13,441	15,705	30,510	19,112	12,923	31,407	53,371	9,134
1945	15,420	20,372	32,784	22,741	14,923	33,026	63,235	9,808
1950	17,840	23,652	36,179	29,824	18,890	35,504	77,376	11,386
1955	20,393	27,797	41,133	36,805	20,773	40,660	92,013	13,170
1960	23,693	33,192	45,493	41,858	23,162	42,984	106,654	14,512
1965	28,081	38,212	51,303	48,835	26,025	46,324	124,965	16,189
1970	33,732	45,205	55,803	59,534	31,205	49,593	144,182	19,307
1975	42,000	52,834	62,264	78,725	38,941	56,300	163,157	25,143
1979	44,796	58,202	67,119	94,687	45,380	62,913	179,992	30,222

*States within each region

1. NORTHEAST   Maine, New Hampshire, Vermont, Massachusetts, Connecticut, Rhode Island, New York.
2. MID-ATLANTIC New Jersey, Pennsylvania, Delaware, Maryland, District of Columbia, Virginia, West Virginia.
3. GREAT LAKES Ohio, Michigan, Indiana, Illinois, Wisconsin.
4. SOUTHEAST Arkansas, Texas, Oklahoma, New Mexico, Arizona.
5. MIDWEST MOUNTAIN Minnesota, Iowa, Missouri, Kansas, Nebraska, South Dakota, North Dakota, Montana, Wyoming, Colorado, Utah, Nevada, Idaho.
6. PACIFIC Alaska, Washington, Oregon, California, Hawaii.

APPENDIX 2 B
WORLD MEMBERSHIP BY GEOGRAPHICAL REGION

Year	RUSSIA/USSR	S. AMERICAN	OCEANIA	N. AMERICAN	MIDEAST	INTERAMERICAN	EUROPE	ASIA	AFRICA
1870				5,390			50		
1875				7,842			200		
1879				13,777			364		
1885				19,476			826		
1890			655	27,031			1,947		78
1895	591	153	1,465	41,951		175	3,125		220
1900	767	1,056	2,495	56,017	121	391	5,397	12	425
1905	1,720	1,873	3,151	59,260	91	2,352	8,158	258	580
1910	3,952	3,386	4,172	60,945	236	3,475	12,707	722	1,213
1915	6,480	4,903	5,654	77,805	430	5,105	29,889	4,092	2,449
1920	8,200	8,711	8,061	96,037	429	6,736	45,996	7,705	2,705
1925	12,434	16,514	9,800	109,029	451	9,163	65,956	19,127	8,515
1930	13,719	20,782	11,965	120,560	473	14,392	81,576	30,344	20,442
1935	13,709	29,607	16,864	157,507	594	25,110	99,375	44,166	36,036
1940	16,513*	37,073	20,378	185,788	748	33,498	102,032	60,125	48,597
1945	16,513*	47,224	22,930	212,514	835	48,563	104,714	67,125	55,960
1950	21,611	64,695	28,656	250,939	1,373	68,425	141,105	84,649	95,259
1955	40,000	133,650	40,964	293,448	2,045	95,849	145,283	119,256	176,450
1960	40,000*	130,566	55,831	332,364	2,161	122,040	154,808	166,617	240,738
1965	40,000*	197,223	74,431	380,855	2,510	167,626	157,563	230,258	328,038
1970	40,000*	318,433	93,432	439,726	3,745	233,771	166,738	318,433	437,336
1975	40,000*	428,671	119,728	520,842	3,540	371,391	177,345	415,694	589,273
1979	40,000*	558,395	138,479	585,050	2,744	515,226	186,663	523,648	757,986

*Estimate from Previous Figures due to Conditions and Inability to Receive Figures

APPENDIX 2 C
TOTAL MEMBERSHIP

1870	5,440
1875	8,042
1879	14,141
1885	20,547
1890	29,711
1895	47,680
1900	67,131
1905	77,433
1910	90,736
1915	136,807
1920	184,580
1925	245,220
1930	314,253
1935	422,968
1940	504,472
1945	576,378
1950	756,712
1955	1,006,218
1960	1,245,125
1965	1,578,504
1970	2,051,864
1975	2,666,484
1979	3,308,191

Membership statistics have been compiled from reports appearing in the following sources: *Advent Review and Sabbath Herald,* 1870-1879; *Seventh-day Adventist Yearbook,* 1885-1890; *General Conference Bulletin*, 1895-1900; and General Conference of Seventh-day Adventists annual Statistical Reports, 1905-1979.

NOTES TO PREFACE

1. Sydney Ahlstrom, *A Religious History of the American People* (New Haven: Yale University Press, 1972), p. 1021.

2. Gottfried Oosterwal, "The Seventh-day Adventist Church in the World Today," in *Servants for Christ: The Adventist Church Facing the 80's*, ed. Robert E. Firth (Berrien Springs, MI: Andrews University Press, 1980), pp. 1-2.

3. J. N. Loughborough, *The Great Second Advent Movement: Its Rise and Progress* (Washington, D.C.: RHPA, 1905; M. Ellsworth Olsen, *A History of the Origin and Progress of Seventh-day Adventists* (Washington, D.C.: RHPA, 1925); Arthur Whitefield Spalding, *Origin and History of Seventh-day Adventists*, 4 vols. (Washington, D.C.: RHPA, 1961–62); see also the recent college-level text: Richard Schwarz, *Lightbearers to the Remnant* (Mountain View, CA: PPPA, 1979).

4. Harold O. McCumber, *Pioneering the Message in the Golden West* (Mountain View, CA: PPPA, 1946).

5. David Mitchell, *Seventh-day Adventist: Faith in Action* (New York: Vantage Press, 1958), pp. 245-319; Booton Herndon, *The Seventh Day: The Story of the Seventh-day Adventists* (New York: McGraw-Hill, 1960), pp. 43-59.

6. Richard W. Schwarz, *John Harvey Kellogg, M.D.* (Nashville: SPA, 1970).

NOTES TO CHAPTER 1

1. Ernest L. Tuveson, *Redeemer Nation: The Idea of America's Millennial Role* (Chicago: University of Chicago Press, 1968), p. 16; Ernest R. Sandeen, *The Roots of Fundamentalism: British and American Millenarianism, 1800–1930* (Chicago: University of Chicago Press, 1970), p. 4.

2. *The Logic of Millennial Thought: Eighteenth-Century New England* (New Haven: Yale University Press, 1977), pp. 75-78.

3. Sandeen, *Roots of Fundamentalism*, pp. 21-22. On the history of prophetic interpretation, see also LeRoy Edwin Froom, *The Prophetic Faith of Our Fathers*, 4 vols. (Washington, D.C.: RHPA, 1946–54), 2: 651-54.

4. Sandeen, *Roots of Fundamentalism*, pp. 42-49; see also N. Gordon Thomas, "The Second Coming: A Major Impulse of American Protestantism," *AH* 3 (Winter 1976): 3-9; Ira V. Brown, "Watchers for the Second Coming: The Millenarian Tradition in America," *Mississipi Valley Historical Review* 39 (December 1952): 441-58.

5. William Miller, *William Miller's Apology and Defense* (Boston: Joshua V. Himes, 1845), pp. 1-4 (hereafter cited as Miller, *Apology and Defense*).

6. Sylvester Bliss, *Memoirs of William Miller* (Boston: Joshua V. Himes, 1853), p. 65 (hereafter cited as Bliss, *William Miller*).

7. Ibid., pp. 70-76; Miller, *Apology and Defense*, pp. 10-12.

8. Whitney R. Cross, *The Burned-over District* (New York: Harper and Row, 1965), p. 291.

9. Sandeen, *Roots of Fundamentalism*, pp. 52-53; see also David L. Rowe, "Comets and Eclipses: The Millerites, Nature, and the Apocalypse," *AH* 3 (Winter 1976): 10-19 and J. F. C. Harrison, *The Second Coming: Popular Millenarianism, 1780–1850* (New Brunswick, NJ: Rutgers University Press, 1979), pp. 194, 206.

10. Miller, *Apology and Defense*, pp. 17-18; Bliss, *William Miller*, pp. 97-98; James White, ed., *Sketches of the Christian Life and Public Labors of William Miller* (Battle Creek: Seventh-day Adventist Publishing Association, 1875), pp. 79-81 (hereafter cited as White, *Sketches of William Miller*); Arthur Whitefield Spalding, *Footprints of the Pioneers* (Washington, D.C.: RHPA, 1947), p. 23. On the impact of Millerism in Vermont, see David R. Ludlum, *Social Ferment in Vermont, 1791–1850*, Columbia Studies in American Culture (New York: Columbia University Press, 1939), pp. 250-60.

11. Richard Carwardine, *Transatlantic Revivalism: Popular Evangelicalism in Britain and America, 1790–1865* (Westport, CT: Greenwood Press, 1978), pp. 3-56.

12. Ronald G. Walters, *American Reformers, 1815–1860*, American Century Series (New York: Hill and Wang, 1978), pp. 3-15; see also Alice Felt Tyler, *Freedom's Ferment: Phases of American Social History to 1860* (Minneapolis: University of Minnesota Press, 1944) and Edwin Scott Gaustad, ed., *The Rise of Adventism: Religion and Society in Mid-Nineteenth-Century America* (New York: Harper & Row, 1974).

13. *Christian Herald* quoted in *Signs of the Times*, Boston (15 April 1840): 13; Bliss, *William Miller*, pp. 142-43.

14. L. D. Fleming to Joshua V. Himes, 6 April 1840, *Signs of the Times* (15 April 1840): 14; *Christian Reflector*, Boston (24 June 1840): 103.

15. White, *Sketches of William Miller*, pp. 122-23.

16. Miller to Himes, 31 March 1840; *Signs of the Times* (15 April 1840): 14; "Address to the Second Advent Believers," 31 January 1844, p. 196.

17. Josiah Litch, *The Probability of the Second Coming of Christ about A.D. 1843* (Boston: David H. Ela, 1838), p. 157; Isaac C. Wellcome, *History of the Second Advent Message* (Yarmouth, ME: By the author, 1874), p. 71 (hereafter cited as *Second Advent Message*); *Advent Shield*, Boston (May 1844): 53-54; *Signs of the Times* (1 February 1841): 161-62.

18. Litch, *An Address to the Public and Especially the Clergy on the New Approach of the Glorious Everlasting Kingdom of God* (Boston: Joshua V. Himes, 1842), pp. 17, 123-24; *Advent Shield*, Boston (May 1844): 53-54; *Signs of the Times* (February 1841): 161-62.

19. *Second Advent of Christ*, Cleveland (6 June 1843); *Advent Shield*, Boston (May 1844): 50-60; "Fitch's Two Sermons," *Signs of the Times* (15 December 1841): 144; (13 April 1842): 13; Bliss, *William Miller*, pp. 3-7.

20. Bliss, *William Miller*, pp. 139-41; *Advent Christian Times*, Buchanan, Michigan (6 February 1872): 220-21; *Liberator*, Boston (2 October 1840): 159; (16 October 1840): 167.

21. *Liberator*, Boston (2 October 1840): 159; (16 October 1840): 167; *Dial*, Boston (July 1842): 100.

22. *Signs of the Times* (15 July 1840): 63; (2 August 1840): 72; (1 November 1840): 115; (15 January 1841): 157.

23. *Report of the First General Conference*, pp. 1, 7.

24. *Report of the Second Session of the General Conference* (Boston, 1841), pp. 8-12; Dick, "William Miller and the Advent Crisis" (typewritten), pp. 31-44.

25. *Signs of the Times* (1 June 1842): 68-69; *Advent Shield*, Boston (May 1844): 66.

26. Arthur, "Millerism," p. 161.

27. *Signs of the Times* (1 June 1842): 68-69. David L. Rowe points out that anticlericalism in the Millerite movement had its origins in the significant number of Millerites who came from the Christian Connection, for whom antisectarianism was a doctrine, and the Baptists, among whom dissent arose against some specific tendencies within their church. "A New Perspective on the Burned-Over District: The Millerites in Upstate New York," *Church History* 47 (December 1978): 416-17.

28. *Midnight Cry*, New York (18 January 1843): 204; (17 November 1842): 3; (8 February 1844): 228; E. H. Wilcox, secretary, Philadelphia Second Advent Association, to Himes, 18 June 1842; *Signs of the Times* (6 July 1842): 110; Godfrey Anderson, *Outrider of the Apocalypse* (Mountain View, CA: PPPA, 1972), pp. 31, 59.

29. White, *Sketches of William Miller*, pp. 128-29.

30. Litch, *Advent Shield*, Boston (May 1844): 66-67.

31. Ibid., p. 70.

32. Ibid., p. 71.

33. Himes to Charles Fitch, *Signs of the Times* (19 April 1843): 53.

34. *Signs of the Times* (6 September 1843): 20; *Midnight Cry* (2 September 1843): 7; Robert Winter to Litch, 23 September 1843; *Midnight Cry* (2 November 1843): 93. For an examination of the British Millerites, see Louis Billington, "The Millerite Adventists in Great Britain, 1840–50," *Journal of American Studies* 1 (October 1967): 191-212.

35. *Advent Message to the Daughters of Zion*, Boston (May 1844); *Midnight Cry* (23 May 1844).

36. *Millennial Harp and Millennial Musings* (Boston, 1842), preface; Bates, *Autobiography*, pp. 284-91. One stanza of the song the slaves were singing may have been:

> Gabriel blows his mighty trumpet
> Gabriel blows his mighty trumpet,
> Gabriel blows his mighty trumpet
>   in the old churchyard.

Miller's following in the South was small. See Robert W. Olson, "Southern Baptists' Reaction to Millerism" (Th.D. diss., Southwestern Baptist Theological Seminary, 1972), pp. 75-100.

37. *Signs of the Times* (16 November 1842): 69; Bliss, *William Miller*, p. 167; Joseph Bates, *The Autobiography of Elder Joseph Bates* (Battle Creek: SDA Publishing Association, 1868), p. 292; Nathan Gordon Thomas, "The Millerite Movement in the State of Ohio" (M.A. thesis, Ohio University, 1957), p. 30.

38. *Signs of the Times* (15 September 1841): 96; (16 November 1842): 69.

39. Wellcome, *Second Advent Message*, p. 304; *Signs of the Times* (15 February 1841): 173.

40. *Philadelphia Public Ledger* 10 (11 October 1844).

41. *Philadelphia Public Ledger* (1 June 1842): 68; Everett N. Dick, "Advent Camp Meetings of the 1840's," *AH* 4 (Winter 1977): 3-10.

42. *Advent Shield*, Boston (May 1844): 66, 68-69; *Signs of the Times* (22 June 1842): 93; Wellcome, *Second Advent Message*, p. 237.

43. Hiram Munger, *Life and Religious Experience of Hiram Munger*, 2d ed. (Chicopee Falls, MA: By the author, 1861), pp. 54-59 (hereafter cited as Munger, *Life*).

44. *Salem* (Massachusetts) *Gazette* (18 October 1842); *Signs of the Times* (26 October 1842): 44; (16 November 1842): 70.

45. Arthur, "Millerism," in Gaustad, *Rise of Adventism*, p. 157.

46. *Signs of the Times* (13 July 1842): 114; (17 August 1842): 157; (24 August 1842): 164; *Newark Daily Advertiser*, 4 November 1842.

47. O. R. Fassett, *Life of Mrs. O. R. Fassett* (Boston: By the author, 1885), pp. 15-16; Wellcome, *Second Advent Message*, pp. 305, 333-34; Luther Boutelle, *Sketch of the Life and Religious Experience of Elder Luther Boutelle* (Boston: Advent Christian Society, 1891), pp. 38-50.

48. David Leslie Rowe, "Thunder and Triumph: The Millerite Movement and Apocalyptic Thought in Upstate New York, 1800–1845" (Ph.D. diss., University of Virginia, 1974), p. 140.

49. *Signs of the Times* (25 January 1843): 150.

50. Litch, *Advent Shield*, Boston (May 1844): 71.

51. Miller to Himes, n.d.; *Detroit Daily Advertiser*, 25 February 1843; see also Arthur, "Millerism," p. 161 and Sandeen, *Roots of Fundamentalism*, p. 52.

52. *Advent Shield*, Boston (May 1844): 72, 78; Henry Crocker, *History of the Baptists in Vermont* (Bellows Falls, VT, 1913), p. 653; *Signs of the Times* (7 June 1843): 107-08; David L. Rowe, "Elon Galusha and the Millerite Movement," *Foundations: A Baptist Journal of History and Theology* 18 (July-September 1975): 252-60.

53. *New Hampshire Patriot*, Concord, 9 November 1843.

54. *Cincinnati Morning Herald*, 19 December 1843.

55. *Cincinnati Chronicle*, 11 April 1844.

56. *Signs of the Times* (22 February 1843): 179; see also Madeline Warner, "The Changing Image of the Millerites in the Western Massachusetts Press," *AH* 2 (Summer 1975): 5-7; Ira V. Brown, "The Millerites and the Boston Press," *New England Quarterly* 16 (December 1943): 592-614.

57. Francis D. Nichol, *The Midnight Cry* (Washington, D.C.: RHPA, 1944), p. 499.

58. Himes, *Outlook*, New York (October 1894). For an examination of how these stories appeared in later years, see James Ehrlich, "Ascension Robes and Other Millerite Fables: The Millerites in American Literature," *AH* 2 (Summer 1975): 8-13 and Gary Scharnhorst, "Images of the Millerites in American Literature," *American Quarterly* 32 (Spring 1980): 19-36. Clara Endicott Sears, *Days of Delusion: A Strange Bit of History* (Boston: Houghton Mifflin Company, 1924) is the principal source for modern use of these ascension robe stories.

59. *Tenth Annual Report of the State Lunatic Asylum* (Boston, 1843), pp. 40-41.

60. *American Journal of Insanity* (January 1845): 250-51.

61. *Zion's Herald*, Boston (11 September 1844): 147; (18 September 1844): 151.

62. Letter from an unidentified eyewitness, *Christian Watchman*, Boston (21 October 1842): 65; Bates, *Autobiography*, pp. 264, 266-67; Munger, *Life* pp. 96-97.

63. Wellcome, *Second Advent Message*, pp. 386-87.

64. *Philadelphia Public Ledger*, 11 September 1843; Litch, *Signs of the Times* (20 September 1843): 38.

65. Wellcome, *Second Advent Message*, pp. 382-83; White, *Life Incidents in Connection with the Great Advent Movement* (Battle Creek: SDA Publishing Association, 1868), pp. 155-60, 163 (hereafter cited as White, *Life Incidents*).

66. Rowe, "Thunder and Triumph," p. 206.

67. *Midnight Cry* (15 June 1843): 120.

68. Albany correspondent to the *New York Herald*, 1, 3, 5 February 1843; 6 and 12 March 1843.

69. Froom, *Prophetic Faith*, 4: 796-97.

70. Bliss, *William Miller*, pp. 256, 262-63; *Midnight Cry* (9 May 1844): 342; *Advent Shield*, Boston (May 1844): 121-25.

71. *Advent Shield*, Boston (May 1844): 80; Bliss, *William Miller*, p. 264; Thomas, "The Second Coming in the Third New England" (Ph.D. diss. Michigan State University, 1967), p. 123.

72. Spalding, *Captains of the Host* (Washington, D.C.: RHPA, 1947), pp. 83-88; Bates, *Autobiography*, pp. 297-98; Anderson, *Outrider*, pp. 54-55.

73. Miller to Himes, 6 October 1844; *Advent Herald*, Boston (16 October 1844); *Midnight Cry* (10 October 1844); Wellcome, *Second Advent Message*, pp. 358-59, 363.

74. Wellcome, *Second Advent Message*, p. 297; Spalding, *Captains of the Host*, p. 161.

75. Wellcome, *Second Advent Message*, pp. 395-96; Dick, "William Miller and the Advent Crisis," pp. 52-53, 263-64; Himes, editorial correspondence, 29 August 1844, *Midnight Cry* (12 September 1844): 80; White, *Sketches of William Miller*, pp. 363-64.

76. Arthur, "Millerism," p. 162.

77. George Grigg, treasurer, to N. Southard, *Midnight Cry* (31 October 1844): 141-42.

78. *Philadelphia Public Ledger*, 5 October 1844; *Alexander's Express Messenger*, New York (10 October 1844).

79. *Midnight Cry* (3 October 1844): 104.

80. An account of an eyewitness in a Rochester paper, *New York Morning Express*, 28 October 1844.

81. Jonathan M. Butler, "Adventism and the American Experience," in Gaustad, *Rise of Adventism*, p. 178.

82. White, *Life Sketches . . . of Elder James White, and His Wife, Mrs. Ellen G. White* (Battle Creek: SDA Publishing Association, 1888), p. 108 (hereafter cited as *White and His Wife*).

83. White, ed., *The Early Life and Later Experience and Labors of Joseph Bates* (Battle Creek: SDA Publishing Association, 1878), p. 303; Anderson, *Outrider*, p. 59.

84. White, *Sketches of William Miller*, p. 310.

85. Dick, "William Miller and the Advent Crisis," p. 253; Charles Elliott Weniger, "A Critical Analysis of the Public Address of William Miller" (Ph.D. diss., University of Southern California, 1948), p. 339.

86. White, *Life Incidents*, p. 187.

87. *Advent Herald*, Boston (12 February 1845); Spalding, *Captains of the Host*, pp. 147-50.

88. White, *White and His Wife*, pp. 224-25; Wellcome, *Second Advent Message*, p. 400.

89. White, *White and His Wife*, p. 231.

90. Arthur L. White, *Prophetic Guidance in Early Days*, reprinted from *Ministry* (Washington, D.C.: Trustees of the Ellen G. White Publications, n.d.), pp. 8-9; Spalding, *Captains of the Host*, pp. 126-27; Ellen G. White, *Life Sketches of Ellen G. White* (Mountain View, CA: PPPA, 1915), pp. 85-86.

91. Wellcome, *Second Advent Message*, pp. 398-400.

92. Ibid., pp. 515-17; David Tallmedge Arthur, " 'Come Out of Babylon':

A Study of Millerite Separatism and Denominationalism, 1840–1865" (Ph.D. diss., University of Rochester, 1970).

93. Spalding, *Captains of the Host*, pp. 108-10; David M. Young, "When Adventists Became Sabbath-keepers," *AH* 2 (Winter 1975): 5-10.

94. Wellcome, *Second Advent Message*, p. 399.

95. Ibid., p. 419.

96. Ibid., pp. 395-96.

97. Ibid., p. 423. "Jewish fables" is probably a reference to the idea of the return of the Jews to Jerusalem, which was contrary to Miller's thinking. "Commandments of men" and distinctive characteristics of modern Judaism likely refer to Preble's article on the Sabbath, which had come out two months earlier.

98. Arthur, "Come Out of Babylon," pp. 137-39.

99. Bliss, *William Miller*, p. 278.

100. *Midnight Cry* (2 March 1844): 282.

101. Wellcome, *Second Advent Message*, pp. 581-82. One is led to suspect that the correspondent was one of the editors of Millerite papers.

102. Dick, "William Miller and the Advent Crisis," p. 268.

103. Winthrop S. Hudson, "A Time of Religious Ferment," in Gaustad, *Rise of Adventism*, pp. 4-5.

104. Dick, "William Miller and the Advent Crisis," pp. 263-64.

105. Carwardine, *Transatlantic Revivalism*, p. 52.

106. Sandeen, *Roots of Fundamentalism*, pp. 42, 60, 81-84.

NOTES TO CHAPTER 2

1. David Tallmadge Arthur, " 'Come Out of Babylon': A Study of Millerite Separatism and Denominationalism, 1840–1865" (Ph.D. diss., University of Rochester, 1970), pp. 224-27, 280-371.

2. David M. Young, "When Adventists Became Sabbathkeepers," *AH* 2 (Winter 1975): 5-10.

3. Ellen G. White (hereafter referred to as EGW), *Early Writings of Ellen G. White* (Battle Creek: RHPA, 1882), pp. 13-20.

4. A detailed explanation of the process by which the sanctuary doctrine developed appears in P. Gerard Damsteegt, *Foundations of the Seventh-day Adventist Message and Mission* (Grand Rapids: William B. Eerdmans Publishing Company, 1977), pp. 122-32.

5. James White, Editorial (hereafter referred to as JW), "The Work of the Lord," *RH* (6 May 1852): 4-6.

6. Arthur, "Come Out of Babylon," pp. 97-115; Damsteegt, *Foundations*, pp. 105-16.

7. JW, "Our Present Work," *RH* (19 August 1851): 12-13.

8. JW, "Opponents in Confusion on the Sabbath Question," *RH* (4 August 1853): 44-45. A detailed discussion of early Sabbatarian Adventist theology appears in Damsteegt, *Foundations*, pp. 103-64. In 1854 the *Review and Herald* ran the following list of "Leading Doctrines" for eighteen issues:

> The Bible, and the Bible alone, the rule of faith and duty.
> The Law of God, as taught in the Old and New Testaments, unchangeable.

> The Personal Advent of Christ and the Resurrection of the Just, before
>   the Millennium.
> The Earth restored to its Eden perfection and glory, the final Inher-
>   itance of the Saints.
> Immortality alone through Christ, to be given to the Saints at the
>   Resurrection.

9. JW, A Word to the "Little Flock" (Brunswick, ME: Private printing, 1847), p. 22.

10. EGW, Present Truth (November 1850): 86-87.

11. Joseph Bates, "Time to Commence the Holy Sabbath," RH (21 April 1851): 71-72.

12. J .N. Andrews, "The Time of the Sabbath," RH (2 June 1851): 92.

13. J. N. Andrews, "Time for Commencing the Sabbath," RH (4 December 1855): 76-78.

14. JW, "The Word," RH (7 February 1856): 148-49.

15. EGW, Early Writings, pp. 121-22; RH (13 December 1853): 178.

16. EGW, 14 December 1851, Ellen G. White Estate Letter 5, 1851 (photocopy, Heritage Room, Loma Linda University Library).

17. Stephen Pierce, "The Use of Tobacco. Doings of the Church in Vermont," RH (4 December 1855): 79.

18. Robert Haddock, "A History of the Doctrine of the Sanctuary in the Advent Movement, 1800– 1905" (B.D. thesis, Andrews University, 1970), pp. 207-8.

19. J. N. Andrews, "The Use of Tobacco a Sin against God," RH (10 April 1856): 5.

20. J. H. Waggoner, "Tobacco," RH (19 November 1857): 12-13; M. E. Cornell, "The Tobacco Abomination," RH (20 May 1858): 1-2; Cornell, "Tobacco," RH (11 August 1853): 85-86.

21. S. T. Fowler, "Minnesota State Conference," RH (4 March 1862): 112.

22. Joseph Clarke, "Holy," RH (3 September 1857): 144.

23. P. Gerard Damsteegt, "Health Reform and the Bible in Early Sabbatarian Adventism," AH (Winter 1978): 21; see also Ronald L. Numbers, Prophetess of Health: A Study of Ellen G. White (New York: Harper & Row, 1976), pp. 38-76.

24. D. P. Hall, "Man Not Immortal," RH (12 September 1854): 33-36.

25. J. H. Waggoner, "The Atonement," RH (10 November 1863): 189; see also Erwin Roy Gane, "The Arian or Anti-Trinitarian Views Presented in Seventh-day Adventist Literature and the Ellen G. White Answer" (M.A. thesis, Andrews University, 1963), p. 103.

26. RH extra (21 July 1851): 4.

27. JW, Reply to Hiram Bingham, RH (14 February 1856): 158; reprinted in RH (22 January 1857): 96.

28. JW, "The Gifts—Their Object," RH (28 February 1856): 172-73.

29. D. T. Bourdeau letter, RH (22 April 1862): 167; U. Smith, RH (21 January 1862): 62-64.

30. Smith, "The Visions a Test," RH (14 January 1862): 52-53.

31. Andrews, RH (17 December 1861): 22; S. W. Rhodes, RH (6 May 1862): 182; Frederick Wheeler, RH (3 December 1861): 7.

32. RH (27 May 1862): 205.

33. "Business Proceedings of the Conference at Battle Creek," RH (4 December 1855): 76; "Address of the Conference Assembled at Battle Creek," ibid., pp. 78-79.

34. Everett N. Dick, *Founders of the Message* (Washington, D.C.: RHPA, 1938), pp. 224-25.

35. Arthur L. White, *Ellen G. White, Messenger to the Remnant* (Washington, D.C.: RHPA, 1969), p. 53.

36. Jonathan Butler, "Adventism and the American Experience," in *The Rise of Adventism: Religion and Society in Mid-Nineteenth-Century America*, ed. Edwin Scott Gaustad (New York: Harper & Row, 1974), p. 185.

37. "The Two-Horned Beast," *RH* (19 March 1857): 156.

38. *RH* (23 April 1857): 198.

39. R. F. Cottrell, "How Shall I Vote?" *RH* (30 October 1856): 205.

40. *Advent Harbinger and Bible Advocate* (28 February 1852).

41. George Storrs, "Come Out of Her My People," *Midnight Cry* (15 February 1844): 238.

42. JW, "Organization," *RH* (7 January 1862): 44.

43. EGW, *Christian Experience and Teachings of Ellen G. White*, (Mountain View, CA: PPPA, 1922), p. 195.

44. JW, "Yearly Meetings," *RH* (21 July 1859): 68.

45. Cottrell, "What are the Duties of Church Officers?" *RH* (2 October 1856): 173.

46. EGW, *Early Writings*, pp. 97-104.

47. JW, "Gospel Order," *RH* (13 December 1853): 180.

48. JW, "Gospel Order," *RH* (28 March 1854): 76.

49. Loughborough, *RH* (4 September 1855): 40.

50. Matilda Erickson Andross, *Story of the Advent Message* (Washington, D.C.: RHPA, 1926), p. 131; G. W. Amadon, "Sabbath-Schools," *RH* (16 February 1860): 102.

51. JW, "Meeting House in Battle Creek," *RH* (23 July 1857): 96.

52. JW, "Making Us a Name," *RH* (26 April 1860): 180-82.

53. JW, "The New Hymn Book," *RH* (23 January 1855): 165.

54. Waggoner, "Pledges," *RH* (25 November 1858): 8.

55. JW, "The Cause," *RH* (26 May 1859): 8.

56. *RH* (9 June 1859): 20-23.

57. *Good Samaritan*, no. 5 (January 1861); quoted in *RH* (9 April 1861): 164.

58. Dick, *Founders of the Message*, pp. 280-81.

59. EGW, "Duty of Parents to Their Children," *RH* (19 September 1854): 45-56.

60. JW, "Sabbath-Keepers' Children," *RH* (20 August 1857): 125-26.

61. An unsigned note reported that Bell had started the school on June 3 in Battle Creek: *RH* (11 June 1872): 204.

62. JW, "Moving West," *RH* (7 May 1857): 5.

63. Waggoner, "The Cause in the West," *RH* (15 May 1856): 36; (7 August 1857): 109-10.

64. JW, "An Appeal," *RH* (6 October 1863): 148.

65. "The Eastern Mission," *RH* (11 August 1863): 85.

66. JW, "The Third Angel's Message," *RH* (28 August 1856): 132-33.

67. *RH* (18 November 1858): 208. Ronald Graybill has examined the economic status of Adventists between 1858 and 1862 and has found them to be concentrated above the 50th percentile financially in relation to their communities, and to be overwhelmingly rural in character ("Millenarians and Money: Adventist Wealth and Adventist Beliefs," *Spectrum* 10 [August 1979]: 31-41).

68. JW, "Western Tour," *RH* (15 January 1857): 84-85.

69. M. Ellsworth Olsen, A *History of the Origin and Progress of Seventh-day Adventists* (Washington, D.C.: RHPA, 1925), p. 229.

70. Editorial note on the November 16-19 meeting at Battle Creek, *RH* (4 December 1855): 75.

71. Haddock, "A History of the Doctrine," p. 369.

72. Felix A. Lorenz, "A Study of the Message, with Emphasis on the Writings of Mrs. E. G. White" (essay written for SDA Theological Seminary, Washington, D.C., 1951).

73. JW, "The Cause," *RH* (28 August 1860): 116.

74. Editorial note, *RH* (18 March 1858): 144.

75. Bates, "Meetings in Vt. and Mass.," *RH* (6 May 1858): 198.

76. A. Worth, "Views Meriting Consideration," *RH* (12 August 1858): 98-99.

77. Cottrell, "The Present 'Revivals' in Babylon," *RH* (13 May 1858): 206.

78. "Business Proceedings," *RH* (12 November 1857): 4-5.

79. Cottrell, "Making Us a Name," *RH* (22 March 1860): 140; rpt. (26 April 1860): 180.

80. *Advent Harbinger and Bible Advocate*, 16 August 1851.

81. Spalding, *Origin and History*, p. 303.

82. JW, Reply to Seventh Day Baptist letter, *RH* (11 August 1853): 52-53.

83. J. N. Loughborough, "Eastern Tour," *RH* (13 November 1860): 204-5.

84. Mrs. P. P. Lewis, "Extracts from Letters," *RH* (18 August 1859): 103.

85. Loughborough, "Meetings in Parkville, Mich.," *RH* (29 May 1860): 9.

86. O. Nichols, "Organization," *RH* (28 August 1860): 116.

87. Some indication of the importance attached to the meeting can be seen in the publishing of a fairly complete account of it. See *RH* (9 October 1860): 161-63; (16 October 1860): 169-171; (23 October 1860): 177-79.

88. EGW, *The Testimonies to the Church*, Nov. 1-11 (Battle Creek: Steam Press of the Seventh-day Adventist Publishing Association, 1871), pp. 167-69.

89. JW, "Organization," *RH* (16 July 1861): 52.

90. JW, "The Association," *RH* (25 March 1862): 132.

91. JW, "Conference Address," *RH* (11 June 1861): 21-22.

92. JW, "Eastern Tour," *RH* (3 September 1861): 108.

93. *RH* (24 September 1861): 132.

94. Clarke, "Stone of Stumbling," *RH* (18 November 1862): 197-98.

95. "Doings of the Battle Creek Conference, Oct. 5 & 6, 1861," *RH* (8 October 1861): 148-49.

96. Ibid.

97. "The Cause," *RH* (20 May 1862): 196.

98. "To the Ministers of the Michigan Conference," *RH* (27 January 1863): 69.

99. Statistical Report of Seventh-day Adventists 1972, Comp. General Conference Statistical Secretary (Washington, D.C.: General Conference of SDA).

100. D. T. Taylor, *World's Crisis*, January and February 1860.

101. John Byington, "Report of General Conference of Seventh-day Adventists," *RH* (26 May 1863): 204-6; for Byington's background, see John O. Waller, "John Byington of Bucks Bridge: The Pre—Adventist Years," *AH* 1 (July 1974): 5-13, 65-67.

102. Smith, "The Conference," *RH* (26 May 1863): 204.

103. JW, "The Association," *RH* (2 June 1863): 4.

104. JW, "State of the Cause of Michigan," *RH* (2 June 1863): 7.

105. Samuel Treat, *RH* (23 June 1863): 30.

106. Cornell, "Justice to Whom Justice Is Due," *RH* (10 December 1861): 13.

107. Waggoner, *RH* (14 August 1883): 157.

108. JW, "The Nation," *RH* (12 August 1862): 84; "The Views of Seventh-day Adventists Relative to Bearing Arms" (Battle Creek: SDA Publishing Association, 1865), White Estate DF 320a (photocopy, Heritage Room, Loma Linda University Library). For a more complete analysis of the Seventh-day Adventist response to the Civil War, see Peter Brock, *Pacifism in the United States: From the Colonial Era to the First World War* (Princeton, NJ: Princeton University Press, 1968), pp. 852-61.

109. F. Morrow, "The Truth Abroad," *RH* (15 April 1862): 157; JW, "Books to Ireland," *RH* (30 December 1862): 40.

NOTES TO CHAPTER 3

1. P. Gerard Damsteegt, *Foundations of the Seventh-day Adventist Message and Mission* (Grand Rapids: William B. Eerdmans Publishing Company, 1977), p. 296.

2. The standard biographical aid for the study of Seventh-day Adventist leaders is Don F. Neufeld, ed., *Seventh-day Adventist Encyclopedia* (Washington, D.C.: RHPA, 1966) (hereafter cited as *SDA Encyclopedia*). See also Gordon Balharrie, "A Study of the Contributions Made to the Seventh-day Adventist Movement by John Nevins Andrews" (M.A. thesis, Seventh-day Adventist Theological Seminary, 1949); Ella M. Robinson, *S. N. Haskell: Man of Action* (Washington, D.C.: RHPA, 1967).

3. Ellen G. White, though never ordained ecclesiastically, was annually extended ministerial credentials by the General Conference. She is portrayed in W. Homer Teesdale, "Ellen G. White: Pioneer, Prophet" (Ph.D. diss., University of California, n.d.).

4. This paragraph indicates the content trend of Ellen G. White's *Testimonies for the Church*, 9 vols. (Mountain View, CA: PPPA, vol. 1, 465, to vol. 5, 476, written and/or published 1865– 86) (this series hereafter cited as *Testimonies*; the author as EGW).

5. *RH* (20 December 1881): 392.

6. George I. Butler, "The Death of Elder [James] White," *RH* (16 August 1881): 120-21.

7. The foundations of the Indiana Conference were laid by Sands H. Lane's older brother, Elbert B. Lane, and Elbert's wife Ellen; the latter, a licensed minister for a while, sometimes conducted her own evangelistic crusades. See S. H. Lamson, "Eld[er] E. Lane," *RH* (23 August 1881): 143.

8. *Seventh-day Adventist Yearbook* (Battle Creek: SDA Publishing Association, 1886), pp. 103-4 (hereafter cited as *SDA Yearbook*).

9. Ibid., pp. 100-102.

10. Ibid., pp. 105-7. Discussion of the early development of Seventh-day Adventist health ideas appears in Dores Eugene Robinson, *The Story of Our Health Message* (Nashville: SPA, 1943), pp. 45-133; and Ronald L. Numbers, *Prophetess of Health: A Study of Ellen G. White* (New York: Harper & Row, 1976), pp. 31-128;

see also Richard W. Schwarz, *John Harvey Kellogg, M.D.* (Nashville: SPA, 1970), pp. 59-81, for the history of Battle Creek Sanitarium.

11. For the early history of Battle Creek College, see Emmett K. VandeVere, *The Wisdom Seekers* (Nashville: SPA, 1972), pp. 11-52; further information appears in Leigh Johnsen, "Brownsberger and Battle Creek: The Beginning of Adventist Higher Education," *AH* 3 (Winter 1976): 30-38; a documentary history of early Adventist education appears in Maurice Hodgen, ed., *School Bells & Gospel Trumpets: A Documentary History of Seventh-day Adventist Education in North America* (Loma Linda, CA: Adventist Heritage Publications, 1978), pp. 3-27; John O. Waller discusses the teaching of English at Battle Creek College in "Adventist English Teachers: Some Roots," in *Language Matters*, ed. Verne Wehtje (Nashville: SPA, 1978), pp. 123-36.

12. D. W. Reavis, *I Remember* (Washington, D.C.: RHPA, n.d.), p. 110; a more complete description of student life at Battle Creek College is found in Derek C. Beardsell, "George Royal Avery—A Rich Poor Man" (M.A. thesis, Andrews University, 1967).

13. *SDA Yearbook 1886*, pp. 105-6.

14. R. A. Underwood, "Denominational Finance," *RH* (1 May 1919): 8-12; "Symposium of Pioneers," *RH* (4 June 1926): 1-6.

15. U. Smith, "Special Session of the General Conference," *RH* (6 April 1876): 108.

16. *SDA Yearbook 1883*, p. 33; 1886, p. 57.

17. Damsteegt, *Foundations*, pp. 263-308.

18. EGW, *Testimonies* 1: 147.

19. Membership statistics in this chapter derive from reports of annual sessions of the General Conference of Seventh-day Adventists as printed in the *Review and Herald* and the *SDA Yearbook*. No further notes will be given, therefore, to substantiate denominational and conference memberships.

20. Thomas D. Clark, *Frontier America* (New York: Charles Scribner's Sons, 1959), pp. 301, 306; Robert E. Riegel and Robert G. Athern, *America Moves West*, 5th ed. (New York: Holt, Rinehart and Winston, 1971), p. 240.

21. *RH* (18 March 1880): 187.

22. Washington Morse, "History of the Life of Washington and Olive Morse" (handwritten, ca. 1893, in present writer's collection).

23. The story that follows is drawn from W. B. Hill, *The Experiences of a Pioneer Evangelist of the Northwest* (privately published by the author, 1902); this book expanded his preliminary *Experiences of a Pioneer Minister in Minnesota* (Minneapolis: Press of J. A. Folsom, 1892); a photograph of Hill appears in the earlier work.

24. Butler, "A Few Words to My Iowa Friends," *RH* (19 May 1903): 5-6; the Snook-Brinkerhoff affair is recorded more fully in VandeVere, *Rugged Heart: The Story of George I. Butler* (Nashville: SPA, 1979), pp. 18-24.

25. Washington Gardner, *History of Calhoun County, Michigan*, 2 vols. (Chicago: Lewis Publishing Company, 1913), 2: 676-80; the biographical sketch of "Hiland George Butler" includes the Butler family.

26. Butler, "A Few Words to My Iowa Friends," *RH* (5 May 1903): 5-6.

27. S. N. Haskell, "Life Sketch of Elder R. M. Kilgore," *RH* (1 August 1912): 13-14.

28. The following account of California expansion is drawn from Harold Oliver McCumber, *Pioneering the Message in the Golden West* (Mountain View, CA: PPPA, 1946), pp. 28-53.

29. *RH* (3 December 1867): 395.

30. Butler, "Our Conference," *RH* (25 March 1873): 116.

31. Diary of EGW, 17 and 30 July 1872, Ellen G. White Estate, Manuscript File, General Conference of SDA, Washington, D.C. (hereafter cited as White Estate).

32. Ibid., 28-29 July and 18 August 1872.

33. Ibid., 4 September 1872.

34. James White, "Health in the West," *Health Reformer* (April 1874): 97-101 (James White hereafter cited as JW).

35. Lucinda Hall's contribution to the struggling press was described by Haskell thus: "She is the balance wheel of the whole concern. [No one] . . . can take her place." Haskell to W. C. White, 13 May 1879, White Estate Incoming Letter File (hereafter cited as White Estate ILF). (William Clarence White hereafter cited as WCW.)

36. Haskell to EGW, ca. September 1896 (White Estate ILF).

37. J. H. Waggoner to EGW, March 1879 (White Estate ILF).

38. For examples, see: Waggoner to JW, 9 and 24 January and 12 and 21 February 1879; Waggoner to EGW, 5 March, 15 May 1879; Waggoner to WCW, 19 November 1879 (White Estate ILF).

39. Waggoner to WCW, 12 December 1879; Charles H. Jones to WCW, 26 July 1885 (White Estate ILF).

40. Waggoner, "Death of Elder James White," *Signs of the Times* (11 August 1881): 354.

41. Butler to JW, 29 March 1875; Waggoner to JW, 21 March 1879; Haskell to WCW, 24 November 1880 (White Estate ILF).

42. EGW, *Testimonies*, 2: 502; JW (in facsimile) to D. M. Canright, 24 May [1881] (Heritage Room, Andrews University Library); Butler to John Harvey Kellogg, 10 May 1904, 11 June 1905 (John Harvey Kellogg Manuscript Collection, The Museum, Michigan State University); John Orr Corliss to JW, 26 April 1881; Haskell to WCW, 29 December 1880, 17 June 1881 (White Estate ILF).

43. Haskell to EGW, 11 August 1881 (White Estate ILF).

44. Morse, "History of . . . Washington and Olive Morse."

45. Butler to WCW, 17 August 1881 (White Estate ILF).

46. *Battle Creek Daily Journal* 2 April 1885.

47. E. M. Cadwallader, A *History of Seventh-day Adventist Education*, 3d ed. (Lincoln, NE: Union College, 1958), chap. 15; see also VandeVere, *The Wisdom Seekers*, pp. 42-47.

48. Pacific Union College, *Diogenes Lantern 1957* (Angwin, CA: Student Association, 1957), p. 44; Waggoner to WCW, 5 February 1879 (White Estate ILF). A student's view of Healdsburg College appears in Maud O'Neill, "Letters from a Healdsburg College student," *AH* 3 (Winter 1976): 51-57.

49. J. F. Wood, "The North Pacific Mission," *Signs of the Times* (11 June 1874): 16.

50. Adelia P. Van Horn, "A Sabbath in Walla Walla, W[ashington] T[erritory]," *RH* (25 August 1874): 78.

51. A. P. Van Horn to JW, 26 August 1877; Haskell to JW, 4 June 1879 (White Estate ILF).

52. Haskell to JW, 4 June 1879 (White Estate ILF).

53. Isaac Van Horn to JW, 5 September 1877, 12 November 1879 (White Estate ILF).

54. See EGW, *Testimonies*, 4: 286-96 for a description of her 1878 trip to and ministry in Oregon.

55. A. P. Van Horn to "the Review Folks," 5 October 1878 (White Estate ILF).

56. I. D. Van Horn to WCW, 21 September 1876; John N. Loughborough to WCW, 31 October 1877 (White Estate ILF).

57. I. D. Van Horn to WCW, 21 September 1876 (White Estate ILF).

58. A. P. Van Horn to JW and EGW, 8 March 1879 (White Estate ILF). The most detailed account of early entrance into the Pacific Northwest by Seventh-day Adventists is in *Sixty Years of Progress: Walla Walla College* (College Place, WA: College Press, n.d.).

59. Eric Norelius, *Early Life of Eric Norelius* (1833–62), trans. Emeroy Johnson (Rock Island, IL: 1934), p. 76, quoted in Carl Wittke, *We Who Built America* (New York: Prentice-Hall, 1939), p. 266.

60. The dawning idea among Seventh-day Adventists of making converts among foreign-language people in the United States and a developing sense of world mission are traced in Donald Curtiss Bozarth, "An Investigation of the Development of the Concept of Seventh-day Adventist Missions, 1848–1874" (M.A. thesis, SDA Theological Seminary, 1956) and Damsteegt, *Foundations*, pp. 263-308.

61. John Gottlieb Matteson, "The Providence of God in Events Connected with the Life of J. G. Matteson" (typewritten, 1890), pp. 118-29 (Heritage Room, Andrews University Library).

62. Butler to JW, 16 April 1874; Butler to WCW, 1 October 1885 (White Estate ILF).

63. Butler to JW, 14 January 1874 (White Estate ILF).

64. In 1902 these congregations largely migrated to Oklahoma.

65. U. Smith, "General Conference: Business Proceedings," *RH* (3 January 1882): 10-11.

66. Lewis Harrison Christian, *Sons of the North* (Mountain View, CA: PPPA, 1941), p. 137. Christian estimates that the Scandinavians numbered eight hundred; I suggest that the Germans numbered seven hundred.

67. Butler to JW, 14 January 1874 (White Estate ILF).

68. The role of Scandinavians in the Seventh-day Adventist Church is portrayed by Christian, *Sons of the North*, and that of the Russian-Mennonite-Germans by Frank E. Wall and Ava C. Wall, *Uncertain Journey* (Washington, D.C.: RHPA, 1974). Nothing comparable to these books exists for the fatherland Germans. A broad coverage of immigrant Americans is in Wittke, *We Who Built America*.

69. M. B. Czechowski, *Thrilling and Instructive Developments: An Experience of Fifteen Years as Roman Catholic Clergyman and Priest* (Boston: Published for the author, 1862); Jacques Frei, "Recuil de Documents Concernant Michael Belina Czechowski (1971)," (photocopies of these works in Heritage Room, Andrews University Library); see also JW, "The Seventh-day Adventists of Europe," *RH* (30 November 1869): 181; "European Mission," *RH* (11 January 1870): 22; E. Naenny, "Waldensian Pioneer: Literature Evangelist," *RH* (27 December 1973): 20; Rajmund Dabrowski, "M. B. Czechowski: Pioneer to Europe," *AH* 4 (Summer 1977): 13-23.

70. J. O. Corliss, "Experiences of Former Days," *RH* (10 November 1904): 9; J. N. Andrews [correspondence from Switzerland], *RH* (23 September 1875): 92; G. I. Butler, *RH* (29 April 1884): 282; (6 May 1884): 297; (20 May 1884): 328-29.

71. See Andrews, "The Work in Europe," *RH* (28 January 1875): 36.

72. Christian, *Sons of the North*, p. 104.

73. Ibid.

74. EGW, *Life Sketches of Ellen G. White* (Mountain View, CA: PPPA, 1915), pp. 208-9.

75. *RH* (18 November 1884): 728.

76. *RH* (14 February 1871): 68; (4 October 1877): 105; (18 November 1884): 728.

77. Butler, *Leadership* (Battle Creek: Published for the author, 1873), p. 1; Butler to F. E. Belden, 14 March 1907; Butler to C. Creager Crisler, 25 September 1914 (White Estate ILF).

78. JW, "Leadership," *RH* (1 December 1874): 180-181; JW, "Future Labors," *RH* (22 April 1875): 136; EGW, *Testimonies*, 3: 492-509; Butler to Belden, 14 March 1907; Butler to Crisler, 25 September 1914 (White Estate ILF). For General Conference session resolutions, see *RH* (26 August 1875); (4 October 1877).

79. *RH* (26 August 1875): 59; (4 October 1877): 106; JW, "Leadership," *RH* (1 December 1874): 180-81.

80. *RH* (24 September 1867); (1 October 1867).

81. Butler to EGW, 2 June 1882 (White Estate ILF).

82. Butler to EGW, 31 August 1885 (White Estate ILF).

83. EGW, "Sensational Revivals," *Testimonies*, 4: 73-76. A description of frontier extravagances ("jerking, whirling, swooning") is in Catherine C. Cleveland, *The Great Revival in the West, 1796–1805* (Chicago: University of Chicago Press, 1916).

84. Uriah Smith, *Thoughts, Critical and Practical, on the Book of Revelation* (Battle Creek: SDA Publishing Association, 1867); Smith, *Thoughts, Critical and Practical, on the Book of Daniel* (Battle Creek: SDA Publishing Association, 1873); see also Smith, *Synopsis of the Present Truth* (Battle Creek: SDA Publishing Association, 1884).

85. Uriah Smith, *The State of the Dead and the Destiny of the Wicked* (Battle Creek: SDA Publishing Association, 1873), p. 247. *Battle Creek Daily Journal*, 7 October 1879; John H. Kellogg, *Harmony of Science and the Bible on the Nature of the Soul and the Doctrine of the Resurrection* (Battle Creek: SDA Publishing Association, 1879), p. 219; Dudley M. Canright, *Matter and Spirit; or, the Problem of Human Thought* (Battle Creek: RHPA, 1882), p. 57.

86. Waggoner, *The Spirit of God: Its Offices and Manifestations to the End of the Christian Age* (Battle Creek: SDA Publishing Association, 1877), pp. 51-52, 139.

87. Waggoner, *The Atonement: An Examination of a Remedial System in Light of Nature and Revelation* (Oakland: PPPA, 1884), p. 187; cf. *Seventh-day Adventists Answer Questions on Doctrine* (Washington, D.C.: RHPA, 1956), pp. 173, 195, 228.

88. Butler, "The Camp-Meeting Campaign," *RH* (28 October 1873): 157.

89. EGW, *Testimonies*, 1: 141-46, 185-95; 3: 212-21, 424-28.

90. EGW, *Selected Messages*, 2 vols. (Washington, D.C.: RHPA, 1858), 1: 353.

91. Smith, ed., "The Conference [of 1885]," *RH* (24 November 1885): 728.

NOTES TO CHAPTER 4

1. Uriah Smith, Editorial, "The Conference" (24th annual session), *RH* (24 November 1885): 728.

2. Ellen G. White, *The Great Controversy Between Christ and Satan from the Destruction of Jerusalem to the End of the Great Controversy* (Oakland: PPPA, 1884), p. 410 (author hereafter cited as EGW; title hereafter cited as *The Great Controversy*).

3. *Seventh-day Adventist Yearbook* (Battle Creek: SDA Publishing Association, 1884), p. 42 (hereafter cited as *SDA Yearbook*).

4. Eric D. Syme, "Seventh-day Adventist Concepts on Church and State" (Ph.D. diss., American University, 1969), pp. 80-107.

5. G. I. Butler, "The Sabbath Question Coming Before the Arkansas Courts," *RH* (27 October 1885): 666; "The Arkansas Persecution," *RH* (8 December 1885): 768.

6. William A. Blakely, ed., *American State Papers Bearing on Sunday Legislation* (Washington, D.C.: RHPA, 1911), pp. 733-34.

7. "General Conference Proceedings," *RH* (1 December 1885): 744-75.

8. Syme, "SDA Concepts," pp. 103-21.

9. Ibid., pp. 111-25; see also Ben McArthur, "1893, The Chicago World's Fair: An Early Test for Adventist Religious Liberty," *AH* 2 (Winter 1975): 11-21.

10. Syme, "SDA Concepts," pp. 145-48.

11. Jonathan Butler, "Adventism and the American Experience," in *The Rise of Adventism: Religion and Society in Mid-Nineteenth-Century America* ed. Edwin Scott Gaustad (New York: Harper & Row, 1974), p. 194.

12. Substantial monographic interpretations of this theological debate are included in A. V. Olson, *Through Crisis to Victory, 1888–1901* (Washington, D.C.: RHPA, 1966) (hereafter cited as *Through Crisis*); LeRoy E. Froom, *Movement of Destiny* (Washington, D.C.: RHPA, 1971), pp. 148-375 (hereafter cited as *Movement*).

13. Butler to EGW, 20 June and 16 December 1886, Washington, D.C., (General Conference of Seventh-Adventists, Ellen G. White Estate Incoming Letter File) (hereafter cited as ILF).

14. Ibid.

15. Butler to EGW, 16 December 1886 (ILF); "General Conference Session," *RH* (14 December 1886): 779.

16. EGW to Waggoner and Jones, 18 February 1887, Letter 37, 1887.

17. EGW to Butler and Smith, 5 April 1887, Letter 13, 1887.

18. Chester C. McReynolds, "Experiences While at the General Conference in Minneapolis, Minn., in 1888" (manuscript), White Estate Document File 189 (hereafter cited as White Est. DF); R. T. Nash, "The Minneapolis Conference—An Eyewitness Account" (manuscript), 25 June 1955 (White Est. DF 189).

19. McReynolds, "Experiences" (White Est. DF 189); EGW to W. M. Healey, 9 December 1888, Letter 7, 1888.

20. Asa T. Robinson, "Did the Seventh-day Adventist Denomination Reject the Doctrine of Righteousness by Faith?" (manuscript) (White Est. DF 189); Froom, *Movement*, p. 242.

21. McReynolds, "Experiences." Probably the best idea of the messages that Waggoner presented at Minneapolis in 1888 may be found by examining his book *Christ and His Righteousness* (Oakland: PPPA, 1890); see also Froom, *Movement*, p. 189.

22. EGW, "Looking Back at Minneapolis," ca. November 1888, MS 24, 1888; Nash, "Eyewitness."

23. Nash, "Eyewitness"; McReynolds, "Experiences."

24. Nash, "Eyewitness."

25. Butler, *RH* (13 November 1888). It is possible to consider Ole Andres

Olsen something of a Butler protégé and thus entirely acceptable to him as his successor. See Butler to EGW, 28 December 1885 (ILF).

26. *General Conference Daily Bulletin*, 2: 12 (2 November 1888): 2 (hereafter cited as *GC Daily Bulletin*); *RH* (13 November 1888): 713; Dan T. Jones, *RH* (27 November 1888): 749.

27. EGW to Mary White, 4 November 1888, Letter 82, 1888; EGW, "Looking Back at Minneapolis"; EGW to Madison and Howard Miller, 23 July 1889, Letter 4, 1889.

28. EGW to William C. White, 7 April 1889, Letter 1, 1889; EGW ca. late June 1889, MS 30, 1889.

29. EGW to WCW, 7 April 1889, Letter 1, 1889; Olson, *Through Crisis*, pp. 59-62.

30. Charles E. White, "The Ministerial Institutes" (Term paper, Andrews University, 1968). At the 1891 General Conference session Waggoner gave sixteen lectures on Paul's Epistle to the Romans; in 1897 he gave eighteen studies on the Book of Hebrews. At the 1893 session Jones gave twenty-four lectures on the "The Third Angel's Message," followed by twenty-six more on the same topic in 1895. Jones gave seven sermons at the 1899 session and Waggoner three. In 1901, Waggoner spoke twice and Jones once.

31. A. O. Tait to WCW, 7 October 1895 (ILF).

32. Waggoner to WCW, 1 April 1892; Olsen to WCW and EGW, 15 June 1892; A. T. Jones to EGW, 14 August 1893; A. G. Daniells to WCW, 4 August 1901 and 12 May 1902 (ILF). The Huns-Alemanni controversy, once so sharp, appears to have simply faded away in the SDA Church.

33. Butler to S. N. Haskell, 22 April 1893 (copy, ILF).

34. Butler, "Personal," *RH* (13 June 1893): 377. See also Olsen to EGW, 23 July 1893 (ILF).

35. R. M. Kilgore, *RH* (4 December 1894): 764.

36. EGW to Elder and Mrs. J. S. Washburn, 8 January 1891, Letter 32, 1891; EGW, MS 40, 1891.

37. G. A. Irwin to EGW, 13 October 1897 (ILF); see also Olson, *Through Crisis*, p. 102n.

38. Olsen to EGW, 21 March 1893; W. A. Spicer to WCW, 24 February 1893 (ILF).

39. D. T. Jones to Olsen, 27 November 1894 (copy, ILF).

40. Butler to EGW, 13 May 1885; 23 August, 30 September, 7 October 1886; 24 February 1887 (ILF).

41. Butler to EGW, 30 September 1885 (ILF).

42. Olsen to WCW, 1 February 1892; Olsen to EGW, 23 May 1892 (ILF).

43. Olsen to EGW, 7 November 1895 (ILF).

44. Daniells to WCW, 23 August 1901 (ILF).

45. Daniells to WCW, 17 May 1903 (ILF).

46. Daniells to WCW, 18 April 1905 (ILF).

47. Irwin to EGW, 20 January 1899 (ILF).

48. Haskell to EGW, 10 November 1899 (ILF).

49. Haskell to EGW, 27 July 1900 (ILF).

50. Daniells to EGW, 10 September 1903 (ILF).

51. Waggoner to WCW, 20 November 1885; A. T. Jones to WCW, 4 December 1885; J. N. Loughborough to EGW, 6 December 1885 (ILF). This incident is discussed in Arthur L. White, "Revivals—the Time When God and Satan Work," *RH* (2 August 1973): 4-7.

52. Olsen to WCW, 9 October 1891; Olsen to EGW, 10 March 1892; Haskell to EGW, 3 October 1899 (ILF).

53. Hetty H. Haskell to EGW, 18 September 1899; S. N. Haskell to EGW, 3 October 1899; 24 January 1900 (ILF) (S. N. Haskell hereafter cited as Haskell; his wife as H. Haskell).

54. G. B. Thompson to Daniells, 7 August 1901 (General Conference Publishing Department Historical Files, Daniells folder 2).

55. Haskell to EGW, 3 October 1899 (ILF).

56. Daniells to WCW, 16 March 1905; Daniells to Spicer, 25 August 1905 (copy, ILF).

57. Haskell to EGW, 10 November 1899 (ILF).

58. Haskell to EGW, 23 November 1899; P. T. Magan to EGW, 24 November 1899 (ILF).

59. Waggoner, "Spirit of Prophecy" (sermon), *GC Daily Bulletin* (17 February 1899): 13.

60. Haskell to EGW, 25 September 1900 (ILF).

61. Daniells to WCW, 16 May and 2 September 1901 (ILF).

62. Don F. Neufeld, ed., *Seventh-day Adventist Encyclopedia* (Washington, D.C.: RHPA, 1966), s.v. "Albion Fox Ballenger" (hereafter cited as *SDA Encyclopedia*).

63. Dudley M. Canright, *Seventh-day Adventism Renounced*, 5th ed. (Cincinnati: Standard Publishing Company, 1889), pp. 137, 151, and passim; Butler to EGW, 17 February 1887 (ILF).

64. Butler to EGW, 30 September 1885; 16 December 1886; 17 February 1887 (ILF).

65. Butler to EGW, 17 February 1887 (ILF); *RH* (22 March 1887): 185; *SDA Encyclopedia*, s.v. "Dudley Marvin Canright."

66. Canright to EGW, 29 July 1887; Butler to EGW, 16 November 1886; 6 March 1888 (ILF).

67. Haskell to EGW, 5 April 1897; Daniells to EGW, 29 March and 5 April 1897; Daniells to WCW, 6 July and 22 August 1902 (ILF).

68. Spicer to WCW, 20 April 1893; Olsen to EGW, 23 July 1893 (ILF); *RH* (22 August 1893): 530-31; (29 August 1893): 546-47; (5 September 1893): 562-63; (12 September 1893): 578-79.

69. EGW, "Meeting the Claims of False Prophets," *Selected Messages from the Writings of Ellen G. White*, 2 vols. (Washington, D.C.: RHPA, 1958), 2: 72-84 (hereafter cited as *Selected Messages*); H. Haskell to EGW, 27 February 1900 (ILF).

70. Haskell to EGW, 4 January 1893, 9 March and 10 October 1893 (ILF).

71. F. M. Wilcox to D. A. Robinson, 8 March 1894 (copy); Olsen to EGW, 29 March 1894; Haskell to EGW, 20 and 22 April 1894 (ILF). Ellen White's views of this incident are given in "The Visions of Anna Phillips," *Selected Messages*, 2: 85-95.

72. Irwin to EGW, 16 March 1900; H. Haskell to EGW, 27 February and 20 October 1900 (ILF).

73. For a comprehensive study of this aspect of Adventist thought, see Erwin Roy Gane, "The Arian or Anti-Trinitarian Views Presented in Seventh-day Adventist Literature and the Ellen G. White Answer" (M.A. thesis, Andrews University, 1963); this matter is also treated substantially in Froom, *Movement*.

74. EGW, *The Desire of Ages* (Oakland: PPPA, 1898), pp. 73, 213, 469, 470, 483.

75. Examples of these ideas may be found in the presentations of these three men at the 1897 General Conference session. See also W. W. Prescott, "True

Education," *GC Daily Bulletin* (16 February 1897): 36; Waggoner, "Studies on the Book of Hebrews," *GC Daily Bulletin* (16 February 1897): 45; and Kellogg, "God in Man," *GC Daily Bulletin* (18, 19 February 1897): 76-84.

76. EGW, "A Message of Warning," MS 70, 1905 (a transcript of a talk presented at the 1905 General Conference session). The progression of Kellogg's thought during these years is conveniently and convincingly presented in James W. Zackrison, "The Development of Dr. J. H. Kellogg's Theological Ideas up to 1903" (term paper, Andrews University, 1973) (hereafter cited as "JHK Ideas").

77. Daniells to WCW, 22 December 1903 (ILF).

78. Tait to EGW, 22 March 1898 (ILF).

79. Zackrison, "JHK Ideas," pp. 25, 28, 33, 34; Butler to Kellogg, 31 July 1904 (Kellogg Papers, The Museum, Michigan State University).

80. Daniells to WCW, 29 September 1903 (ILF).

81. Daniells, "How the Denomination was Saved from Pantheism" (stenographically reported statement), 12 March 1935 (White Est. DF 15a); see also Daniells to WCW, 25 March 1902 (ILF), in which the number of *Living Temple* to be sold is stated as four hundred thousand.

82. Daniells to WCW, 29 September 1903 (ILF).

83. Ibid. See also Haskell to WCW, 29 September 1903; E. J. Dryer to Daniells, 28 August 1903 (ILF); Haskell to Kellogg, 16 September 1903 (Kellogg Papers, MSU).

84. Daniells to WCW, 29 September 1903 (ILF).

85. Daniells to WCW, 23 October 1903 (ILF); see also Daniells to WCW, 8 October 1903, and Daniells to EGW, 20 October 1903 (ILF). A published version of these events is given in Daniells, *The Abiding Gift of Prophecy* (Mountain View, CA: PPPA, 1936), pp. 336-40.

86. Daniells to WCW, 23 October 1903 (ILF).

87. Daniells to WCW, 29 October 1903 (ILF).

88. Daniells to WCW, 27 December 1903; 1 and 8 January 1904, ILF; Kellogg to Butler, 27 June 1904 (Kellogg Papers, MSU).

89. Daniells to WCW, 4 January 1904; Daniells to EGW, 22 February 1905 (ILF).

90. Arthur Whitefield Spalding, *Origin and History of Seventh-day Adventists*, 4 vols. (Washington, D.C.: RHPA, 1961), 1: 262 (hereafter cited as *Origin and History of SDA*).

91. A. L. White, "Adventist Responsibility to the Inner City," *RH* (5 November 1970): 1-2.

92. Ibid. See also Butler to EGW, 20 June 1886; Haskell to the General Conference Assembled, 17 March 1903 (ILF); *RH* (1 December 1885): 746; and Michael McGuckin, "The Lincoln City Mission: A. J. Cudney and Seventh-day Adventist Beginnings in Lincoln, Nebraska," *AH* 2 (Summer 1975): 24-32.

93. E. W. Farnsworth, "Chicago Mission Training School," *GC Daily Bulletin* (29 October 1888): 2, 3.

94. Loughborough to EGW, 7 January 1893 (ILF).

95. Haskell to WCW, 21 June 1892; Haskell to EGW, 30 November 1893 and 3 February 1894 (ILF).

96. EGW to "Dear Brethren Engaged in Labor in Nimes," 24 August 1886, Letter 48, 1886; see also Haskell to EGW, 9 September 1886 and 11 April 1887 (ILF).

97. Richard W. Schwarz, "Adventism's Social Gospel Advocate: John Harvey Kellogg," *Spectrum* 1 (Spring 1969): 18-20; Richard Rice, "Adventists and Welfare Work: A Comparative Study," *Spectrum* 2 (Winter 1970): 22-32.

98. Rice, "Adventists and Welfare Work," pp. 20-24; Schwarz, "John Harvey Kellogg: American Health Reformer" (Ph.D. diss., University of Michigan, 1964), pp. 331-33.

99. Schwarz, "JHK: American Health Reformer," pp. 311-12.

100. Ibid., pp. 335-37; Schwarz, "Adventism's Social Gospel Advocate," pp. 24-26; see also A. L. White, "A Shift in Emphasis," *RH* (12 November 1970): 7-10; "Strategy of Diversion," *RH* (19 November 1970): 8-11.

101. A. L. White, "A Work Others Will Not Do," *RH* (26 November 1970): 4-6. Jonathan Butler, "Ellen G. White and the Chicago Mission," *Spectrum* 2 (Winter 1970): 41-51.

102. Haskell to EGW, 11 July 1901; Haskell to the General Conference Assembled, 17 March 1903; Haskell to WCW, 12 November 1905 (ILF).

103. These activities are abundantly documented in letters from the Haskells to Ellen White during the period July 1901 to June 1902 (ILF); they are conveniently summarized in Ella M. Robinson, *S. N. Haskell: Man of Action* (Washington, D.C.: RHPA, 1967), pp. 177-88.

104. Robinson, *Haskell*, pp. 186-88.

105. H. Haskell to EGW, 16 August and 5 September 1902; 7 March 1903 (ILF).

106. Irwin to EGW, 8 November 1900; Haskell to EGW, 17 November 1900 (ILF).

107. Robinson, *Haskell*, pp. 189-95; Daniells to WCW, 28 September and 13 December 1903 (ILF).

108. *SDA Encyclopedia*, s.v. "Stephen Nelson Haskell."

109. Daniells to WCW, 14 October 1904 and 11 April 1905 (ILF).

110. Daniells to EGW, 24 February 1903 (ILF).

111. EGW, MS 62, 1903, quoted in EGW, *Evangelism* (Washington, D.C.: RHPA, 1946), p. 31.

112. Ibid., p. 33, e.g.

113. Spalding, "Lights and Shades in the Black Belt; Containing the story of the South Missionary Society, the Oakwood School and the Hillcrest School" (unpublished book MS, 1913), p. 147 (White Est. DF 376).

114. Ibid., p. 151.

115. EGW, "Our Duty to the Colored People," 20 March 1891, MS 6, 1891, in EGW, *The Southern Work* (Washington, D.C.: RHPA, 1966), pp. 12-13.

116. Ronald D. Graybill, *Mission to Black America* (Mountain View, CA: PPPA, 1971), pp. 14-21.

117. Ibid., pp. 20-28.

118. Olsen to WCW, 27 April 1894 (ILF).

119. Graybill, *Mission*, pp. 40-44.

120. Ibid., pp. 45-61.

121. Ibid., pp. 80-86, 120-25; see also Otis B. Edwards, "Origin and Development of the Seventh-day Adventist Work Among Negroes in the Alabama-Mississippi Conference" (M.A. thesis, Andrews University, 1941), pp. 46-47.

122. Graybill, *Mission*, pp. 73-78, 112-14; Edwards, "Work Among Negroes," pp. 52-53.

123. Graybill, *Mission*, pp. 106-8; A. H. Adams to Irwin, 26 September 1899 (copy, ILF).

124. Edwards, "Work Among Negroes," pp. 119-21. Irwin to Olsen, 26 November 1895 and 7 May 1896 (copies); Irwin to Leroy T. Nicola, 15 April 1896 (copy, ILF); Spalding, "Lights and Shades," pp. 248-49.

125. Irwin to Nicola, 15 April 1896 (copy); see also Irwin to Olsen, 5 February and 7 May 1896 (ILF).

126. Irwin to Olsen, 21 January 1897 (copy); Irwin to EGW, 30 January 1898 (ILF); Spalding, "Lights and Shades," pp. 262-63, 306-7.

127. Spalding, "Lights and Shades," pp. 301-4; Edwards, "Work Among Negroes," pp. 65-71; see also Jacob Justiss, "Origin and Development of the Seventh-day Adventist Health Message Among Negroes" (M.A. thesis, Andrews University, 1945), pp. 16-22, 37-40.

128. Olsen to WCW, 8 November 1894 (ILF).

129. Irwin to Olsen, 19 September 1895 (copy); Irwin to Nicola, 6 January 1896 (copy, ILF).

130. Irwin to Olsen, 25 August and 22 December 1896 (copies); Irwin to EGW, 30 January 1898 and 26 March 1899 (ILF). Ellen White's position is comprehensively covered in Ronald D. Graybill, *Ellen G. White and Church Race Relations* (Washington, D.C.: RHPA, 1970).

131. *Outline of Mission Fields Entered by Seventh-day Adventists* (Washington, D.C.: Mission Board of Seventh-day Adventists, 1905), pp. 25, 33, 43-44, 52.

132. Ibid., p. 32; Haskell to Wilcox, 8 December 1894 (copy); Haskell to WCW, 29 October 1905 (ILF).

133. *Outline of Mission Fields*, p. 26; Haskell to WCW, 13 September 1894; Haskell to Wilcox, 8 December 1894 (copy); Haskell to Olsen, 1 January 1895 (copy); Olsen to WCW, 26 February 1895 (ILF).

134. *Outline of Mission Fields*, pp. 45-46; Haskell to WCW, 16 April 1893; Daniells to "Dear Fellow Worker," 23 October 1904 (ILF).

135. James A. Scherer, *Missionary Go Home! A Re-appraisal of the Christian World Mission* (Englewood Cliffs, NJ: Prentice-Hall, 1908), p. 33; see also *RH* (26 February 1901): 135.

136. *Outline of Mission Fields*, passim; Robinson, *Haskell*, pp. 57-120, 130-59; see also Spicer to WCW, 24 February 1893 (ILF). That attention to being paid (at the 1893 General Conference session then in progress), Spicer thought, was due to the presence of workers who had served or were serving in these areas.

137. Olsen to WCW, 4 December 1894 (ILF).

138. Olsen to WCW and Prescott, 9 December 1895 (ILF).

139. Spicer to WCW, 13 July and 8 September 1893 (ILF).

140. *SDA Encyclopedia*, s.v. "Pitcairn"; Fred M. Harder, "Pitcairn: Ship and Symbol," *AH* 6 (Summer 1979): 3-15.

141. Haskell to WCW, 19 September 1887; Haskell to EGW, 27 July 1893; Haskell to Olsen, 7 September 1895 (copy); Olsen to WCW, 1 September 1892; Daniells to EGW, 8 March 1892; Daniells to EGW, 8 March 1896; Daniells to WCW, 3 July 1900 (ILF).

142. Daniells to EGW, 26 June 1894 (ILF).

143. Haskell to WCW, 18 September 1885; Olsen to WCW, 23 May 1895; Olsen to I. H. Evans, 22 February 1900 (copy); Irwin to EGW, 3 October 1898; Daniells to EGW, 2 June 1902 (ILF).

144. Daniells to WCW, 3 April 1900 and 9 October 1901; Daniells to E. H. Gates, 23 May 1901 (copy, ILF).

145. Haskell to EGW, 23 August 1899; Haskell to WCW, 26 December 1899 and 9 March 1900 (ILF).

146. Olsen to WCW, 22 February 1892, 19 June 1894, and 10 September 1896; Harmon Lindsay to EGW, 16 August 1894 (ILF).

147. Irwin to Nicola, 9 August 1896 (copy, ILF).

148. Haskell to EGW, 25 March 1892; Haskell to WCW, 14 October 1894; Haskell to Olsen, 1 January 1895 (copy); Haskell to Wilcox, 26 January 1896 (copy); Daniells to EGW, 9 June 1900 (ILF).

149. Olsen to WCW, 19 April 1892; Olsen to Prescott, 22 September 1896 (copy); Irwin to EGW, 11 December 1900; Magan to WCW, 19 September 1901; Daniells to WCW, 13 April 1902 (ILF).

150. The development of the tithing principle is described in *SDA Encyclopedia*, s.v. "Systematic Benevolence" and "Tithe." From Butler in 1885 to Daniells in 1905, all General Conference presidents were concerned with getting the people to pay an honest tithe. See Butler to EGW, 27 January 1885 and Daniells to WCW, 12 January and 12 February 1905 (ILF).

151. Butler to EGW, 30 September and 8 October 1885 (ILF). This situation was not remedied until 1905, when the General Conference arranged for the surplus tithe from a conference to be available to meet the salaries of overseas missionaries. See *RH* (11 May 1905): 9.

152. Butler to EGW, 30 September 1885; Irwin to EGW, 28 September 1899; Daniells to WCW, 8 June 1904 (ILF).

153. Butler to EGW, 25 January 1886; Spicer to WCW, 4 January 1893; Tait to "Dear Friend of the Cause," 7 September 1893; Evans to WCW, 4 January 1898 (ILF). *SDA Yearbook 1894*, pp. 62-63; *RH* (14 December 1886): 778.

154. Spalding, *Origin and History of SDA*, 2: 74-75; *SDA Yearbook 1904*, p 9.

155. H. Haskell to EGW, 12 September 1899; Daniells to WCW, 30 November 1904 and 16 March 1905; Daniells to J. E. White, 10 March 1905 (copy, ILF).

156. Irwin to Daniells, 10 October 1901 (copy); Daniells to Edwin White, 10 March 1905 (copy, ILF).

157. Butler to WCW, 1 October 1885; Evans to EGW, 20 November 1901 (ILF).

158. Haskell to M. C. Wilcox, 4 February 1896 (copy); H. Haskell to EGW, 6 December 1899; Daniells to C. P. Bollman, 9 February 1905 (copy, ILF).

159. Prescott to EGW, 30 July 1896; Daniells to EGW, 7 June 1901; Daniells to WCW, 26 June 1903 (ILF).

160. Irwin to EGW, 28 September 1899 and 12 April 1900; Daniells to Members of General Conference Committee, 2 August 1901 (ILF).

161. Daniells to WCW, 13 December 1903 (ILF).

162. Irwin to EGW, 27 October and 21 December 1899; Irwin to WCW, 25 December 1899; Evans and J. N. Nelson to Irwin, January 1900 (copy); Olsen to Irwin, 21 February and 10 April 1900 (copy); Olsen to EGW, 4 March 1901 (ILF).

163. Evans to EGW, 17 March 1898; Daniells to WCW, 4 August 1901; Irwin to Daniells, 11 August 1901 (copy, ILF). The financial position of the General Conference was so bad that on December 31, 1898, it had in cash on hand and in the bank only $61.20; see A. G. Adams, "Financial Report," *GC Daily Bulletin* (17 February 1899): 11.

164. Daniells to WCW, 6 July and 24 August 1902; Irwin to E. R. Palmer, 30 December 1901 (copy, ILF).

165. Haskell to WCW, 12 December 1899; Irwin to EGW, 12 April 1900 (ILF); Daniells, *GC Daily Bulletin* (31 March 1903): 18-19.

166. Daniells to WCW, 12 May 1902 (ILF).

167. Haskell to EGW, 3 September 1904; Haskell to WCW, 1 September 1905 (ILF).

168. Daniells to Prescott and E. A. Sutherland, 15 May 1902 (copy, ILF); see also Butler to WCW, 30 October 1885; Magan to WCW, 29 December 1892; Prescott to EGW, 8 November 1893; Olsen to WCW, 18 June 1895; H. Haskell to EGW, 30 March 1898 (ILF).

169. M. Ellsworth Olsen, A History of the Origin and Progress of Seventh-day Adventists, 2d ed. (Washington, D.C.: RHPA, 1926), p. 426.

170. Magan to EGW, 24 November 1899 (ILF); see also A. T. Jones to EGW, 28 December 1898; Daniells to WCW, 2 September 1901 (ILF). One report places the amount of commercial work being done by the Review and Herald at this time as 80 percent of the total, but this seems excessive. Irwin to EGW, 10 November 1899 (ILF).

171. Evans to WCW, 16 July 1901; Daniells to Palmer, 23 August 1901 (copy, ILF).

172. Kellogg to Butler, 1 July 1904 (Kellogg Papers, MSU).

173. Daniells to C. C. Nicola, 30 July 1906 (copy, ILF).

174. Olsen to WCW, 21 May 1896 (ILF).

175. C. C. Crisler, Organization: Its Character, Purpose, Place, and Development in the Seventh-day Adventist Church (Washington, D.C.: RHPA, 1938), pp. 121-33.

176. GC Daily Bulletin (21 November 1887): 1-2.

177. Crisler, Organization, pp. 136-37.

178. Ibid., p. 138.

179. GC Daily Bulletin (27 and 28 January 1893): 20; SDA Encyclopedia, pp. 29-30, 37, 528, 806, 1068, 1080, 1124; Olsen to WCW, 28 August 1892; Olsen to EGW, 1 September 1892 (ILF).

180. Crisler, Organization, pp. 139-43. The plan for district conferences seems to have originated with Will White. See Olsen to WCW, 25 January 1892 (ILF).

181. Crisler, Organization, pp. 145-48. The departmental plan had been vigorously discussed at the 1889 General Conference session. It was first tried under the leadership of Asa T. Robinson in South Africa. So effective did it seem that Robinson carried the idea with him to Australia in 1897. See SDA Encyclopedia, pp. 936-37.

182. Olsen to WCW, 9 March and 16 July 1896; Olsen to EGW, 18 June and 9 December 1896; Waggoner to EGW, 28 November 1898; Prescott to EGW, 9 August 1896 and 15 November 1897 (ILF).

183. GC Daily Bulletin (2 March 1897): 213-15; Crisler, Organization, pp. 152-53; A. V. Olsen, Through Crisis, p. 172.

184. Evans to EGW, 17 March 1898 (ILF).

185. GC Daily Bulletin (23 February 1899): 60-64; 73-77.

186. GC Daily Bulletin (26 February 1899): 85-94.

187. Daniells to WCW, 23 August 1900; Prescott to WCW, 26 October 1899; Prescott to EGW, 26 April 1900 (ILF).

188. EGW, quoted in Crisler, Organization, p. 158.

189. GC Daily Bulletin (3 April 1901): 27.

190. GC Daily Bulletin (11 April 1901): 185; (12 April 1901): 201.

191. GC Daily Bulletin (15 April 1901): 232; (18 April 1901): 316; (31 March 1903): 18.

192. Emmett K. VandeVere, The Wisdom Seekers (Nashville: SPA, 1972),

pp. 90-98; Olsen to WCW, 30 November 1895; Haskell to EGW, 26 December 1899; Magan to EGW, 16 August 1900; Daniells to WCW, 1 July 1901 (ILF).

193. Kellogg to EGW, 6 September 1901; Daniells to WCW, 1 July 1901 (ILF).

194. O. J. Graf, quoted in May Cole Kuhn, *Leader of Men: The Life of Arthur G. Daniells* (Washington, D.C.: RHPA, 1946), p. 9.

195. Daniells to WCW, 31 May and 1 July 1901 (ILF); GC *Daily Bulletin* (10 April 1903): 146-64.

196. Daniells to WCW, 2 September 1901; Daniells to W. T. Knox, 31 January 1902 (copy, ILF); Schwarz, "JHK: American Health Reformer," pp. 380-81.

197. GC *Daily Bulletin* (3 April 1903): 67; (6 April 1903): 73-82.

198. GC *Daily Bulletin* (10 April 1903): 158-59; *RH* (1 June 1905): 9; Daniells to WCW, 3 February 1905 (ILF). The idea of departmental organization had been around for a long time; see Olsen to WCW, 4 August 1892 (ILF).

199. Daniells to W. S. Hyatt, 14 July 1901 (copy, ILF).

200. Daniells to Irwin, 9 July 1905 (copy, ILF).

201. G. C. Tenney to WCW, 7 November 1893; Waggoner to EGW, 28 November 1898; H. Haskell to EGW, 22 November 1899 and 29 October 1900 (ILF).

202. Daniells to WCW, 31 January 1902 (ILF).

203. GC *Daily Bulletin* (6 April 1903): 84-88; Spalding, *Origin and History of SDA,* 3: 68-75.

204. Daniells to EGW, 15 May 1903; Daniells to Palmer, 22 May 1903 (copy); Daniells to WCW, 21 June 1903 (ILF).

205. Daniells to EGW, 23 and 27 July 1903; Daniells to WCW, 14 August and 23 October 1903 (ILF).

206. Daniells to WCW, 13 June and 13 December 1903; Daniells to EGW, 5 July 1903; Daniells to Butler, 24 December 1903 (copy, ILF).

207. Daniells to WCW, 30 November 1904 and 3 February 1905 (ILF); *SDA Encyclopedia,* p. 294.

208. Daniells to WCW, 24 March and 4 April 1904; 3 February and 19 March 1905 (ILF); *SDA Encyclopedia,* pp. 1393-94.

209. Daniells to WCW, 13 January and 25 December 1904, and 21 February 1905; Daniells to EGW, 18 January 1904 (ILF).

210. Daniells to WCW, 23 and 26 February; 10, 16, and 21 March; and 13 April 1905 (ILF).

211. For a more complete discussion of the Kellogg controversy, particularly as it concerned the last two issues, see Schwarz, "The Kellogg Schism: The Hidden Issues," *Spectrum* 4 (Autumn 1972): 23-39, esp. 26-28, 30-31.

212. Butler to EGW, 23 August and 16 December 1886 (ILF).

213. Haskell to EGW, 30 March and 27 April 1887 (ILF). The stenographer in question was Spicer, later to be General Conference secretary; see Butler to EGW, 16 December 1886 (ILF).

214. Olsen to Kellogg, 21 February 1892 (copy); Olsen to EGW, 23 May and 4 October 1892; Kellogg to WCW, 27 December 1892 (ILF); see also Schwarz, "The Kellogg Schism," pp. 23, 25, 30.

215. Olsen to EGW, 7 November 1895; 27 May and 9 October 1896 (ILF).

216. For Kellogg's rather devious methods to assure his continued control of the Battle Creek Sanitarium, see Schwarz, "The Kellogg Schism," pp. 27-28.

217. Irwin to EGW, 30 January, 3 October, and 10 November 1898 (ILF).

218. Irwin to EGW, 21 January and 26 March 1899; Kellogg to EGW, 8 March 1899 (ILF).

219. Irwin to EGW, 15 February 1900 (ILF); Schwarz, "The Kellogg Schism," pp. 32-33.

220. Irwin to EGW, 19 July 1900 (ILF).

221. Haskell to WCW, 9 May 1900; Haskell to EGW, 13 and 25 September 1900; Daniells to WCW, 1 November 1900 (ILF).

222. Daniells to Farnsworth, 12 January 1901 (copy); Daniells to Prescott and Olsen, 11 July 1901 (copy); Daniells to WCW, 28 October 1904 (ILF).

223. Daniells to WCW, 6 July 1902; 24 February and 3 March 1903; 2 July and 28 October 1904 (ILF).

224. Daniells to WCW, 24 December 1903 (ILF).

225. Daniells to WCW, 29 April and 23 October 1903 (ILF).

226. Daniells to WCW, 13 April 1904; 3 and 12 October 1905 (ILF).

227. Daniells to WCW, 24 April 1903; 3 July 1905 (ILF).

228. Magan to Prescott, 21 April 1896 (copy); Olsen to EGW, 22 May 1896; Daniells to WCW, 17 May 1903 (ILF).

229. Daniells to WCW, 9 and 30 August and 10 September 1903; 21 February and 22 March 1905; Daniells to EGW, 11 October 1905 (ILF); see also Schwarz, "JHK: American Health Reformer," pp. 384-85.

230. Daniells to WCW, 22 March 1905 (ILF).

231. Daniells to WCW, 26 October 1903 (ILF).

232. Daniells to EGW, 30 July 1903 (ILF).

233. Daniells to WCW, 16 February 1905 and 16 January 1906; Daniells to Irwin, 3 July 1905 (copy, ILF); Schwarz, "JHK: American Health Reformer," pp. 402-5.

234. Daniells to WCW, 16 and 23 February 1905 (ILF). It seems that for some time Jones had pictured himself in the role of a "whip" to bring both sides of the conflict into line. See also Daniells to WCW, 23 February 1905 (ILF).

235. *SDA Encyclopedia*, pp. 814, 1181.

NOTES TO CHAPTER 5

1. John J. Robertson, "Arthur Grosvenor Daniells: The Effect of Australasia upon the Man and His Work as Revealed through Correspondence with W. C. White and Ellen G. White" (M.A. thesis, Andrews University, 1966), p. 3.

2. For a brief biographical sketch on Daniells, see Don F. Neufeld, ed., *Seventh-day Adventist Encyclopedia* (Washington, D.C.: RHPA, 1966), s.v. "Daniells" (hereafter cited as *SDA Encyclopedia*).

3. Carl Dicmann Anderson, "The History and Evolution of Seventh-day Adventist Church Organization" (Ph.D. diss., American University, 1960), pp. 192-96, 215; May Cole Kuhn, *Leader of Men: The Life of Arthur G. Daniells* (Washington, D.C.: RHPA, 1946), p. 113.

4. Robertson, *Daniells*, pp. 111-30.

5. Daniells to E. W. Farnsworth, 3 April 1901 (General Conference Publishing Department Historical Files, Daniells folder).

6. F. M. Wilcox, "The Reason for Our Existence as a Denomination," *RH* (21 September 1911): 7.

7. I. G. Bigelow, "Our Missionary Work and Why It Is Important," *RH* (9 January 1913): 4-5.

8. R. C. Porter, "A Missionary Movement," *RH* (2 May 1912): 3-4.

9. C. M. Snow, "Building New Babels," *RH* (23 November 1911): 10-11.

10. W. A. Spicer, "The Enlarging Work," *RH* (9 March 1905): 4.

11. Ellen G. White, "City Work—No. 2," *RH* (25 January 1912): 3-4 (author hereafter cited as EGW).

12. William Covert, "Aggressive Missionary Work," *RH* (9 January 1913): 6.

13. "The Key-Note of the General Conference," *RH* (22 May 1913): 3.

14. Daniells, "The President's Address," *RH* (13 May 1909): 11.

15. Ibid.

16. Ibid.

17. *RH* (1 June 1905): 8-9.

18. "The General Conference," RH (8 June 1905): 6. Another possible reason for establishment of a foreign department appears in a letter from Daniells to William C. White (hereafter cited as WCW). Daniells referred to the agitation of Germans, Swedes, and Norwegians in the Midwest for a separate organization. He believed that such an organization would be a mistake and that the movement was "of the devil"; Daniells to WCW, 6 April 1905 (White Estate ILF).

19. *RH* (22 May 1913): 7. L. H. Christian, *Sons of the North* (Mountain View, CA: PPPA, 1942), pp. 173-79; Emma E. Howell, *The Great Advent Movement* (Washington, D.C.: RHPA, 1935), p. 109; Marley Soper, " 'Unser Seminar,' The Story of Clinton German Seminary," *AH* 4 (Summer 1977): 44-54.

20. Kuhn, *Leader of Men*, p. 82.

21. Howell, *Great Advent*, p. 82; Arthur Whitefield Spalding, *Christ's Last Legion* (Washington, D.C.: RHPA, 1949), p. 125; Matilda Erickson [later Andross], *Missionary Volunteers and Their Work* (Washington, D.C.: RHPA, n.d.), p. 27; Nathaniel Krum, *The M. V. Story* (Washington, D.C.: RHPA, 1963), pp. 38-41.

22. Erickson, *MVs and Their Work*, p. 25.

23. *RH* (10 June 1909): 21.

24. See Ronald D. Graybill, *Ellen G. White and Church Race Relations* (Washington, D.C.: RHPA, 1970); see Graybill, *Mission to Black America* (Mountain View, CA: PPPA, 1971), for the story of Edson White and the riverboat *Morning Star*.

25. See C. Vann Woodward, *The Strange Career of Jim Crow*, 2d ed. rev. (New York: Oxford University Press, 1966), pp. 67-109.

26. *RH* (17 June 1909): 7; Louis H. Hansen, *From So Small a Dream* (Nashville: SPA, 1968), p. 205.

27. *RH* (19 June 1913): 12.

28. *RH* (14 June 1926): 5.

29. Joe Mesar and Tom Dybdahl, "The Utopia Park Affair and the Rise of Northern Black Adventists," *AH* 1 (January 1974): 34-41.

30. *RH* (19 June 1913): 8.

31. Daniells, "The President's Address," *RH* (11 May 1905): 10.

32. Daniells, "The Philadelpia Ministerial Institute," *RH* (6 April 1911): 15.

33. Howell, *Great Advent*, p. 105; Matilda Erickson Andross, *Story of the Advent Message* (Washington, D.C.: RHPA, 1926), p. 117.

34. *RH* (2 May 1918): 13, 18-19.

35. *RH* (15 June 1922): 28-29.

36. *RH* (4 June 1926): 7.

37. *RH* (5 June 1913): 11.

38. Ibid., 6-7.

39. Ibid., 7.

40. Ibid.

41. Ibid., 11-13; see also *RH* (19 June 1913): 6.

42. *RH* (12 June 1913): 17.

43. *RH* (2 May 1918): 22.

44. Schwarz, *Light Bearers to the Remnant* (Mountain View, CA: PPPA, 1979), p. 375; *RH* (18 April 1918): 11.

45. *RH* (9 June 1926): 4.

46. *RH* extra (5 June 1922): 2; *RH* (8 June 1922): 24-27.

47. *RH* (5 June 1930): 169; (13 June 1930): 236.

48. To describe the growth of the church precisely in this time period is very difficult, for the rapid developments in organizational structure wrought major changes in the bodies making the reports and in operational practices affecting methods of reporting statistics. Hence reports from particular union or division conferences often do not reflect the same geographical areas. Likewise, the definition of church members may or may not include those who did not belong to an organized local church, though they were baptized; and the definition of what constituted a church "worker" was not the same for all areas. Nevertheless, the figures in the statistical reports indicate roughly how the church grew and where it concentrated its missionary efforts.

49. *RH* (17 June 1909): 12; (6 December 1906): 7; (10 June 1909): 8; Sabbath School Department, Seventh-day Adventist Church, *The Sabbath School: Its History, Organization, and Objectives* (Washington, D.C.: RHPA, 1938), pp. 25-26; Arthur Whitefield Spalding, *Origin and History of Seventh-day Adventists*, 4 vols. (Washington, D.C.: RHPA, 1962), 187-95; M. Ellsworth Olsen, *A History of the Origin and Progress of Seventh-day Adventists* (Washington, D.C.: RHPA, 1925), pp. 714-15.

50. A. T. Jones, *Some History, Some Experiences, and Some Facts* (n.p., 1906), pp. 17-18 (hereafter cited as *Some History*).

51. Ibid., pp. 19-21, 37, 43, 45.

52. Executive Committee, General Conference of Seventh-day Adventists, *A Statement Refuting Charges Made by A. T. Jones Against the Spirit of Prophecy and the Plan of Organization of the Seventh-day Adventist Denomination* (Washington, D.C.: General Conference Committee, 1906), pp. 17-18, 25-28, 39 (hereafter cited as *Statement Refuting Jones*).

53. Ibid., p. 34.

54. Jones, *The Final Word and a Confession* (n.p., n.d.), pp. 31-38 (hereafter cited as *Final Word*).

55. Jones, "Evening Sermon," *General Conference Bulletin*, extra no. 2 (4 April 1901): 37-42.

56. Jones, "Bible Study," *GC Bulletin*, extra no. 4 (7 April 1907): 103.

57. Richard W. Schwarz, "John Harvey Kellogg: American Health Reformer" (Ph.D. diss., University of Michigan, 1964), p. 380.

58. Anderson, "History and Evolution," pp. 243, 450. This interpretation is based on rumor; no evidence in support has been found to date.

59. Spicer, "The General Conference Committee Council at Gland, Switzerland," *RH* (27 June 1907): 5.

60. Spicer, "Gospel Order—No. 8," *RH* (13 May 1909): 8; Spicer, "The Doctrine of Christ," *RH* (14 November 1907): 3; W. E. Haskell, "Organization," *RH* (12 January 1911): 5; J. H. Morrison, *A Straight Talk to Old Brethren*, 2d ed. (n.p., n.d. [1913? 1915?]), pp. 92ff.

61. Jones, *Some History*, pp. 53-61.

62. Ibid., p. 66.

63. Ibid., p. 70.

64. Jones to EGW ([Riverside, CA: The Gathering Call] n.d.), p. 31.

65. Jones, *Final Word*, p. 28; see also Jones, *An Appeal for Evangelical Christianity* (n.p., n.d.), p. 67.

66. W. S. Sadler to EGW, 26 April 1906 (copy, John Harvey Kellogg Collection, The Museum, Michigan State University).

67. *An Authentic Interview Between Elder G. W. Amadon, Elder A. C. Bourdeau and Dr. John Harvey Kellogg in Battle Creek, Michigan, on October 7th, 1907* ([Riverside, CA: The Gathering Call] n.d.), p. 37 (hereafter cited as *An Authentic Interview*).

68. Charles E. Stewart, *A Response to An Urgent Testimony from Mrs. Ellen G. White Concerning Contradictions, Inconsistencies and Other Errors in Her Writings*, 2d ed. ([Riverside, CA: The Gathering Call] n.d.), pp. 87-88.

69. Schwarz, *JHK: American Health Reformer*, pp. 360ff.

70. *An Authentic Interview*, p. 42.

71. Ibid., pp. 45, 47.

72. General Conference, *Statement Refuting Jones*, p. 10.

73. Ibid., p. 86.

74. Ibid., p. 87.

75. In their references to pantheism, *Review* writers seem to have been thinking primarily of evolutionary Christianity as presented by Lyman Abbott in *The Outlook*; for an explanation of this position, see Ira Brown, *Lyman Abbott, Christian Evolutionist: A Study in Religious Liberalism* (Cambridge, MA: Harvard University Press, 1953), pp. 139-49.

76. "Creator and Redeemer," *RH* (26 January 1905): 4. Numerous editorials against this "pantheism" appeared during the last few years of Prescott's editorship of the *Review*; and similar ideas appeared often in sermons and articles published on the same issue.

77. "Unchristian Science," *RH* (30 August 1906): 3-4; Spicer, "The Overspreading Curse," *RH* (8 August 1907): 4.

78. Snow, "The Higher Critic and God's Word," *RH* (28 November 1907): 4-5.

79. L. A. Smith, "Modern Criticism of the Decalogue," *RH* (26 January 1905): 6.

80. "The Infallible Word," *RH* (2 November 1905): 3.

81. "Revelation and Speculation," *RH* (9 February 1905): 5; "The Platform," *RH* (27 February 1908): 3; "The Infallible Guide," *RH* (6 May 1909): 3.

82. E. A. Rowell, "Higher Criticism the Enemy of Seventh-day Adventists," *RH* (9 November 1911): 7; see also W. W. Prescott, "The God of the Bible and the God of the Sabbath," *RH* (6 April 1911): 12; C. H. Edwards, "Facing the Crisis," *RH* (18 May 1911): 4.

83. Prescott, "The Ultimate of Pantheism," *RH* (5 April 1906): 5.

84. "Notes and Comments," *RH* (28 June 1906): 6.

85. H. E. Phelps, "A Steadfast Faith," *RH* (9 August 1906): 8-9.

86. S. N. Haskell, "The Gift of Prophecy," *RH* (13 September 1906): 9.

87. "The Mask of Apostasy," *RH* (28 June 1906): 3-4.

88. D. H. Kress, "More Than a Prophet," *RH* (1 November 1906): 9.

89. Haskell, "The Spirit of Prophecy and Our Relation to It," *RH* (5 September 1918): 5.

90. G. I. Butler, "Special Evidences that the Gift of the Spirit of Prophecy was Necessary for the Success of this Message," *RH* (7 September 1916): 11.

91. F. M. Wilcox, "The Position and Work of Mrs. E. G. White," *RH* (17 March 1921): 4-6.

92. Wilcox, "The Gift of the Spirit of Prophecy," *RH* (10 June 1915): 7.

93. Wilcox, "The Study of the Bible," *RH* (3 February 1921): 2.

94. Porter, "The Spirit of Prophecy," *RH* (13 September 1906): 10-11.

95. George O. States, "Lessons from Past Experiences—No. 12," *RH* (28 February 1907): 9.

96. G. I. Butler, "The Work of Mrs. E. G. White," *RH* (30 May 1918): 9.

97. States, "Lessons from Past Experiences—No. 2," *RH* (9 August 1906): 9.

98. States, "Lessons from Past Experiences—No. 9," *RH* (6 December 1906): 11.

99. G. A. Irwin, "The Spirit of Prophecy," *RH* (22 November 1906): 9.

100. My statement here is impressionistic; someone trained in sampling techniques might produce precise documentation by studying the *Review* issues of this period.

101. Wilcox, "Our Refuge in Sorrow," *RH* (29 July 1915): 6; "Prophetic Succession," *RH* (19 August 1915): 3-4.

102. Wilcox, "Prophetic Succession." An account of a disastrous attempt to succeed Ellen White as the Adventist prophet appears in Larry White, "Margaret A. Rowen: Prophetess of Reform and Doom," *AH* 6 (Summer 1979): 28-40.

103. Daniells, "The Bible Conference," *RH* (21 August 1919): 3.

104. "The Use of the Spirit of Prophecy in Our Teaching of Bible and History," Bible and History Teachers Council, July 30, 1919, Takoma Park, Washington, D.C. (copy, Heritage Room, James White Library, Andrews University).

105. "Inspiration of the Spirit of Prophecy as Related to the Inspiration of the Bible," Bible and History Teachers Council, 1 August 1919, pp. 29-31. The sessions dealing with Ellen White are reprinted in *Spectrum* 10 (May 1979): 27-57.

106. *San Francisco Chronicle*, 22 May 1922, p. 5.

107. Ibid.

108. *San Francisco Chronicle*, 23 May 1922, p. 9; *San Francisco Examiner*, 23 May 1922, p. 5; *San Francisco Call*, 23 May 1922, pp. 2-3.

109. Wilcox, "The True Significance," *RH* (28 December 1911): 9-11; Prescott, "The New Cardinals," *RH* (30 November 1911): 8-9.

110. Prescott, "The Roman Peril," *RH* (23 November 1911): 11-12.

111. Snow, "Rome Never Changes: The Doctrine of the Immaculate Conception," *RH* (3 December 1914): 8-10.

112. Prescott, "A Challenge to Protestantism," *RH* (29 February 1912): 9.

113. Snow, "Rome's Claim on America," *RH* (23 April 1914): 8-9.

114. John Higham, *Strangers in the Land: Patterns of American Nativism, 1860–1925* (New Brunswick, NJ: Rutgers University Press, 1959), pp. 179-82.

115. Snow, "Church Unity," *RH* (19 February 1914): 6-7.

116. Smith, "The Hopelessness of the Effort to Reform Politics," *RH* (6 April 1905): 5.

117. Porter, "The World's Armageddon Battle in Prophecy," *RH* (24 July 1913): 702.

118. G. W. Reaser, "Preparation for Armageddon," *Watchman Magazine* (October 1913): 473.

119. For an example see "Unseen Forces in the European War Storm," *Signs of the Times* (15 September 1914): 576.

120. P. T. Magan, "The Old Eastern Question Is Dead," *Watchman Magazine* (March 1917): 30.

121. *The World's Crisis in the Light of Prophecy* (Washington, D.C.: RHPA, n.d.), p. 36.

122. "A Time to Pray," *RH* (13 August 1914): 6.

123. FMW, "A World of Changing Emphasis," *RH* (30 January 1919): 3-4. For a fuller examination of Seventh-day Adventist attitudes toward World War I, see Gary Land, "The Perils of Prophecying [*sic*]," *Adventist Heritage* 1 (January 1974): 28-33ff.

124. LeRoy Edwin Froom, *Movement of Destiny* (Washington, D.C.: RHPA, 1971), p. 375 (hereafter cited as *Movement*).

125. Bruno William Steinweg, "Developments in the Teaching of Justification and Righteousness by Faith in the Seventh-day Adventist Church after 1900" (M.A. thesis, SDA Theological Seminary, 1948), pp. 18-37 (hereafter cited as "Developments"); Norval F. Pease, *By Faith Alone* (Mountain View, CA: PPPA, 1962), p. 182.

126. Froom, *Movement*, pp. 377-80.

127. Ibid., p. 391.

128. Prescott, *The Doctrine of Christ*, 2 vols. (Washington, D.C.: RHPA, n.d.), 1: 2.

129. Ibid., pp. 96-111.

130. *Victorious Life Studies*, rev. ed. (Philadelphia: Christian Life Literature Fund, 1918). An indication of some of the controversy, from a Fundamentalist standpoint, appears in George Dollar, *A History of Fundamentalism in America* (Greenville, S.C.: Bob Jones University Press, 1973), pp. 267-69. Timothy L. Smith also comments on this controversy in *Called Unto Holiness; The Story of the Nazarenes: The Formative Years* (Kansas City: Nazarene Publishing House, 1962), pp. 319-20. On Prescott's relationship to McQuilken, see Robert J. Wieland and Donald K. Short, *1888 Re-examined* (Strafford, MO: Gems of Truth, n.d.), p. 220.

131. Steinweg, "Developments," pp. 38-54.

132. Froom, *Movement*, pp. 375-76.

133. Ibid., pp. 392, 395; Steinweg, "Developments," pp. 44-48.

134. Froom, *Movement*, pp. 397-98.

135. Steinweg, "Developments," pp. 60-61.

136. Ibid., pp. 61-65; Froom, *Movement*, pp. 400-401; see also Pease, *By Faith Alone*, pp. 183ff.

137. Wieland and Short, *1888 Re-examined*. Further criticism of the Victorious Life movement within Adventism appears in Geoffrey J. Paxton, *The Shaking of Adventism* (Grand Rapids: Baker Book House, 1978), pp. 74-75. McQuilken argued for the "second blessing" in *Victorious Life Studies*, pp. 82-93. On the "second blessing" doctrine during the Second Great Awakening, see Timothy L. Smith, *Revivalism and Social Reform in Mid-Nineteenth Century America* (New York: Abingdon Press, 1957), pp. 25, 103-13.

138. Prescott, *The Saviour of the World* (Washington, D.C.: RHPA, 1929), pp. 36, 38.

139. William H. Branson, *The Way to Christ* (Washington, D.C.: RHPA, 1928), p. 28.

140. Daniells, *Christ Our Righteousness* (Washington, D.C.: Ministerial Association of SDA, 1926), p. 31.

141. Meade MacGuire, *The Life of Victory* (Washington, D.C.: RHPA, p. 7.

142. MacGuire, *His Cross and Mine* (Washington, D.C.: RHPA, 1927), pp. 126, 133.

143. Froom, *The Coming of the Comforter* (Washington, D.C.: RHPA, 1928), p. 171.

144. In addition to the comments cited, the following give a representative sampling: J. L. Shuler, *Christ the Divine One* (Washington, D.C.: RHPA, 1922), pp. 7, 94-95, 104-5; Daniells, *Christ Our Righteousness*, pp. 22-23, 115, 118-23; Branson, *The Way to Christ*, pp. 86-88, 112, 120; M. C. Wilcox, *Studies in Ephesians* (Mountain View, CA: PPPA, 1927), pp. 45-46; M. C. Wilcox, *Studies in Romans* (Mountain View, CA: PPPA, 1930), pp. 39, 60; Prescott, *The Saviour of the World*, p. 75. For further examples of the second-experience idea, see Froom, *The Coming of the Comforter*, pp. 144, 180; MacGuire, *His Cross and Mine*, p. 148; MacGuire, *The Life of Victory*, pp. 8, 73-74.

145. On Fundamentalism, see Stewart G. Cole, *The History of Fundamentalism* (New York: Richard R. Smith, 1931); Norman F. Furniss, *The Fundamentalist Controversy: 1918–1931* (New Haven: Yale University Press, 1954); Ernest R. Sandeen, *The Roots of Fundamentalism* (Chicago: University of Chicago Press, 1970); and Dollar, *History of Fundamentalism*.

146. Prescott, "As to Evolution," *RH* (5 August 1909): 3-4; Prescott, "Denying the Advent Doctrine," *RH* (22 July 1909): 3-4. For earlier Adventist attitudes toward evolution, see Ronald L. Numbers, "Science Falsely So-called: Evolution and Adventists in the Nineteenth Century," *Journal of the American Scientific Affiliation* 27 (March 1975): 18-23.

147. Harold W. Clark, "Geology Supports the Flood," *RH* (13 August 1925): 4; see also Alonzo L. Baker, "The San Francisco Evolution Debates, June 13-14, 1925," *AH* 2 (Winter 1975): 22-32.

148. Snow, "Religious Apathy and the Reason for It," *RH* (17 October 1912): 7-8.

149. F. M. Wilcox, "Nothing to Offer," *RH* (5 October 1911): 10.

150. L. L. Caviness, "The Inspiration of the Bible," *RH* (31 December 1941): 4-5.

151. Snow, "An Attack Upon God," *RH* (24 October 1912): 11; see also Smith, "The True Basis for a Genuine Revival," *RH* (5 January 1905): 5; M. C. Wilcox, "Fundamentalism or Modernism—Which?" *RH* (15 January 1925): 3.

152. Caviness, "The Triumphs of Prohibition," *RH* (3 January 1918): 5.

153. Otto M. John, "The Benefits of Prohibition," *RH* (3 July 1919): 2.

154. E. R. Palmer, "The Value of Prohibition," *RH* (30 August 1928): 4; see also Larry White, "The Return of the Thief: The Repeal of Prohibition and the Adventist Response," *AH* 5 (Winter 1978): 34-46.

155. "The Seventh-day Adventist Stand on Certain Fundamental Doctrines of the Bible," *RH* (13 May 1925): 3.

156. F. M. Wilcox, "Forsaking the Foundations of Faith," *RH* (28 November 1929): 13-14.

157. Ronald L. Numbers, "Sciences of Satanic Origin: Adventist Attitudes Toward Evolutionary Biology and Geology," *Spectrum* 9 (January 1979): 24.

158. George McCready Price, "The Significance of Fundamentalism," *RH* (12 May 1927): 13-14.

159. Calvin P. Bollman, "Christian Fundamentals," *RH* (3 July 1919): 5-7.

160. M. C. Wilcox, "Fundamentalism or Modernism—Which?" *RH* (2 April 1925): 5.

161. Snow, "Has Protestantism Failed?" *RH* (12 June 1924): 8.

NOTES TO CHAPTER 6

1. M. E. Kern, "Report of the Autumn Council of the General Conference Committee," *RH* (27 November 1930): 6-17.

2. E. Kotz, "Report of the Autumn Council of the General Conference Committee," *RH* (26 November 1931): 6-16.

3. C. H. Watson, "President's Address," *RH* (28 May 1936): 7-10.

4. William L. Shirer, *The Rise and Fall of the Third Reich* (New York: Simon and Schuster, 1960), p. 2. The response of the German Adventists to Nazi power is examined in Jack M. Patt, "Living in a Time of Trouble: German Adventists Under Nazi Rule," *Spectrum* 8 (March 1977): 2-10, and Erwin Sicher, "Seventh-day Adventist Publications and the Nazi Temptation," *Spectrum* 8 (March 1977): 11-24.

5. A. V. Olson, *RH* (16 November 1939): 14-15.

6. H. L. Rudy, "Our Work in Europe," *RH* (19 October 1939): 19.

7. F. Lee, "Echoes from the Fall Council," *RH* (14 November 1940): 3-4.

8. Victor T. Armstrong, "The Far East and the Reconstruction Plan," *RH* (18 January 1945): 12.

9. W. H. Branson, "The China Division," *RH* (19 July 1950): 164-66, 175; Armstrong, "The Far Eastern Division," *RH* (23 July 1950): 236-39.

10. Branson, "The China Division"; *Actions of the Autumn Council*, 1949, pp. 8-9 (hereafter cited as *Autumn Council*).

11. Ralph and Beatrice Neall, "The Rains Descended and the Floods Came: A Survey of the Seventh-day Adventist Church in Communist China" (Term paper, Andrews University, 1971), pp. 9-10.

12. Ibid., pp. 12-19.

13. Ibid., pp. 39-42.

14. S. J. Lee, "Adventism in China: The Communist Takeover," *Spectrum* 7 (No. 3): 16-22; David Linn, "Years of Heartbreak: Lessons for Mission by a China Insider," *Spectrum* 7 (No. 3): 22-33.

15. E. D. Dick, "The Autumn Council of 1942," *RH* (3 December 1942): 13.

16. Girouard v. United States, 328 U.S. 61, *Supreme Court Reporter*, 66, October Term (St. Paul: West Publishing Co., 1947), pp. 826-34.

17. Everett N. Dick, "The Adventist Medical Cadet Corps as Seen By Its Founder," *AH* 1 (July 1974): 18-27.

18. E. D. Dick, "The Autumn Council of 1942," *RH* (3 December 1942): 12.

19. *New York Times*, 12 May 1945, p. 3; 9 Oct. 1945, p. 10; 12 Oct. 1945, p. 3; 13 Oct. 1945, p. 3; Booton Herndon, *The Unlikeliest Hero* (Mountain View, CA: PPPA, 1967), pp. 143, 162.

20. Don F. Neufeld, ed., *Seventh-day Adventist Encyclopedia* (Washington, D.C., RHPA, 1966), s.v. "National Service Organization" (hereafter cited as *SDA Encyclopedia*).

21. Christian P. Sorensen, interview with Reynolds, 24 October 1974.

22. *Autumn Council*, 1950, p. 15. Actually, the first Seventh-day Adventist chaplain was Floyd E. Bresee, who entered the service in September 1942, even though he did not have the required denominational endorsement. See Everett N. Dick, "The Military Chaplaincy and Seventh-day Adventists: The Evolution of an Attitude," *AH* 3 (Summer 1976): 33-45.

23. Clark Smith to Reynolds, 1 October 1974. Smith was director of the National Service Organization at the General Conference of Seventh-day Adventists.

24. Carlyle B. Haynes, "Adventists and Labor Unions," *RH* (6 December 1945): 17-18. For the roots of Adventist attitudes toward labor unions, see Carlos A. Schwantes, "Labor Unions and Seventh-day Adventists: The Formative Years, 1877—1903," *AH* 4 (Winter 1977): 11-19 and Eugene Chellis, "The *Review and Herald* and Early Adventist Response to Organized Labor," *Spectrum* 10 (August 1979): 20-30.

25. Joe Mesar and Tom Dybdahl, "The Utopia Affair," *AH* 1 (January 1974): 34-41, 53-54.

26. Ibid.

27. *Autumn Council*, 1961, pp. 12-13; Harold D. Singleton to Reynolds, 2 April 1974. Singleton was secretary of the North American Regional Department, General Conference of SDA, Washington, D.C.

28. J. J. Strahle, "Report of Food Distribution in Europe," *RH* (9 June 1946): 80-79.

29. Adolf Minck, "The Central European Division," *RH* (16 July 1950): 103-5.

30. Branson, "If Bombs Fall," *RH* (14 June 1951): 1.

31. J. I. Robison, "1956 Autumn Council Report," *RH* (29 November 1956): 5-10, 21-24.

32. J. L. McElhany, "Answering the Needs of a Suffering World," *RH* (6 December 1945): 1.

33. McElhany, "Our World and Its Needs," *RH* (25 November 1943): 3-6.

34. My observation as a participant.

35. My observation as a participant.

36. Lee, "Paris Youth Congress," *RH* (9 August 1951): 1; Lee, "European Youth on the March," *RH* (16 August 1951): 3-5.

37. Two and three years later I was to hear again the lively gospel songs these young people learned in Paris—once while I was at an Alpine school overlooking the city of Geneva, and once in Egypt, floating down the Nile on a summer night in a dhow crowded with youngsters from Cairo churches. All of these were multilingual singers, the Egyptians having added Arabic translations of their own.

38. *Church Manual* (Washington, D.C.: General Conference of SDA, 1932).

39. General Conference Minutes, 29 December 1930; "Proceedings of the General Conference: Revision of the Church Manual," *RH* (14 June 1946): 197-99.

40. A. W. Cormack, "The 1941 Autumn Council," *RH* (4 December 1941): 5-17.

41. *Manual for Ministers* (Washington, D.C.: General Conference of SDA, 1942).

42. "Proceedings of the General Conference: Standards of Christian Living," *RH* (16 June 1946): 216-220.

43. Branson, "The Bible Conference," *Ministry* 25 (July 1952): 4-5.

44. Raymond F. Cottrell, "The Bible Research Fellowship: A Pioneering Seventh-day Adventist Organization in Retrospect," *AH* 5 (Summer 1978): 39-52.

45. Reynolds to Cottrell, 14 January 1951.

46. General Conference of SDA, *Our Firm Foundation*, 2 vols. (Washington, D.C.: RHPA, 1954), 1: 58.

47. Ibid., p. 30.

48. Ibid., pp. 29-30.

49. Ibid., pp. 36-41.

50. *Our Firm Foundation* contains all of the papers presented at the 1952 Bible Conference.

51. Francis D. Nichol, "Looking Back on the Bible Conference," *RH* (23 October 1952): 10-11.

52. *Autumn Council*, 1952, p. 20.

53. Nichol, ed., *The Seventh-day Adventist Bible Commentary*, Commentary Reference Series, 8 vols. (Washington, D.C.: RHPA, 1953-57), 1: 11-13.

54. T. E. Unruh to Donald G. Barnhouse, 28 November 1949 (personal files of T. E. Unruh, Grand Terrace, California).

55. Barnhouse to Unruh, 22 December 1949.

56. Barnhouse, "Spiritual Discourse, or How to Read Religious Books," *Eternity* (June 1950): 42-44.

57. Details are from my interviews with Unruh, December 1975; see also T. E. Unruh, "The Seventh-day Adventist Evangelical Conferences of 1955–1956," *AH* 4 (Winter 1977): 35-46.

58. Donald Gray Barnhouse, "Foreword," in Walter Ralston Martin, *The Truth about Seventh-day Adventism* (Grand Rapids: Zondervan, 1960), p. 8 (hereafter cited as *Truth About SDA*); Barnhouse, "Are Seventh-day Adventists Christians? A New Look At Seventh-day Adventism," *Eternity* (September 1956): 6-7, 43-45; Martin, "The Truth About Seventh-day Adventism," *Eternity* (October 1956): 6-7, 38-40; Martin, "What Seventh-day Adventists Really Believe," *Eternity* (November 1956): 20-21, 38-43.

59. *Seventh-day Adventists Answer Questions on Doctrine* (Washington, D.C.: RHPA, 1957), pp. 7-10. Some church members objected strongly to what they regarded as a capitulation to the Evangelicals and a departure from distinctive Seventh-day Adventist beliefs; see M. L. Andreasen, *Letters to the Churches*, Series A (Baker, OR: Hudson Printing Company, [1959]).

60. Martin, *Truth About SDA*, p. 9.

61. Ibid., pp. 117-219.

62. Ibid., pp. 10, 111, 113.

63. Ibid., pp. 236-37. Seventh-day Adventists replied to Martin in Ministerial Association, General Conference of Seventh-day Adventists, *Doctrinal Discussions* (Washington, D.C.: RHPA, n.d.).

64. Harold Lindsell, "What of Seventh-day Adventism?" *Christianity Today* 11 (14 April 1958): 13-15.

65. Frank A. Laurence, "Exhaustive Research," *Christianity Today* 4 (4 July 1960): 36; a more recent critique appears in Anthony Hoekema, *The Four Major Cults: Christian Science, Jehovah's Witnesses, Mormonism, Seventh-day Adventism* (Grand Rapids: William B. Eerdmans Publishing Company, 1963).

66. Merwin R. Thurber, "Revised D & R in Relation to Denominational Doctrine," *Ministry* 27 (May 1945): 3-4, 30.

67. "Action of General Conference Committee, Spring Council, May 4 1931: Evangelistic Decorum," *Ministry* 4 (July 1931): 7.

68. Howard B. Weeks, *Adventist Evangelism in the Twentieth Century* (Washington, D.C.: RHPA, 1969), pp. 161-62 (hereafter cited as *Adventist Evangelism*).

69. Ibid.

70. Ibid., p. 173.

71. *Autumn Council*, 1941, pp. 7-9.

72. Weeks, *Adventist Evangelism*, pp. 193-94.

73. Ibid., p. 180.

74. *Autumn Council*, 1938, pp. 7-10.

75. Weeks, *Adventist Evangelism*, p. 186.

76. Nichol, "The Great Layman's Congress," *RH* (20 September 1951): 3-5.

77. Weeks, *Adventist Evangelism*, pp. 186-87.

78. Ibid., p. 249.

79. *Autumn Council*, 1951, pp. 17-18.

80. Weeks, *Adventist Evangelism*, p. 272.

81. Ibid., p. 273.

82. *Autumn Council*, 1947, pp. 9-10.

83. Ibid.

84. Weeks, *Adventist Evangelism*, p. 264.

85. Ibid., p. 282.

86. Ibid., p. 139.

87. Ben Glanzer, "Your Radio Doctor," *Ministry* 27 (April 1954): 8-9.

88. E. J. Folkenberg, "New Frontiers in Medical Evangelism," *Ministry* 35 (June 1962): 27-30.

89. G. E. Peters, "The North American Colored Department," *RH* (13 June 1946): 194-95, 207.

90. G. Nathaniel Banks, interview with Reynolds at Monrovia, Liberia, November 1950.

91. Duane V. Cowin, interview with Reynolds at Kumasi, Gold Coast, November 1950.

92. Leo B. Halliwell, *Light in the Jungle* (New York: David McKay Company, 1959).

93. W. R. Beach, "The General Conference Secretary's Report," *RH* (22 June 1958): 28-39.

94. Loma Linda University, Minutes of the Health Evangelism Committee, n.d.

95. Saleem A. Farag, Karl C. Fischer, Lester Lonergan, Harold N. Mozar, Ruth M. White, "Health Problems of the Waha," *Medical Arts and Sciences*, 12 (1958): 116-22; 13 (1959): 41-45; 16 (1962): 109-14.

96. *Autumn Council*, 1945, p. 26.

97. *Statistical Report of Seventh-day Adventists*, 1960 (Washington, D.C.: General Conference of SDA), p. 18 (hereafter cited as *SDA Statistical Report*).

98. Ibid., p. 32.

99. *SDA Statistical Report*, 1930, p. 20; 1960, pp. 26-27.

100. *SDA Statistical Report*, 1960, pp. 26-27.

101. Ibid.

102. *SDA Statistical Report*, 1930, pp. 21, 23; 1960, p. 23.

103. General Conference of SDA, Board of Regents, "Bulletin," 21-24 February 1929, pp. 1-2.

104. Kotz, "Report of the Autumn Council," *RH* (26 November 1931): 8-10.

105. Ibid.

106. Walton J. Brown, comp., *Chronology of Seventh-day Adventist Education* (Washington, D.C.: Department of Education, General Conference of SDA, 1972), p. 39.

107. Department of Missionary Volunteers and Department of Education, *Seventh-day Adventist Youth at the Mid-Century* (Washington, D.C.: General Conference of SDA, 1951).

108. Pacific Union College, Minutes of the Board of Trustees for 31 March and 28 April 1953; official documents of the president's office, Pacific Union College, California.

109. Brown, *Chronology*, pp. 136, 130.

110. *SDA Encyclopedia*, s.v. "Andrews University: III. History of the Seventh-day Adventist Theological Seminary."

111. Ibid.

112. *Autumn Council*, 1954, p. 21; 1957, p. 25.

113. *Autumn Council*, 1958, p. 6; *SDA Encyclopedia*, s.v. "Andrews University"; Emmett K. VandeVere, *The Wisdom Seekers* (Nashville: SPA, 1972), pp. 243-66.

114. For the history of Loma Linda University, see *AH* 5 (Winter 1979).

115. Loma Linda University, Minutes of the Board of Trustees, 15 December 1960; 29 June 1961.

116. Minutes, 3 April 1967.

117. Minutes, 25-26 September 1962.

118. Minutes, 20 October 1963.

119. G. M. Mathews to Reynolds, August 21, 1974.

120. *SDA Yearbook 1930* (Washington, D.C.: RHPA, 1930), pp. 344-56.

121. *SDA Yearbook 1960*, pp. 280-302.

122. "Institutional Medical Workers' Council held at Boulder, Colorado, November 29 to December 4, 1940" ([Washington, D.C.]: Medical Department, General Conference of SDA, 1940) (mimeographed copy at Heritage Room, Loma Linda University Library).

123. *Autumn Council*, 1941, p. 35.

124. "Report of Medical Council Held at Boulder, Colorado, April 25-30, 1949" ([Washington, D.C.]: Medical Department, General Conference of SDA), p. 8 (Heritage Room, Loma Linda University Library).

125. Nichol, "Sanitariums or Hospitals," *RH* (5 September 1974): 6-7.

126. R. C. Cabot and R. L. Dicks, *The Art of Ministering to the Sick* (New York: Macmillan Company, 1936); Dicks, *Principles and Practices of Pastoral Care* (Englewood Cliffs, NJ: Prentice-Hall, 1963), pp. 18-21.

127. Charles W. Teel, interview with Reynolds, 12 November 1974, at Loma Linda University. Teel, the first Adventist to qualify with the national accrediting body, initiated and directed the instructional program in clinical pastoral care at the University Medical Center.

128. O. Montgomery, "Voting for Prohibition," *RH* (4 August, 1932): 732-33; W. A. Scharffenberg, "Revival of the American Temperance Society," *RH* (10 July 1947): 16-18.

129. *SDA Encyclopedia*, s.v. "International Commission for the Prevention of Alcoholism"; s.v. "National Committees for the Prevention of Alcoholism."

130. George Rosen, "Trends in American Public Health, from the Colonial Period to the Present," in Felix Marti-Ibatinez, *History of American Medicine, A Symposium* (New York: MD Publications, 1958), p. 157.

131. René J. Dubos, *Mirage of Health* (New York: Harper and Bros., 1959); *Proceedings of the White House Conference on Health*, 3-4 November 1965 (Washington, D.C.: Government Printing Office), pp. 405-7; see also Dysinger, "Ecology Can Be a Way of Medical Practice," *Medical Arts and Sciences*, 26 (1972): 3-5.

NOTES TO CHAPTER 7

1. Gottfried Oosterwal, "The Seventh-day Adventist Church in the World Today," in *Servants for Christ: The Adventist Church Facing the 80's*, ed. Robert E. Firth (Berrien Springs, MI: Andrews University Press, 1980), pp. 31-32.

2. Oosterwal, "Patterns of S.D.A. Church Growth in North America," Research Report No. 1, December 1974 (Berrien Springs, MI: Andrews University Department of World Missions, 1974), pp. 20-30.

3. Dean M. Kelley, *Why Conservative Churches are Growing: A Study in the Sociology of Religion* (New York: Harper & Row, 1972), pp. 1-35.

4. Sydney Ahlstrom, *A Religious History of the American People* (New Haven: Yale University Press, 1972), p. 959.

5. Oosterwal, "A Lay Movement," *RH* (7 February 1974): 9-11.

6. Russell L. Staples, "Seventh-day Adventist Mission in the 80's," in *Servants for Christ,* p. 107.

7. Oosterwal, "The Seventh-day Adventist Church in the World Today," p. 38.

8. R. M. Reinhard, "The Trend is Down, Down, Down," *RH* (18 November 1971): 10; E. L. Becker, "Membership Growth and Giving Patterns," *RH* (30 December 1976): 9-11; Kenneth H. Emerson, "Greatest Days Ahead," *AR: General Conference Bulletin No. 3* (21 April 1980): 12-13.

9. Robert H. Pierson, "Dollar Devaluation and the Church's World Work," *RH* (24 February 1972): 4-5; (19 October 1972): 22; Herbert E. Douglass, "1973 Annual Council," *RH* (15 November 1973): 5.

10. *RH* (17 November 1977): 19-21; Walter R. Beach, "Preserving Unity World Wide," *AR* (1 November 1979): 8-10; Beach, "More on Preserving Unity Worldwide," *AR* (27 December 1979): 12-13.

11. *RH* (11 December 1969): 18; see also Chuck Scriven, "The Case for Selective Nonpacifism," *Spectrum* 1 (Winter 1969): 41-44; Donald R. McAdams, "A Defense of the Adventist Position," ibid., pp. 44-49; Emmanuel G. Fenz, "The Case for Conscientious Objection," ibid., pp. 50-55.

12. Martin D. Turner, "Project Whitecoat," *Spectrum* 2 (Summer 1970): 55-70; "Project Whitecoat," *RH* (27 November 1969): 2-4; Seymour Hersh, "Germ Warfare: for Alma Mater, God and Country," *Ramparts* (December 1969): 21-24.

13. *RH* (14 May 1970): 32.

14. *RH* (17 June 1971): 20-21.

15. Richard C. Osburn, "The Establishment of the Adventist Forum," *Spectrum* 10 (March 1980): 42-58.

16. F. D. Nicol, Editorial, "The Church and Social Reform," *RH* (15 April 1965): 14-15. G. Clouzet, Editorial, "The Social Gospel versus Christ's Gospel," *AR* (7 June 1979): 14.

17. *RH* (10 August 1967): 32; (20 June 1968): 22; (4 July 1968): 22; Roy Branson, "Christian Ministry for the Disadvantaged," *RH* (17 April 1969): 5-7; (25 March 1971): 20-21.

18. *RH* (29 April 1965): 8; F. D. Nichol, Editorial, "Important Series Begins," *RH* (24 March 1966): 12; (23 June 1966): 17.

19. *Christianity Today* (3 July 1970): 3; *RH* (18 June 1970): 18.

20. *RH* (4 June 1970): 9-10, 15; Minutes, General Conference Committee, 1 March 1979 (copy, Heritage Room, James White Library, Andrews University); "Should the Church Organize Black Unions in North America?" *AR* (7 September 1978): 4-7; (30 November 1978): 14, 18; (25 January 1979): 24; see also the collections of articles on black unions appearing in *Spectrum* 2 (Spring 1970): 21-60 and 9 (July 1978): 2-22.

21. Leona G. Running, "The Status and Role of Women in the Adventist Church," *Spectrum* 4 (Summer 1972): 54-62; Gerhard F. Hasel, "Equality From the Start: Women in the Creation Story," *Spectrum* 7 (No. 2): 21-28; *RH* (7-14 August 1975), General Conference Bulletin No. 10, p. 23; *Christianity Today* (29

August 1975): 42-43; Janice Eiseman Daffern, "How Long Must Women Wait? Prospects for Adventist Church Leadership," *Spectrum* 12 (June 1982): 39-43.

22. Tom Dybdahl, "Merikay and the Pacific Press: Money, Courts and Church Authority," *Spectrum* 7 (No. 2): 44-53; Elvin Benton, "Lawsuits and the Church: Notes on the Vienna Decision," *Spectrum* 7 (No. 3): 2-8; "Church Settles Court Cases," *Spectrum* 9 (March 1978): 2-5; Douglas Welebir, "Is the Church Above the Law? God and Caesar in the California Lawsuits," ibid., pp. 6-15; Ron Walden, "How Hierarchical Views of the Church Emerge," ibid., pp. 16-22; John Van Horne, "Why Did Church Lawyers Use Hierarchy Language?" ibid., pp. 23-29; "Neal Wilson Talks About the Lawsuits," ibid., pp. 30-37; Tom Dybdahl, "Court Verdict on Pacific Press Case," *Spectrum* 10 (July 1980): 14-17; "Update: Pacific Press Case," *Spectrum* 12 (June 1982): 63-64. For Merikay Silver's personal account, see Merikay McLeod, *Betrayal* (Loma Linda, CA: Mars Hill Publications, Inc., 1985).

23. *RH* (18 July 1975): 9; (4 December 1975): 4; Elvin Benton, "Suing the Church," *Spectrum* 11 (July 1980): 8-9.

24. Geri Ann Fuller, "The New Adventist Health Care Corporations," *Spectrum* 11 (June 1981): 16-22.

25. "The Lord Will Do Wonders," *RH* (17 November 1966): 1, 6-9; "Is the Lord Among Us?" *RH* (14 November 1968): 2-5; "Now Is the Time," *RH* (31 July 1975): 5-7; "To God be the Glory," *RH* (11 July 1975): 7.

26. W. R. Beach, "Worldwide Revival and Reformation," *RH* (1 December 1966): 4-5; "An Earnest Appeal From the Annual Council," *RH* (6 December 1973): 1, 4-5.

27. "Evangelism and Finishing God's Work," *RH* (2 December 1976): 14-15.

28. K. H. Wood, Editorial, "F.Y.I." *RH* (18 November 1977): 2, 13.

29. Douglass, "Concepts of Jesus Affect Personality," *RH* (31 August 1972): 12.

30. Editorial, "Making the Sabbath More Meaningful," *RH* (19 April 1973): 12.

31. Editorial, "Jesus—the God-Man," *RH* (5 May 1977): 2, 12; see also Herbert E. Douglass, "Paxton's Misunderstanding of Adventism," *Spectrum* 9 (July 1978): 32-33.

32. The foregoing history is drawn principally from Geoffrey J. Paxton, *The Shaking of Adventism*, rpt. (Grand Rapids: Baker Book House, 1978), pp. 85-145; see also Desmond Ford's correction of Paxton, "The Truth of Paxton's Thesis," *Spectrum* 9 (July 1978): 42; other historical accounts include Norval F. Pease, *By Faith Alone* (Mountain View, CA: PPPA, 1962), pp. 212-21, and Arthur Leroy Moore, *Theology in Crisis or Ellen G. White's Concept of Righteousness by Faith as it Relates to Contemporary SDA Issues* (Corpus Christi, TX: Life Seminars Incorporated, 1980), pp. 1-9. The "Palmdale statement" was published as "Christ Our Righteousness," *RH* (27 May 1976): 4-7.

33. Paxton, *Shaking of Adventism*, pp. 130-33; K. H. Wood, Editorial, "F.Y.I." *RH* (21 October 1976): 2.

34. H. K. LaRondelle, "A Profile of the Biblical Doctrine of Sanctification," *RH* (6 January 1977): 6-7.

35. "An Interview with Paxton," *Spectrum* 9 (July 1978): 59; *AR* (7 September 1978): 24; *AR* (22 November 1979): 23; Neal C. Wilson, "An Open Letter to the Church," *AR* (24 May 1979): 4-5. The "Consultation" on righteousness by faith took place on October 3 and 4, 1979; *AR* [22 November 1979]:23).

36. *AR* (31 July 1980): 3-7.

37. "Paxton and the Reformers," *Spectrum* 9 (July 1938): 46.

38. "A View from the Outside," *Spectrum* 9 (July 1938): 31.

39. Neal C. Wilson, "Testimony Countdown," *RH* (28 August 1969): 8-9; D. A. and Evelyn Delafield, "Promoting the Spirit of Prophecy in Europe—Part 1," *RH* (18 January 1973): 17-18; D. A. and Evelyn Delafield, "The Attitude of Adventists to Ellen G. White," *RH* (25 January 1973): 17.

40. "Ellen White: A Subject for Adventist Scholarship," *Spectrum* 2 (Autumn 1970): 30-33.

41. "A Textual and Historical Study of Ellen G. White's Account of the French Revolution," *Spectrum* 2 (Autumn 1970): 66.

42. "Ellen G. White and Her Writings," *Spectrum* 3 (Spring 1971): 48, 61.

43. "How Did Ellen White Choose and Use Historical Sources?" *Spectrum* 4 (Summer 1972): 49-53.

44. *Prophetess of Health: A Study of Ellen G. White* (New York: Harper & Row, 1976), pp. 49-53.

45. *Time*, 2 August 1976, p. 45; Kenneth H. Wood, Editorial, "An Important Challenge to the Faith?" *RH* (19 August 1976): 2; "A Discussion and Review of Prophetess of Health" (Washington, D.C.: Ellen G. White Estate, 1976); *A Critique of Prophetess of Health* (Washington, D.C.: Ellen G. White Estate, 1976).

46. *Critique*, pp. 10, 93.

47. These articles appeared in *Spectrum* 8 (January 1972): 2-36.

48. Quoted in Donald R. McAdams, "Shifting Views of Inspiration: Ellen G. White Studies in the 1970's," *Spectrum* 10 (March 1980): 34.

49. Ibid., pp. 34-36.

50. Ibid., pp. 36-38; Arthur L. White, "Toward an Adventist Conception of Inspiration," *AR* (12 January 1978): 4-6; (19 January 1978): 7-8; (26 January 1978): 6-8; (2 February 1978): 6-8; Arthur L. White, "The E. G. White Historical Writings," *AR* (12 July 1979): 4-7; (19 July 1979): 7-9 (26 July 1979): 5-10; (2 August 1979): 7-11; (9 August 1979): 7-10; (16 August 1979): 6-9; (23 August 1980): 6-9.

51. Douglas Hackleman, "G. C. Committee Studies Ellen White Sources," *Spectrum* 10 (March 1980): 9-15.

52. "This I Believe about Ellen G. White," *AR* (20 March 1980): 8-10.

53. *Los Angeles Times*, 23 October 1980, sec. 1, pp. 1ff.; *Christianity Today* (12 December 1980): 61; *Newsweek* (19 January 1981): 72. Rea published his findings in Walter T. Rea, *The White Lie* (Turlock, CA: M & R Publications, 1982).

54. Joseph J. Battistone, "Ellen White's Authority as Bible Commentator," *Spectrum* 8 (January 1977): 37-40; Jonathan Butler, "The World of Ellen G. White and the End of the World," *Spectrum* 10 (August 1979): 2-13.

55. McAdams, "Shifting Views," p. 39.

56. Raymond F. Cottrell, "Sanctuary Debate: A Question of Method," *Spectrum* 10 (March 1980): 16-19.

57. For example, see Donald F. Neufeld, Editorial, "No Sanctuary, No True Adventism," *AR* (9 November 1978): 20-21.

58. Walter Utt, "Desmond Ford Raises the Sanctuary Question," *Spectrum* 10 (March 1980): 4-5; see also Edward E. Plowman, "The Shaking Up of Adventism?" *Christianity Today* (8 February 1980): 64-67.

59. Utt, "Desmond Ford," pp. 5-6.

60. *AR* (20 December 1979): 23.

61. Richard Lesher, "Truth Stands Forever," *AR* 13 (March 1980): 7.

62. Desmond Ford, "Daniel 8:14 and the Day of Atonement," *Spectrum* 11 (November 1980): 36. This article is a summary of Ford's manuscript presented

to the Sanctuary Review Committee. This manuscript with a new introduction was published as *Daniel 8:14, The Day of Atonement and the Investigative Judgment* (Casselberry, FL: Evangelion Press, 1980).

63. William G. Johnsson, "Overview of a Historic Meeting," *AR* (4 September 1980): 4-7; "Editorial Perspectives," *Ministry* 53 (October 1980): 4-10; Raymond F. Cottrell, "The Sanctuary Review Committee and its New Consensus," *Spectrum* 11 (November 1980): 2-26; "Sanctuary Delegates Report Progress, Confusion," *Evangelica*, 1: 5-6; "Statement on Desmond Ford Document," *AR* (4 September 1980): 8-11; "Christ in the Heavenly Sanctuary," ibid., pp. 12-15; "The Role of the Ellen G. White Writings in Doctrinal Matters," ibid., p. 15.

64. Tom Minnery, "The Adventist Showdown: Will It Trigger a Rash of Defections?" *Christianity Today* (10 October 1980): 76-77; *Newsweek* (19 January 1981): 72; Eric Anderson, Jonathan Butler, Molleurus Couperous, Adrian Zytkoskee, "Must the Crisis Continue?" *Spectrum* 11 (February 1981): 44-52.

65. *Newsweek* (7 June 1971): 65-66; K. H. Wood, Editorial, "The Newsweek Story," *RH* (1 July 1971): 2.

66. Harold Lindsell, *The Battle for the Bible* (Grand Rapids: Zondervan, 1976).

67. For example, see W. J. Hackett, "The Church in an Era of Change," *RH* (16 May 1968): 1, 8-9; Robert H. Pierson, "The Old Message Is Always New/True," *RH* (1 January 1970): 2-3.

68. W. J. Hackett, Editorial, "Preserve the Landmarks," *RH* (26 May 1977): 2.

69. Richard Rice, "Dominant Themes in Adventist Theology," *Spectrum* 10 (March 1980): 66.

70. "A Response from PUC," *Spectrum* 8 (August 1977): 43-44; "The West Coast Bible Teachers: A Statement of Concern," ibid., pp. 44-47; "Introduction," ibid., pp. 37-38.

71. "Some Reflections on Change and Continuity," ibid., p. 42; "West Coast Bible Teachers," ibid., p. 46.

72. Rice, "Dominant Themes," pp. 66-67.

73. *AR* (1 May 1980); *General Conference Bulletin* No. 9, p. 23; see also Lawrence Geraty, "A New Statement of Fundamental Beliefs," *Spectrum* 11 (July 1980): 2-13.

74. Rice, "Dominant Themes," p. 69; this article surveys Adventist theological developments in the 1970s and provides extensive bibliographical information.

75. *RH* (23 July 1970): 24.

76. Heshbon reports appeared in such journals as *Annual of the Department of Antiquities of Jordan, American Schools of Oriental Research Newsletter, Biblical Archaeologist, Palestine Exploration Quarterly*, and *Revue Biblique Benedictine*; for a general article, see *International Standard Bible Encyclopedia*, vol. 2 (Grand Rapids: William B. Eerdmans Publishing Company, 1982), s.v. "Heshbon," by Lawrence T. Geraty.

77. *AR* (26 October 1978): 1, 10-11.

78. Donald R. McAdams, "The 1978 Annual Council: A Report and Analysis," *Spectrum* 9 (January 1979): 7-8. A sociological perspective on Adventist sectarianism appears in Bryan Wilson, *Religious Sects: A Sociological Study*, World University Library (New York: McGraw Hill, 1970), p. 103, and Bryan Wilson, "Sect or Denomination: Can Adventism Maintain Its Identity?" *Spectrum* 7, No. 1 (1975): 34-43.

79. "The Seventh-day Adventist Church," *Ecumenical Review* 19 (January 1967): 2-28; Cosmàs Rubencamp, "The Seventh-day Adventists and the Ecumen-

ical Movement," *Journal of Ecumenical Studies* 6 (Fall 1969): 534-48; Raoul De-
deren, "An Adventist Response to 'The Seventh-day Adventists and the Ecumenical
Movement,' " *Journal of Ecumenical Studies* 7 (Summer 1970): 558-563; B. B.
Beach, "An Adventist Reaction," *The Ecumenical Review* 23 (January 1971): 38-43;
24 (April 1972): 200-207; K. H. Wood, Editorial, "F.Y.I." *RH* (26 July 1973): 2;
Ella M. Rydzewski, "The World Council of Churches and Seventh-day Adventists," *Spectrum* 5, No. 3 (1973): 33-41.

     80. "The Jerusalem Conference in Retrospect," *RH* (29 July 1971): 1, 7-8.

     81. *RH* (30 December 1976): 21.

     82. *RH* (16 July 1977): 16-17.

     83. Jerry L. Pettis, "An Adventist in Congress," *Spectrum* 2 (Winter 1970):
36-40.

     84. For example, see R. F. Cottrell, Editorial, "To Vote or Not to Vote,"
RH (21 October 1976): 9-10.

     85. "1978 Annual Council," p. 8.

     86. Luke 19:13.

BIBLIOGRAPHICAL ESSAY

For the scholar wishing to pursue Seventh-day Adventist history, the number of serious studies is limited. Of the general histories of the church, Richard W. Schwarz's college-level text *Lightbearers to the Remnant* (Mountain View, CA: PPPA, 1979) is the most useful, although M. Ellsworth Olsen's *A History of the Origin and Progress of Seventh-day Adventists* (Washington, D.C.: RHPA, 1925) remains a valuable account of the denomination's history into the early twentieth century. J. N. Loughborough gives a participant's view in *The Great Second Advent Movement: Its Rise and Progress* (Washington, D.C.: RHPA, 1905); and a primarily anecdotal approach appears in Arthur Whitefield Spalding's *Origin and History of Seventh-day Adventists*, 4 vols. (Washington, D.C.: RHPA, 1961–62). C. Mervyn Maxwell's *Tell It To The World: The Story of Seventh-day Adventists* (Mountain View, CA: PPPA, 1976) emphasizes the distinctive elements of Adventist theology as they emerged in the nineteenth century. Emmett K. VandeVere has compiled an interesting collection of documents in *Windows: Readings in Seventh-day Adventist Church History, 1844–1922* (Nashville: SPA, 1975). *The Seventh-day Adventist Encyclopedia*, ed. Don F. Neufeld (Commentary Reference Series, Vol. X; Washington, D.C.: RHPA, 1966) is an indispensable reference work.

The Millerite movement has stimulated the richest body of literature on the history of Adventism. Most of the myths about Millerism appear in Clara Endicott Sears's *Days of Delusion: A Strange Bit of History* (Boston: Houghton Mifflin Company, 1924), which is answered by Francis D. Nichol's thoroughly researched but strongly apologetical *The Midnight Cry* (Washington, D.C.: RHPA, 1944). Everett N. Dick undertook the first scholarly examination of the movement in "The Advent Crisis of 1843–1844" (Ph.D. diss., University of Wisconsin, 1930); this dissertation should not be confused with Dick's typescript volume, "William Miller and the Advent Crisis, 1831–1844" (1932). These works have now been largely superceded by David T. Arthur's " 'Come Out of Babylon': A Study of Millerite Separatism and Denominationalism, 1840–1865" (Ph.D. diss., University of Rochester, 1970) and David L. Rowe's "Thunder and Trumpets: The Millerite Movement and Apocalyptic Thought in Upstate New York, 1800–1845" (Ph.D. diss., University of Virginia, 1974). An Advent Christian account of the Millerite movement and development of the Advent Christian denomination to 1860 is Clyde E. Hewitt, *Midnight and Morning* (Charlotte, NC: Venture Books, 1983). The social context of Adventism is examined in Whitney Cross, *The Burned-Over District: The Social and*

Intellectual History of Enthusiastic Religion in Western New York, 1800 – 1850 (Ithaca, NY: Cornell University Press, 1950); Richard Carwardine, *Transatlantic Revivalism: Popular Evangelicalism in Britain and America, 1790 – 1865* (Westport, CT: Greenwood Press, 1978); and Edwin Scott Gaustad, ed., *The Rise of Adventism: Religion and Society in Mid-Nineteenth-Century America* (New York: Harper & Row, 1974). Gaustad's work contains the most thorough bibliography of Millerism available. Ernest R. Sandeen discusses the millenarian ideas of the nineteenth century in *The Roots of Fundamentalism: British and American Millenarianism, 1800 – 1930* (Chicago: University of Chicago Press, 1970). A Seventh-day Adventist view of the social and intellectual context of the Millerites appears in LeRoy Edwin Froom, *The Prophetic Faith of Our Fathers: The Historical Development of Prophetic Interpretation*, 4 vols. (Washington, D.C.: RHPA, 1954) and Jerome Clark, *1844*, 3 vols. (Nashville: SPA, 1968). A useful participant's account of Millerite history is Isaac C. Wellcome, *History of the Second Advent Message and Mission, Doctrine and People* (Yarmouth, ME: I. C. Wellcome, 1874).

Among topical studies, theological concerns predominate. An apologetic approach characterizes LeRoy Edwin Froom's background study on *The Conditionalist Faith of Our Fathers: The Conflict of the Ages Over the Nature and Destiny of Man*, 2 vols. (Washington, D.C.: RHPA, 1965 – 66) and the same author's *Movement of Destiny* (Washington, D.C.: RHPA, 1971), which examines the development of Adventist Christology. A. V. Olsen's *Through Crisis to Victory, 1888 – 1901: From the Minneapolis Meeting to the Reorganization of the General Conference* (Washington, D.C.: RHPA, 1966) is another useful if apologetic work on the Adventist understanding of righteousness by faith. B. W. Ball, *The English Connection: The Puritan Roots of Seventh-day Adventist Belief* (Cambridge: James Clarke, 1981) provides a scholarly approach, while W. L. Emmerson, *The Reformation and the Advent Movement* (Washington, D.C.: RHPA, 1983) offers a popular treatment of Adventism's relationship to earlier Christianity. Two sharply contrasting examinations of early Adventist belief are P. Gerard Damsteegt's detailed description, *Foundations of the Seventh-day Adventist Message and Mission* (Grand Rapids: William B. Eerdmans Publishing Company, 1977) and Ingemar Linden's highly critical *The Last Trump: A Historico-Genetical Study of Some Important Chapters in the Making and Development of the Seventh-day Adventist Church* (Frankfurt: Peter, Lang, 1978). Paul A. Gordon, *The Sanctuary, 1844, and the Pioneers* (Washington, D.C.: RHPA, 1983) is a worthwhile popular study. Other Adventist concerns are surveyed in Dores Eugene Robinson, *The Story of Our Health Message: The Origin, Character, and Development of Health Education in the Seventh-day Adventist Church* (Nashville: SPA, 1943) and Eric B. Syme, *A History of S.D.A. Church-State Relationships* (Mountain View, CA: PPPA, 1946). Howard B. Weeks's *Adventist Evangelism in the Twentieth Century* (Washington: RHPA, 1969) is an excellent study of that subject. The history of black American Adventists is told in Louis B. Reynolds, *We Have Tomorrow* (Washington, D.C.: RHPA, 1984). Harold Oliver Mc-

Cumber's *Pioneering the Message in the Golden West* (Mountain View, CA: PPPA, 1946) is a popularization of a doctoral dissertation. There is no adequate history of Adventist education, although Maurice Hodgen's *School Bells & Gospel Trumpets: A Documentary History of Seventh-day Adventist Education in North America* (Loma Linda, CA: Adventist Heritage Publications, 1978) is a fine collection of primary sources and George R. Knight, ed., *Early Adventist Educators* (Berrien Springs, MI: Andrews University Press, 1983) provides several short biographies. Histories of individual Adventist colleges include David D. Rees and Everett Dick, *Union College: Fifty Years of Service* (Lincoln, NE: Union College Press, 1941); Walter C. Utt, *A Mountain, A Pickax, and A College* (Angwin, CA: Alumni Asssociation, Pacific Union College, 1968) on Pacific Union College; and Emmett K. VandeVere, *The Wisdom Seekers* (Nashville: SPA, 1972) on Andrews University. Lowell Tarling surveys the various groups that have broken off from Seventh-day Adventism in *The Edges of Seventh-day Adventism* (Barragga Bay, Bermagui South, Australia: Galilee, 1981).

Nearly all of the biographies of individual Adventists concern nineteenth-century figures. Sylvester Bliss sought to correct the public image of Miller in *Memoirs of William Miller Generally Known as a Lecturer on the Prophecies, and the Second Coming of Christ* (Boston: Joshua V. Himes, 1835). A founder of Seventh-day Adventism is the subject of Godfrey T. Anderson's careful biography, *Outrider of the Apocalypse: The Life and Times of Joseph Bates* (Mountain View, CA: PPPA, 1972). An increasing number of works examine Ellen G. White: Arthur L. White's six volume *Ellen G. White* (Washington, D.C.: RHPA, 1982–86) is a useful source of information but lacks analytical interpretation, while Ronald L. Numbers's *Prophetess of Health: A Study of Ellen G. White* (New York: Harper & Row, 1976) critically examines the development of the Adventist leader's health ideas, particularly their relationship to the nineteenth-century health reform movement. Richard W. Schwarz's *John Harvey Kellogg, M.D.* (Nashville: SPA, 1970) is useful, but the scholar should also consult the same author's "John Harvey Kellogg: American Health Reformer" (Ph.D. diss., University of Michigan, 1964). Informative popular biographies include Robert Gale, *The Urgent Voice: The Story of William Miller* (Washington, D.C.: RHPA, 1975); Ella N. Robinson, *S. N. Haskell: Man of Action* (Washington, D.C.: RHPA, 1967); Virgil Robinson, *James White* (Washington, D.C.: RHPA, 1976); Emmett K. VandeVere, *Rugged Heart: The Story of George I. Butler* (Nashville: SPA, 1979); Eugene F. Durand, *Yours in the Blessed Hope, Uriah Smith* (Washington, D.C.: RHPA, 1980); Merlin L. Neff, *For God and C.M.E.: A Biography of Percy Tilson Magan* (Mountain View, CA: PPPA, 1964); and Harold W. Clark, *Crusader for Creation: The Life and Writings of George McCready Price* (Mountain View, Ca: PPPA, 1966).

Spectrum: Journal of the Association of Adventist Forums (1969–) frequently publishes articles on Adventist history and reviews books in the field. Articles of a primarily narrative nature appear in *Adventist Heritage: A Magazine of Adventist History* (1974–).

CONTRIBUTORS

Everett N. Dick, now retired from teaching history at Union College, wrote his dissertation in the 1920s on the Millerite movement. Since that time, he has published several significant works on the American West, including *The Sod-House Frontier*, has written Adventist history for young people, and has contributed to *Adventist Heritage*.

Godfey T. Anderson served as president of Loma Linda University and is currently spending his retirement as the university archivist. He has written *Outrider of the Apocalypse: The Life and Times of Joseph Bates* and contributed articles to *Adventist Heritage*.

Emmett K. VandeVere is now retired after teaching history for over thirty years at Andrews University. His publications on Seventh-day Adventist history include *The Wisdom Seekers*, a history of Andrews University; *Windows: Readings in Seventh-day Adventist Church History*; and *Rugged Heart: The Story of George I. Butler*.

Richard W. Schwarz is Vice President for Academic Affairs at Andrews University. In addition to serving for several years as the chairman of the history department at Andrews, he has written *John Harvey Kellogg, M.D.* and *Light Bearers to the Remnant*, a college-level denominational history text.

Gary Land is professor of history at Andrews University. He is coeditor of *Adventist Heritage* and has contributed several articles on Adventist history to *Spectrum*. Author of articles and papers on American intellectual and popular culture history, he is currently collaborating on a historical survey of American thought and culture.

Keld J. Reynolds is now retired after serving as an associate secretary in the education department of the General Conference of Seventh-day Adventists and as a teacher and administrator at Loma Linda University.

Index

Adventist Review. See Review and Herald

Albany Conference, 33

Anderson, Roy, 189 – 91

Andrews, John, 42, 49, 52, 60, 67, 88

Andrews University, 129, 199 – 200, 229

Association of Adventist Forums, 211 – 12

Australia, 89, 105, 117, 126, 139

Barnhouse, Donald, 185 – 86

Bates, Joseph: health reform ideas of, 69; and Millerite movement, 10, 12, 27, 30; and Sabbatarian Adventism, 38 – 39, 41 – 42, 58

Battle Creek: Adventist institutions established at, 50, 54, 70 – 71; Adventists move from, 131; conferences held at, 57, 59, 63; as denominational center, 68

Battle Creek College, 71, 104, 129, 137

Battle Creek Sanitarium, 70, 110, 137

Bell, Goodloe, 54, 70

Bible Research Fellowship, 182 – 83

Bourdeau, Daniel, 77

Bradley, W. Paul, 220

Branson, Roy, 211, 219

Branson, William, 178, 183

Butler, George: in California, 79; in Europe, 88; as General Conference President, 67, 100, 133; as Iowa Conference President, 75 – 76; and John Kellogg, 133; and righteousness by faith, 98, 101; writes *Tract on Leadership*, 90

Byington, John, 63

California, 76 – 82

Canright, Dudley, 79, 104 – 5

China, 172 – 73

Christian Connection, 9, 22, 43

Church Manual, 180, 213 – 14

College of Medical Evangelists. *See* Loma Linda University

Conditional immortality, 32, 36 – 37

Conradi, Louis, 86

Cornell, Merritt, 42, 44, 79

Cottrell, Roswell, 42, 57, 64

Czechowski, Michael, 87

Daniells, Arthur: conflict with Kellogg, 136 – 38; criticized by Jones, 151; elected chairman, General Conference Committee, 129; leaves General Conference presidency, 161; financial views of, 121; missions interest of, 139 – 41; and righteousness by faith, 165 – 66

Doss, Desmond, 174

Douglass, Herbert, 216 – 17

Edson, Hiram, 30, 33, 39

Emmanuel Missionary College. *See* Andrews University

Fagal, William, 191

Figuhr, Reuben, 176

Fitch, Charles, 8, 11, 14

Five-day Plan, 193

Ford, Desmond, 217 – 18, 223 – 24

Franke, Elmer, 112 – 13

Fundamentalism, 168 – 69

General Tract and Missionary Society, 68

Girouard v United States, 173

Glacier View, Colorado, 224 – 25

Graybill, Ronald, 220, 228

Hackett, Willis, 226

Halliwell, Leo, 195

Haskell, Stephen, 68, 79, 88, 111 – 12

Healdsburg College, 81

Hetzell, M. Carol, 213

Hill, William, 74 – 75

Himes, Joshua: brings Miller to the cities, 9, 12; and Great Disappointment, 30 – 31; and John Starkweather,

23 – 24; independent of Evangelical Adventists, 37; publishes *Advent Herald*, 36

Insight, 211

Irwin, George, 127, 134

Jones, Alonzo: becomes *Review* editor, 101; converts to Adventism, 83; criticizes Ellen White, 153 – 54; criticizes General Conference, 150 – 53; supports Kellogg, 137; theology of, 92 – 93, 98

Kellogg, John: begins welfare missions, 110 – 11; conflict with Seventh-day Adventists, 133 – 38; relationship with Ellen White, 155 – 56; theology of, 106 – 9

Kellogg, Merritt, 77

Litch, Josiah, 8, 11, 13, 19

Loma Linda University, 174, 195 – 96, 200 – 201, 227

Loughborough, John, 58, 77

McAdams, Donald, 221 – 23

McElhany, J. Lamar, 176, 178

Marsh, Joseph, 37

Martin, Walter, 185 – 88

Matteson, John, 84 – 85, 88

Medical Cadet Corps, 173 – 75

Medical Missionary and Benevolent Association, 126, 129, 137

Michigan Conference, 62, 73

Millerites: attitudes toward denominations, 28; camp meetings of, 16 – 18; in cities, 12 – 15; conferences of, 9 – 11; denominational affiliations of, 34; fanaticism in, 22 – 25; and Great Awakening, 34 – 35; and Great Disappointment, 29 – 30; reaction to, 20 – 21, 28; size of, 34; and date of Second Coming, 25 – 28

Miller, William: 3 – 6; and date of Second Coming, 20, 26, 28; death of, 34; and Great Disappointment, 30 – 1; and Millerites, 10, 19; preaching of, 7 – 8

Mission Institute, 209

Morrison, J. H., 99

Munger, Hiram, 17

Nichol, Francis, 184, 203

Numbers, Ronald, 220 – 21

Olsen, Ole, 100, 125 – 27

Oakwood Industrial School, 115

Pacific Press, 79 – 80

Pacific Union College, 223 – 24, 227

Paris Youth Congress, 179

Paxton, Geoffrey, 217 – 218

Peterson, William, 219 – 20

Pettis, Jerry, 230

Pierson, Robert, 215, 225 – 26, 229

Preble, Thomas, 32, 38

Prescott, William, 164 – 65

Prohibition, 168

Rea, Walter, 222

Regional Conferences, 176

Review and Herald, 40, 44, 49, 146, 163, 216, 224

Review and Herald Publishing Association, 68, 124, 131 – 32

Richards, H. M. S., 189 – 90

Righteousness by faith, 98 – 102, 164 – 67, 215 – 19

Rural Health Retreat, 81

Sabbatarian Adventists. *See* Seventh-day Adventists

Sabbath, Seventh-day, 32, 38, 41 – 42, 229

Sadler, William, 154

Sanctuary doctrine, 39, 223 – 25

Second Coming of Christ, 1 – 4, 229

Second Great Awakening, 6, 34 – 35

Seventh-day Adventist Bible Commentary, 184

Seventh-day Adventists: camp meetings, 91; develop educational system, 53 – 54, 102, 197 – 201; emphasize evangelism, 109 – 13, 188 – 93; financial support of, 52 – 53, 72, 119 – 23; growth of, 55, 73 – 82, 89, 147 – 50, 208 – 10; health teachings and practices of, 42 – 43, 69 – 70, 202 – 4, 214 – 15; missions of, 5, 72 – 73, 116 – 19, 139 – 41; organization of, 46 – 54, 57 – 65, 125 – 29, 131 – 33, 141 – 46, 182 – 84; publishing of, 68; and racial problems, 113 – 16, 176 – 77, 212 – 13; and relationship to society, 45 – 46, 56 – 57, 65, 96 – 97, 162, 167 – 78, 205 – 6, 210 – 11, 229; theology of, 40 – 41, 43, 92 – 93, 98 – 109, 157 – 67, 180 – 81, 185 – 87, 215 – 23, 226 – 28

Shut door doctrine, 31
Signs of the Times, 79
Silver, Merikay, 213 – 14
Smith, Uriah: as editor, 50; as General
    Conference officer, 59, 63, 100; the-
    ology of, 92, 98
Snow, Samuel, 27
Spicer, William, 161
Spectrum, 211, 219 – 20, 226
Starkweather, John, 23 – 24
Stewart, Charles, 155
Storrs, George, 24, 32
Sunday laws, 96 – 97

Takoma Park. *See* Washington, D.C.
Turner, Joseph, 31, 37

Unruh, T. Edgar, 185

Vandeman, George, 180 – 191
Van Horn, Isaac, 82 – 83
Victorious Life, 164 – 66

Waggoner, Ellet, 98 – 100
Waggoner, Joseph, 42, 64, 79, 92 – 93
Ward, Henry Dana, 9, 11

Washington, D.C., 108, 131 – 33
Western Health Reform Institute. *See*
    Battle Creek Sanitarium
White, Edson, 113 – 16
White, Ellen: accepts seventh-day Sab-
    bath, 38; appeals for missions, 55 –
    56, 109 – 13; death of, 166; debate
    over, 44, 105 – 6, 153 – 61, 219 – 23;
    and denominational organization, 47,
    60, 67, 123, 128, 131; educational
    views of, 54, 70 – 71; and John Kel-
    logg, 135; marries James White, 39;
    theology of, 42, 93, 98 – 100, 108;
    travels of, 78, 83; visions of, 39, 55 –
    56, 69
White, James: death of, 81; and denom-
    inational organization, 47 – 50, 54,
    61 – 63; as General Conference pres-
    ident, 67; illness of, 69; leadership of,
    55 – 56, 63 – 65, 68; and publishing,
    40, 51 – 52, 79 – 80; and seventh-day
    Sabbath, 38, 42
Wilcox, Francis, 140, 159, 180
Wilson, Neal, 211, 217 – 18
Wood, Kenneth, 216 – 17

Youth's Instructor, The, 49, 211